D1729792

Playing Gods

Playing Gods

OVID'S *METAMORPHOSES* AND
THE POLITICS OF FICTION

Andrew Feldherr

PRINCETON UNIVERSITY PRESS

PRINCETON AND OXFORD

Copyright 2010 © by Princeton University Press

Published by Princeton University Press, 41 William Street, Princeton,
New Jersey 08540
In the United Kingdom: Princeton University Press, 6 Oxford Street,
Woodstock, Oxfordshire OX20 1TW

press.princeton.edu

Library of Congress Cataloging-in-Publication Data

Feldherr, Andrew, 1963–
Playing gods : Ovid's Metamorphoses and the politics of fiction / Andrew Feldherr.
    p.   cm.
Includes bibliographical references and index.
ISBN 978-0-691-13814-5 (hardcover : alk. paper) 1. Ovid, 43 B.C.–17 or 18 A.D.
Metamorphoses. 2. Fables, Latin—History and criticism. 3. Politics and literature—
Rome. I. Title.
PA6519.M9F45 2010
873'.01—dc22   2010010198

British Library Cataloging-in-Publication Data is available

This book has been composed in Sabon and Caslon Open Face

Printed on acid-free paper. ∞

Printed in the United States of America

10 9 8 7 6 5 4 3 2 1

For Erich Gruen and in memory of Joan Gruen

Contents

Acknowledgments

Versions of some material presented here have been published before: part 2 of chapter 1 in P. Hardie, ed., The Cambridge Companion to Ovid (Cambridge, 2002), 163–79; part 2 of chapter 2 in Arethusa 37 (2004): 77–87; the latter half of chapter 4 in MD 38 (1997): 25–55; chapter 5 in M. Moller, ed., Vom Selbst-Verständnis in Antike und Neuzeit/ Notions of the Self in Antiquity and Beyond (Berlin and New York, 2008), 33–47; and part 1 of chapter 7 in Hermathena 177–78 (2004–5): 126–46. I am grateful to Cambridge University Press, the Johns Hopkins University Press, Fabrizio Serra Editore, Walter de Gruyter, and Trinity College, Dublin, respectively, for permission to include this material here. Thanks, too, to the anonymous readers of several of these journal submissions for their valuable suggestions.

Philip Hardie has read through several versions of this project with unsettling acumen and unflagging generosity. If he ever feels the need to read it again, he will see how much I owe him. Detailed suggestions on the entire manuscript were also offered by Carole Newlands and Denis Feeney. Stephen Hinds gave valuable comments as well. I was extremely fortunate to have the anonymous referees assigned by Princeton University Press; their comments succeeded in making me think again about many aspects of this work at a time when that was the last thing I wanted to do—though of course they couldn't work miracles. Audiences at Berkeley, Leeds, Trinity College Dublin, Williams, Lehigh, Birmingham, Münster, and New York University all provided inspiration and advice. Simon Price shared a draft of his then unpublished article on local religions in Asia Minor, and Barbara Kellum another on the art of freedmen. The scholars named above will race to distance themselves from much that they find in this book, and these expressions of gratitude should not be construed as placing obstacles in their path.

It would be an exaggeration to say that I could not have written this book anywhere but Princeton, but both the process and the product would have been much poorer and less interesting without the colleagues and students I have known here. I hope that such friends as Mark Buchan, Elaine Fantham, Bob Kaster, Josh Ober, Ruth Webb, and Froma Zeitlin will recognize with more pleasure than distress the impact they have had on my work.

Of them all, I single out Denis Feeney for special thanks. Few authors are lucky enough to have their ideal reader just down the hall. And if this could have been a mixed blessing, Denis's friendship and belief that this project would and should eventually be finished have more than compensated for the frustration of his already having said most of what I wanted to and for my despair at ever matching the standards set by his own work.

By contrast, my daughters Rebecca and Miriam have made practically every stage of writing slower and more difficult. But—in retrospect—I love them all the more for that.

I also owe a great debt to Rob Tempio at Princeton University Press for his patience and very valuable advice during the revision process. Thanks too to Nathan Carr for his help in seeing the manuscript through its final stages and to my copy editor Brian MacDonald for frustrating my intentions by making the argument a little more comprehensible. Meredith Safran helped in preparing the index.

Although I have not specifically asked for their help on this project, working on it has made me remember with particular gratitude three of my teachers at Berkeley. It was a pleasure to read Ovid in the text prepared by W. S. Anderson, and his own commentaries and articles on the poem have established him in my mind as the scholar I would be most reluctant to disagree with. I have no idea what Tom Rosenmeyer would have made of this book, but I am very sad not to be able to ask him. Finally, the inspiring teaching of Tom Habinek lies behind everything I will ever write about Latin literature.

It is in general an excellent idea to dedicate books to eminent figures in the field. Except in the hardest cases, such a move will effectively keep them from ever telling you honestly what they think of your work. It certainly disqualifies them from reviewing it. Here, though, I am at a disadvantage since, much as I hope to profit from the pietas of his legions of students, friends, and colleagues, Erich Gruen himself possesses relatively little clout in Ovidian studies. Nor can I think of any particular aid or advice he has given me on this book—aside from his decade-long campaign to make sure I remained employed to complete it. I offer it, nevertheless, to Erich and to Joan's memory, in gratitude for many years of friendship and for the example of their life together.

Playing Gods

Ovid begins the *Metamorphoses* by promising his readers, quite literally, the world. The gods who inspire the poet's song are asked to lead his narrative "from the first creation of the cosmos to my own times" (1.3–4). Alongside the grandeur of the project they set in motion, however, the lines already signal a number of questions that Ovid's audience will have to confront throughout the fifteen books that follow. To start with, the technical terms used to describe the composition of the work present it as a kind of hybrid, paradoxically claiming the qualities of two antithetical poetic forms: on the one hand, the song will be "unbroken" (*perpetuum*, 1.4) like the extended, homogeneous narratives of epic—and, indeed, the *Metamorphoses* marks Ovid's first use of the distinctive meter of epic poetry, the dactylic hexameter. On the other, the word that means "lead down" (*deducite*, 1.4) also means "spin fine" and was used in this meaning by Latin poets to describe the writing of short, exquisitely crafted pieces. How can Ovid's poem be at once short and long, grand and refined? The contradictory formal expectations raised by this description relate to a distinction in strategies of reading that are at the core of this book and that are complemented by the second paradox the brief proem sets in play. The word *perpetuum* applies both to the narrative form of the work, which will not be disassembled into a sequence of individual poetic units, and to the material that it describes, the history of time that connects past with present in an unbroken chain. Conversely, the suggestion of "fine spinning" in *deducite* directs attention above all to the nature of the poetic product itself, its artistry and style. Without crudely reducing the poem to an epic subject treated in a refined style, this opposition broadly raises the question of how much the reader should focus on the content of the work, the story it tells, and how much on Ovid's poem itself as a literary artifact.

The issue of the relationship between the subject matter and its artistic representation emerges more dramatically in the poem's first two lines:

> *In nova fert animus mutatas dicere formas*
> *Corpora: di, coeptis (nam vos mutastis et illa)*
> *Adspirate meis . . .*
>
> (1.1–3)

> My mind drives me to speak of forms changed to new bodies: gods, favor my beginnings, for you have changed them too.

The external universe is to be characterized above all by changes of form: the gods invoked to aid Ovid's composition are appropriately those who produce change. This already suggests not only that the poetic artifact is to be coextensive in time with the material it describes (it moves from the beginning to the now, just as time itself has done) but that it will in a sense be subject to the same "physical" laws as the world it describes. In fact, the first changed form we encounter comes not in a story the poem tells but in its own linguistic structures. As the reader unravels the opening sentence, his initial impulse may be to construe the first four words as a complete syntactical unit: "My mind drives me into new things."[1] He would be encouraged in this interpretation by the learned poet's conventional promise of originality, to avoid the well-trodden path according to the precepts of Callimachus, a crucial poetic predecessor. However, the word *corpora* that begins the second line cannot fit in this construction and reveals that the only syntactically possible meaning of the sentence is "my mind impels me to speak of forms changed to new bodies." This transformation in the linguistic surface of the text already suggests that the literary work itself comprises an entity parallel to the outer universe. And if Ovid seems initially to subordinate his creation to this external reality by making its development dependent on the same animating forces, the gods, that created the real world,[2] the repeated first-person pronouns create an undertow of distance and separation, drawing attention to the author's own role in making and defining the world he describes. Ovid's "beginnings" stand juxtaposed to the "first origin of the world," and Ovid's time (*mea tempora*), time as defined and measured by the author,[3] forms the work's conclusion. To blur the distinction further, when Ovid begins his narrative with the creation of the cosmos, he does so in terms that make the divine creator's actions resemble the forging of the Shield of Achilles in Homer's *Iliad*.[4] This effect emphasizes the analogous roles of the artist and god as creators but also, more fundamentally, reverses

---

[1] Kenney 1973.117; 1976. Treated in detail by Wheeler 1999.8–30.

[2] The priority of the external world is also suggested by the expression *animus fert dicere*. *Animus fert*, as von Albrecht 1961 has shown, represents a claim to the epic objectivity of the Homeric narrator, inspired by a reality outside himself, while the verb *dicere*—as opposed to the Vergilian "*canere*" or "*loqui*"—suggests the religious language of the *vates* as prophet, as interpreter of the god's will. See Spahlinger 1996.29–32.

[3] An effect reinforced by self-citation since, as Barchiesi 1991.6 points out, the word links the final goal of the diachronic *Metamorphoses* to Ovid's synchronous poetic treatment of the Roman calendar, the *Fasti*, which begin with the word *tempora*. For a full discussion of the implications of the significance of the pronoun in *mea tempora*, see Feeney 1999.

[4] Wheeler 1995.

the priorities of literary representation and what it represents. Here it is not simply a question of the literary text reproducing or imagining an external event set in motion by the divine actor; rather, the actions of the god himself appear as a reflection or imitation of an earlier literary representation. The originary text of classical literature thus comes to mold the origins of the world itself.

To return to where we began, if Ovid does begin by promising his readers the world, he makes it unclear which world that is, the world of our external experience whose history and shifting form become accessible through the poem, or the poem as world, an artificial creation whose extent and diversity make it an equivalent to the larger cosmos, and whose vivid "realizations" of the stories told can assume the appearance of reality for the audience. This opposition in turn helps shape the strange oscillation of styles that has subjected Ovid's text to so many contradictory critical responses. For, as we shall discover, Ovid characteristically combines passages of great "realism"—in the sense that his representations come to seem real to the readers, drawing them into the narrative, and allowing them to recognize sympathies between themselves and the characters whose experiences are described—with continual reminders of the poet's own manipulating presence and of the artifice through which he shapes the text, reminders that redirect the reader's attention to the work's artistic surface. The connection between these alternative ways of reading and the question of the priority of world and work with which we began is itself far from straightforward. To be absorbed into the narrative can be construed as passing through the text to enter the governing "reality" behind it or as the ultimate proof of the capacity of the literary artist to make a fiction that counts as real. Conversely, those passages that seem to draw attention precisely to the constructive role of the artist undercut the very point they make by anchoring the reader's perspective outside the poem and reminding him of the status of the text in the "real" world: this is, after all, only a poem. My first aim in this book is to draw attention to this opposition as an informing principle of Ovidian narrative and to show how the tension created between these two modes of reception generates the hermeneutic and emotional complexity of so much of his text.

Ovid's suggestion of the potential autonomy of his own fiction, while central to the poetics of the *Metamorphoses*, is hardly unique to it. Works from Chaucer's *Book of the Duchess* to *Harold and the Purple Crayon* imagine a text made world, as the creative process produces an actual space for the reader to enter. The device of the "book within the book" or *mise en abyme*, though not restricted to fiction,[5] can also create a

---

[5] For the phrase and the now classic explication, see Dällenbach 1977.

reader in the text whose experience, to the extent that it resembles and differs from that of the work's actual readers, can make them at once less and more conscious of the activity in which they are engaged. These techniques have become defining characteristics of contemporary "magic realism," where, as in Ovid's poem, the blurring of the boundary between fiction and reality complements intrusions of the fantastic into a narrative unwilling to relinquish the claim to represent events located in the world of our own experience. One obvious explanation for the omnipresence of such phenomena is that they expose something essential about the reception of all fiction: a suspension of disbelief that is never quite total, that even in the case of the most "absorbing" play, film, or novel always exists in counterpoise to an awareness of who and where one is.[6]

But an appeal to a universal law of fiction fails to exhaust the importance of this phenomenon as it operates in any single text. Even if the experience of fiction is always at some level the same, its significance in a given set of historical and cultural circumstances will vary dramatically. Indeed, the choice to make the workings of fiction explicit can often herald some pressure on, or demand reexamination of, the role that fictional representation plays in a society. Thus, magic realist representations of readers drawn into the plot of what they read—such as Julio Cortazar's "The Continuity of Parks," where a man sits down to read a murder novel only to discover that he is the victim—have been understood as a way not so much of demonstrating a book's absorptive powers but rather of claiming for it a status beyond that of mere entertainment, of warning off the reader looking only for diversion. This impulse in turn can be interpreted as a reflex of these works' postcolonial origins—a reaction to the sense that one's own experience has already been scripted by the texts of a distant culture—or related to the operations of the marketplace, where outsiders rely on the entertainment value of their works to reach the lucrative markets of the West.[7] How might Ovid's construction of his poem's fictionality make sense in the context of Augustan Rome and what it can tell us about the terms in which the text can participate in that culture?

The very posing of such a question about Ovid still needs some defending. For one of the most beguiling responses to Ovid's assertions of the constructive power of art and the alterity of the world of his fictions is to take them at face value. Critics working along these lines have suggested an analogy between Ovid's procedures and aestheticizing *l'art pour l'art* movements of the nineteenth century. Projecting these conclusions back to the political context of late Augustan Rome, they depict a

---

[6] Feeney 1991.224–49, citing Newsom 1988.134–35.
[7] Thiem 1995.

poem whose aim is to provide sophisticated amusement and escape for the disaffected upper classes. Like Ovid, members of a generation too young to remember the serious struggles of the civil wars, these frivolous young nobles were also excluded from meaningful occupations by the growing self-aggrandizement of the imperial family.[8] The artificial reality of the Ovidian text irresistibly recalls those other illusionistic retreats, the luxurious villas whose painted landscapes and trompe-l'oeil gardens open up comparable imaginary vistas.[9] Yet recently scholars have been reminded that such elaborate interior spaces, when viewed in the context of the Roman house, were never purely aesthetic monuments set back from the outer world but also stage sets where the very public identities of their owners were forged and displayed.[10] In a similar way, if we do not focus exclusively on the illusions the poem creates but also remember the social realities of the text itself—and we shall repeatedly see that the very conspicuousness of Ovid's disclaimers invites us to do just that—efforts to isolate the poem from any kind of context become less tenable.

Those who have read a political agenda in Ovid's poem have frequently identified that purpose as the expression of authorial attitudes toward the regime of Augustus. The most dramatic and best-known incident in the life of the poet, his relegation to the Black Sea in 8 CE, validates such investigation by suggesting that there was indeed a political component to the poet's activities, whether personal or artistic, and that they were regarded negatively by the emperor. While the fact of relegation fuels efforts to uncover anti-Augustan elements in the poetry, the self-justifications Ovid sent back from exile use the *Metamorphoses* itself as testimony to the poet's glorification of Augustus.[11] As Stephen Hinds has pointed out, the most potent aspect of Ovid's allusions to the regime is precisely their indirectness. The comparison of Jupiter's assembling the gods to the emperor's summoning the Senate (1.163ff.), for example, sets in motion an analogy that follows the conventions of panegyric but can seem less flattering, given the cruel and indulgent acts of Jupiter that receive so much attention in Ovid's work. The poetry can sustain either point of view while distancing both from the authority of the poet. For Hinds, Ovid's technique of political commentary heralds the only form that criticism of the emperor can take under an increasingly authoritarian

---

[8] Above all, Little 1972, also Lyne 1984 and even Rosati 1983. Comparable are the conclusions of Due 1974.88 that Ovid "has nothing against praising the emperor: praise, even flattery was a becoming part of good manners. But Ovid thoroughly lacked any deeper understanding of true Augustanism."

[9] Bernbeck 1967.135–38.

[10] In particular by Wallace-Hadrill 1996.

[11] For a review of the arguments and bibliography up through 1993, see Bretzigheimer 1993.

regime, an ostensible panegyric seeded with irony, although, as he admits, the very nature of his argument makes it impossible ever to prove Ovid's intentions.[12]

Though he ultimately opted for a subversive Ovid, Hinds's analysis pointed toward an important redefinition of the terms in which the poetry's political aspect was discussed as attention was directed away from the intentions of the author toward the effect on the audience. Many recent studies, including this one, start from the premise that poetry puts in play contrasting views of the emperor so that it becomes a touchstone for the audience to consolidate or reconsider its own position in relation to the center of Roman power. For Denis Feeney, the questions that the poem opens up about the believability of fictions ultimately flow into a discourse about the summit of imperial self-representation, the claim to divinity. "With an apparent guilelessness that never entirely vanishes, Augustus' repeated assertions of his quasi-divine status are taken at face-value by Ovid, and nobody—not Augustus, nor Ovid, nor any reader—can circumscribe the limits at which the implications of this status cease to register."[13] Alessandro Barchiesi ends his discussion of the effects of closure in both the *Metamorphoses* and the *Fasti* with the position that far from simply responding to external conditions, favorably or unfavorably, Ovid's work has itself summoned up the debate between Augustans and anti-Augustans through the very fact of its "erratic irony,"[14] crystallizing alternative responses to the regime through its own ambiguity.

As both of these comments make clear, what had been a position of weakness, with the poet forced to renounce his own authority—or too self-evidently making such a gesture to indict his loss of liberty—has become one of strength. From imagining a poet unable to express his own views without indirection in the face of repressive forces from outside, we have moved to a poem that determines its audience's definitions of that "outside." The impact of new historicism, and in Latin studies the work of Duncan Kennedy in particular,[15] has sharpened the recognition that literature exists within the larger political culture rather than commenting on it from some distant vantage point, and that therefore to focus analysis on the mere transmission of authorial opinion about seemingly external events and practices provides only a limited perspective on the political efficacy of any text. The "Augustus" that previous scholars would have Ovid support or oppose himself bears a name whose meaning is determined by a process of discourse in which the text participates

---

[12] Hinds 1987b.24–31.
[13] Feeney 1991.224.
[14] Barchiesi 1997b.272.
[15] Kennedy 1992.

and in which any positive statement summons up a host of alternatives from its diverse audience.

My project in this book is informed throughout by these new readings of Ovid. The "politics" of *Metamorphoses* it addresses does not mean the same thing as Ovid's politics, and readers will find no explicit discussion of the attitudes of the poet toward the emperor. Rather my goal is to expand our understanding of the modes by which the work facilitates the audience's reflection on and redefinition of the hierarchies operative within Roman society. (If relatively few episodes in the poem refer directly or transparently to Augustus, it is surprising how many hinge on inequalities in power relations more generally, as superiors and inferiors alternately punish, exploit, confer benefits on, and deceive one another.) A good example of this difference in emphasis comes in my treatment of the poem's self-proclaimed subject, metamorphosis. Metamorphosis can easily find an external referent that allows it to be read as part of a commentary on contemporary politics. In the face of a regime then intensely interested in manifesting its stability and permanence, the voices within the poem that insist on change as the only immutable law seem to offer a dangerous challenge. Conversely, the persistence of identity that sometimes seems within the poem to survive even the most radical changes of form gibes with Augustus's repeated assurances that he had restored the past rather than replacing it. The question of what metamorphosis means—and in chapter 1 I argue for the impossibility of pinning down a stable view of metamorphosis—does indeed impact on the audience's understanding of contemporary politics. But metamorphosis is more than just a term to be defined, whose definition can then be extended outward from text to world. Within the poem, the experience of metamorphosis becomes a means by which characters and audiences apprehend the workings of a variety of forces. Metamorphosis, as a tool for deception, as the immortalization of the subject, as justified punishment, or as cruel victimization, confronts characters with the fact of their vulnerability or power and its conflicting meanings and consequences. And, as I demonstrate in part 2, a connection with the world outside the text exists for this aspect of metamorphosis as well in the spectacles and sacrifices that similarly gave audiences the choice of identifying with victims or victors, and of recognizing a self in the captive works of art that adorned the imperial city. In this way, the poet not only mobilizes reflection on the imperial regime but creates a new space for the experience of power. Ovid is not just writing about the emperor; he is, in this sense, writing as emperor.

In addition to expanding our view of the techniques by which Ovid engages his audience in examining its place in and understanding of Roman society, it is equally important to expand our awareness of the breadth of that society. The debate about Ovid's "Augustanism" has further skewed investigation of the political dimension of Ovid's work by defining politics almost solely in terms of the emperor.[16] That is not to say that the name of Augustus will be absent from the pages that follow—far from it. But as opposed to reading the poet's treatment of Augustus primarily to ascertain the author's opinions of the regime, or even, as Feeney and Barchiesi have done, to demonstrate the multivalent portraits that mobilize the audience's judgments of the new empire, I will be arguing, above all in the second chapter, that by highlighting his own efforts to represent Augustus Ovid invites attention precisely to the capacity of his poem to become an element in political discourse. The presence of Augustus within the poem involves much more than the question of whether the stories the emperor tells about himself are credible. As a figure who is so undoubtedly a real presence in the extratextual experience of Ovid's readers, Augustus's appearance in the text also compels an evaluation of the extent and capacities of the poem's constructions of the world. And more than a poetic strategy is at work here, for the emperor's omnipresent self-representations transformed how members of all classes constructed their public identities. One of the consequences of such an environment will emerge as a blurring of the boundary between the author and the audience, as reception becomes itself a context for display. Thus, it is no accident that the poet's most distinctive definition of his own role as a poet depends precisely on the way he stages his own response to Augustus.

But the new historicist perspective that blurs the distinctions between text and context also brings a risk of distortion, particularly when applied to Ovid's poem. For triumphal assumptions about the broad political role of all texts and the position they occupy in making rather than reflecting political discourse were not ones that the writer of the *Metamorphoses* or its audience would have taken as a given. Rather, as I have already suggested, the idea of the text in the world, so to speak, always exists in tension with a view of the creative capacities of poetry, of its ability to make a world that seems real but ultimately, and importantly, is not. If we hold fast to our own orthodoxies, either about the segregation of "poetry and life" or about their interpenetration, we will miss the experience the *Metamorphoses* offers of having such assumptions challenged. We will also overlook the genuine uncertainties with which Ovid probes the boundaries between reality and illusion and his acute awareness of the vulnerability and impotence of mere words.

---

[16] See Habinek 2002, esp. 56: "Indeed the overattention to the relationship between poet and princeps that characterizes much recent work on Ovid comes close to being an avoidance of politics altogether."

The model of the poem's place in the world offered here draws its inspiration from the paradoxes presented by its form and content. The oscillations generated by the narrative between absorption in a fictional world and awareness of the text as a present artifact find an echo in the rival images of the cosmos within the poem, of an ephemeral world where everything changes in contrast with the permanent forms that so many of its characters assume. So we shall see Ovid respond to the realia of experience with a transparent textualization that charges them with new mythical associations and views them from new perspectives by placing them back in a narrative about change.

But at the same time as the *Metamorphoses* points out the fluidity of hard facts, the invocations of the immediate physical world of its audience anchor in the here and now a work that has sometimes seemed to float free in space and time. The constant appeal of the *Metamorphoses* in different epochs has sometimes been attributed to Ovid's decontextualization of myth. But as Feeney has recently argued, it is better to call the resulting narrative "universalizing" than "universal," for it treats myth not as pure story addressing aspects of human experience independent of particular cults or cultures but as something to be regrafted onto the specific local environment of the reader.[17] The trees, animals, and statues that precipitate from his narrative become not just the products of literary description to be seen in the mind's eye; rather, real objects bring the distant world of his stories into the present. And this effect would have been all the more immediate to the poem's first readers, whose homes and cities were filled with the physical traces of Ovid's tales also in the form of artistic representations.

The weight it gives to this second aspect of textual "metamorphosis" also differentiates my work from the many important recent studies that have stressed the poet's ability to generate belief and "absent presences" through the illusions of representation. As opposed to looking at this illusionistic capacity from the text out, my emphasis will be to imagine how these efforts appear from the outside in, that is, from the horizons defined by the material and social circumstances of its first readers. Such an attempt raises two immediate difficulties. First is the infinite diversity of "realities" that first audience would have brought to its reading, and the absence of any evidence allowing us to gauge the range of responses that even a single artifact might have evoked. The semantic complexities of the text itself compound these problems: even if all readers did apply the same set of outside references to the interpretation of the poem, the way they would use them to construe its meaning would again be irre-

[17] Feeney 1998.74.

coverably varied. Any project like mine must therefore be subjective and partial; I am not claiming the ability to recover even one Augustan reading as a historical fact. But that the poem was read by that first audience and that it formed an element in their reading of the world around them are historical phenomena whose interest and importance, both for Augustan culture as a whole and for our conception of Ovid's poem, are not diminished because they must be approached through the imagination.

Having said something about what I mean by politics, I also want to offer a brief defense of a second key term in my title, fiction. For although the word derives transparently from the Latin verb, *fingo*, meaning to mold or shape, an ancient theory of fiction has become something of a holy grail for literary critics. Scholars of the ancient novel in particular, the classical form that seems tantalizingly like the modern genre we most reflexively think of when we hear the term fiction, have used the virtual absence of any Greek or Roman account of what these works do to make us aware at once of the complex bundle of terms contained in our word fiction and the distance that separates it from any ancient categories of narrative. In light of this, one might have preferred to speak of "illusion" in describing Ovid's crafting of images that are accepted as reality. Yet, aside from the practical inconvenience that this word has recently featured in the title of another monograph on Ovidian poetics,[18] "illusion" also throws disproportionate emphasis on but one aspect of the phenomenon I am studying here. Illusion certainly connotes the approximation of art to the status of the real, the blurring of the boundary between what one is made to see or hear and what is. And the very mention of illusion does indeed create precisely the hermeneutic tension between knowing that something is not there and thinking that it is or, in Philip Hardie's terms, between seeing the illusion as a presence or as an absence. "Fiction," by contrast, adds an emphasis on the uncanniness and improbability of the whole experience by stressing not so much the perceptions of the audience, or even the craft of the artist, but the fundamental "not-there-ness" of what is represented. Illusions surprise us by not being real, fictions by seeming to be.

My emphasis on the distance between fictional narrative and reality helps overcome any anachronism imported by the term fiction by moving us closer to the ancient categories of narrative. Ancient rhetoricians divided narratives into three classes according to their relationship to reality: histories (*historiae*) told what actually happened; *argumenta*, exemplified by the plots of new comedy, presented plausible stories, things that might have happened; and, finally, "tales" (*fabulae*) describe events that are not only "untrue, but separated even from the appearance of

[18] Hardie 2002c.

truth" because they are unnatural or impossible.[19] This last category, frequently exemplified by tales of transformation, would self-evidently be the one into which Ovid's own narratives would fall.[20] However, what in this system seems a straightforward progression, from not being real to not seeming real, in fact folds together two potentially distinct modern criteria for marking off fiction from reality: that it is not "true" and that it is not realistic, or "make-believe." Their absence of verisimilitude would seem to set Ovid's stories of transformation programmatically in the category of *fabulae*, by ancient reckoning the one most removed from reality. And yet for all Ovid's gesturing in this direction, his stories, like so much of what we call "myth," combine elements of different narrative "genres" in perplexing and challenging ways.[21] Thus, while their essential subject matter falls in the category of the unbelievable, not only do these narratives contain passages of great verisimilitude, sometimes leading into obvious anachronism, but they possess the chronological framework of history itself.[22] And the very questions of whether anthropomorphized gods were either "real" or "believable" would inevitably depend on the predispositions of the audience and the context in which they were represented. Another important factor that generally makes reading fictional narratives more complex and problematic for ancient audiences was the general absence of a context, like that of the modern novel for example, in which men told fictions without relinquishing a claim to cultural authority and prestige; without this the line between fictions and simple falsity in describing reality (i.e., lies) becomes much harder to negotiate.

[19] For examples of this classification, see Sext. *Gramm.* 1.263, *Rhet. ad Herr.* 1.13, Cic. *Inv.* 1.27, and Quint. Inst. 2.3.4 (quoted in the text).

[20] Thus, Sextus (1.264) includes the tales "of the companions of Diomedes changed into sea birds, of Odysseus changed to a horse, and of Hecuba to a dog," in this class, and Martianus Capella (486.16H.) presents the transformation of Daphne as a paradigmatic *fabula*.

[21] On the problem of classifying mythical narratives in this schema, see Konstan 1998. In this article Konstan also employs a different criterion for describing fiction, referentiality, that has interesting consequences for Ovid's text as well. He argues that what makes the ancient novels different from other ancient narratives is the absence, for all their verisimilitude, of any external referent in relation to which claims can be judged as true or false: there is simply no Daphnis or Chloe outside the text "for Longus to have been mistaken about." If we accept Konstan's claims that both mythical events and conventional figures, including the "cunning slave" of comedy, can also serve as such referents, then Ovid in the *Metamorphoses* adopts a diametrically opposite fictional strategy to the novelists, whose work, Konstan argues, responds to the same set of historical circumstances. Whereas the novels offer "realistic" narratives that nevertheless describe figures with no existence outside of the specific text in which they appear, Ovid tells unbelievable stories whose referentiality is almost overdetermined—by their engagement with myth, their "historical" framework, and the variety of real objects, species, and practices that accrue from them.

[22] See Wheeler 2002; also Cole 2004.

PART ONE

Fiction and Empire

CHAPTER 1

===

Metamorphosis and Fiction

The aim of this first chapter is to offer a fuller description of the distinctive nature of Ovidian fictionality. A close reading of the extensive narrative sequence that occupies the last quarter of Ovid's first book—the interlocked tales of Io, Argus, and Syrinx—highlights how Ovid's strategies of keeping the reader at once aware of the external reality of his text and absorbed by the reality it describes are thematized within the story and reciprocally linked to the emergence of distinctive internal points of view. Two specific features of the poem especially further this play between the positions of internality and externality available to the reader: the subject matter of metamorphosis itself and what seem to be extratextual exhortations toward skepticism delivered by figures within the narrative. By suggesting how a Roman reader's approach to such issues would be colored by different assumptions about the role and nature of poetic fiction, we can attempt to historicize our reading further.

I. Io and Syrinx

The account of how Jupiter transforms Io into a cow to conceal her from his jealous wife, of her experiences in her new form, and finally of how Mercury rescues her by slaying her hundred-eyed guard Argus takes up roughly the last third of the poem's first book. I have chosen it as an introduction to the complexities of the poem's narrative because Ovid himself uses it to train his readers to balance a connoisseurial awareness of the poem's elaborate verbal texture with an empathy for the characters that allows them to penetrate the surface of the text and "enter" into the story it tells. The tale of Io also provides a useful starting place because it is just the kind of episode that has over the past several decades provoked antithetical critical responses to Ovid's work. One reading focuses on the kind of close psychological observation that gives Ovid's portrayals of suffering a verisimilitude almost unique in Latin literature; the other presents the poet as a verbal gamester for whom even the greatest suffering offers only an occasion for the display of wit and a forensic cleverness.

Here is Ovid's account of the moment when Juno hands Io over to be guarded by Argus:

> *Centum luminibus cinctum caput Argus habebat:*
> *inde suis vicibus capiebant bina quietem,*
> *cetera servabant atque in statione manebant.*
> *constiterat quocumque modo, spectabat ad Io.*
> *ante oculos Io, quamvis aversus, habebat.*
> *luce sinit pasci; cum sol tellure sub alta est,*
> *claudit et indigno circumdat vincula collo.*
> *frondibus arboreis et amara pascitur herba*
> *proque toro terrae non semper gramen habenti*
> *incubat infelix limosaque flumina potat.*
> *illa etiam supplex Argo cum bracchia vellet*
> *tendere, non habuit quae bracchia tenderet Argo,*
> *et conata queri mugitus edidit ore*
> *pertimuitque sonos propriaque exterrita voce est.*
>   (1.625–38)

Argus's head was girded with a hundred eyes, which slept in pairs while the others guarded her and remained at their post. Wherever he stood, he looked at Io: he had Io before his eyes even when he turned away. By day he lets her graze; when the sun goes beneath the deep earth, he shuts her in and encloses her undeserving neck with a chain. She feeds on the leaves of trees and bitter grass and in place of a couch, reclines on the earth—and that not always even covered with sod—and drinks from slimy rivers. Even when she wished to stretch her arms to Argus as a suppliant, she found that she had no arms to stretch out to him. When she tried to lament, she gave forth a moo; she feared the sound and was terrified by her own voice.

Io's terror at her own voice reproduces, as a classic article of the 1970s pointed out, a clinically observed effect of the experience of rape.[1] It is one of the more telling psychological touches in the poem, conveying the full horror of Io's situation. But the passage as a whole seems hardly the place to look for such horror. In fact, the girl's baffled attempt at communication becomes part of a set of human endeavors rendered impossible by her new form, the kind of clever catalog that has made Ovid infamous. Each human pleasure yields a new bovine discomfort: grass replaces food (and here Ovid makes his narrative fulfill the prediction

---

[1] Curran 1978.

made in an earlier Latin treatment of Io);[2] earth takes the place of a bed, and muddy rivers provide her drink. Argus's physical peculiarity gives rise to another witty figure of thought, the paradox that he gazes at Io even when he turns away. The very lines are also elaborately patterned: like Argus's eyes they work in pairs, with the description of cow cultural practices—signaled by the enjambed *incubat*—marking the only three-line unit. Descriptions also tend to end with a pleonastic doubling: *in statione manebant* amplifies *servabant, indigna … collo* does more or less the same for *claudit*, and the pattern continues even in the account of the girl's pathetic self-alienation, where the second half of the hexameter restates the first.

Another level of literary self-consciousness appears in the description of Argus. The language describing the grotesque monster comes very close to the traditional depiction of the lover in Latin love elegy. The persistent lover must endure all sorts of hardships, encamped on his beloved's threshold; Argus would prove remarkably well equipped for such a lifestyle, able to snatch sleep while remaining "at his post," a conventional transposition of military language to describe amatory "warfare." His ocular endowments also mean that, like the lover, he keeps the image of Io always before him. Indeed, when line 630 begins, the reader may be tempted to assume that *luce* is an ablative of means and that Argus will feast his eyes on the image of his beloved. This invocation of the genre in which Ovid made his literary reputation can serve to amplify by contrast precisely the horrific aspects of Io's plight. If only Argus were merely a lover, if only he were subject to the sympathy that the elegiac lover traditionally feels for his beloved's misfortune,[3] if only the entire grotesque situation were susceptible to the stock descriptions of elegiac convention. But at the same time, for the informed reader who has followed the invitation issued in the poem's preface to pay attention to the interaction between epic and the slighter genres, there is a delightful appeal in seeing elegiac conventions foisted back on precisely the kind of mythological scenes that earlier love poets had used to provide ironic foils to their own fictive affairs. And, as an alternative to interpreting the depiction of Argus as lover as a technique for highlighting the pathetic content of the episode, we can see the self-referential literary game as determining even Io's terror of her own voice. Her discovery that she can only moo offers a parallel for the poet's own witty advertisement of the fact that his elegiac language has been strangely distorted into an epic roar. Io wants to lament, *queri*, the very task of an elegist, in fact the programmatic one,

[2] Calvus, fr. 9 Courtney: *a virgo infelix, herbis pasceris amaris*. See Barchiesi 2005.219.
[3] Cf., e.g., Gallus imagining Lycoris's tender feet hurt by Alpine ice (Verg. *E.* 10.48).

because elegy as a genre was believed to derive from lamentation. So too, the moo that comes out instead recalls the hollow rumblings conventionally used to disparage windy epic utterance.

It should be clear that my point is not to privilege one of these readings over the other—though it should also be clear how trivial, not to say offensive, the reduction of Io's silence to merely another literary sport will be to critics with a serious interest in Ovid's portrayal of the victims of the god's sexual imperialism and conversely how strained this alternative reading might seem to critics interested above all in Ovid's poem as a showpiece of sophisticated generic play.[4] Rather I want to stress that the narrative makes both responses available to the reader and indeed correlates them with the perspective from which Io's plight is viewed. For the humor that comes from the narrative derives from another kind of superficiality than simply the attention to the obtrusive effects of the narrative surface. Here, as elsewhere in Ovid, it is the visual overexplicitness with which the poet describes the unusual forms of the two nonhuman figures as they are measured against the standard of conventional human behaviors that produces the cleverness.[5] The many-eyed giant who keeps Io in his sight resembles the elegiac lover except when we remember those hundred eyes, in which case the metaphorical meaning of the phrase "he had her always before his eyes" becomes quite literal. Similarly, as long as we, like Argus, keep Io's bovine form before our eyes, the incongruity of the cow acting as a human amuses.

But not the least important of the passage's doublings comes when Io's own perspective emerges in counterpoise to that of the watcher Argus. As the repetition of the name Io at the end of the line and at the following caesura marked the account of Argus's response to Io (1.628–29), so her actions toward Argus call forth a symmetrical pattern of repetition (Argo at line end, 636; Argo at caesura, 635). This mirroring within the text reminds us how different things look when viewed from out of the cow's eye, and how disorienting our experience of the narrative becomes when such a possibility enters into it. Io, unlike Argus, does not take her cow form for granted; she acts as though she were human and finds that her form baffles and frightens her and frustrates her intentions.[6] We have been reading a narrative that similarly seemed to present fantastic forms as commonplace, but once we measure these fantastical forms subjectively, against our own expectations of experience, as Io's perspective on her form invites us to do, a kind of recognition makes us feel the full

[4] Fränkel 1945.79–80.

[5] See Galinsky 1975.179–84 and Hinds 1987b on overexplicitness.

[6] On this discrepancy between psychological state and external appearance, see esp. Rosati 1983.109–14.

strangeness of this fantastic world. We heard without demur that Argus "had" a hundred eyes; Io raises her arms, in the natural assumption that she possesses them, only to discover that she "has" none. Between the beginning and the ending of the passage, we have moved from the distant perspective of the watcher, for whom any fantastical image can be marveled at with equanimity, to that of the participant for whom this fantasy has become all too vivid.

Our discovery in this passage of an overlap between the reader's experience and the alternative perceptions of the characters within the poem receives confirmation when in the very next scene a written text makes possible the recognition of Io. The transformed Io arrives at the stream of her father, the river god Inachus. Lacking a human voice, she first tries to make her identity known through gestures. She acts as a daughter by following after her father and sisters, by allowing herself to be touched, by licking and kissing his hand, and by weeping. Yet although such gestures provoke astonishment (*admirantibus*, 1.644), they are interpreted through her bovine form and, in the absence of language, cannot convey a human identity within it. A friendly cow may be uncanny, but precisely because it is a cow. Finally, she resorts to the expedient of writing, an intrinsically human activity.[7] The act of tracing her name with her feet at once reveals her identity, draws attention to the remarkable ingenuity of the poet, and, appropriately for such a doubly valent gesture, brings to the fore problems of reading and interpretation. The very letters that make up Io's name have in Greek another signification; they mean "alas," and such an expression of sorrow is perfectly suited to her situation. In fact, one might say that to recognize Io necessitates the cry alas. Lest anyone miss this point, Ovid works another clarifying transformation on the inscribed text, translating written Greek into spoken Latin in the reply of Inachus—*me miserum*! Inachus's words here reveal fully what is at stake in recognizing Io, not just the acknowledgment of her identity but a kind of sympathy that literally makes him the vehicle for her voice. *Me miserum* not only translates bovine Greek into comprehensible Latin— making clear for Ovid's reader's what Io has written; it also conveys Inachus's own emotional response to the discovery. Inachus intends *me miserum* to represent his own suffering: however, in context the *me* is Io.[8] But this optimistic reading of reading as a way by which writing literally restores a lost identity is unfortunately only part of the story. For Inachus's subsequent speech reveals that it is very much his own sor-

---

[7] See Santini 1998.

[8] *me miserum* as a translation of *io* has now also been observed by Barchiesi 2005.221. As P. Hardie points out to me, *per litteras*, the other "transformation" Io's text has undergone is one of gender, for Inachus *me* is grammatically masculine: "Even in the act of self-reflection the male reader is inevitably distanced from the female subjectivity."

rows that are on his mind. Far from empathizing with Io's misfortune, Inachus is interested only in what his daughters new form means for him. Like any demigod—or Roman father—on the make, he had hoped to advance his status through his daughter's marriage. Now, however, the opposite will be the case: his son-in-law will be a bull, and his grandchildren cattle—just the kind of humor we have already seen to depend on an inability to penetrate Io's form.

Not surprisingly, Ovid signals the parallel between this first representation of reading in the poem and the audience's task of interpreting his work as text. Io's writing is described as the sign of her new form, *corporis indicium mutati*, a citation of the poem's definition of its subject matter in lines 1–2. Indeed, the closely related word *index* can itself mean the title or summary of a literary work, a point that gives a further level of self-referentiality to Io's "citation," because the poem as a whole might well be indexed as something like *mutata corpora*.[9] If *indicium* makes us think of the actual label hanging on a book roll, that will not be the only reminder of the materiality of Ovid's text in the passage. For the word *corpora* itself has already been subject to change here. What Io sees when she looks at herself reflected in the stream is new horns, *nova cornua*. Not only is this a variant for the poem's opening theme—where *corpora* is also modified by *nova* and occurs at the same emphatic position in the line—but *cornua* were themselves the wooden knobs at the ends of the papyrus role.[10] But beyond the suggestion that Io herself, transformed into a book roll, becomes a real presence to every reader, the scene where Io sees herself mirrored in the stream introduces an even greater level of reflexivity between the various levels of audience. For the mirror through which Io sees herself is in a very literal sense none other than the reader of her words. The stream is the Inachus, and Inachus is the very river god who, in crying out *me miserum*, mirrors Io's own writings. This moment of self-recognition as a cow, then, comes when she literally sees herself as others see her, and those others are her readers, and yet the very same device makes the reader himself a reflection of Io, and so gives access to her experience as perceiving subject.

What this passage shows above all is how closely the question of narrative form is bound up with the changing "forms" that make up the poem's content. A loose parallelism between the two has been a staple of Ovidian criticism: as the universe it describes is constantly in flux, so

[9] *OLD* s.v. *index* § 3. Ovid himself will use the tag phrase, *corpora versa*, at Trist. 2.64 to refer to the *Metamorphoses*. See Horsfall 1981.104.

[10] A pun elsewhere observed by Barchiesi 1997a.187, and with particular panache by Wheeler 1999.92–93 in reference to the horns of the bull that carries away Europa, see the introduction to chapter 6.

the tone and configuration of Ovid's poem oscillates before the readers eyes, veering between the comical, the grotesque, the tragic, and the philosophical. His interest in form has also been connected to an Ovidian impulse to "change the shape" of the narratives that he inherits from earlier authors, introducing comic elements into an epic narrative, for example.[11] Here though, the way the characters themselves respond to Io's changed shape offers a model for precisely the kind of ambiguity that the surface of the text produces: as the narrative of the poem generates two apparently incompatible readings, so Io's own form constitutes a puzzle or problem, capable of eliciting divergent responses from characters depending on how and from whence they view it.[12] And as Io's shape alone can suffice to categorize and define her, so too the poem's linguistic play, the attention it attracts to its own form, can seem to take over the narrative content, partly, in the sense we have seen, in that the story that is told can seem to be so self-referential that it does nothing but provide an allegory for the style of the narrative itself. But that is not all there is to the relationship between narrative form and the form of the characters. The problem of Io's changed form offers more than a paradigm for how the reader can interpret the text of the Io story. His own understanding of Io's form plays a crucial role in determining the reader's response to the narrative itself: to focus on Io as cow opens up one possibility for reading; to be aware of her humanity, quite another. Put another way, as the reader enters into each level of narration—in this case by moving from an awareness of his role as reader of the Ovidian text to an interest in and acceptance of the perspective of Argus, he encounters another enigma that juxtaposes the same potentials for external wonder and sympathetic identification as the first. And the two levels of interpretation required influence one another reciprocally—thus the reader fascinated by the poet's wit will perhaps be less inclined to achieve the final identification with Io; conversely, it is precisely Argus's conviction that Io is just a cow that is required to appreciate the humor of the poem.

Argus's role as a model, or foil, for the reader's interpretation of the narrative serves as a preparation for the next episode, in which Argus quite explicitly becomes the audience for a typically Ovidian narrative. After Io has encountered and been recognized by her father, Jupiter can at last no longer endure her misfortunes. (Perhaps he himself has come to adopt a different perspective on Io; at any rate, his response here seems

---

[11] Galinsky 1975.4–6, citing *AA* 2.127–28, where Ovid has Odysseus tells Calypso the story of the fall of Troy over and over again always varying it, *referre idem aliter*. See also Galinsky 1975.62–63.

[12] Cf. again Rosati 1983.109–114.

directly opposite to the last time he saw [*viderat*] Io departing from her father's stream, when he was impelled to rape her, thus beginning her misfortunes.) He sends his son Mercury off to kill Argus, and the divine messenger, after a quick change of costume, appears before Io's guardian as a shepherd. After much conversation, the god attempts to put Argus to sleep by playing on the panpipes. Argus asks the origin of this strange instrument, and is rewarded with the story of Pan's desire for the nymph Syrinx. Halfway through the tale however, Ovid abruptly changes from the direct report of the god's words into indirect discourse, through which he completes the tale of the nymph's transformation into reeds to escape Pan's pursuit. What has happened, of course, is that Argus has fallen asleep while listening to Mercury's words, and the god wastes no more time but immediately slits his throat and hurls him from the rock he sits on.

Here Argus literally hears the same story as Ovid's audience, but his failure as a listener to be absorbed by the narrative results from just the kind of "superficial" interest that distinguished his response to Io.[13] David Konstan has argued that Argus's fascination with the pipes points out his responsiveness to the artistry of the god's song and to the music of his performance, in contrast to his utter lack of interest "in the human narrative that lies behind [the instrument the poet uses]."[14] He then goes on to locate the alternatives of mere admiration for the technical skill of the narrator, of his *ars*, and the kind of absorption possible when the narrattee recognizes himself in the narrative in ancient theories of aesthetic response, going back as far as the *Odyssey*. In Plato's *Ion*, for example, the rhapsode's ability to enter sympathetically into the Homeric poems he performs differentiates him from the philosophical listener or, more precisely, watcher (*theates*), a term that perhaps suggests the distance required for the thoughtful analysis of the poem's content. Indeed, Konstan suggests that Argus, who is, as we have seen, all eyes, can "almost" be read as a parody of the philosophical spectator, who tunes out when his quite technical question about the origin of the pipes turns out to provide no material to engage his interest. Aristotle's account of the emotions roused by tragedy also hinges on the capacity of those in the audience to perceive themselves in the position of the character whose suffering they see represented. Thus, for example, pity depends on some perceived likeness between the character depicted and the audience, while genuine fear comes when we fully accept an identification

---

[13] Galinsky 1975.174 treats Argus not as a foil for the reader but as a reminder of precisely the response demanded of the Syrinx story, which is merely the transposition of the narrative of Daphne and so all too well known to the audience.

[14] Konstan 1991.19.

with such characters to the point of identifying a danger to them as a danger to ourselves.[15]

But to return to the question of what sort of audience Argus provides, and how and why he differs from the poet's own audience, we can begin by noting the trust he places in appearances and in artifacts. Again, the ground is laid for Argus's fatal lapse of attention when the creature fails to recognize the god Mercury, assuming that he is a fellow shepherd because of the attributes he bears. In the same way as Konstan points out, the artifact of the panpipes and the physical sensation they produce work upon him, just as the same artifact prompts his request for the tale of its origins. The song, as it were, takes priority over and generates its narrative content. But once the story begins—or, more specifically, once the god's narrative comes to introduce other characters who perceive—Argus loses interest entirely.[16] The beginning of the story is entirely descriptive; when the figure of Pan ceases to be described and begins actively to see (*videt*) and to speak (*verba refert*), Mercury can stop narrating because his audience is asleep.

Is Ovid then inviting his audience to go beyond Argus's limited perceptions? To the extent that he continues telling the story of Syrinx, he presumably expects them to be more interested in it than Argus was. On the other hand, the way the narrative is continued, the elaborate game of putting the rest of the story in indirect discourse, advertises the artfulness with which the poet has contrived his own narrative structures. The audience, if it is expected to be interested in the narrative itself, is also supposed to be awake to the function it fills within the poet's own artifice. For if we accept Argus as the model of the reader who sees only the surface of the narrative, there is another model interpreter within the narrative complex who makes the opposite set of cognitive mistakes, the god Pan himself. As Argus mistook a god for a shepherd because of his staff, so Pan initially seems to mistake a nymph for a goddess, despite the telltale difference in their attributes. Similarly, later in the story Pan hears the same sound as Argus, the wind playing through the reeds, and is similarly "captivated" by it. As opposed to Argus, though, who can

---

[15] Another connection between the way Ovid has constructed the role of the reader here and this tradition of ancient narratological theory comes when Io's changed form becomes a figure for the narrative's own deceptive surface. Not only do strange or incredible appearances become a defining feature of *fabulae*, but these narratives themselves are sometimes figured as presenting a strange or implausible "form" to the reader. Thus, Quintilian defines *fabulae* as narratives remote even from the form of truth (*a forma veritatis*, 2.4.2).

[16] Indeed, his incapacity to identify with the perspectives of either of the characters in the Pan and Syrinx story is precisely what qualifies him to act as Io's guard. He can neither recognize or identify with the metamorphosed object of the god's desire nor, like Pan, can he desire her himself. He can only watch.

respond only to the instrument itself and cannot hear whose "voice" it is, the god makes the mistake of overly subjectivizing what is really just a clump of reeds. He hears the wind moved by his sighs passing over the reeds[17] and, because the resulting sound resembles a lament, interprets it as the expression of the vanished nymph, even though it is nothing other than the transformation of his own voice, and assumes that it will make possible a "conversation" (*conloquium*) that it has in fact prevented.

Argus's function in constructing the reader's response to Ovid's narrative, then, is not so simple as an injunction to "absorption" in the inner narrative. For Argus is guilty not only of a lack of interest in the story but also of a lack of awareness of his present circumstances, of the context in which the tale is told. Falling asleep, after all, is hardly the connoisseur's response to a poet's technical craft. He fails in both the aspects of the task that Ovid has set for his reader of being at once inside and outside the story. Thus, Argus's failure to enter into the narrative comes not simply from a lack of psychological engagement with the narrated events but also from the passive assumption that he is outside or beyond the reach of the narrative, when in fact the tale of Syrinx is very much a part of his story. What is so shocking when the report of his death finally comes is the reminder of the connection between the various levels of narrative.[18] One effect of the way Ovid has deferred the climax of Argus's story is that his own reader becomes so absorbed in the narrative that, like Argus in a different sense, he loses an awareness of the larger story and sees the terrible risk an audience runs for not recognizing the reciprocity between the tale and its telling, between audience and narrated event.

But are we justified in using a term like risk, or is the "punishment" of Argus such a grotesque exaggeration of the consequences of bad reading that it can be read only as a joke that further separates Ovid's readers from the characters he describes?[19] After all, the poet is not still lurking

---

[17] So Anderson 1996.217 interprets lines 1.707–8: *dumque ibi suspirat, motos in harundine ventos / effecisse sonum tenuem similemque querenti.* Contra Hardie, *per litteras*, who sees the passage as an allusion to Lucr. 5.1382–85, where it is precisely the natural effect of the wind blowing over reeds that teaches man the use of the panpipes. The juxtaposition of the (onomatopoetic) *suspiria* with the description of the wind as "moved," however, makes me think that here Ovid is reversing rather than following the Lucretian model.

[18] As Anderson 1996.216 points out, the shift between levels is initially blurred at the juncture when Ovid resumes telling the story. *Restabat verba referre* certainly marks an interruption, but who has been interrupted? Is the one who has left his words unfinished Pan, who has been prevented from delivering his speech, perhaps by the flight of the nymph? (After all, the reader has already seen Apollo unable to finish his address to Daphne on account of her precipitous departure [*plura locuturum timido Peneia cursu / fugit cumque ipso verba inperfecta reliquit*, 1.525–26]). Or is it, as later proves to be the case, Mercury?

[19] Cf. Thiem 1995, esp. 243, on how such writers use the fiction of the reader absorbed into the text to reject reading that is merely ludic.

around the corner with his curved sword. What such momentous effect can a narrative, and a narrative whose very subject matter marks its distance from the world of actuality, possess for the reader's experience of reality? That is the question that the book as a whole will try to answer, but we can make a start by looking at one last element of this elaborate set of tales, the panpipes themselves. This instrument first offers an apt image for the Ovidian text itself, with its unequal lengths welded into a harmonic whole by the skill of the artist.[20] In another sense as well, they return the reader to the generic issues we met in the introduction. For, as an archetypal symbol of the bucolic genre, they represent a distorting intrusion into the epic fabric of the poem. And as before, the generic question is part of the larger issue of the relation between the tale and the telling, for the whole Syrinx tale can be read as a rustic modulation of a story the poet has already told, the tale of Daphne and Apollo. As we have seen too, the very nature of the artifact focuses attention on this relationship between the telling and the tale, between the voice of the speaker and the voices of the figures whose stories he tells. The sound of the syrinx comes literally from the voice of the artist, but at the same time the music makes us hear voices. Like Pan, we can hear the nymph's lament in what the poet then pointedly reminds us is simply the sound of the god's own sighs played through the reeds. And, as in the earlier account of Io's sufferings, the question of which frame of reference we adopt plays a large part in how we answer that question, whether we hear the story through the real object, or whether we grant priority to the fabulous narrative the god tells, and then allow it to change perceptions of reality. Is it the syrinx, an object that forms part of the inner audience's (viz. Argus's) experience of the real, as Ovid's own artifice exists as text in the real world, that prompts and generates the story, or does the story form an aetion that explains and interprets reality, so that the syrinx really does bring Syrinx into the present? Within the narrative, the story itself is offered as an explanation, as though it were a true account, but the suggestion arises that Mercury and/or Ovid may quite literally have spun the tale out of the instrument. This is in fact the earliest surviving account of the tale of Pan and Syrinx, and even if Forbes-Irving is right in assuming that Ovid did not simply invent it, we can certainly say that it was far from being an uncontested or canonical explanation for the origins of the instrument.[21] Not only does the syrinx lie at the cusp of all these questions but, correspondingly, it is this instrument that forms the bridge be-

---

[20] *disparibus calamis compagine cerae inter se iunctis nomen tenuisse puellae* (1.711–12). Note the resemblance to another artisanal product with programmatic overtones, the wings of Daedalus, which are explicitly compared to panpipes (8.189–95).

[21] Forbes-Irving 1990.277–78.

tween the three levels of narration: it is present to Pan in Mercury's story, to Argus in Ovid's, and, if we accept it as a figure for the poem itself, it also confronts the poet's audience outside the tale. The instrument acts as a kind of narrative firebreak, the material legacy of an earlier story that, by its very presence, seems to mark that story as complete, and yet the set of pipes, precisely because it still exists, reminds us that none of the stories is over and that no audience can ever be truly outside their embrace.

II. Metamorphosis

The narrative of the Io episode has shown how the changed body of Io figures at the center of the interpretative complexities of the episode. In a manner already predicted by the poem's first lines, where the text's form and its subject matter are subject to change, reading Io's own "changed body" becomes at once a metaphor, and a very real starting point, for reading the narrative about her. The transformative power of metamorphosis for the reader's experience of the text demonstrates the multiple ways in which the phenomenon itself links the inside and the outside of the poem's narrative. From outside, that is to say from the set of expectations a reader brings to the poem, metamorphosis becomes a narrative element that compels a reexamination of the "form" of the text before one. Is it an epic poem or something much slighter? Is it the kind of narrative that should be read as true or that one can approach with the comfortable distance of self-acknowledged fiction? Does metamorphosis function as a kind of natural law that different philosophical systems can make sense of? Does its presence correspondingly signal that Ovid's work is to be understood as in some way an allegorical account of the nature of things? The cognitive problems that any story about metamorphosis raises, especially given its associations for an ancient reader, mirror and accentuate the hermeneutic puzzle that the metamorphosed figures within the poem pose for an inner audience and often for themselves. And here, too, the problem becomes one of surface and depth. Is the new form as it appears from the outside all that matters? Or can we identify, and identify with, some essence within the new figure that preserves traces of the old? As I argue, no law of metamorphosis diminishes the impact and puzzlement of each new change, which will have to be made sense of on its own terms. This power of metamorphosis to draw the reader into the narrated experience of the poem, and simultaneously to project the poem's influence outward into the real in turn, drives the work's ideological engine, for assumptions made about the nature of change and its resulting products translate directly, though never simplistically, into an understanding of the kind of world the work portrays and the role it claims within it. This fundamental ambiguity of metamorphosis will thus be at the center of my reading of the poem because it at once reflects, and helps bring about, the transformation of Ovid's text into a dynamic locus for defining and codifying political and social roles.

The large functional claims I am making for metamorphosis must be defended at the outset against two strong tendencies in modern scholarship, one of which treats metamorphosis too lightly, whereas the other takes it too seriously. Karl Galinsky's 1975 study of the poem has provided an influential formulation of the first of these tendencies. Galinsky finds a double link between the poem's theme and its literary form: the emphasis on change mirrors the poem's own shifts in language, tone, and subject matter as well as its relentless pursuit of novelty in retelling well-known tales in new ways. Indeed, no small proof of Ovid's narrative virtuosity is his bending over backward to include accounts of transformation in tales where it would seem to have no place. The occasionally tangential nature of the metamorphosis element in Ovid's narratives leads to Galinsky's second, more fundamental claim about its role in the poem. Metamorphoses help establish the poem's "imaginative and tonal qualities,"[22] by wresting myth away from the kind of serious moral investigations prompted by the tragic potential of the tales he tells. Not only does transformation provide a soft option to death and annihilation as a closural element; more significantly, it translates myth to a realm of fantasy that loosens our engagement with the issues it raises. The idea of metamorphosis as a way of draining off the moral qualities of myth also featured in Joseph Solodow's 1988 book on the poem, although in a move that anticipates my own interpretation, he points out that the poem's very refusal to pin down the moral consequences of transformation—whether it is a punishment or a reward, and, in either case, whether it is deserved—can invite the audience to examine precisely these issues.[23]

The tradition of using the metamorphosis theme to emphasize the poem's essential lack of seriousness begins with Ovid himself, who in a later work tells us that his tales of transformation were "not to be believed" (Trist. 2.64), a claim that highlights the first assumption a contemporary reader might bring to any such story. The rhetorical categorization of narrative took metamorphosis tales as exemplary of stories removed even from the appearance of reality. But against the assumption that the pres-

[22] Galinsky 1975.61.

[23] Solodow 1988.170–72. Two key features differentiate my interpretation of metamorphosis from Solodow's: first, my emphasis on the transformed image itself as the generator of hermeneutic ambiguities and, second, my attempt to interpret those ambiguities not only in terms of what happens inside the text (whether, for example, Daphne's transformation should be seen as a reward or punishment) but also as a way in which the poet positions his poem in relation to the world outside it.

ence of metamorphosis offered an escape to fantasy that automatically programmed a particular response in the reader, perhaps the multiple ways in which metamorphosis is construed in the poem, the many literary genres in which it is at home, and the many intellectual models available for understanding changes of shape, from skeptical disbelief to allegorization, make it something that opens the text to reevaluation rather than shutting it down. The authorial tendency to dismiss metamorphosis as by its nature unbelievable, always of course an available option, becomes also a foil that raises the stakes of not abiding by its prescriptions. In this case, we may also be guided by our own responses to fantastic elements in modern literature, where, as Todorov powerfully shows, their effect is to demand speculation, on the part of those within the narrative and of its audience, about the nature of the experience described, precisely because of their assumptions about the way things happen in the real world: "The fantastic is that hesitation experienced by a person who knows only the laws of nature, confronting an apparently supernatural event."[24]

As a first demonstration of how Ovid uses metamorphosis to keep the reader alert to the essential ambiguities of his text, we can turn to the question of literary genre. The claims to alternative generic allegiances in the poem's first lines open up very different possibilities for understanding the choice of metamorphosis as a subject. If we are to read the work as a series of discrete, refined narratives such a topic would seem entirely appropriate.[25] Although their works are almost completely lost, Ovid's most important predecessors for building tales of metamorphosis into larger poetic units seem to have worked very much in the tradition of Callimachean brevity. In the second century BC, for example, Nicander of Colophon, whose only surviving works are a pair of didactic poems about snakebites and antidotes, produced the *Heteroioumena* (Transformations), in which he collected what seem to have been particularly obscure metamorphoses associated with the monuments and rites of far-flung cities and usually featuring local rustic divinities rather than the Olympian gods. While we are not in a position to tell what kind of larger structures Nicander used to organize his material, it is fairly clear that the poem was on a significantly smaller scale than Ovid's: five books, probably, as opposed to fifteen. Nothing can be said for certain about the scope, or even the date, of another source and antecedent of the *Metamorphoses*, the *Ornithogonia* (Bird Origins) of Boios, but his apparent aim of demonstrating that every species of bird was at one time a man

---

[24] Todorov 1975.25.

[25] For a general discussion of the treatment of metamorphosis in earlier literature and detailed accounts of Nicander and Boios, see Forbes-Irving 1990.7–37. See also Hardie 1999 for a discussion of metamorphosis as a way of commenting on the representational strategies of earlier epics.

again indicates a much more restricted canvas than Ovid's universal history. The entirely lost *Metamorphoses* of Parthenius of Nicaea, a Greek poet brought to Rome as a slave and an important influence on the development of Roman poetics in the first century BCE, was probably an important influence in Romanizing this tradition.

By contrast to its suitability to these catalog poems, the fabulous aspect of metamorphosis tales made them very difficult to reconcile with the aesthetic principles of serious epic, where supernatural solutions to human problems are pointedly avoided. In the Homeric poems, for example, stories of metamorphosis occur either in Odysseus's account of his wanderings, a narrative space reserved for all sorts of miraculous figures, or in passages whose very strangeness marks them out as communications from the gods, like the serpent and the bird's nest turned to stone mentioned in *Iliad* 2.301–29. And even these examples do not form a part of the poet's own narrative; they are described and interpreted by characters within the poem.[26]

In the works of Ovid's immediate epic predecessor Vergil, the phenomenon of metamorphosis assumes a more prominent but deeply ambiguous role, one that in many respects looks ahead to its complex function in the *Metamorphoses*.[27] On the one hand, Vergil seems to give an ideological dimension to Homer's reticence about transformation stories. Beyond raising questions about the plausibility of the narrative, metamorphosis suggests a world of unstable ephemerality that can only be at odds with the poem's motion toward the foundation of Rome as the center of a stable cosmos and indeed comes to be associated with the dehumanizing violence and immorality of Rome's civil wars. The bleeding bush that manifests the presence of Polydorus, a Trojan prince murdered by an avaricious and impious Thracian king, at the beginning of book 3 and the howling of the bestialized inhabitants of Circe's realm (*Aen.* 7.10–24) signpost regions where neither Aeneas's mission nor Vergil's narrative should go.[28] Vergil swerves just shy of metamorphosis in another sense when one of the poem's final similes figures Aeneas and Turnus, in the climactic duel that decides the fate of Italy, as battling bulls (*Aen.* 12.715–22). Animal rage and undifferentiated violence are hardly the stuff from which the reader expects the tapestry of Roman history to be woven. But because this is just a figure of speech, it can always be read as but a partial, imprecise image of the combatants, or even as a foil to them. However, metamorphosis within Vergil's poem is not merely the

---

[26] On the avoidance of the miraculous in Homer, see Griffin 1977.

[27] For a fuller treatment of metamorphosis in the *Aeneid*, see Hardie 1992.

[28] For the reemergence of these Circean dangers later in book 7, see Putnam 1995.100–120.

favored modus operandi of the forces of darkness and dissolution. On the contrary, the victory of Aeneas—and, by implication, the emergence of Roman order from the chaotic final books of the poem—is in a sense a tale of metamorphosis, requiring the hero's transformation from the last remnant of a city doomed to fall to the founder of a civilization fated to endure. And in one important instance, his account of how the goddess Cybele saves the Trojan ships from destruction by turning them into nymphs (*Aen.* 9.77–122), Vergil highlights his inclusion of a miraculous transformation to make clear the special status of his epic. The passage has jolted Vergil's readers since antiquity, and even within the poem characters struggle to make sense of it.[29] The poet himself seems to hold the story at arm's length, presenting it as a legend, yet the transformation as an event is anchored in the plot of his epic.[30] But rather than regard Vergil's treatment of the episode as either halfhearted or misjudged, we can take it as a self-conscious deployment of the vexed status of metamorphosis within epic, alerting readers all too ready to dismiss the tale as fantasy that Aeneas's divinely guided foundation of Rome requires a different poetics than the exploits of Homer's mortal heroes. As Ovid will later, Vergil here makes metamorphosis an occasion to reorient his readers' expectations of the poem.

If metamorphosis generally marks the limit of what is consistent with the moral seriousness of heroic epic, this is the line on which *Metamorphoses* dances. The poem's meter, size, and incorporation of the Trojan and Roman subject matter of epic invite the reader to view the poem in its entirety as a rival to those earlier works. Should we read metamorphosis through epic eyes, with an even greater awareness of its essential unbelievability and trivializing effect? Can the epic form even save the *Metamorphoses* from itself by transfiguring its fabulous subject matter into a grand history of the Augustan world, just as Vergil allows metamorphosis a new role in his poem? Or is the work fundamentally an antiepic, lending the gravity of the Homeric and Vergilian form to an antithetical vision of man's place in the cosmos? Or, a final alternative, should we simply avoid the question by allowing the poem to decompose itself into a Hellenistic assemblage of separate tales? Because Ovid often posi-

---

[29] Thus, Servius Danielis mentions two slightly different objections to the passage: one implies that the poet should never make up anything so remote from truth (*Ad Aen.* 3.46), and the other, though allowing poetic fictions, insists that they should have some precedent in earlier authors (9.81). On the episode of the nymphs, see esp. Fantham 1990.

[30] The verb *fertur* ("it is said," 9.82) provides the most obvious sign of this authorial distancing—although even that can be treated as a learned reference to an earlier poetic authority. According to Servius Danielis, "some have objected to this '*fertur*' because it denies authority to the tale; others have praised it as a sign that the poet was unwilling to lend authority to an unbelievable event" (*Ad Aen.* 9.81).

tions metamorphoses at the end of episodes, the transformations within the narrative tend to occur precisely where the structure of the work as a whole is most up for grabs. In deciding whether each metamorphosis marks an ending, or merely a transition, readers are continually confronted with the question of what kind of work they are reading.

But it is not only the alternative genres of continuous epic and Hellenistic narrative catalog that react with the phenomenon of metamorphosis. If metamorphosis initiates a cognitive challenge for both reader and internal figure, demanding a matching between appearance and reality, surface and depth, then it is appropriate to think of that other literary experience in which recognition plays a crucial role, tragedy. Ingo Gildenhard and Andrew Zissos in a series of articles soon to be united in a book, have gone a long way toward rebutting the characterization of the *Metamorphoses* as essentially untragic, by showing how closely and explicitly the poem refigures central concerns and themes of the genre of Attic tragedy.[31] In a discussion of Actaeon's transformation into a deer and subsequent dismemberment by his own hounds, they link the pronounced discrepancy between the way Actaeon thinks of himself and the stag's appearance that makes him unrecognizable to the performative medium of tragedy, where the actor's masked impersonation of the other creates a similar gulf between seeming and reality. What makes this performance practice meaningful is the analogy it creates between the form and plot of tragedy, for the latter too, as Aristotle points out, ideally centers on a moment of recognition. The recognition of Sophocles' Oedipus, to take the classic example, as the murderer of his father shocks largely because it requires the protagonist's own acceptance of the fact that the sacrilegious monster he knows through the speech of others and the pious king he thinks himself to be are one in the same.[32]

Both the epistemological problem created by metamorphosis and the way that this problem links audience and character in a similar bind thus recall the operation of tragedy. More important still, this capacity for those in the audience to recognize themselves in the figures they see on the stage not only provides the key effects of tragedy on its audience, pity and terror, but also arguably provides a link between the aesthetic workings of tragedy and its ability to evoke such ritual experiences as sacrifice. The ritual dimension of tragic recognition marks a difference in emphasis between my own approach to the parallels between tragedy and metamorphosis and the work of Gildenhard and Zissos. Whereas they stress how Ovid's narrative self-consciously signals its incorporation and as-

---

[31] Gildenhard and Zissos 1999a.

[32] Gildenhard and Zissos 2000b invoke a similar account of the *Oedipus* in their discussion of its relevance to the episode of Narcissus.

similation of the defining concerns of the tragic genre and, in the case of the allusions to the Oedipus play in the Narcissus episode, show how the narrative draws attention to the fundamentally Ovidian problem of intertextual adaptation, I explore how the inclusion of tragic modalities expands our understanding of the effects of Ovid's poem on its own audience. Specifically, I argue for a close link between metamorphosis and sacrifice which reveals metamorphosis as a potential narrative equivalent for tragedy's dramatic evocation of ritual practice (see chapter 3).

If recognition in the case of Oedipus at once reveals a tragic instability of human aims and undermines the roles and relationships that ground human society, recognition in comedy performs the opposite function of reestablishing the status quo by restoring the lost or enslaved child to his or her legitimate place in the social order. The tale of Io shows how the dynamics of recognition necessitated by metamorphosis gain from being read against the capacity of comic recognition to highlight a sameness between the new and the old. The tale of Io, in fact, is a pure new comedy plot, from the rape occasioned by the casual sight of a maiden venturing from her home, to the miscalculated use of disguise and deception to conceal its effects, to the deployment of a clever servant to get round the girl's fearsome guardian.[33] Here though, the father's recognition of his long-lost daughter in the guise of a cow has precisely the opposite consequences of the usual comic resolution: there will be no marriage to an equal in status, and no legitimate offspring—rather than return to her old status, this lost maiden is stuck in her new role as cow. While obviously evocation of the supremely realistic genre of new comedy at this point adds humor to the passage, it also points out more significant differences between this story and the conventional comic plot. Even when Io returns to her human form, there can be no marriage here because, fundamentally, unlike comedy, this is not an encounter between social equals, and while Io may be granted divine status, she is never returned to her native land but remains by the Egyptian Nile, as opposed to the paternal stream (*patrio flumine*, 1.588) from which she was returning when seen

---

[33] The catalog of comic features could be continued to include the role of Juno as the comic wife interfering with her husband's plans for erotic amusement, noted by Anderson 1996.208—a plot feature that further casts Io in a low-status role, for the husband's plans, because they cannot ever result in a legitimate marriage, always involve an (apparent) slave, and are never consummated. The exception to the rule against the successful seduction of a freeborn woman who is not available to become a bride is a telling one: Jupiter's adulterous impregnation of Alcmena in Plautus's *Amphitruo*. Note too that as in Plautus's comedies the deception of the pimp frequently invites metatheatricality, as the clever slave practices his deception through "playacting," so here Mercury uses narrative, indeed a specifically Ovidian story, to overcome Argus. Though again the parallel raises new questions, because Mercury's victory ends in a kind of violence unthinkable on the comic stage.

by Jupiter.[34] So too, though the violated maiden in comedy is often an equally silent character, the genre relies on an assumption that she does indeed love and will happily marry her violator, an assumption that is much more difficult to make in Ovid's rape narratives. The capacity to recognize a maiden beneath a new form imposed by metamorphosis also involves comic resolution in the earlier Daphne episode, where the ability for the new tree to count as a spouse equivalent depends upon the recognition of Daphne within its bark.

New Comedy's focus on an essential sameness of identity that can survive any series of misfortunes and changes of state brings me to the second general approach to metamorphosis I want to challenge. So far we have seen, by a brief account of some of the genres that can color a reading of a metamorphosis narrative, that the very presence of a miraculous change of shape does not automatically reduce any tale that contains it to a merely entertaining fiction. The opposite tendency is a too-confident generalization about the nature of Ovidian metamorphosis, a generalization that often then provides the basis for a political reading of the poem. Metamorphosis is a topic that cannot help but engage reflection on larger political issues in the climate of Augustan Rome, an era that had witnessed enormous, sometimes violent, social change and the enforced idealization of stability. And so it is no surprise to find that previous attempts at defining Ovid's politics have relied heavily on the significance of the metamorphosis theme and have offered very different views of what matters in a metamorphosis narrative. In general, readers inclined toward an anti-Augustan view of the work have focused on the process of metamorphosis more than the product: the poem displays a world where appearances are deceptive and where, in the words of the problematic figure Pythagoras, "everything changes," though "nothing perishes" (omnia mutantur, nihil interit, 15.165). This law of universal mutability calls into question not only Rome's own claims to eternity, especially when it is none other than Pythagoras who reports the foundations of Rome as a proof that Troy has not entirely vanished, but also the Augustan project of establishing boundaries, for classes, provinces, even the empire itself, and then supporting these boundaries as natural.[35] Pythagoras's contrasting insistence that nothing perishes can also be read as establishing an opposition between the soul and the material world that provides scope for an individual resistance to the imposition of external authority. Such a reading gains force when the poet ends his work with

[34] Complementing this theme, the following tale, Phaethon, focuses on a return to the lost father.

[35] This is admittedly very much a shorthand account of a much broader interpretation of Augustan ideology. For the coalescence between natural history and Roman history, the best starting point is Hardie 1986.

the assertion that his better part will survive no matter what the "anger of Jove" and other destructive forces may do to his body.

Those who see the poem as supportive of Augustan ends place the emphasis rather on what results from metamorphosis: change is something that happened in the past and has brought about the comprehensible, ordered, normal world in which we live, or, as Habinek puts it, "from the standpoint of the poem the only changes that matter are those that produce the world as currently configured."[36] Karl Galinsky has suggested a new parallel between Ovid's view of metamorphosis and the emperor's account of his own societal goals by pointing out that Augustus himself emphasizes the newness of his laws and institutions.[37] Galinsky's summation of Augustus's political and religious program as the use of the new to revitalize the old accords well with a common view of Ovidian metamorphosis as a change that preserves, a process that ends up with an immutable new manifestation of some essential quality of the being that has been transformed.[38] My objection to such readings, those which picture Ovid either as an oppositional figure or as consummate Augustan, comes neither from their move outside the poem to the realm of politics nor from the equations they make between the consequences of metamorphosis in the poem and the external political system. Many of these connections are plausible and productive. Rather, my resistance stems from these critics' initial assumption that the poem articulates a specific view of what metamorphosis is and what matters in it. On the contrary, the process of defining metamorphosis continues throughout the reading of the work, and to readapt the language of Habinek, the poem offers many different standpoints on change, and what matters in each metamorphosis depends very much on which the reader adopts. Thus, the political impact of the poem comes not through recognizing metamorphosis itself as a monovalent political allegory but as a narrative device that by its nature makes available shifting ways of construing a highly charged term. Carolyn Walker Bynum has recently explored the many different accounts of change constructed in the twelfth and thirteenth centuries as the product of a period when "concepts of change itself tended to change."[39] In a similar way, I contend that Ovid's poem emerges in a political context where the concept of change itself becomes central to a configuration of the political world and one's place in it and that Ovid's poem will put competing views about change in dialogue with each other.

---

[36] Habinek 2002.52.

[37] Galinsky 1999.105 citing the programmatic *legibus novis* at *Res Gestae* 8.5.

[38] Such a parallel between the nature of Augustus *imperium* and Ovid's poetics also features in Wheeler 1999. For metamorphosis as clarification, see Solodow 1988.174.

[39] Bynum 2001.21.

Before more explicit demonstrations of how Ovid's narratives of transformation activate these contrasting understandings of the poem's political function and further comments on the social significance of change in this period, let me first develop my assertion that the poem offers no clear prescription for understanding the phenomenon of metamorphosis. Galinsky's account of change in the poem as a clarification of some preexisting quality, already present in the old form but more sharply revealed in the new, is here based directly on a specific reading of the poem's first lines developed by Lothar Spahlinger,[40] but it is similar to other optimistic efforts to define some positive law of change. Solodow for example, directly defines metamorphosis as a process of clarification,[41] and Dörrie, in a particularly influential article, connected the workings of metamorphosis in Ovid with the doctrine of identity developed by the stoic Posidonius: all things have a kind of substance that is destroyed by material change, but "peculiarly qualified individuals" (e.g., individual persons) also possess a substance that endures despite alterations to their physical makeup—for example, Socrates is still Socrates even if he gains weight. Ovidian metamorphosis reveals this second kind of abiding existence.[42] Many of these interpreters cautiously limited the applicability of their formulations. But rather than measure the success of any theory of metamorphosis by the number of examples it fits, as though this were a scientific problem, we might rather stress that metamorphosis throughout the poem is something that must be continually reimagined. Any "key," whether derived from the language of the poem itself or taken from a preexisting philosophical debate, will be refined and challenged by the reader's experience of the poem, rather than simply providing a template to solve its problems. Thus, for example, all the existence of the Posidonius passage really proves is that the relationship between identity and material form was important in Hellenistic philosophy and that this formulation was available as a model for understanding what happens in metamorphosis. There were also, of course, others, and someone reading the poem with, for example Aristotelian or Epicurean assumptions about the nature of physical change might be more inclined to question the survival of a distinctive identity after metamorphosis.

But does Ovid himself offer a theory of metamorphosis that ought to guide us in how to read what follows? In his interpretation of what he takes as the programmatic definition of metamorphosis in the first two lines of Ovid's poem, *in nova ... mutatas dicere formas ... corpora,*

[40] Spahlinger 1996.28–29.
[41] Solodow 1988.176–83.
[42] Dörrie 1959.

Spahlinger tries to differentiate *forma* and *corpus*, arguing convincingly that the two terms are not juxtaposed simply to avoid repetition: the latter, he says, connotes the material reality of a body, in terms of both its physical dimensions and its substance. *Forma*, by contrast, suggests the outward appearance of an entity as a defining characteristic of a person or object, especially with reference to its function or role, the surface of an entity as apprehended or defined by others through perception or use, or the shape or pattern in and of itself, a "form" with or without content. On the basis of this distinction, Spahlinger assumes that what happens in metamorphosis is that "an individual being with a distinctive *forma* obtains through transformation a new body, is thus changed in his physical presence, respecting his externally visible material appearance, without any effect to his psychic existence, his individual mental make-up."[43] His interpretation depends then, on the reader having a strong enough sense of this particular distinction, to assume that everything that defines a *forma* against a *corpus* (i.e., its particularizing, defining capacity) is unaffected by the change. Yet, if such a reading is possible, it is by no means inevitable. The Latin does seem strongly to suggest that it is in fact the *forma* that undergoes change (*mutatas formas*), and therefore is precisely what does not survive to preserve the distinctive character of the prior being. An emphasis on the loss of *forma* might in turn shift attention to the distinction between identity as defined by external features and by inner perceptions; thus Actaeon, to take a classic example, retains an awareness of who he is but has lost the outward signs that make him recognizable to others.

The emphasis on permanence and preservation in Spahlinger's formulation, even more apparent in the use Galinsky makes of it,[44] also relies heavily on one particular reading of words with a wide range of meanings. If, for example, we stress that forms are turned *into* bodies, then other kinds of distinctions become relevant. *Forma* can also be used very much in the sense that we use form, to define a pattern or type that can exist in the mind independent of any physical manifestation. It was in fact the word Cicero chose to render Platonic "forms" into Latin.[45] *Corpus*, by contrast, despite its suggestions of solidity, can also denote the softer and inherently changeable parts of the human body, the "flesh" as opposed to both the bones and the spirit.[46] When forms become bodies,

---

[43] Spahlinger 1996.29.

[44] Galinsky 1999.105.

[45] Cic. *Orat.* 10.

[46] Lewis and Short s.v. B. 2 suggest that *corpus* can, in poetry, mean just the opposite of a body without the spirit, a spirit without a body. They cite two lines of Vergil 6.303 and 306, where the term *corpora* is used of the shades of the dead being carried across to the underworld in Charon's bark. But this is very much the exception that proves the rule. The

they can both take on a presence and immanence they would otherwise lack and, at the same time, move from the stability and unchangeability of pure images to the more labile and transitory world of actual existence. Both kinds of transition have relevance to Ovid's representation of metamorphosis.

That the poet's own definition of change is itself changeable finds support in the well-known story of Pygmalion and his statue. The transformation of the ivory statue of an ideal maiden into a flesh and blood creature makes one look again at what can happen during a metamorphosis and, in particular, at the very language used to describe transformation in the poem's first lines. Here the metamorphosis involves no change whatsoever to the statue's outside shape but only to its substance. To put it another way, we might say that here a form has not been obliterated but literally changed into substance. In fact, the terms in question figure largely in the episode. The statue is *formosa* (10.266), and Pygmalion gives it a "*forma* with which no woman was ever born" (10.248–49)—a phrase that, beyond employing the word in its specialized sense of beauty, also connotes the world of Platonic "forms" or models that no single manifestation ever perfectly reproduces. Ovid describes the moment of metamorphosis itself, or rather the moment when Pygmalion recognizes that a metamorphosis has taken place, with the phrase *corpus erat* (10.289); and this realization recalls the sculptor's earlier uncertainty about the "content of the form," his question about whether the statue really was ivory or flesh (*corpus*, 10.255). Shapes abide, but what they consist of, what they denote, can change, and this change very much depends on the eye of the beholder, who has only the *forma* to go on. My purpose in introducing this reading is not, of course, to supply a new paradigm for all metamorphoses—one might argue for instance that this passage becomes all the more engaging precisely because it reverses the standard protocols—but to suggest the fluidity of how the process can work and the importance of the reader's awareness of this fluidity and of the constant attention required to make sense of each change.

The poem's very first account of the transformation of a human being into an animal, the tale of Lycaon (1.209–43), provides a sense of what is at stake ideologically in the differing responses to metamorphosis offered by the poem. This story follows after the poem's account of the formation of the cosmos, a process that involves not the creation of new substances out of nothing but rather the sorting of elements already present in the confused mass of primordial chaos into an ordered hierarchy. At first, this

---

weightlessness of the "*corpora*" of the dead here contrasts with the living body of Aeneas, whose mass makes the boat groan and leak (6.413–14). The *corpora* of the dead are bodies that are no bodies.

story will seem to further the suggestion that metamorphosis itself serves as a tool for imposing a familiar, stable order on things, as opposed to signifying a world in a state of unaccountable flux. Jupiter has heard of the impious behavior of human beings, and in hopes of finding the story is false, he disguises himself as a mortal and descends from Olympus to investigate. When he enters Lycaon's realm, he gives signs of his divinity and begins to receive the worship of the people. The king however refuses to acknowledge Jupiter as divine and plots to prove him mortal by killing him in his sleep. He also kills a hostage and attempts to serve his cooked limbs to the god. In punishment, the god destroys the palace, and Lycaon is driven into exile, at which point "he wails and tries in vain to speak. His countenance takes upon itself all his madness; he turns his innate love of slaughter against sheep and even now rejoices in blood. His clothes turn into hair; his arms into legs. He becomes a wolf and preserves the traces of his old form. There is the same grayness, the same violent countenance. His eyes still gleam, and the appearance of bestiality remains" (1.233–39).

Jupiter's account suggests that Lycaon has been quite literally put in his place. He had violated human norms by murdering a hostage and even attempted to usurp Jupiter's prerogative here by imposing his own test on the god. He subsequently undergoes a transformation that seems at once to punish his attempt to take on the god's role in the story and to express his own innate bestiality. (Notice that Jupiter never claims responsibility for the transformation, which appears to happen spontaneously.) Just as the creation of the world involved the separation of the lighter elements from water and earth, so here this wild beast that had somehow been grouped among men has finally been returned to his rightful category. The change that has taken place is merely one of form. And Lycaon's new shape not only more clearly reveals his essence but also manifests and enforces the cosmic hierarchies he has violated. The wolf itself becomes a reminder of the consequences of behaving as either a beast or a god. There is also a more narrowly political significance to the metamorphosis. Before recounting this story, Jupiter had been compared to the emperor Augustus, and the assembly of gods he addresses takes on the form of the Roman Senate. The little epiphany of order that results from his metamorphosis, in which the natural world as we know it becomes a sign of the proper distribution of authority of gods and men, also serves as a reminder of the specifically Roman order that now, as Augustan artistic imagery so often implied, had embraced the cosmos itself.[47] The very name Lycaon means wolf in Greek, again suggesting

[47] For a good introduction to this pattern of imagery in the visual arts, see Zanker 1990.183–92 and Nicolet 1991.29–56, and for an example of its development in literature, see Hardie's (1986.336–76) reading of the Vergilian shield of Aeneas.

that metamorphosis is above all a clarification of who he really is[48] and that, because of metamorphosis, even verbal signs now more clearly represent the world. But, of course, in Ovid's text, Lycaon has not become a wolf but a *lupus*: metamorphosis as cosmic clarification depends on the translation of Greek into Latin.

Such readings as this have produced a sense that the real emphasis in Ovid's poem of changes should be on stability, the view represented by Habinek's suggestion that metamorphosis in the past results in a firm natural and political order in the present. And, indeed, by narrating stories of this type, Ovid seems to be contributing to the semantic clarification and revelation that Jupiter sets in motion, by offering a world whose natural elements, like wolves, become transparent to human qualities and divine actions. But the very neatness of this interpretation results precisely from the tale's univocality and from the erasure of alternative points of view. Indeed, this is the one story in the poem narrated by Jupiter himself, the ultimate representation of authority in the epic universe. But the very metamorphosis that seems to provide such unanswerable closure in fact allows competing readings back into the text precisely because it makes the shutting down of alternative points of view so explicit. The first thing that happens to Lycaon is that he loses his power to speak—precisely the eloquence that allows Jupiter to tell his version of events. The last body parts mentioned are Lycaon's shining eyes, eyes that are depicted only as seen, not as seeing. Points of view opposed to Jupiter's would have been ready to hand for an informed reader of the text. For, as nearly as we can tell, no other account of Lycaon is so relentless in its condemnation of the king. Greek versions in fact present a highly ambivalent figure whose outrageous treatment of the gods is balanced by his role as a civilizing hero, an institutor of religious practices, whose name would be preserved not just by the wolf but by the cult of Zeus Lykaios, which he founded.[49] Even within Ovid's Jovian account, the boundaries between gods, humans, and animals seem dangerously permeable. Jupiter sets the plot in motion by his own shape shifting, the assumption of human form—a disguise that anticipates the paradox of the final metamorphosis by simultaneously masking and revealing his divine nature. Indeed, it might even be argued that Lycaon's outrage results less from his attempt to deprive the gods of the honor due them than from his scrupulous belief in the reality of appearances and his efforts to use those appearances to distinguish different orders of being. His very plot to kill Jupiter shows

---

[48] Solodow 1988.174 defines "clarification" as the central function of metamorphosis.

[49] For earlier accounts of the Lycaon story, see Forbes-Irving 1990.90–15 and 216–18; see also Barkan's (1986.24–17) integration of the legend of Lycaon the sacrificer with Ovid's story. See also chapter 3, section 1.

that he has taken his disguise seriously: far from attempting to dishonor the god, he assumes that the figure before him is a mortal impostor. And if Lycaon's error is really a failure to recognize that gods can disguise themselves as men, his experience is very relevant to Ovid's own readers, who are making their first acquaintance with anthropomorphized gods in the work.[50] If they attempt to apply the same criterion of truth to their reading, then the entire epic machinery that underlies the moralizing or politicizing interpretation of the story would be called into question. To expose the gods as mere projections of human authority is to shortcircuit their political use to glorify any individual human potentate—a central issue in Augustan iconography.[51]

Another tale from the first book reveals even more clearly how interpretation of the poem's thematic emphases hinges on the reading of a metamorphosis. When the nymph Daphne realizes that she will never win the footrace against Apollo and will forfeit her virginity, she prays to be transformed and so to lose the external form (*figura*) that has caused her downfall by arousing the god's desire: "Scarcely had she ended her prayer when a heavy sluggishness took possession of her limbs; her soft breast clothes itself in thin bark. Her hair grows into leaves, her arms into branches. Her foot once so swift cleaves to sluggish roots. A bough holds her face; only her beauty remains" (1.548–52). Here the relationship between the new shape and the old becomes much more complicated. Far from fixing her in a state that permanently expresses her essential qualities, Daphne's metamorphosis strips her of the swiftness by which she has been characterized in the narrative; Ovid figures the transformation itself as a process of occlusion and possession. To read this metamorphosis according to the Lycaon paradigm by stressing the persistence of her beauty raises new problems, for it was her external attractiveness that warred against her desire to remain a virgin (*uotoque tuo tua forma repugnat*, 1.489). Indeed, if anything has been preserved of Daphne it is the tragic discrepancy between her inner will and outer appearance. To read her metamorphosis as a clarification, then, implies that her essence lay in what she seemed to others to be rather than recognizing her as subject in her own right.

Such a reading is put forward by the divine interpreter within the poem, none other than Apollo himself, the god who pursued her on account of her form: "Though you cannot be my wife, you will be my tree. My locks will always possess you, laurel, so will my lyre and my quiver.

---

[50] For another adversarial reading of Jupiter's account of Lycaon, see Anderson 1989; for the balance between contrasting readings in the story, see Wheeler 1999.171–81.

[51] For a discussion of how Ovid's hyper-anthropomorphized gods undercut imperial religious innovations, see Feeney 1991.205–24.

You will accompany the Latin chiefs when the joyful voice sings 'Triumph' and the Capitoline witnesses long (triumphal) processions.... And as my youthful head is perpetually unshorn, so you will always retain the honor of leaves" (1.557–65).

Apollo's response to Daphne's metamorphosis in a sense completes the processes of the transformation by converting her form into a symbol, yet a symbol that recalls not so much who Daphne was as who Apollo is. It is his hair that her leaves are now made to recall, not her own once disordered tresses. Apollo's strategy also bears on the question of the poem's genre: by placing Daphne's transformation in an extensive historical context, recalling the broad temporal sweep proclaimed in the poet's prologue, and converting her into an instrument of praise, Apollo epicizes her story.[52] In doing so, he fits it into the continuum prepared by the poet himself, who introduced the story as an explanation for how the laurel tree came to be the sign of victory in the games that celebrated Apollo's conquest of the Python. Thus, the tale that might have been thought to show how the god lost an archery contest with Cupid and was forced to shed his typical attributes by assuming the role of a lover, becomes instead a celebration of his once and future triumphs. For Daphne, though, does her metamorphosis mark the beginning of her epic significance, or is it in fact the end of the story? Again her changed form holds the key. The final lines at first appear to close the gap between Daphne's perspective and Apollo's by suggesting that Daphne herself consented to the role Apollo offered her by nodding her bough "as if it were a head." But perhaps the bough is just a bough. In other words, perhaps Daphne's will has been masked completely by her new form, and the attempt to claim her participation in this future as though she were still there marks merely the final stage in her possession.

The readings offered so far suggest that the event of metamorphosis in Ovid mobilizes two coherent interpretations of the poem and that the choice between them depends on the point of view adopted on the transformation itself. First, to focus on the new shape, which is often a form familiar from the actual experience of the reader, in several senses normalizes metamorphosis, subordinating a manifestly unbelievable process to an undeniably real product. The world is, reassuringly, not a place where metamorphosis happens every day, and the very stories Ovid tells about wolves and laurel trees give them a new significance as the representations and preserving exempla of cosmic and political order. In depicting metamorphosis from this perspective, not only is Ovid in several senses doing the lord's work, but he is also making his poem function

---

[52] For an introduction to the sophisticated pattern of generic play in this story, see Nicoll 1980 and the discussion in chapter 2, section 2.

like Vergilian epic, granting legendary events a privileged function for explaining the here and now, and conversely exalting the here and now by linking it to the grand sagas of past myth.[53] The reader's distance from the narrative, his recognition that this story by its nature must be a fiction, becomes anything but a disadvantage. Lycaon's tale, for example, readily lends itself to allegorization, an interpretative strategy that allows the dubious motives of Jupiter as character to fade from view. The alternative, to continue to recognize the human subjects of metamorphosis, dissolves the epic structure of the poem by making metamorphosis seem ultimately both inexplicable and very much the end of the story. Each transformation appears less a stage in the history of the cosmos than the shutting down of an individual consciousness, locked in opposition to the ordering forces of the universe. Here, far from retaining a comfortable position in the world after metamorphosis, the reader is drawn back into the unstable past, entering into the fiction rather than marking it off as such.

The pair of internal *Metamorphoses* that Ovid places at the beginning of his sixth book, in which the goddess Minerva and her human rival Arachne assemble stories of transformation for the two tapestries they weave in competition with each other, enshrine these polar alternatives for interpreting the process, for again the ideological differences between the two "texts" result not just from the discursive use each artist makes of metamorphosis but from the perspective they present on the process itself (6.1–145).[54] Minerva depicts four tales of metamorphoses, designed explicitly to warn Arachne of the dangers of rivaling the gods, symmetrically at the corners of a tapestry whose centerpiece depicts her own triumph in a contest with Neptune for possession of Athens. In each case, only the name of the victim and the final form they have assumed are indicated. By contrast the gods themselves are depicted in forms that, like the disguise Jupiter assumes in the Lycaon tale, are at once anthropomorphized and authentic. "His own appearance marks each god: Jupiter's is the image of a king" (6.73–4). In answer to Athena's use of metamorphosis as a warning against human presumption, Arachne presents a catalog of the animal forms the gods have used to deceive the victims of their lust. Here, rather than being final, metamorphosis appears as a fleeting mechanism of deception, proof not only of the crimes of the gods but of the unreliability of appearances. The artist freezes each story at the moment when the god's bestiality is exposed and enshrines the human countenances of the victims (in contrast to the many rape victims the

[53] On etiology in Ovid, see Graf 1988.62.

[54] Leach 1974, Vincent 1994, Feeney 1991.190–94, and now Oliensis 2004 offer particularly stimulating readings of this much-discussed episode: see also chapter 2, introduction.

poem presents who end up transformed into other shapes).[55] So too, her realistic descriptive technique—or rather Ovid's technique for presenting her depiction as narrative—works to draw the viewers into this world of deceptive fictions, which is significantly the same thing as granting them access to the victim's point of view: thus, in describing how the god Jupiter took on the form of a bull to abduct Europa, he comments that "you would think it was a real bull," as if "you" were Europa.

While the metamorphic subject matter of the poem helps to energize the possible responses of its readers, much more was at stake for an ancient audience in entering into the world of transformations it offers than might be immediately apparent to us. As Maurizio Bettini points out in an essay on Plautus's *Amphitruo*, perhaps Latin literature's most extensive pre-Ovidian treatment of shape changing, the possibility of surreptitious transformation figures rather largely in ancient anxieties about witchcraft. Thus, a curse tablet from Portugal calls down vengeance on anyone who steals an article of clothing by "transforming" it.[56] And in contrast to modern clinical experience, which suggests that dreams about being the victim of transformation are practically restricted to cases of psychosis, ancient texts on dream divination devote a proportionately much greater amount of space to dreams about changes of shape. This may however be simply because such dreams were so good to think with, allowing the interpreter to adduce any number of interpretations based on the properties of men, women, or animals, rather than indicating that such dreams were actually more common in antiquity.[57] But the most compelling and extensive proof of a wide-ranging and definitive link between metamorphosis and magic in the ancient world comes from the *Metamorphoses* of Apuleius, where shape changes of a very Ovidian kind feature as the most glamorous deeds of the Thessalian witch who has become the host of the hero Lucius, and it is his desire to experience precisely such marvels that lures him into the disastrous error that turns him into an ass. None of this should be taken as proving that metamorphosis was after all less fantastic to Ovid's original audience because of their beliefs in magical forces really out there ready to change the shape of their victims. What it does suggest, though, is that even if no one thought such stories were true—and it is suggestive to note in Apuleius's narrative how much the will to believe involves a desire to move beyond the intellectual horizons of an upper-class education by going native—their prominence in the Roman imaginary gives metamorphosis some cultural significance

---

[55] *omnibus his faciemque suam, faciemque locorum | reddidit,* 6.121–22.

[56] *Immudavit,* CIL 2.462, discussed by Bettini 1991.29–30.

[57] Bettini 1991.36–37 citing Artemidorus *On.* 1.50 for the ancients against Devereux 1976.xxv–xxvi for the moderns.

as the definition of what it is that we do not believe is out there, just as one can learn much about contemporary U.S. culture through its obsession with UFOs.

But to speculate on what was so threatening about shape changing will bring us back to more tangible historical forces. The broad social changes of Augustus's half century of dominance manifested themselves on an individual level by the potential for considerable changes in status, especially for the Italian upper classes from which Ovid came, as did many other prominent literary figures. At the same time, the class structure itself was being made more rigid and more publicly conspicuous through an increasing imperial concern for legislating who was entitled to what rank and creating more contexts for its display. A preeminent example of such institutionalized status display was Augustus's theater legislation, which established new and more elaborate patterns of reserved seats for the upper orders at public festivals. This was a period, in other words, where forms were at once more subject to change and assumed an increasing role in defining who one was. Transformation begins at the top, and it is no accident that one of the most convenient shorthands for writing the history of the Augustan regime is to chronicle the various transformations undergone by the *princeps* himself, as he takes on new names and titles, while preparing for the ultimate change that would perpetually validate his regime, apotheosis. On a slightly more mundane level, personal transformation figures largely in the way that poets of the great generation before Ovid's construct their own poetic autobiographies.[58] From a freedman's son in the *Satires*, Horace will become nothing less than a *princeps* in the *Odes*. And as Ovid's poem will always put us on the lookout for identity as well as difference between the new and the old, so "Vergil"'s proem to the *Aeneid*—if indeed the apocryphal lines were already current in Ovid's day—assures us that it is "the very same I who once composed to the graceful pipe, and having left the forest compelled the neighboring fields to obey the farmer, howsoever greedy, a gratifying work for the husbandman, now sing the terrifying arms of Mars and the man." Ovid himself was among the most metamorphosed of poets: his first efforts were afflicted by the god Cupid who stole one foot away from every second hexameter, rendering epic love elegy, and that collection later became three books instead of five. But, more important, his political persona undergoes changes in status equivalent to these literary transformations. *Tristia* 4.10 describes Ovid's life even before the momentous

---

[58] On the autobiography in the *Tristia* as modeled on the life story of the *princeps*, and possibly alluding to the *Aeneid* preface, see Fairweather 1987, esp. 191–96. For Ovid's persistent references to the *Aeneid* "prologue," see now Farrell 2004.

relegation to Tomi as a series of changes of state and draws special attention to the visible markers of his shifting fortune. Thus, when at the age of manhood he stakes claim to the status of a senator, an advance over his ancestral rank of knight, the poem portrays this by noting the broad stripe on his tunic, while again insisting that, despite the new form, his enthusiasm for poetry remained: *induiturque umeris cum lato purpura clavo / et studium nobis, quod fuit ante, manet* (*Trist.* 4.10.29–30). A few lines later his reassumption of the earlier status manifests itself in a corresponding change of form: the measure of his stripe contracts (*Trist.* 4.10.35).

The well-known importance of outward appearance as a marker of status in Roman culture, acquiring as it did even more prominence thanks to Augustus's reforms, in and of itself both gives an additional cultural resonance to the dichotomy between identity and its external manifestations we have found in the poem's transformations and hints at why such transformations become so suitable for engaging questions of power and one's place in a larger hierarchy. Such suggestions are not by their nature provable, but a glance back at an earlier transformation text, Plautus's *Amphitruo* again, will provide further material for examining how responses to changes of shape themselves varied according to social status. Three orders of character are separated from their recognizable appearance in the play: the gods who, as they do in Ovid, change shape at will to gratify their own desires at the expense of mortals, the slave Sosia, and his high-status master Amphitruo. Neither of these latter is actually transformed, though Sosia assumes that he has "lost his *forma*," but the effect is the same in that they are expelled from their places in the household by the gods who have assumed their appearances. This is, of course, a disconcerting experience for the slave Sosia, who spends many lines trying to prove his identity to his new double. But the encounter remains very much within the bounds of comedy. The slave's identity was always a changeable property, because his only role in society was as the possession of his master, who may well have given him his very name. The physical violence that could be inflicted on a slave, in contradistinction to the ideal untouchability of the citizen, takes on its own metamorphic quality thanks to Plautus's exuberant tropes. Thus, Mercury, who has literally taken the shape of Sosia, says in a stage aside to himself that "the person you skim with your fist ought to take on another form" (*Amph.* 316), which Sosia later translates into the realization that Mercury wants to "de-bone me like an eel" (*Amph.* 319), with an assonantal pun on the word for face (*os*). But even after Sosia inevitably fails to reclaim his identity from the god, he can console himself with the prospect of a further metamorphosis. If no one recognizes him, he can simply shave his head and take on the cap of a freedman. In contrast to Sosia's easy acceptance of a world of shifting identity, his master Amphitruo has much more at stake in keeping control over his appearance. He wages war with his own double by an appeal to all kinds of visible proof, seals and witnesses, ultimately invoking a judge whose very name means Mr. Eyelid. The divergence in treatment between the two cases of mistaken identity reminds us that a high-status Roman might well read the poem with a much more sharply defined sense of how closely outward appearance and position were linked and the consummate importance of maintaining control over one's own face.[59]

III. BEYOND BELIEF

Ovid claimed in a later poem that "unbelievability" was a programmatic element of the *Metamorphoses*, whose subject he defined as *in non credendos corpora versa modos* (*Trist.* 2.64). This dense phrase at once simply recapitulates the miraculous nature of metamorphosis and also, if we remember that "*modos*" can mean poetry as well, hints at unbelievability as a special quality that Ovid himself has bestowed on previously substantial "bodies" by turning them into verse.[60] Earlier, though, I argued that such claims acted more as a provocation than a description. Now I want to develop that point by looking briefly at Roman conceptions of the nature and function of fiction and how Ovid consistently throughout his works turns the traditional demotion of fiction on its head, giving a new power to fiction precisely because of its unbelievability. The issue of believability is raised in the *Metamorphoses* itself, in the much-studied response to the river god Achelous's account of the miraculous origins of the islands near his mouth. Discussion of this passage shows how the text uses the questions of belief to highlight the contrast between the internal and external points of view defined earlier and, at the same time,

---

[59] For a different way of relating metamorphosis to the fact of slavery, see Fitzgerald 2000.87–114. Fitzgerald focuses on how the changeability of the slave's fortune and the fundamental question of what happens when one becomes a slave—does the mind become servile?—address anxieties about the nature and limits of ethical decision making on the part of the masters. Like Ovidian metamorphosis then, the process of enslavement raises the issue of the recognizability of a true self that survives the change into the legal equivalent of a beast, and this issue in turn has the power to draw every individual who confronts it into an evaluation of the natural stability of his own position in the face of external circumstances. The stoic assertion that the true self of a wise man could never be enslaved—and, correspondingly, that real virtue was always recognizable, never more so than when the brave man withstood enslavement itself—provides a kind of insurance against precisely the circumstances of *Amphitruo*.

[60] *OLD* s.v. 8b, as opposed to 11c, the primary definition of *modus* in play here.

gives this contrast a new role in defining the distinctive kind of authority Ovid's fictional discourse takes upon itself.

As an introduction to first-century BCE Roman views on the nature of poetic fictions, how they were to be read and what kind of representation they offered, we can consider a conversation, itself fictional, depicted at the beginning of the *de legibus* as taking place on the country estate of the ex-consul Cicero, in the highlands of southern Latium, some ten years before Ovid's birth. Cicero's brother Quintus and brother-in-law Atticus are discussing a scene in the poem *Marius*, written by Cicero himself, where the statesman Marius was encouraged by the propitious omen of an eagle flying off to the east after defeating a serpent. Atticus begins the conversation with the assertion that the oak tree he sees before him is the very one where Marius saw his omen. Quintus responds that the poetic oak tree "endures and will always endure, for it was sown by genius. No farmer's care can plant a tree as long-lived as that sown by a poet's verse" (1.1.). He then turns to the example of the olive tree in Athens, or the palm on Delos, claimed to be the very one that Ulysses saw on his voyage. Because of the poetic fame of these trees, there will always be some actual tree that will be pressed into service as a real-world corollary. At this point, Atticus addresses the poet himself, and the issue of the tree's authenticity emerges as the prologue to a broader question about the veracity of poetry: "Did your verses really sow that tree, or are you passing down a story you heard about Marius?" (1.2). In other words: were we right to define the tree merely as a poetic tree, or was there some real, historical tree that provided the basis for your description? Given that this is for us such a natural thing to ask of a "historical fiction," as Cicero's *Marius* was, the response is striking. For Cicero claims not simply a poet's license to embellish and elaborate; he also asserts that only inexperienced readers would even ask about the truthfulness of any datum presented in a poem: "They betray their ignorance when in such a case they demand the truth of a poet, as they would of a witness.... In historical writings all things are evaluated according to their truth, in poetry according to the pleasure that they give" (1.4).

The privileging of the poet's ability to create fictions thus goes together with, in fact depends on, the corollary discrimination of the poet's world from the real world. The poet is given the power to sow the tree, and his own tree granted epistemological priority over any existing tree, only on condition that we remember that the tree Ulysses saw is not in fact really present. For Cicero, the response to poetry by skilled readers therefore becomes an unproblematic receptivity to fictions, unproblematic because the question of the actual truth of what is being described is literally rendered out of court. But the interest of the Cicero passage for a reading of Ovid is that Ovid's poem systematically undercuts the foundations of this normative view of how poetry is to be read.[61] As we have already seen from our reading of the Syrinx passage, Ovid's text calls into question Cicero's neat dichotomy between real "this" and poetic "that" by suggesting much more powerful connections between representation and reality. Correspondingly, the easy acceptance of fictions that results precisely from not considering the question of veracity is one that Ovid deliberately shuts off for his readers.

Also essential to Cicero's claim, and to Ovid's response to its implications, is the link between the fictionality of an utterance and its social status. Cicero deliberately exempts the poet from the economies of truth and authority that obtain in significant social settings where the truth matters, like court cases, in which the prestige of the "witness" determines whether his account is to be believed. Such a move makes perfect sense in a culture where our concept of "serious fiction" would have been felt as an oxymoron. As we have seen, the nature of their subject matter, neither factually true nor resembling truth, would have put Ovid's narratives of metamorphoses in the category of *fabulae*.[62] But not only were *fabulae* at the greatest remove from actual reality; in the hierarchy of narrative types, they were also to be separated from the major prose genres of oratory and history, where the truth content or at least the plausibility of the stories told at once depended on and enhanced the credibility of the narrator. A speaker or historian whose words were self-evidently false fell into the same category as the actor, a mere impersonator, whose utterances were *levis* (light), lacking the *gravitas* that conferred authority. The word *fabula*, which could be used equally of an incredible narrative and of a stage play, points to a conceptual overlap, between fiction and the

[61] I am not arguing that Ovid's overturning of the limits of fiction responds specifically to Cicero's formulations. However, it is interesting that Feeney 1999.23–24 points to another case where Ovid seems to play with Ciceronian definitions about how far fiction can go. At *Rep.* 2.28, one of the characters in the dialogue asks about the legend that the Roman king Numa had known Pythagoras. Scipio responds that such a story is not only a fiction (*fictum*) but an ignorant and ridiculous fiction (*imperite absurdeque fictum*). Yet Ovid allots five hundred lines of his final book to Pythagoras's instruction of Numa.

[62] Ovid himself explicitly alludes to the generic distinction in an earlier poem (*Amores* 3.12) where he protests that poets should not be treated as if they were witnesses in a courtroom (19–20). He then proves his point that the "license of poets" is not constrained by the criterion of credibility that applies to the genre of history (*historica fide*, 42) by cataloging the miraculous mythological stories to be found in their works. In most of these tales, the unbelievable element is precisely metamorphosis. Yet the context of the poet's plea not to be believed undercuts its ostensible message: Ovid has portrayed his (fictional) mistress in such terms that now everyone is in love with her and he himself is jealous. He therefore demands that his readers understand his praise of her as false. For the poem's manipulation of the rhetorical categories of believable and unbelievable stories, see McKeown 1979.

realm of the theater, and this overlap became more and more apparent in the early empire as mythological pantomimes, drawing on a repertoire of subjects very like those of the *Metamorphoses*, became a major theatrical form.[63] Those who wanted their voices to matter in the Roman polity often defined their work against the category of *fabulae*; thus the orator, however much he employs the techniques of the stage, is emphatically no actor, and historians relegate *fabulae* to the entertainment of children and mere thrill seekers.[64] Tellingly, the theoretical defenses of fiction in antiquity, if they can be called that, take the form of paradox: Gorgias, speaking of tragedy, which, relying as it does on verisimilitude, is very different in effect from the overt incredibility of Ovidian fiction, calls it a "deception where the one who deceives is more just than the one who does not and the one who is deceived is wiser than the one who is not."[65] The very terms of this defense play off against a common ancient association between producing veristic representations of false events and deceptive and unjust behavior.

Though it assumes such a negative perspective on this kind of representation, Gorgias's statement also recalls the associations of the poetic tradition with justice and wisdom, and above all reminds us of the uncanny persuasive capacity of fiction, which can invert and reconfigure moral and epistemological assumptions. And in Roman culture, fiction and play develop an enormous prestige, outside of the realities of power but linked to it by both likeness (the actors played at being kings and gods) and association (they were specially connected to the real centers of Roman social power, particularly the imperial family). Thus, the reminder that the poet is writing incredible stories and injunctions to place his work in that category of *fabulae* tends to diminish and trivialize the social value and seriousness of his project; on the contrary, the absorption into fiction itself testifies to the poet's power, absolute in the manipulation of his created world.

The tension between the external definition of poetic fiction, represented by Cicero, as valuable only when it makes no claim to truth, and the internal claim to significance—internal both because it is made from within the poetic tradition and, I would argue, because it requires a capacity to enter into the perspective of the poetic representations itself—repeatedly informs Ovid's construction of his own poetic identity. An excellent example of this comes in the "autobiographical" poem, *Tristia*

---

[63] See Galinsky 1996.265–66 and 1999.103–4, with Habinek 2002.52–54.

[64] For orators, see Edwards 1993.117–19; for historians cf. Sempronius Asellio, fr. 2 Chassignet.

[65] Plut. *Mor.* 348c. See Feeney 1991.24.

4.10, written after Ovid's banishment to the Black Sea. First comes the question of language itself: every time Ovid tried to write in the respectable medium of prose, the training necessary for social and monetary advancement, the words miraculously came out verse. Ovid then describes how he was on the verge of entering the Senate but was temperamentally unsuited to the strains of political competition: "My body was not tough enough; my mind unfit for labor, and I shunned troublesome ambition. The Muses urged me to seek out safe tranquility, which was also my own predilection" (*Trist.* 4.10.37–40). But this traditional image of poetry as a haven from the storms of politics acquires ironic overtones in a poem written from exile. Far from offering him a safe refuge, poetry would cause him to undergo labors far more taxing than running for office, and this reluctant politician ends by presenting himself as a new Aeneas, tossed by trouble on land and sea (*Trist.* 4.10.107–8; note the play between *fugax* and *fuga*), even a new Augustus presenting posterity with an account of his *acta* (4.10.92).

A similar manipulation of audience expectations about the powers of fiction, on a smaller scale, comes in *Amores* 3.12. In this poem, the speaker ironically laments the power of his own poetry to make all his readers fall in love with Corinna; the poets, precisely because they can describe things that never existed, take on the punishing power of the gods: "We stretched out Tityos to measureless extent, and we gave three faces to the snaky dog." Whenever poets go beyond the credible, breaking the links that bind their representations to the standards of an external reality, they become the masters of their fictional domains. Nor does their dominion remain confined to the text because the point about these two examples in particular is the immense coercive power that images of divine punishment have really exercised in human history, making it all the more fitting that the poet himself should now be punished by jealousy for making his readers believe in his fictions. Thus, the fiction-making capacity of poets is itself a slippery property, offering at once the refuge of unbelievability and lack of weight and at the same time a claim precisely to transform impressions of the world "out there."

As we have seen, Ovid parades the *Metamorphoses*' fictional status before the reader: "bodies transformed in incredible ways" (*in non credendos corpora versa modos, Trist.* 2.64). Yet the very point Ovid is making in the passage where this line occurs, part of a justification of his poetic career addressed to no less a person than Augustus, is not that the poem is negligible or irrelevant because fictional. On the contrary, unlike Cicero, who will not demand of poets the same kind of truth as he does of witnesses, Ovid uses the poem precisely as testimony of his loyalty toward the regime. The emperor in the midst of all the miracles will find many "presages of your fame, and pledges of my intention," all of which the poet invites him to read as true. Yet what is particularly interesting about this claim is that what is true in the poem, the signs of the real-world relationship between the poet and the emperor, are those that maintain Ovid in the subservient status of loyal subject, whereas, as we have already seen and shall consider more fully in the next chapter, the fictions, which he here explicitly points out as such, change the balance of dominance. Perhaps a hint of this comes here in the reminder that the *Metamorphoses* was still "without end": as every reader of the *Aeneid* knew, the absence of a limit was the ideal condition of Rome's own empire (*imperium sine fine, Aen.* 1.279) and a defining characteristic of the power of the gods within the poem.

But the most explicit and complex way in which the poem problematizes its own status as fiction comes through its manipulation of narrators and audiences within the poem. We have already seen in the Io and Syrinx stories, a series of "readers" within the text from Inachus to Argus, whose attempts to distance themselves from unbelievable transformations conspicuously fail. Elsewhere in the poem, characters within the narrative will baldly state that a tale is unbelievable—and be chastised or punished for their incredulity. The most famous of these dramas of disbelief comes in the very center of the poem. When at a banquet the river god Achelous has described how the islands that form the background to the scene were in fact once nymphs, one of his guests, Pirithous, whom the narrator presents not as skeptical but indeed as impious, bridles and treats the god's tale as unbelievable, only to be cautioned against such scoffing by the sage Lelex:

> *Amnis ab his tacuit. factum mirabile cunctos*
> *moverat: inridet credentes, utque deorum*
> *spretor erat mentisque ferox, Ixione natus*
> *"ficta refers nimiumque putas, Acheloe, potentes*
> *esse deos," dixit "si dant adimuntque figuras."*
> *obstipuere omnes nec talia dicta probarunt,*
> *ante omnesque Lelex animo maturus et aevo,*
> *sic ait: "inmensa est finemque potentia caeli*
> *non habet, et quicquid superi voluere, peractum est."*
>
> (8.611–19)

The stream fell silent, and the astonishing deed moved all listeners: but the son of Ixion, a spurner of the gods and fierce in his mind, mocked the believers: "Fictions is what you are telling, Achelous, and you reckon the gods to be too powerful, if they give and take away shapes." Everyone was aghast and rejected such words. Above all, Lelex, as mature in his mind as he was by age, spoke like this: "The power of heaven is unmeasurable and has no limits. Whatever the gods will is accomplished."

Typical of the poem are both the voice of the narrator, weighing in strongly on the side of the "old believer" Lelex, and the sense that by the mere fact of raising the issue of credibility, and of taking a position so much in keeping with contemporary assumptions about the kinds of tales being told, it is Pirithous whose position ought to be more sympathetic to the poem's actual audience and author.[66] One response to the seemingly contradictory injunctions toward skepticism and belief is to resolve them in favor of one or the other possibility, with skepticism usually predominating because internal admonitions toward credulity can easily be read as ironic.[67] Graf's model of an essentially skeptical author manipulating a credulous narrator has been adopted as a particularly satisfactory way of creating coherence in the work. However, when the issue is put in terms of effects of the narrative rather than the attitudes and intentions of the author, coherence has come to seem a less desirable goal. More recent treatments of belief and disbelief in Ovid's poetics, especially those of Feeney, Barchiesi, and Wheeler, no longer attempt to resolve the conflict but rather argue that the important thing in Ovid's narrative is to experience the tension between the alternative reading strategies that the work makes available. Moreover, all three critics have found in the problem of the reader's belief a crucial connection between the narrative dynamics of the poem and its contemporary political effectiveness. For Feeney, the continual formulation of poetic assertions in a medium whose changeability and unreliability stand in such high relief inspires a constant interrogation of the power of the literary tradition to make belief. And all three writers present the emperor Augustus's own assimilation of himself to a god as the ultimate test case for the reader's willingness to accept fictions.[68] Indeed, Wheeler finds in the poet's construction of an audience sternly recalled from invitations to disbelief by authorial reminders of the criminality of such views a model for the actual experience of his

---

[66] Graf 1988.

[67] Skepticism: see esp. Galinsky 1999; a notable exception is Spahlinger 1996, who argues that the emphasis on belief delineates an Ovidian ideal of the pious artist.

[68] Cf. esp. Feeney 1991.224: "Deeply engrained attitudes towards the power of the gods are questioned and explored by the movement of the *Metamorphoses*. At the climax, the currents of this questioning flow into the organization of the contemporary world, to cap the poem's repeated confrontation of human and divine power. The princeps is as august, and as mighty, as the gods he has made his own." Also crucial to this discussion has been Hinds 1987b.23–29.

own audience, which is forced to decide for itself how much to disbelieve under the policing eye of the emperor.[69]

My own emphasis in discussing the effects of these provocations toward skepticism is on the process of reading they stimulate rather than on the ends of intellectual decision making. Thus, in place of arguing that the skepticism generated by the poem is eventually directed toward some external reality, a figure, ideology, or narrative that demands to be taken as authentic by its audience, like the divinity of the emperor, I concentrate on the ways in which explicit challenges to the credibility of internal narratives sharpen the double vision that I have described whereby the planes of reception generated by internal narratives veer away from conventional expectations of fictionality. This complication of the audience's understanding of what they are doing when they read the poem has at least as many consequences for their view of Ovid as of Augustus. It is another striking example of how his narrative breaks the bounds that ought to contain it. And while it is true that crucial programmatic passages in the poem, the Lycaon and Daphne story in book 1 and the complex ending of the work, do bring the emperor directly on stage, in the vast majority of metamorphoses narratives, there is no specific Augustan element in the content of the story. Whether we believe that Io was turned into a cow or Syrinx into a reed will only in the very broadest sense bear on our interpretation of the imperial regime. To argue either that the programmatic links to political issues are sufficient to code every unbelievable narrative as a test of our faith in the empire or that these other episodes are hermeneutic dry runs for more ideologically charged narratives would be to distort the work in the quest for political relevance. A more important point is that in the politics of fictional belief it is not always clear on which side believers and nonbelievers should stand. Thus, for Wheeler, rejecting the tales of an Achelous can be connected with an impious failure to believe in "official fictions."[70] A contrary position might be that the refusal to enter into fictions at all, to be duped by a trickster poet, represents a clearheaded unwillingness to let go of an actuality in which the emperor is fully in charge.[71] Thus, if we do agree that working out what is to count as true within the poem becomes a political exercise, this is not only because it challenges assent to fixed articles of faith but precisely because it involves a more radical refiguring of the very terms under debate, opening up a hall of mirrors

[69] Wheeler 1999.165–77.

[70] Wheeler 1999.181.

[71] Thus, for Barchiesi 1997a.181, it is the voice of the "credulous" reader who has been tricked too many times that sounds suggestively "imperial"; see discussion in Wheeler 1999.166–67.

where emperor and poet stand now on one side, now on another, now together, now apart.

As an example of the many ways in which the issue of belief, far from simply inviting the audience to question its own credulity, exposes the multiple paradoxes of Ovid's fiction and the reader's position in relation to it, I want to take a closer look at the Pirithous episode. The first question to ask is just what it is that Pirithous is disbelieving. Achelous, a classic "split divinity"[72] who appears in the narrative both as a personification and as the actual river that bears his name, has just told two quite similar stories in very different ways. The first describes the Echinades, a group of nymphs who forget to sacrifice to Achelous as a god. "I swole with rage, and as great as ever when I am at my full, enormous both in my spirit and in my waves, I ripped forest from forest and field from field and together with the place itself, I hurled the nymphs—who didn't neglect me then—into the sea. And my waters and those of the sea, eroded the soil and little by little divided them with channels into as many Echinades as you see" (8.583–87). The transformation in this case is not miraculous at all; in fact, the god seems at pains to offer a rationalization for a possibly unbelievable metamorphosis. The nymphs are carried away in a flood that has created a new set of islands, and the god's power and wrath take the form of a purely natural phenomenon operating in ways familiar to us from observable experience—a flooding river breaking new channels. What challenges belief here comes from assuming that some personal presence, an angry river god, lies behind these natural phenomena; and indeed the punning language, by which the same word can without strain express both the influx of rage and the swelling of a river, exposes Ovid's audience to just such a conundrum.[73] The issue is not in fact that different from the one that Atticus faces at the beginning of de legibus: he sees a tree and wants to know whether that actual tree has a corollary in some miraculous narrative. Indeed, the entire tale is spun out of a simple request for information about a feature of the landscape that is literally before the audience's eyes (subiecta oculis, 8.574): Theseus asks the name of the island he sees in the distance, but at the very moment of asking his question, the perils of relying on simple autopsy emerge. Just as Achelous wants to make natural islands signifiers of something much more than can be seen—the emotions of anthropomorphic gods—so too channels open up within the scene, and the one island, as it had seemed when Theseus began his question, becomes many—so does "separation cheat discernment." Seeing does not always equal believing, in a world where barrier islands can conceal such divine wrath.

[72] For the phrase, see Solodow 1988.96.
[73] See Hardie 2002c.230–31 and Tissol 1997.18–26 on syllepsis.

If the Echinades story challenges us by, to pick up one of Ovid's own puns, animating the immanent, the contrasting story of Perimele, a nymph whom Achelous loved, raped, and, when her father has punished her by casting her off a cliff, persuaded Neptune to save by changing her too into an island, works in precisely the opposite direction. Here the actions of the god within the story are such that they can be performed only in human guise—we may imagine a river falling in love as well as being angry, but having sex and speaking require some measure of human form. The transformation here, though it contains elements of the same pathetic fallacy in the image of the land "embracing the limbs" of the maiden, is genuinely miraculous. There is no question of natural phenomena—the nymph's limbs are changed. Human actions are now clothed in immortal guise, and in contrast to a real natural feature providing the space for the exploits of anthropomorphic gods, a miraculous tale struggles toward actuality by leaving a physical trace, as the nymph's own limbs acquire *gravitas* by becoming an island. Indeed, the god himself offers authenticating strategies equivalent to autopsy to establish the reality of the second story. First comes the absurd introduction of witnesses to establish the name of the island ("sailors call it Perimele") where surely he is the best authority,[74] and then the etymological play of the final lines, where the changed limbs of the nymph as the island accrues around them recall her Greek name "Peri-mele." In growing into the island, she also grows into the name that now comes to validate her story. Or, if we think how autopsy and argument from observable facts were thrown into doubt by the Echinades story, she calls it into question. And it may be that this *factum mirabile*—a highly ambiguous expression that suggests both reality and incredibility[75]—is what prompts Pirithous's dissent, when he was perfectly able to cope with the first narrative.

Except, in a curious way the second story of a god in love would perhaps be at least as credible to the internal audience as that of the river in flood. For Theseus and his fellow travelers have themselves encountered the stream in two irreconcilable guises that correspond to his modes of action in the different stories. First, the river Achelous itself, in flood as it happens, has blocked their return from Calydon; then, the same river in personified form emerges as a courtly host to welcome them to a banquet. If we consider, then, the second half of this encounter, and remember that it is this anthropomorphic figure who is equally before the eyes of the audience, then the transformation involved in this story, told, as it is, as a miracle, may be at least as easy to accept as the mental transformation of their gentle narrator into the cross natural phenomenon described

[74] So Hollis 1970.102.
[75] As noted by Feeney 1991.230.

in the Echinades story. Not only is the god in the second narrative a remarkably human figure, who finds himself in a situation that, for example, the human hero of a new comedy might well encounter. He is also an extraordinarily powerless one, and like so many human lovers in the poem, Pygmalion and Iphis, for example, he has recourse to prayer to a god to bring about his miracle. The effect of this doubling is not just to cast doubt on any strategies of evidence and rationalization we might use to make fictions more plausible, or to point out the dramatic incongruity in Ovid's own narrative, and in many other epics, of setting a river god beside his own stream. Beyond this, the effect of Pirithous's question is to make us remember the difference between what is believable to us and what is believable to the audience within the narrative and in this more nuanced way as well both to explicate and to confuse the perspectives of those within the story and those outside it. The first story assumes a perspective that is perfectly harmonious with that of the poem's real-world audience—we could go to the mouth of the Achelous today and see just that scene—but tries to make us believe that appearances conceal supernatural events. The second story will seem incredible to us, unaccustomed as we are to dining with river gods, but to the internal audience it might be initially more credible, involving as it does both the human narrator that they see before them and correspondingly a distinctively human set of problems and solutions.

If reflection on the content of the two stories makes the poem's audience think about how deeply they have penetrated into the poem's fictional structures, the river Achelous in a different sense as well flows from the realms of fiction into fact. That is, when Pirithous's question is voiced, we are perhaps initially unsure what level of narration it is describing. Though addressed to Achelous, will it also be heard as a criticism of Ovid himself? After all the gods' giving and taking away, *figurae* is the self-proclaimed subject of the entire poem. So too, Perimele and the Echinades are not the only examples of changed form involved here; Achelous himself, just as he appears in irreconcilably different guises within his own stories, is a notorious mythological shape changer.[76] Thus, in this case to ask about the veracity of the narrative is simultaneously to ask about the narrator as well; content and narration blend into one another, and this blending, given the way Pirithous's language recalls the proem, extends to that of the actual narrator of the *Metamorphoses*. Here then, at the very moment that Pirithous himself tries to shake both audience and Ovid's readers outside the narrative by reminding both of the difference between fiction and reality, comes a reminder of how inextricably

---

[76] The reading of Achelous himself, the raging river, as a poetological metaphor for epic further conflates the teller and his tale.

the two are intertwined. And this reminder contains a final twist if we look back at the proem itself. We have been interpreting the scene so far in terms of real literary phenomena, in which Ovid the author creates the character Achelous. But in the proem it is the gods in their transforming capacity who are made responsible for the changes Ovid's poem undergoes: from that perspective it is Achelous who is responsible for Ovid rather than the other way around.[77]

One argument that has sometimes seemed to give extratextual authority to the case against Pirithous comes from the charge, made both by the character Lelex and by the narrator himself, that his skepticism is an act of impiety. By characterizing Pirithous as a "spurner of the gods," Ovid has been taken to be trying to alienate the sympathies of his audience from the character, discouraging us from reading as he does. While the connection between disbelief and impiety may be self-evident to us, to some ancients the claim that to disbelieve poetic fictions about the gods was irreverent would have appeared as a very paradoxical one. In his discussion of poetic representations of the gods, the first-century BCE Roman scholar Varro strikes a note very familiar in ancient theology: "In this [poetic system of representing the divine] many things have been made up [ficta] contrary to the dignity and nature of the immortals. For it describes how one god is born from a head, another from a thigh, and another from drops of blood: it describes how the gods have grown angry, how they have committed adultery, how they have been enslaved to men. In sum, everything that can befall not only a man but a very base man is attributed to the gods."[78]

Measured against Varro's statement, Lelex's caution about slighting gods who are at once unnatural and hyperhuman is very much piety through the poetic looking glass. It assumes that the gods of poetry are the real gods and, to that extent, keeps the reader's perspective grounded within the text's fictions.

Denis Feeney has similarly interpreted the debate between Pirithous and Lelex as articulating the "two possible audience reactions to the divine stories of the *Metamorphoses*" in a manner that complements the reading offered here.[79] Against those who had argued that Ovid endorses either skepticism or credulity, Feeney agrees with the theorist of fictions Robert Newsom that a kind of divided belief, with half our consciousness anchored in the real world and half surrendered to the narrative, describes the ideal state of all readers of fiction. To be fully receptive readers

---

[77] For a different interpretation of book 8 as a whole, and this passage in particular, as an invitation for the reader to reflect on her experience of the narrative, see now Boyd 2006.

[78] Varro *Ant. Div.* fr. 7.

[79] Feeney 1991.229–32.

of the poem, Feeney argues, we must play both Pirithous and Lelex. But such a double reading may prove harder to achieve than Feeney's analysis suggests. For Newsom's argument about the operation of fictions is more important for clarifying what Ovid's narrative does not do. He is speaking of the effect of veristic fiction that never reminds the reader of its own fictionality.[80] What he attempts to describe is the paradoxical state of the little boy at a horror movie who can scream in terror but continue eating his popcorn. This is not the conscious choice or continuous oscillation between perspectives that Ovid's poem seems to demand but a living with ambiguity that relies essentially on a failure to make explicit the logical processes involved. Thus, where Feeney presents a constructive response to the Pirithous story, in which the exposure to polarized alternatives reminds us that both perspectives are required of the reader and so becomes an injunction toward the ideal double vision Newsom describes, I see the effect as more destabilizing.[81] Ovid allows us to sink comfortably into the attitude of neither a Pirithous nor the other members of the audience who willingly suspend their disbelief. It is not Newsom's passive acquiescence in paradox that the passage encourages but an active grappling with the different perspectives available on the poem and its subject matter, which can exist neither together nor apart.

My reasons for stressing the difficulty of what Ovid seems to require of his audience here take us back to the Cicero passage with which this section began. On the basis of the account of reading offered there, it would seem that the problem Ovid or any other Roman recounter of *fabulae* faces is not to coax readers into entering into the fiction in the first place. This is easy for such readers as Cicero wants to construct; they are reading for pleasure, and this knowledge makes it possible to let themselves go because their reading has no consequence. On the contrary, the challenge for Ovid is to get his audience to suspend disbelief without such trivializing distancing. By continually holding up the real-world categories that define his text as mere *fabulae*, and inviting the audience to entertain the perspectives of all manner of credulous audiences within the fiction, Ovid destabilizes these assumptions in two related ways. First, he makes it impossible to settle comfortably into the role of poetic audience that Cicero defines precisely by continually reminding the audience of

---

[80] Cf. Newsom's (1988.108) comment: "Fictions whose fictionality is plain are bad fictions."

[81] Feeney's (1993.238) formulation of the tensions involved in ancient responses to fiction even more closely anticipates the position I take here, for there he views Newsom's "duality" as "one way of coming to terms with the apprehension that art is something crafted *and* emotionally compelling or immediate." Yet here too his emphasis is on how these different levels of awareness can work together in their effect on the reader. My emphasis, by contrast, is on what happens when they do not.

what it is doing and where it is. In this way, the transformation between internal and external perspectives is never hermeneutic business as usual but appears as the powerful manipulation that it is.[82] Alternatively, if we allow such conscious manipulations of audience response to open a gulf between internal and external audience, to provide the reader with a perch from which to observe the operations of fictions without being himself subject to them, and indeed to regard any claims for the potency of mere stories as ironic, then that reader encounters an equally novel reading experience, precisely by continuing in the real-world perspective that sees the actual mechanics of poetic fictions. Returning to the address to Augustus in the *Tristia*, we might now claim that the emperor's capacity to recognize the poem as testimony of the poet's loyalty and as a presage of his own power comes from a reading that refuses to entertain its fictions. Although it is by no means addressed to the emperor, the *Metamorphoses*' concluding prediction of the *princeps*'s own future greatness allows the poem as an artifact to be seen as a component of the "traffic in praise," anchoring literary production to real-world exchanges of duties and favors that defined status. But in this sense as well the continual shifting between external and internal perspective makes it less certain which aspect of the poem matters, the actual text irrespective of its content, that transparently participates in defining the power of Augustus even if it does so in a way that emphasizes the subordination of the poet, or the fictional space it promises to create, where the poet can seem either to break free of the secondariness that necessarily subjects his work to imperial evaluation or simply to have fallen back into the expected behavior of an author who can never make any such claims because he has adopted a self-evidently trivial form of expression, fiction.

[82] This is not, of course, to claim that the destabilization of a fictional narrative by drawing attentions to the real-world conditions in which it is produced and experienced is a uniquely Ovidian phenomenon. An anonymous reader highlights, as two of many possible examples, the introduction to Plato's *Symposium* and "the Roman poets' use of the epistolary form." Both of these examples, however, do help define by contrast the effect I am describing in the *Metamorphoses*. For in the case of the *Symposium*, a veristic narrative highlights its own potential distance from reality through being staged as a memory of a memory. In Ovid's case, the material he narrates is by its nature impossible to read as anything but imaginary. And in the case of epistolary form, the conventions of reception—this is a letter of x to y—can itself easily be read as part of the fiction as well: thus while the device certainly raises questions about the limits of fiction, it does not in my view generate such a starkly external perspective.

CHAPTER 2

Wavering Identity

In artistic terms, the weaving contest between Arachne and Minerva ends in a draw. Even the most hostile possible judge, Minerva herself, can find no fault with her rival's tapestry. But art does not count for everything, and the fact that Arachne has so ably vindicated her abilities fails to prevent her tale too from becoming another example of the folly of rivaling the gods. The tapestry may be perfect but Minerva destroys it[1] and beats the girl with her spindle. Unable to endure this indignity, Arachne hangs herself. Minerva at that point feels pity, but her sympathy manifests itself strangely, as she turns the girl into a spider and assures her that this penalty will travel down through her whole line. The extraordinary dynamic of this ending, with its many unexpected twists and oscillations between stiffening revenge and relaxation into sympathy, helps focus the tale's concern with the power of art in a very material sense and with how the capacity to produce such perfect representations relates to status. At first, art and power may seem caught up in a cycle of conflict that is literally unbreakable. Art represents the crimes of the gods. The gods destroy the tapestry, but only to have their jealous vengeance represented in the very act by another artistic "text," Ovid's own poem, which in consequence exposes itself and its author to retribution. However, certain elements of the narrative complicate this battle between "art" and "reality." First the goddess is herself an artist. Indeed, the instrument of her vengeance is the very tool of her art, the boxwood spindle with which she has produced her own weaving. Such a light object—boxwood was proverbial for its use to make toys and known as the wood from which Catullus fashioned the ship that brought him home from the East, a metaphor for poetry in the slightest vein (4.13)— could not have inflicted such damage were it not for the aspirations of the human artist Arachne. She herself recognizes no clear distinction between the realms of art and power and uses her skill to advance her

---

[1] The motion from "criticism" to revenge hangs on a pun in the term *carpere*, noted by Feeney 1991.192, which can mean both criticize and, literally, pluck apart. This verbal similarity could suggest an essential continuity between what the goddess does as connoisseur, and what she does as outraged divinity, or it could signal that her power comes with a shift from the metaphoric and figurative to the literal and physical.

status, specifically to achieve immortality herself despite her low birth (6.12–13). The overlap between art and power also emerges in the way that each artist's tale gives its distinctive "spin" to her own experience. Minerva's emphasis on divine vengeance provides a narrative and social template for interpreting the punishment of Arachne as the justified and inevitable return for an inferior's hubris: Arachne's catalog of crimes of divine passion offers a rubric under which her own life story, as it turns out, could be easily classed.[2]

In this chapter, I explore the consequences of the complex relation between social authority and artistic representation sketched here for Ovid's act of literary creation. By stressing the interactions between personal status and artistic roles, I hope to replace an old model of Ovid's self-representation as enacting a clear-cut, indeed timeless, battle between the resistant artist and all-powerful tyrant with a more specific and complex picture of the pressures and constraints acting on the writer in a society where the emperor was already an artist and the artist uses his text as a way of pursuing an immortality very like that sought by the *princeps* himself. The argument frequently returns to differing manifestations of the double vision sketched out in the first chapter. Like the spectators for Arachne's own artistic productions, we keep one eye on what the artist makes, and another on the very real act of creation itself. Sometimes the grand fictions the poem discloses seem to be the artist's way of controlling and containing empire as well as emperor; at others, the comparative triviality of the artistic product is balanced by the recognition of the real stature of the artist. Thus, whatever it is that Arachne may portray on her tapestry and despite the fact that she works with "fluff,"[3] the very act of weaving assimilates her to the gods who created the world.[4] Indeed, the uncertain shifting between work and world both produces and reflects the status of the literary artist in late Augustan Rome, where, I suggest, every act of creation depends on a process of recontextualization with the power to limit as much as to exalt.

[2] Indeed, Ovid suggestively questions the bounds between representation and reality by leaving the phrase "divine crimes," *caelestia crimina*, hanging in his account of Minerva's revenge, 6.131. The words could stand in apposition to the content of the pictures, which provides a kind of justification for Minerva's anger; or to the pictures themselves, suggesting how the very act of rivaling the god as a weaver makes art itself a crime; or finally to the actions of Minerva, making her own anger a fit continuation of Arachne's work. For a complementary critique, strongly differentiating art from power in the episode, see now Oliensis 2004.

[3] Note the emphasis in the description on such proverbially worthless and insubstantial material as wool and clouds, as well as the lightness of her thumb and the tinyness of her tools, spindle, and needle.

[4] Parallels noted by Feeney 1991.191 and Wheeler 1995.

The role of metamorphosis and the emphasis on fictionality it brings take on a new aspect in this discussion. We have seen how, by inviting the audience to redraw the boundaries between fact and fiction and give assent to the poet's representation of the cosmos in priority to the world of experience, the marvelous elements of Ovid's narrative at once claim and deny a new seriousness for *fabulae* in relation to a variety of discourses ranging from more conventional epic to the public speech of the politician. A consequence of this will be to turn the poet himself into an unstable figure whose identity, like those of the characters subjected to metamorphosis, undergoes a continual transformation from servile to imperial, depending on the perspective from which his art is viewed. In this way, the shifting shape of the poet allows Ovid, again in the context of a work that seems most remote from the social context of Augustan Rome, to explore the position of the artist with a complexity that rivals that of the *Satires* and *Epistles* of Horace. Thus, where Fränkel coined the phrase "wavering identity" to describe the psychological fluidity of the characters within Ovid's poem, I reapply it here to the external, social identity of the author.

To begin the argument, I want to return to the link between fiction and authorial status discussed at the end of the preceding chapter by offering a reading of the *Metamorphoses'* conclusion. By referring to its own status as a work of art (*iam opus exegi*, 15.871), the poem marks its transition from the reality represented within the text to the reality within which the physical text exists. Ovid simultaneously seems literally to surpass himself by rivaling the real figure of Augustus even as that emperor stands on the verge of further ascent towards divinity. Out of this abundant material, which has prompted some of the most penetrating recent readings of the *Metamorphoses*, I focus only on the last 135 lines, describing what is arguably the poem's last metamorphosis, the catasterism of Caesar and its imagined sequels, the apotheosis of Caesar's successor Augustus and the immortality that the finished poem will give to Ovid himself. My point is to demonstrate how the different kinds of finality the poem claims for itself sketch a paradoxical and shifting relation between reality and representation centering on the figures of the emperor and poet. The second half of the chapter then relates this mutual emulation to the broader reception and dissemination of artistic representations in Augustan Rome and its political ramifications. This will be "fleshed out" in turn by analyses of scenes of rivalry between gods and human artists in the poem, especially Marsyas's flaying by Apollo and Daedalus's flight from Minos through the imitation of bird's wings. Read with an interest in the social contexts of artistic production in Augustan Rome, these tales take on new significance for understanding the poet's ambiguous self-fashioning as creator and imitator.

I. Imitations of Immortality

I start by offering a basic road map of the poem's final book as a whole and the structure of its last narrative. Book 15 begins just after the death of Romulus with a question about succession that, as Philip Hardie has shown,[5] links the poem's narrative with the central political preoccupation of the time: who will come next? But the glance toward Rome and the future prepares for another regression, as the destined second king Numa abandons his fatherland to visit the Greek city of Croton, and the narrative is taken over by an inset tale describing that city's foundation (15.11–59). The reason for Numa's journey is a desire to supplement his knowledge of the rites of his own native place with an understanding of the nature of things as a whole, and for that he turns to the Greek philosopher Pythagoras. Pythagoras does not disappoint, giving a speech of more than four hundred lines (15.75–478) that can only be described as totalizing. This longest speech in the poem moves from a comprehensive picture of the functioning of the cosmos, based on perpetual flux and the transmigration of souls, to a prophecy of Rome's metamorphosis into the "head of the world." Numa leaves Pythagoras in order to fulfill his own historical destiny, which takes up four lines, one one-hundredth of the space dedicated to the meeting with Pythagoras. Then another Greek refugee, Hippolytus, takes center stage as he vainly attempts to console Numa's divine consort after the king's death with the account of his tragic fate before being reborn as the Italian god Virbius (15.493–546). The six hundred years between Numa's death and the assassination of Caesar provide only two narrative episodes. The first of these, the tale of Cipus (15.565–621), who selflessly withdraws from Rome after miraculous horns, a sign of his future kingship,[6] sprout on his head. Just as it is unattested in the main historical narratives of early Rome and has no fixed date, this story stands outside the main stream of Ovid's narrative: Cipus's amazement at his new horns merely offers a point of comparison for Hippolytus's response to Egeria's transformation into a spring. The advent of the god Aesculapius (15.622–744), the next tale, by contrast is more solidly anchored both in the historical record—it can be dated to 292 BCE[7]—and in the architecture of the poem because it follows a formal evocation of the muses, who also guarantee its truth. But if these features should make the tale seem more real than its predecessor, the narrative itself requires yet another retreat to Greece, and the ambiguous god enters Italy by way of the home of Circe, who turns men into beasts.

[5] Hardie 1997.

[6] For a darker view of the Cipus story, see Barchiesi 1997a.186–87.

[7] Noted by Barchiesi 1997a.188.

Imported Aesculapius provides a foil for Caesar, Rome's homegrown god (15.745–851).

This brief schema makes clear how the final book highlights the play between contrasting pairs on the level of style and content: Greece versus Rome, history versus myth, movement into the present versus a retreat into etiological legend, narrative versus digression.[8] The difficult relationship between these opposing terms especially comes to the surface when the elaborate internal speeches of fantastically displaced characters like Pythagoras and Virbius bump up against the Roman historical events within which they are interwoven. Thus, Pythagoras's rejection of animal sacrifice, which would seem to make the natural philosophy he espouses irreconcilable with Numa's native rites, leads to Numa's return to Rome to institute sacrifices.[9] Virbius's speech has no discernible consoling effect on Egeria.

The narrative's continual feints and retreats from Roman history to the world of Greek legend, and its reliance on so many dubious voices, have guided a number of different scholars toward the view that the final book demonstrates a triumph of textualization. The bulk of space taken up by other voices in the poem, which, as Stephen Wheeler has observed, completes a trend throughout the work of giving an increasingly large proportion of the text over to internal narrators, opens up a series of *mises en abyme*, inviting increasing speculation about the reliability of any reported fact or interpretation.[10]

Perhaps the most striking example of this deferral of authority comes with the figure of Pythagoras, whose words are explicitly described as "learned but not believed." The climax of that performance comes in another act of ventriloquism, as Pythagoras predicts the future glory of Rome and the apotheosis of its ultimate founder, Aeneas, by recounting the prophecy of the Trojan seer Helenus. Such crucial assertions about Rome's destiny not only occur as the poet reports a meeting that historical chronology ruled impossible (the Roman king Numa lived some hundred years before Pythagoras came to Italy) but also rely on the philosopher's own misremembering of words he heard when he was literally someone else.[11] Pythagoras seems to be misremembering because of the difference between his version and the direct report of Helenus's prophecy in the

---

[8] In a sense the whole book is a digression—the second word *interea*, "meanwhile," locates its starting point as a turning away from the apotheosis of Hora, time herself (14.851) whose distinctive Romanness is marked by her "conjunction" with Quirinus.

[9] Galinsky 1998.317 shows that Ovid gives no endorsement to the minority view, represented in Plut. *Numa* 8.8, that Numa's sacrifices too were bloodless.

[10] Wheeler 1999, esp.162–65.

[11] This analysis of Pythagoras's speech as a deconstruction of poetic authority was developed by Hardie 1997.185–87.

Aeneid, which Ovid has him cite.[12] Thus, the moment that signals the fallibility of Pythagoras report also encourages us to transfer its model of imperfect reproduction from the philosopher's speech to the poet's text, because Ovid is here varying his "authoritative" model. When the content of the poem matters most, in the sense that it comes closest to describing directly the immediate present and, more than that, to becoming prophecy itself by looking to the future, the text exposes its own reliance on mere words. The victory of Ovidian narrative falsehood over established tradition and the authority of texts like the *Aeneid* takes another form in the very obvious and well-documented transformations of emphasis as Homer and Vergil are Ovidianized through the later poet's foregrounding of the erotic and of verbal play.[13] It is not just that this manipulative fancy pits Ovidian fiction against history and tradition, but, as Hardie has stressed,[14] the Ovidian model infects all those previous stories: words are all there ever were, and Ovid's impossible Pythagoras comes to seem a paradigm of all utterance claiming to be true.

This tendency to view Ovid's poem as leading to a progressive "writing of the world," where the supreme power of the poet comes from breaking the ties between representation and reality even as the text shows its ability to engulf everything, has elements to attract many modern readers. It lends itself to easy politicization, especially for those with an anti-Augustan sensibility, as the master of the world has his domain and, as we shall see, his very identity snatched away by the master representer. At the same time, this reading evokes an idealized separation of art and politics: the poet's victory means becoming a book. But, as so often with Ovid, there is another side to this picture, one that presents a very much less optimistic view of the encounter of text and world and acknowledges the impossibility of the one ever dispensing with the other. Ovid's exposure of imperial fictions to poetic deconstruction will be balanced by an anxiety that he has made himself emperor of nothing, that the type of immortality he creates for himself depends entirely on his own words, that is, on keeping the reader's perspective located within his literary horizons. And the book is too full of examples of the irrelevance of its most impressive verbal performances to its historical "plot" for the loss involved in such a victory to escape notice.

An example of such play between omnipotence and powerlessness comes again in the final book's opening line: *Quaeritur interea, quis*

---

[12] *nate dea*, 15.439 ~ *nate dea*, *Aen.* 3.374. Helenus's speech in the *Aeneid* conveys nothing of the ultimate destiny of Rome but focuses on the necessities of Aeneas's coming voyage. For further inconsistencies between Pythagoras's "citation" and its Vergilian source, see Hardie 1997.188.

[13] See Tissol 2002 for a recent treatment of this subject.

[14] Hardie 1997.

tantae pondera molis / sustineat tantoque queat succedere regi ("Meanwhile there is a question about who will support the weight of so great a task and be able to succeed so great a king"). The present tense is entirely compatible with the narrative's own time frame as a historical present describing speculation after the death of Romulus. But there is nothing to keep it from being felt as a true present either, especially when we learn that the subject of the inquiry is succession. Kenney observes the ring composition that links this initial mention of Numa as successor to Romulus with Augustus as successor to Caesar.[15] Yet hearing a reference to present speculations dramatically breaks into the neat textual preserve such a ring would mark off. What is being asked about "now" is not who will succeed Caesar but who will succeed Augustus. In the case of Numa, prophecy can indeed come to the rescue with a report, predictive of truth, that acquires immediate acquiescence[16] because it is simply "history in the future tense." And if the present tense of *quaeritur* does suggest that this question has become a matter of interest to Ovid's readers, it is a powerful testimony to his narrative accomplishment: so absorbed are they in the flow of the narrative, driven by a desire to learn "what next," that they forget they already know.[17] But once we look outside the circle of the poem, the stakes for prophecy become much higher. What will happen after Augustus is still an open question, which the poet is powerless to answer. This aspect of the book's opening also finds a corollary at its conclusion, not in the confident narrative of Caesar's deification, but in the prayer for Augustus's.

This final section of the book itself directs attention to the persuasive and representational capacities of speech and offers its many different sketches of the ways in which words relate to things as possible models of the Ovidian text. The promise that with the deification of Caesar the poem has finally escaped its interest in exiles and transference to discover an autochthonous god in the present tense, one who needs no explanation or etiology, is immediately thwarted. Caesar's divinity appears very much not to rely on his own authority, and correspondingly opens the door to yet another series of literary regressions, as the end of Ovid's poem seems to become the beginning of another epic—the *Aeneid*. The apotheosis of Caesar, then, will be performed by language in two related senses.

---

[15] Kenney 1986.459–60.

[16] This despite the inevitable suspicions of falsehood that the word *fama* brings after the ecphrasis in book 13 and its analysis by Zumwalt 1977, Feeney 1991.247–49, and Hardie 1997.194 and 2002c.236–38.

[17] For another example of a "metanarratological" what next in the poem, see Wheeler's (1999.91–93) reading of the transition between books 2 and 3.

First and most notoriously, it relies on an obvious and tautological gambit on the part of Augustus who has made his father, a relationship that is itself not a natural given because Caesar became his father only by posthumous adoption, a god so that he could himself be something more than mortal.[18] In this respect Caesar's metamorphosis into a star, flying higher than the moon and "dragging its fiery hair along a vast track" (*flammiferumque trahens spatioso limite crinem*, 15.849), may put us in mind of another of the poem's opening metamorphoses, featuring the hair of a maiden who flees slower than the sun. As Daphne's own metamorphosis conceals what made her distinctively memorable to glorify the god Apollo, so here Ovid ensures that the deification of Caesar is anything but a memorial to him, for the personal accomplishments for which a Roman leader would claim to be remembered, *bella* and *res gestae*, are made subordinate as grounds for immortality to the fact of having Augustus as his son (15.748). Essentially, Caesar's problem also bears a close resemblance to Ovid's: how much will his own poem's conquest of the world, or more precisely transversal of the conquered world, redound to his own glory, and how much will it become a vehicle for Augustus's? And Augustus himself wears a double aspect anticipating his position in much of what follows. He is at once a figure for the poetic capacity to make something out of nothing, and he is the figure of real power who stands very much at the pole of reality as against representation.

The second way in which the ending addresses the role of language in accomplishing Caesar's apotheosis is in some ways more conventional: apotheosis is itself at once miraculous and foreign—being distinctly based on the practices of Hellenistic monarchs, as the allusions to Callimachus's *Coma Berenices* never lets us forget[19]—and Roman and historical.[20] Correspondingly, the representation of apotheosis relies on an unlikely combination of Roman religious and legal imagery and the language and conventions of heroic epic. It replicates on the level of genre the larger problem that the ending as a whole addresses: what happens when a hexameter epic capable of accommodating the most miraculous tales of a foreign mythology reaches the present?

In the first instance, the two generic codes remain in tension with one another. Augustus's own act of self-aggrandizing god-making leads us directly to Venus begging for the aid of other gods to defend her descendant on the basis of past wrongs she has suffered. The gesture has many antecedents and seems to take us back to the unwarlike Aphrodite of the

---

[18] Feeney 1991.210–11.
[19] Barchiesi 1997a.196; Knox 1986.75–76.
[20] See Feeney 1991.218–19.

Iliad (an odd defender of Caesar, *Marte praecipuum*) and perhaps even to the "Viennese" Venus, begging her son for aid in the *Argonautica* of Apollonius.[21] A more specific and interesting parallel, though, is Juno. As Venus here catalogs past sufferings to present herself as uniquely unable to protect those she loves, Juno begins the *Aeneid* (1.37–49) and punctuates its halfway point (7.294–322) with the complaint that she alone among the gods cannot avenge the wrongs done to her. Seeing Venus speaking the language of her enemy and referring precisely to that enemy while doing so (15.774) add to the effect of returning to an earlier narrative world: we are watching an *Aeneid* where the roles are inverted, and we are watching it in reverse. But what is most striking about Venus's speech is its rhetorical success. Juno famously failed to win the aid of the gods and so was forced to "move Acheron." Here Venus does move the gods (*superosque movet*, 15.780), but that successful act of persuasion is rendered vain (*nequiquam*, 15.799) because it comes up against another kind of language, the official Roman-sounding decrees (*decreta*) of the fates (a word never used in the *Aeneid*).

The generic confrontation is repeated in Venus's next effort. With an insistence on repetition perhaps emblematic of heroic epic as a genre, after the failure of the omens to avert disaster, Ovid's narrative seems to double back on itself by returning to a distraught Venus rummaging through a bag of conventional epic tricks, now preparing to whisk away her favorite concealed in a cloud (15.803–6). Venus's proposed rescue of Caesar here implies the continuity of a pattern of epic action—she rescued Paris this way in *Iliad* 3, Aeneas in *Iliad* 5, and again wrapped her son in a cloud to protect him from the Carthaginians in *Aeneid* 1. To be sure, miraculous rescues of mortals by the gods are not uncommon in Homer, and the terms in which the personal intervention of Aphrodite is described in the scenes she recalls do not place an undue strain on the narrative conventions of the *Iliad*. Any competent reader of Homer would be able to understand them, and they do not seem, at least from the scholia, to have attracted any lightning bolts of skepticism. But the application of such epic devices to recent Roman history invites one to look at these conventions from outside, to imagine them applied to the experiences of the way things are.

Bound up with the question of the plausibility of such divine interventions is their effectiveness as panegyric. Describing a human achievement as the result of divine intervention can magnify the human actor, implying that his deeds are godlike, or perhaps simply that he is of sufficient stature to be a concern to the gods; conversely, it can have a deflating effect: the human hero cannot do it on his own. The latter interpretation will

---

[21] The phrase comes from Johnson 1976.43.

be all the more likely when the hero involved is not achieving victory but sneaking away from defeat and is also a Trojan.[22] We may thus ask how flattering an epic rescue of this sort would have been for Caesar.[23] Again, under pressure from real historical circumstances, Venus's language fails to persuade. A gesture that might glorify the hero of an epic poem seems both to threaten the upward course of Roman history and to take on a different rhetorical valence when applied to a real person.

History quite literally blocks the course of Venus's plans in the form of Jupiter's speech. Not only does he contrast the way things might have been in the *Iliad* with the way things will be in first-century Rome, giving a résumé of Augustus's career in lines 15.820–839 that includes the most recent history treated anywhere in the poem, but he validates his account with an appeal to the Fates' "public records office" (*tabularia*, 15.810), an image that belongs much more to the realm of Roman political affairs and indeed is just the sort of place to which a historian might have recourse. The shift from "epic" description to historical prophecy comes to involve much more than the question of the right literary register for representing figures like Caesar and Augustus; it also has to do with a shift in the kind of authority the text claims for itself and the kind of representation it offers. Here, a curious difference emerges from the corresponding prophecy of Roman glory delivered at the beginning of the *Aeneid*: Ovid's Jupiter seems far more concerned to establish his speech as the record of an externally verifiable reality. Vergil's Jupiter speaks of "unrolling the fates' mysteries" (*fatorum arcana volvere*, *Aen.* 1.262), an image that compares the foretelling of the future to the reading of a scroll but does not necessarily require a preexistent "book of fate." "Unrolling the fates" could simply be a metaphor for narrating the future—moving forward in time, as if toward the end of a book. In any case there is no question about the force that will actualize that future; it is none other than the will of Jupiter himself: "I have given Rome empire without end." Thus, for all the legitimate insistence from Vergilian scholars that Jupiter is himself textualized, no more than a character among other characters, and that there is no absolute guarantee for the reader that the god speaks the truth, rhetorically the effect is powerful indeed—the prophet himself is the one who will make (has already made—*dedi*) his words true. In Ovid's case, though, Jupiter's role is quite different. His first words, "Will you alone surpass the fates?" imply that not even he has such a power.

[22] See Feeney 1991.53–54.

[23] Cf. Bömer's (1986 ad loc) citation of the argument that a comparison to Paris, and to Aeneas himself under these circumstances would have instantiated precisely the kind of Trojan legacy the Julians would have wanted to avoid. My point is not that Ovid is himself casting veiled aspersions at Julius but that he is considering the implications of what this rejected language would have been.

Correspondingly his own authority, in the sense of his role as author of the speech, depends on another text. And not only is this text not metaphorical, but Jupiter takes some pains to establish its own existence and indelibility, as though any threat to the material substance of the inscription also imperiled the future that it predicted. So too, Jupiter's words stress the fidelity of his speech to that real inscription: "I myself have read it, and 'notated' it in my mind, and I shall report it" (*legi ipse animoque notavi et referam*, 15.814–15). If the world is indeed made text in Ovid's poem, then, as the technical scribal language of this passage suggests, it is also the case that the text dictates the world, and the highest authority comes from being an accurate reporter of it. The father of the gods has become an antiquarian.

But on every level Jupiter's speech leaves questions unanswered in ways that alert us to the impossibility of any such total grounding of authorial responsibility. Most obviously, he remains very much an epic figure and so draws attention to the continuity of Ovid's work as hexameter epic. His words also seem to stop at the very edge of what is knowable as history in Ovid's time: is the culmination of the prophecy he records that Augustus would live to a ripe old age, which was already a fact when Ovid wrote these words, or is it his divinization, which requires some real knowledge of the future (15.838–39)? And as Jupiter emerges as very much a poetic creation, so his role as mere reporter of the indestructible text of the fates, as opposed to inventor and rhetorical manipulator, also requires some qualifications. For all the insistence on the primacy of an absolutely determinative text, the more real that text becomes, the less accessible it is: Venus is allowed immediately to confirm Jupiter's report by autopsy: *intres licet ipsa sororum tecta trium ...* (15.808–9). She may have this power—and it is very suggestive that at the end of Ovid's poem the power of the gods is specified not as their ability to change fate but as their access to an accurate account of what fate will be—but we obviously have no such recourse. The word fate of course derives from the root that means "speak," and for every attempt to fix the Fates' decrees as an unchangeable text, speech they remain.

The tension between the facticity guaranteed by the Fates' written record and the way the truth it professes is qualified when those "*tabularia*" are refashioned as the speech of a character in an epic poem provides insight into the complex relationship between Ovid's epic telling and the world of historical reality, particularly the central "fact" it records: that Julius Caesar became a god. The poet says of Caesar's deification that "it was not so much his wars ending in triumph, and his domestic achievements [*resque domi gestae*] and the speeding glory of his accomplishments that turned him into a new star and trailing comet as his offspring" (15.747–50). Already in this passage the language of historiography (*bella, res gestae*), not to say of reality (*res, rerum*), bumps up against a distinctly Ovidian miracle, metamorphosis (*vertit*) into a star. As subject of that verb, *vertit*, Augustus here becomes at once the cause and perhaps the author of the metamorphosis Ovid narrates. This seemingly simple statement, though, offers many handles for skepticism. First, how was it exactly that Augustus was responsible for the deification? In human, historical terms, he was perhaps the agent of it, but Ovid's language makes us think not of the particular act of deification as of its grounds: being Augustus's father was the most divine of Caesar's actions. And both of these possibilities in turn cry out for qualification. First, it was not strictly speaking Augustus who declared Caesar a god, but all of the triumvirs acting together (Dio 47.18.3–19.3). And though Augustus had been formally adopted as Caesar's son, the biological sense of *progenies* draws attention to the fact that this offspring was himself the product not of nature but of an official act. Ultimately, of course, as Hardie emphasizes,[24] the treatment of Caesar's divinization reveals a tautological "poetics of divinity" by which Caesar makes the son who makes him a god in order that he himself should not be of mortal birth.

Ovid's narrative, however, significantly occludes the central facts behind this mutual exaltation society. He never acknowledges the adoption of Augustus or the official proclamation of Caesar's divinity. Rather, he tells the story as an epic poet would, with the gods as actors and agents. It is no longer Augustus (not to speak of Antony or Lepidus) who made Caesar a god, but Jupiter, and while the end result was to magnify Augustus further, again the aim belongs to the god, not to the man. We might take this purposeful avoidance as itself contributing to an ironic intent: by not referring to these proclamations Ovid presents the story that results from them in a way that draws attention to its own constructedness. But this is not all there is to it. An alternative reading might stress instead how Ovid's version exalts rather than exposes the fact-making power of words. Just as he moves away from recounting the stuff of history (not only decrees of adoption but also Caesar's *res gestae*, and indeed the whole annalistic history of the republic, as he proceeds not from consul to consul but from apotheosis to apotheosis), so he naturalizes the products of that history by presenting a story that makes them result not from mere convention but from the way things are. Caesar may have declared Octavius his *filius*, but Ovid makes him his offspring (*progenies*). And Caesar may have been proclaimed a *deus*, but it is left for a poet (with a long history of learned panegyric behind him) literally to turn him into a star. And in narrating the story this way, the epic poet also confuses the priority of the historical and epic narratives. We may say that Ovid

[24] Hardie 1997.189–95.

writes this story because political authorities at Rome have prescribed Caesar's divinization, and Ovid's acknowledgment of this—significantly expressed, as Hardie notes, through the literary language that makes Augustus Caesar's *maius opus*[25]—reveals the extent to which he defers to their precedence. Yet the story he tells, like every other aetion, claims priority to the reality that records it; Ovid tells us not that Caesar became a god but how and why he did, and the real causes are to be found not in historical *Realpolitik* but in a poem whose miracles precisely resist its translation into fact. If Ovid has acknowledged the historical prompt for his poetry in Caesar's *acta*, he has simultaneously refashioned the emperors themselves into his own image as poets. A similar generic tension between history and epic also shapes the dynamics of the work's reception: the unbelievable aspect of Ovid's narrative can either expose the fictionality in what history proclaims as true (that Caesar is a god and Augustus a *divus filius*) or, reading from the poetic inside out, provide the right language for making such claims and supplant history as the way to describe succession, which is wholly at home in the unhistorical world of Ovidian poetry. This example illustrates how the juxtaposition of epic and historical registers allows Ovid at once to intervene in political discourse and explicitly to stage that intervention by drawing attention to the various ways of positioning his poetry in relation to history.

Jupiter's speech also calls attention to the shuttling between historical representation and epic fiction, and the importance of these alternations for reading the poem's politics, because it contains the poem's most explicit presentation of the emperor Augustus:

> ... *natusque suus, qui nominis heres*
> *inpositum feret unus onus caesique parentis*
> *nos in bella suos fortissimus ultor habebit.*
> *illius auspiciis obsessae moenia pacem*
> *victa petent Mutinae, Pharsalia sentiet illum,*
> *Emathiique iterum madefient caede Philippi,*
> *et magnum Siculis nomen superabitur undis,*
> *Romanique ducis coniunx Aegyptia taedae*
> *non bene fisa cadet, frustraque erit illa minata,*
> *servitura suo Capitolia nostra Canopo.*
> *quid tibi barbariam gentesque ab utroque iacentes*
> *oceano numerem? quodcumque habitabile tellus*
> *sustinet, huius erit: pontus quoque serviet illi!*
> *Pace data terris animum ad civilia vertet*

[25] Hardie 1997.191.

iura suum legesque feret iustissimus auctor
exemploque suo mores reget inque futuri
temporis aetatem venturorumque nepotum
prospiciens prolem sancta de coniuge natam
ferre simul nomenque suum curasque iubebit,
nec nisi cum senior meritis aequaverit annos,
aetherias sedes cognataque sidera tanget.
(15.819–39)

… and his son, who as heir of his name will also bear the burden of his murdered parent, will, as a mighty avenger, count us on his side in war. The walls of besieged Mutina, conquered under his auspices, will seek peace. Pharsalia will experience him, and Thessalian Philippi will twice be drenched in slaughter, and the great name Magnus will be bested on the Sicilian waves, and the Aegyptian wife of a Roman commander, too confident in her marriage, will fall and will have threatened in vain that our Capitol would be a slave to her Canopus. Why should I number barbary for you and the nations east and west? Whatever habitable territory the earth supports will be his, and the sea will be his slave. And once peace has been achieved on earth, he will turn his attention to civil laws and, as the fairest author, will propose legislation and by his example will guide morality, and providing for the future and for his descendants to come, he will order the offspring born from his sanctified wife to bear his name as well as his cares. Nor will he reach the heavens and the stars that are his kin until as an old man he will have made his years equal to his achievements.

Not only do Jupiter's words bring Augustus's accomplishments before the reader, but Augustus himself emerges as a speaker within the passage, as Jupiter's language comes very close to the emperor's own account of his deeds. The passage in lines 832–34, as has been long noted, approximates the phrases of the *Res Gestae*, which would be inscribed on Augustus's mausoleum and in many other prominent places throughout the empire.[26] The poem's incorporation of this language, in the context of a

---

[26] See discussion in Hardie 1997.192. The chronological problem involved in such "allusions" has never quite been solved. Fairweather 1987.193, on echoes of the *Res Gestae* in *Tristia* 4.10, presumes that Ovid would have had access to none of the drafts of Augustus's *elogium* before it was inscribed after his death and that both texts have a common source in Augustus's autobiography of 25 BCE. But this solution would not account for either of the echoes in the *Metamorphoses* (*RG* 8.5, as a reference to laws passed by the emperor would itself seem to postdate 25 BCE. On the second echo, at 6.195, see chapter 7, section 1; again the reference is to a historical event, the deaths of Gaius and Lucius much later than the date of the autobiography). Without being able to prove it, I consider the possibility either that

speech within a speech and thus doubly embedded in the uncertainties of epic representation, has seemed the ultimate mark of its power to make everything a part of its own text. But the immanence of the emperor in the real-world context of the poem has the power to change everything. At precisely the moment when he becomes one of the most remote of the poem's figures, separated from the actual audience by two levels of re-ported speech (the narrator reporting Jupiter's words), he also possesses a presence that differentiates him not only from the mythological char-acters of the early portion of the poem, and even from its now dead and/ or deified historical personages, but especially from the very god, Jupi-ter, whose conventional power as prophetic god adds luster to his deeds. The penultimate passage of the poem ends with a prayer that Augustus's stay on earth may be further prolonged, before he "aids those entreating him as an absent divinity" (*faveatque precantibus absens*, 15.870). When he does so, he will join a set of gods that includes both central figures of Roman cult, like Vesta, and figures whose deification the poem itself has narrated, like Romulus/Quirinus, and the protagonists of the poem's strictly mythological tales, like Jupiter himself. But until that moment, he occupies quite a different realm, as the poem's only god whose presence is achieved by something other than representation.

This presence complicates the all-encompassing sweep of Ovidian nar-rative. Now, rather than becoming a character like any other and having his *Res Gestae* become, in Hardie's words, "just another kind of text to quote," in a context that has highlighted the distance between all texts and reality, Augustus becomes the reality that guarantees the text. We can read the *Res Gestae* through the lens of epic utterance, or we can see the real inscription as giving an extraordinary affirmation of the correctness of Jupiter's prophecy, one that lifts this particular speech to a whole new plane. But such exaltation comes with a price, because words gain such authority only by borrowing it from the emperor.

This positioning of the emperor inside and outside of the text emerges in other ways in the speech. It is no accident that the particular passage of the *Res Gestae* quoted stresses the overlap between the emperor's role as representation and as representer. Augustus both culls all of history for examples worthy of imitation and, partly perhaps by doing so, offers himself as an example to be imitated. As Ovid's pairing of the verb *reget* with the instrumental *exemplo* suggests, the emperor's power to com-

---

the earlier versions of the *Res Gestae* were more public than Fairweather suggests or, more likely, that the final version of the inscription contains language already familiar from the official self-presentation of the *princeps* sufficiently plausible to make the similarity to the *Res Gestae* in this passage worth discussing.

mand itself closely coexists with this ability to perpetuate images. But by positioning this quote at the culmination of his survey of Augustan accomplishments, Ovid also locates this movement into representation, so to speak, with the point at which the real emperor's life ends and the present gives way to the future.[27]

The evocation of the metamorphosis theme in the passage also raises questions about the historical emperor's superiority to the world of representation. Augustus's principate effects a change that is at once global and present, tempting one to read it, as we saw in the preceding chapter, as the historical phenomenon that the poem's very emphasis on transformation allegorically figures. Indeed, the many different ways in which the poem has taught us to view change open out contrasting responses to Augustus's accomplishments. The pacification of the world, carefully segregated into its components of land, sea, and sky, recalls the ordering of chaos with which the poem begins. Similarly, Augustus, exercising divine "providence," aims for this ruling process to extend into the future as well, (15.834–35) so as to plant change itself solidly in the past and make the future preserve the quiet face of its final results. At the same time, such peace is brought about only through the chaos of civil war, which, as the *iterum* in line 824 stresses, implies the possibility of repetition. Against an image of the world where change is viewed as something that is over, the account of civil wars reintroduces a cosmos where everything flows. The poem itself begins with a sweeping account of the world we know that bears all the signs of finality, but by a few hundred lines into the second book, this ordered cosmos will twice have lapsed into chaos.

While reiterating the larger question of the finality of change, Jupiter's prophecy of imperial Rome also introduces the same kind of narratological problems as other metamorphoses: how much do we see transformation from the distant perspective of hindsight, and how much does the persistence of a recognizable identity between before and after allow for a kind of narrative absorption that resists the unidirectional flow of history?

In the case of this particular passage, the figure who brings such questions to a head is Augustus. For beyond being the force, at once poetic and divine, that produces change, the emperor himself undergoes metamorphoses, transformed from the mere avenger of his human father to one who shares his immortality. In terms of the historical Augustus, the most obvious transformation, perhaps, comes at the moment of the pacification of the earth, when he "turns his mind" to internal matters and to the future: that very phrase *animum ... vertet* makes the emperor's

----

[27] Hardie 1997.193–95.

mind the object of the poem's most common verb for "change."[28] Also very relevant to this process is the issue of naming. Changes of titulature from Octavius to Caesar Octavianus, to Augustus, to, presumably, Divus Augustus (contrast Divus Iulius in Jupiter's closing line 15.842), provided one of the most powerful ways for the emperor himself to demarcate the different phases of his life. But as we have learned to ask how much of the past self survives in any new shape, the language of the passage, which abounds in references to naming, raises the question of how final the "word" can really be. In addition to becoming Augustus, an unprecedented honorific title all his own, the *princeps* must also become another Caesar, both in name and, by staining the Thessalian plains again with slaughter, in deed. In addition to the possibility of reading back to Caesar through Augustus, the references of any of the titles Augustus takes on turn out to be very fluid. When Octavian distinguishes himself from the other triumvirs, by becoming the only (*unus*) heir of Caesar, he also takes on the immediately juxtaposed *onus* of a slaughtered man (*caesi*, as opposed to the tale of the comet, *caesaries*, that manifests his divinity in the sky, *caelum*). And the repetition of the slaughter in Thessaly adds an equally unwelcome active element (*caede*) to the assassination that defines what it means to be a Caesar.[29] In summary, as the producer of change it is Augustus who, like the gods in the poem's first lines, has created the changes that the poet merely records. But as a figure undergoing change, Augustus is bound up within the text of the poem; he has become part of its subject matter rather than its source, and our interpretation of him is subject to its rules.

To this point, we have seen the question of priorities between poetic representation and historical reality played out through an insoluble generic struggle between epic fiction and historical reality. The way we read this struggle has important consequences for the political status of Ovid's

[28] Ninety-two examples; see Anderson 1963.2. And the composition of a peaceful world undertaken by Augustus as *auctor* begins with a textual transformation that echoes Ovid's own beginnings: in the poem's first lines the enjambed *corpora* forces the reader to reconstrue the grammar of the sentence. Here a similar enjambment marks an important transformation in the reader's expectations. We might expect the adjective *civilia* (15.832) to modify the noun *bella*, but here as peace comes to the world, civil wars are rewritten as civil laws, *iura*.

[29] These puns on the name of Caesar are treated in detail by Ahl 1985.86–91. There is perhaps no better sign of the emperor's subordination to textuality than the changes the poet rings on the very titles the emperor uses to define himself—the celebration of the authorizing power of the written word contrasts with a destabilization of meaning that comes about precisely through puns. Yet the paradox, as we shall see, is that, as Augustus's words move beyond his control, there is no one the emperor resembles so much as the poet himself, whose own position of poetic maker will be constantly threatened by the danger that his words merely echo another's.

text in part because the two cast such different lights on Augustan accomplishments. These accomplishments either are themselves caught up in a matrix of changeability and misrepresentation or emerge as the supreme truth Ovid's poem works to reflect. Additionally, the extent to which we read Augustan reality through Ovid itself demands reevaluation of the relative prestige and control wielded by the author. This politics of textualization, so to speak, gives a new color as well to the ending's interest in the issue of succession. It is not just that the ultimate expression of mortal power, whether of a poet or a prince, is the ability to escape the condition of mortality by self-perpetuation, but successor and predecessor, as imitation and model, each define and limit the status of one another. We observe this process at work in the case of Julius and Augustus. In a positive reading, both sustain one another's reputation without any regard for their own. Thus, Caesar's new status as star not only glorifies the dictator by making him conspicuous but also makes the father bear witness that his son's accomplishments are greater. As an "eye in the sky," he "testifies that the good deeds of his son surpass his own and rejoices to be conquered by him" (15.850–51). Augustus, by contrast, forbids his own deeds to take priority over his father's, but the free speech of the evaluators refuses to acknowledge this priority. Yet Ovid's phrasing here is so fraught with paradox that it cannot but suggest the very rivalry whose possibility it has so explicitly precluded. Can the leader famous for the phrase *veni, vidi, vici* really rejoice to be conquered (*vinci gaudet*, 15.851), or does the suggestion that he can do so drive a further wedge between the real Caesar and the one commemorated? In the case of Augustus, the very existence of dissenting speech flatters the restorer of the republic, yet its one overt appearance in the closing panegyric makes disobedience the means only of further praising the emperor.

As the voice of the narrator becomes the mouthpiece for *libera fama* by indulging in his own comparisons between father and son, the reference to *tituli* (15.855, at once "honors" and, specifically, "inscriptions") reminds us how much the emperor dictates Ovid's poetic procedures. The comparison enacted in the passage is one that Augustus himself invited and indeed gave as the purpose for the erection of galleries of inscribed statues in his own forum: in an edict of his own, he claimed to have set up the statues, "so that against the [standard] of these men, as if an exemplar, both he himself while he lived and the *principes* of coming ages would be measured by the citizens" (Suet. *Aug.* 31.5). Here, too, the past is given a guiding power over the future, and even the present. But what would it look like from the future? What if one of Augustus's successors similarly surpasses his own virtues?

The dynamics of imitation addressed here is crucial to my investigation of the links between art and social status represented in and involving Ovid's text. We have seen the issue played out in parallel sequences both by the emperor as successor to Julius and Romulus and Aeneas—all, incidentally, figures literally present in the Forum of Augustus—and by Ovid in relation to Vergil and Homer. But it also affects the relationship between the two spheres, as the very account of Caesar's yielding to Augustus makes clear. Ovid catalogs a number of mythical fathers whose renown was surpassed by their children: Atreus's by Agamemnon, Aegeus's by Theseus, and Peleus's by Achilles. The culmination of the catalog comes with Saturn and Jupiter, as Ovid points out with the phrase, "that I might use exemplars matching [the comparands] themselves." This interesting borrowing of the emperor's own term, exemplar, makes it clear that not only father and son are being compared here; the poetic comparison is set against its historical original. Here again we should note how specifically different Ovid's set of models is from those selected by the emperor in his forum. All of Ovid's pairs come from the world of poetry and myth, and indeed the last image may well be read as more antagonistic to the imperial self-image than any that have gone before: Jupiter, precisely because he is an immortal, cannot naturally and peacefully succeed his father but must overthrow him. This mythological parallel thus threatens to supplant the panegyric tendencies of the preceding lines, even as Jupiter does Saturn. Such a rivalry between image and reality, as a poetic succession myth obtrudes into the very Roman space of the forum signals again the mirroring between poet and emperor as Ovid shifts from spectator in the forum, indulging in the free comparison facilitated by the *princeps*'s own constructs, to the role of imperial successor seeking to match the virtues there depicted. By a parallel metamorphosis, the very comparison allows Augustus figuratively to supplant his own father: the simile begins with Augustus in the role of Jupiter as son, but its validity is affirmed with the final flourish that Jupiter and Augustus—as both their names necessitate—each act as *pater et rector*.

Before turning to the poet's epilogue, let me give a brief summary of the ways that emperor and poet function to define one another in book 15. The poet "writes" the emperor in the sense that he incorporates both Augustus and Augustus's representation of himself within a verbal construct whose authority continually slips away, which has no proof of what it says except in the saying. But viewed a different way, the emperor gives precisely that proof: if the real-world power of Augustus is taken as a given—and the strict illogicality of this move might not have seemed so inevitable in the predeconstructionist days when the emperor sat on the Palatine—then his emergence from the text and the congruence that develops between his own monuments and inscriptions and the poem's language lend the poet's words an extratextual support that the literary tradition itself cannot. To read the text from within, with the emphasis on its own constructive powers, means seeing the emperor anew as a character in this all-embracing narrative: Ovid is the master of this world, although, appropriately we only see that after, when we look up from the text, but it is a world whose truth and reality must constantly slip away. On the other hand, to start with a recognition of the real presence of the emperor and to judge Ovid by whether, as the poet puts it, he "uses examples matching the realities" anchor the poet's representation in the solidity of the here and now, but it is Augustus who plays the god. Correspondingly, neither quite departs from the sphere of the other, so that the rubrics of literature and life cannot ever be fully disengaged: we never stop looking at Ovid's words or Augustus's from inside the tradition of hexameter epic. But we never look at them merely that way.

As the text's narrative self-referentiality generates this ambiguity about whether the poet and his work have become everything or nothing, so too does the curious play between script and speech in the poem's famous epilogue:

> Iamque opus exegi, quod nec Iovis ira nec ignis
> nec poterit ferrum nec edax abolere vetustas.
> cum volet, illa dies, quae nil nisi corporis huius
> ius habet, incerti spatium mihi finiat aevi:
> parte tamen meliore mei super alta perennis
> astra ferar, nomenque erit indelebile nostrum,
> quaque patet domitis Romana potentia terris,
> ore legar populi, perque omnia saecula fama,
> siquid habent veri vatum praesagia, vivam.
> (15.871–79)

And now I have wrought a work that neither the anger of Jupiter, nor fire, nor the sword, nor devouring age will be able to wipe away. Whenever it wills, let that day which has power over nothing but this body end the uncertain span of my life. Nevertheless, with the better part of myself I shall be born above the stars, eternal, and my name shall be indestructible. Wherever Roman power extends over conquered lands, I shall be spoken of by the people, and if the predictions of singers have any truth, I shall live in speech through all ages.

In having "completed a monument," Ovid advances a double comparison, both to the literary model Horace (C. 3.30.1), whose own claim to immortality he has emulated and updated with the initial iam ("Now that's a monument"), and to the inscribed monuments of the emperor, which the account of Julius's apotheosis has put in play. In particular, though, the language invites analogies between Ovid's text and another piece of writing contained within it: the inscription in the house of the fates that guarantees the apotheosis of Caesar and predicts the Augustan present:

> *cernes illic molimine vasto*
> *ex aere et solido rerum tabularia ferro,*
> *quae neque concursum caeli neque fulminis iram*
> *nec metuunt ullas tuta atque aeterna ruinas;*
> *invenies illic incisa adamante perenni*
> *fata tui generis.*
>
> (15.809–14)

You will see there on a vast construction the records of events in bronze and solid iron, which dread neither the clashes of the sky nor the wrath of the thunderbolt nor, as they are secure and everlasting, any collapse; and you will discover there, inscribed in ageless adamant, the destiny of your race.

At first, the poem may again seem to struggle to become as resistant to the elements as the adamant letters of the fates, even to be the very text described there. And yet another perspective reveals an important difference that places the two on either side of a crucial divide. Ovid's poem will not be destroyed by iron or time, but fate's inscription is iron and time. Not only, then, does the poet's work not partake of the same kind of materiality, but the inscription's very substance seems to emblematize some of the forces that threaten to destroy Ovid's text. In retrospect, this opposition should not surprise us, because poets traditionally favorably compared their works to physical monuments to stress that words lasted longer than marble or bronze. Time has legitimate power only over this *corpus*, but what *corpus* is that? Just the poet's physical body, and not the "body" of his work, a disembodied body? So too, when we read of the poet's indestructible name, we wonder whether it is materially indestructible, harder even than the adamant letters of the fates, or whether it is indestructible precisely because there is nothing there to destroy. The name is only there because the poet says it is—quite literally, because Ovid's immortalization epitomizes the poem's self-authorizing fictions. His life depends on nothing other than his own prophetic voice containing something of reality. And that is precisely what we are not sure it does.

Of course, it is possible, even obvious, to read the scripted and spoken as complements: no physical text, no prompt for speech. No speech, and the text is never reanimated in the now. And, as the word *corpus* especially suggests, no speech can totally break the thread that ties it to the physical world. The slighter that thread becomes—paper instead of iron—the more liable it is precisely to destruction. But by following up Ovid's hint at the opposition between the two ways of conceptualizing his work, we perceive more clearly how the ending brings to a fitting culmination the essential paradoxes of its poetics. It is most powerful when it is nothing, when it lives only on breath and the shifting doubleness of *fama*.

This much more guarded evaluation of the triumph of the book at the poem's close stands in contrast to the optimistic readings even of those very critics who have themselves drawn greatest emphasis to the poem's preoccupation with the limits to any text's power. Feeney, for example, argues that the lines show the poet committing himself entirely to the slippery world of literary *fama*. It is the poet's words, as the last line makes clear, that alone guarantee his immortality, but this puts him on the side of the masters of language, as opposed to those who rely on *fama* to preserve their deeds.[30] Hardie too promotes the kind of self-produced immortality Ovid projects for himself over the emperor's claims to live on through deification and through the production of an heir like himself, a process that requires a control over future *fama* that no one can possess, except of course the poet who puts the very words in his readers' mouths.[31] His position acknowledges that Ovid's trick works only if "the World has been completely reduced to Text"[32] but perhaps downplays the poem's ambiguity about such a reduction: "The matchless poet at the very end, with no anxiety about *his* succession, stands in pointed contrast to finding an imperial successor."

The sense of a poetic trumping of the "historical" immortality of the divinized emperor comes above all from Ovid's vow to be carried above the stars; if Caesar was star quality, so to speak, Ovid has surpassed him. But other elements of the ending set out a set of likenesses and differences to the imperial gods that qualify such a view. Both poet and emperor are to achieve the tricky state of the absent presence. But the emperor works in part through monumental complexes like the Forum Augustum as well as inscriptions like those on his mausoleum. If Ovid shows these artifacts to be less reliably predictive of the precise terms fame will use to record the emperor, they at least make him impossible quite to ignore. The poet's material presence is much harder to pin down. Ovid's final account of his completed *opus* has been claimed to approximate such imperial constructs,[33] but another glance back at the Horatian in-

---

[30] "Ovid presents himself as a new repository for the *Fama*, which future generations will inherit. Some of the inhabitants of the House of Fame suffer oblivion; but Ovid will live, as his last lines defiantly proclaim, with the final verse containing a last ironic explosion of the doubt over the truth of words." Feeney 1991.248.

[31] Hardie 1997.194.

[32] Hardie 1997.194. "Augustus' problem, we may grant, is more difficult."

[33] Wickkiser 1999.

tertext complicates this impression. Horace unambiguously spoke of his text as a *monumentum*; Ovid employs the much broader *opus*, making the building metaphor less insistent, if still available. The physicality of the poet's *opus* diminishes further when we notice Ovid's transference of the specific properties Horace gave to his. The *monumentum* of the lyric poet was to be lofty (*altius*) and eternal (*perennis*); Ovid appropriates for his *opus* some of the proofs of this longevity—resistance to time, for example—but when these particular adjectives appear, back to back at the end of line 875, the point of reference is no longer the *opus* itself but the "eternal" soul of Ovid that rises above the "lofty" stars as it leaves the world behind.

My point is that the Ovidian ascent is alternatively imperial, borrowing the language and means of imperial self-propagation, and poetically insubstantial, consisting, as Feeney and Hardie describe, of a self-produced *nomen*. Script and speech, which as images symbolically spell out this opposition, do so functionally as well. The reception of the text as written artifact gives it "presence" but highlights the separation of audience and author.[34] By contrast, the absorbed hearing of the text succeeds in bringing the author to life, but with the prospect of a much less certain future. The two words that frame the epilogue, *iam* and *vivam*, help to put these alternatives into play. For the absorbed reader, the idea of *iam* becoming the now of her present provides one of the most compelling examples of Ovidian magic, as the temporal horizon of the audience merges with the speaking voice of the author at the point of his own metamorphosis. Yet just at the moment that that voice proclaims its immortality, it stops. If this model of reception, depending on reading the poem from within, marks *vivam* out as the ending, a consciousness of the material artifact of the text highlights a different kind of metamorphosis that can indeed make the end of the work its own beginning.[35] The epilogue marks the moment at which the production of the poem ends, and the life of the poem as a completed written text begins. In this case, though, the value of the *iam* changes to that of a marker for a single historical point, now in the past, in which the present object was created.[36] The presence of the text increases with the absence of the author, and vice versa. Like any other metamorphosis, the poem's ending invites opposed reading strategies, which cast very different lights on what the poet has achieved. The two conceptions may indeed be easily reconciled, but in holding them apart for an instant, we gain a clearer

---

[34] This point is anticipated in Farrell 1999.128–33, and see Hardie 2002c.97.

[35] See too Barchiesi 1997a.195, especially on the anagram *incip*, marking first five lines of the poem's *envoi* (15.871–75), which thus begin to be a beginning, but only in their written, not their oral, form.

[36] On *iam*, cf. Feeney 1999.30.

sense of the extent to which fiction and empire inevitably define one another throughout the work.

II. Reception and Social Identity

The poem's ending, as the preceding section has shown, highlights the degree of assent granted to its fiction as a political question not merely through incorporating real political figures and their words into its own dubiously reliable matrix of representation but because the continual balancing of the material reality such a figure as Augustus conjures up against the evanescent manipulations of fiction brings to the fore an evaluation of the kind of authority we grant to the poet himself. Now it is time to deepen the significance of this question of priorities by making our own transition from work to world. I want to suggest that the kind of interpretative choices required of Ovid's audience really do imitate and reproduce the hermeneutic challenges that lay at the core of the political impact of the emperor's actual monuments. The threatened imperial appropriation of Ovid's poem that comes about when we see Ovid as imitator of an Augustan reality thus finds its corollary both in the poem's reinterpretation of actual monuments of the emperor as artist and also in the very recentering on his own work of an aesthetic experience that was anything but apolitical. This competition between imperial artist and artistic emperor, which already elides the boundaries between power and art, will also help us understand Ovid's concern with artistic priority as something more than a literary preoccupation with the anxiety of influence. Rather, status and social capacity in Augustan society can be mapped by artistic roles, by the extent to which one is a producer, an imitator, or a reader of images. The figure of the poet, therefore, the extent to which he emerges from his own "changed forms," becomes, like the disguised Io, one in which contemporary audiences could also recognize themselves.

The conception of the emperor as himself the practitioner of a cosmic poetics is one whose force would have escaped no contemporary. Crafted images like the map erected by Agrippa depicting the shape of the world occupy prominent positions in the imperial city. The emperor's own account of his accomplishments, the *Res Gestae*, is studded with geographic references that summon up an image of the ordered empire as the prime monument of Augustus's accomplishment.[37] And this geography was not just something for the reader to imagine. The *Res Gestae*, inscribed at the entrance to the mausoleum of the imperial family, formed part of an

---

[37] Nicolet 1991.15–27.

even larger monumental complex whose function as a representation of cosmic order was made explicit by the dominating presence of a giant obelisk, spoils of the victory over Egypt that literally united the world by ending the schism between East and West. The shadow of this obelisk served as the marker on a solar meridian and also formed the visual organizer for a complex of monuments, including the emperor's tomb and the Ara Pacis.[38] As Ovid's proem seems to call the cosmos into being by representing it, so the emperor's depictions of the world in Rome recall his literal shaping of territory through conquest, administrative organization, and building programs. For beyond iconographic associations of imperial power with the ordering of the world, his mark was apparent in the actual landscape of empire, from the straight roads that gave shape to provincial domains to the apportionment of the land belonging to colonies in rectilinear plots.

If this coalescence between representation and represented reality lends even greater authority to Augustus's deployment of cosmic imagery, another issue involving the status of imitations can undercut its message. For Augustus occupies the curious double position of creator and artistic subject here—again like Ovid—providing the ultimate authority attesting to his own power. What does it mean to link the conquest of Egypt to the proper ordering of time? That the event has a role to play in some cosmic scheme preordained by some higher power, or that Augustus himself is that power? Is he the architect, or the subject, of the cosmic plan? Both ideas can exalt; both can even be made compatible with one another, but they need not be. And if they are not they reveal the same fact that Ovid's own accounts of Augustus make more explicit, the emperor's own role in the creation of the mythical props for his authority.

How far this kind of oppositional reading was pursued by any individual viewer is of course an unanswerable question, but the very possibility of constructing such an interpretation reveals that the presentation of imperial power through visual images was a much more uncertain business than used to be imagined. Far from constituting mere propaganda, valuable because it reveals the public image Augustus chose to present, the artistic and architectural projects of the period, amounting to an almost total transformation of Rome's visual environment, make the reception of images increasingly the locus for a complex dialogue about the nature of the Roman state. Participation in this act of viewing—inevitable for anyone with eyes, Roman or barbarian, free or slave, male or female—both depended on and defined position within the civic sphere.

Recent scholarship has illuminated a number of aspects of this process that were truly dialogic, that involved not just the projection outward of

---

[38] See Heslin 2007, esp. 15–16.

a prepackaged self-image, but the definition of that image on the part of a number of participants. Paul Zanker,[39] for example, has stressed that the very production of Augustus's image was not monolithically controlled from the center but the result of a collaborative effort on the part of artists, patrons, poets, and moneyers, each of whom may or may not have been following trends or trying to give the *princeps* what he wanted, but who could also fashion the emperor as they wanted him to be. And these images, whatever their origins, far from merely representing reality or a version of it, could also come to constrain and shape it.[40] Even one of the monuments that most transparently reflected Augustus's authority, the Forum of Augustus with its exemplary statues of the great men of the republic, exerts its own pressure on the emperor's behavior. In principle, the virtuous deeds recorded in the forum may appear subsumed by the accomplishments of Augustus, as his forum provides the locus for their display; they enshrine qualities that he has already made his own. But as we saw in the preceding section, the emperor's own account of the purpose of these monuments, disseminated by edict, puts things quite differently: there he claimed to have set up the statues, "so that against the [standard] of these men, as if an exemplar, both he himself while he lived and the *principes* of coming ages would be measured by the citizens." The emperor's words here may be regarded as a backhanded assertion of his own excellence. He, after all, would not have set the test unless he could pass it. Yet, of course, the emperor was absolutely right: every laudatory monument put in place raises the stakes for his own behavior. If in the eyes of its viewers that behavior falls short of the imperial public image, the whole elaborate edifice becomes an indictment rather than a glorification of his reign.

As this last point reveals, conceptions of how the "power of images" worked in Augustan Rome depend in turn on an understanding of how the meaning of images is fixed. Those who consider that the image means what the author or producer says it means and that viewers who interpret it differently are getting it wrong naturally tend to view Augustan self-representation more as the unidirectional sending of a coherent message. And coherence and clarity have become the hallmarks of Augustan culture in contrast to the multiplicity of competing systems of visual language typical of the collapsing republic. Others, who make the reader-recipient the arbiter of meaning, open the door to a much wider range of responses and portray the reception of images as a bargaining process that allows for whatever the presenter may have intended a work to say

[39] Zanker 1990.265–74.

[40] See Feeney 1992: the literary corollary of this view of artistic representation will be found particularly in Kennedy 1992.

to be potentially subjected to revision, inversion, and mockery. Attempts to combine a recognition of the multiplicity of an audience's responses with a belief that there does exist a basic, agreed-upon sense of what an image means at first seem to provide a sensible and productive alternative to either extreme position. In particular Karl Galinsky has argued for a model of "authorial" control in Augustan culture based closely on the emperor's methods of exercising political power.[41] As the *princeps* eschewed offices and privileges that would have directly compelled obedience, relying instead on the esteem and authority he enjoyed to make his subjects participants in the aims of his regime, so as an "author" he employs sophisticated and complex representations of his ideals that communicate on many levels. Thus, the viewers work out for themselves what the intention of the image is, guided by their own knowledge and experience, which have in turn been attuned to the visual and mythical language the emperor uses.

For example, the great portico of the Danaids, erected in 25 BCE as part of the temple of Apollo on the Palatine, confronted its viewers with statues of the fifty daughters of the Greek king Danaus killing their bridegrooms and cousins, the sons of Aegyptus, whom they had been compelled to marry. By its nature an ambiguous story, it becomes all the more so in its immediate political context, five years after the defeat of an Egyptian queen who was also, inconveniently, the ally of a Roman triumvir.[42] While the most common interpretation makes the Danaids the heroes of the episode, beating back foreign aggressors as Augustus's troops had overwhelmed the Egyptians at Actium, another places emphasis on the Danaids' own impious act: like Cleopatra herself, these women become unnatural monsters demanding punishment. As Galinsky sees it, the image, despite the potentially troubling overtones of making the instruments of justice violators of the institution of marriage, was chosen precisely because of the nuanced view it gave of the civil wars as a necessary but tragic action made right by subsequent expiation. The surrounding imagery in turn helps guide the audience toward this reading by portraying the victorious god Apollo himself in the act of pouring a purificatory libation.

Galinsky's interpretation has the great virtue of acknowledging that the image can be interpreted in many ways, and surely the subject was not chosen at random by Augustus. But I do not share his confidence that every viewer would have put the many pieces of the puzzle together

[41] Galinsky 1996, esp. 149–55, 222, 231.

[42] See the discussion of Galinsky 1996.220–24, who reviews previous scholarship on the significance of the image.

in the way he describes to arrive at an intended meaning, nor do I want to disregard the validity of viewpoints that fail to do so. The very violence of the story, as well as its deployment of the language of race and gender—contradictory as they are here—can act to polarize rather than reconcile ambiguities. To explore a few possibilities, a woman viewing this image might feel a particular identification with the Augustan victory in seeing its agents compared to other women defending their own purity. Conversely, one who recognized the Danaids themselves as guilty might find herself identifying with the victims of imperial power or continue to view things from the perspective of their punishers. An Egyptian in the Danaid portico might feel the full hostility of the scene, and perhaps the very sight of this monument will confirm his own recognition that he is indeed an outsider in the emperor's city. On the other hand, we might imagine a newly manumitted freedman of eastern extraction, eager to claim an identity as a Roman, willingly, even obliviously, acquiescing in the punishment of the sons of Aegyptus. Even a viewer who applies her intellect in the way Galinsky intends and recognizes the complex, conciliatory meaning of the image may be unable or unwilling to view the scene from the point of view of its imperial author rather than from the embedded perspective of the victim. Nor can we count on the power of context to put her on the right track. On the contrary, rather than assuming that a complex series of interlinked images will smooth over whatever interpretative cracks appear in a single element of the program, one could argue instead that once alternative perspectives are opened up, they tend to destabilize even images that were once clear and unproblematic.

To revise Galinsky's formulation of how Augustus's authority operates through images, we might say that in making sense of a monument like the Danaid portico, an authorial point of view, a viewer's understanding of what the author intended the image to signify, emerges in potential tension with other readings that can reflect the position of the individual viewer—for example, gender, status, attitudes—but can also be prompted and shaped by the points of view of the various characters depicted within the image, such as a Danaid doomed for her valor.[43] Rather than imagining viewing as the intellectual decoding of an author's meaning, however complex and equivocal, we may think of it as a dynamic process in which the individual viewer defines and revises his position in relation to authority through identifying and rejecting the perspectives that

[43] Contra Galinsky 1996.222: "Instead of simple and obvious 'messages,' Augustan art (and poetry) asks for the intellectual participation of the viewer or reader and for their scrutiny of alternative interpretations *in order that the intentions of the creators may be understood all the more thoroughly*" (emphasis added).

the work of art makes available. And rather than invariably offering a guiding hand toward hermeneutic concord, the intentions of the imperial author are themselves there to be accepted or rejected. Accepting them, far from simply making the viewer understand a policy position, co-opts him into an imperial poetics of remaking the world. Acknowledging the political and astronomic significance of Augustus's obelisk requires both the simple transformation of lines and symbols into signs and the re-projection of the resulting mental image of order onto the cosmos. The depictions of the emperor Augustus, to take another example, ceased to age in the twenties BCE. By the time Ovid was writing the *Metamorphoses*, therefore, there would have been a considerable gap between the appearance of the now very old emperor and the classicizing portraits of a young man sacrificing or addressing his troops. To overcome that gap, to see the latter images as Augustus, is in a very real sense to impose a different order on reality, exalting the timeless crafted image above change and decline.

By contrast, the rejection or modification of this point of view is an assertion of the viewer's own power to act as author, fitting both the image and the extratextual intentions that produced it into his own interpretative schema. Thus, the author of the Augustan forum himself becomes one of his own statues in the sense that the viewer constructs an image of him by measuring him against a reading of the exemplary monuments. Or, in the case of the Danaid portico, the interpretations suggested by the points of view made available within the monument become potential rivals to the designs of the creator.

We can see an example of the battle between the shaper and the viewer of images to act as author in the elegiac poet Propertius's account of his own responses to Augustus's temple of Apollo:

> Quaeris cur veniam tibi tardior. aurea Phoebi
>   porticus a magno Caesare aperta fuit.
> tota erat in spatium Poenis digesta columnis,
>   inter quas Danai femina turba senis.
> hic equidem Phoebus visus mihi pulchrior ipso
>   marmoreus tacita carmen hiare lyra;
> atque aram circum steterant armenta Myronis,
>   quattuor artificis, vivida signa, boves.
> tum medium claro surgebat marmore templum,
>   et patria Phoebo carius Ortygia:
> in quo Solis erat supra fastigia currus,
>   et valvae, Libyci nobile dentis opus;
> altera deiectos Parnasi vertice Gallos,
>   altera maerebat funera Tantalidos.

deinde inter matrem deus ipse interque sororem
  Pythius in longa carmina veste sonat.
                    (Prop. 2.31.1–16)

You ask why I am late in coming to you. The golden portico of Phoebus was opened by great Caesar. The whole extended on columns of
Punic marble, among which was the female throng of old Danaus.
Here the Phoebus of marble seemed to me, more beautiful than himself, to open his mouth to sing, though the lyre was silent. And the
herd of the artist Myron stood around the altar, four cows, living
statues. Then, dearer to Phoebus than his native Delos, the temple
rose in the middle, of bright marble. On it, above the pediment, was
the chariot of the sun, and double doors, noble construct of Libyan
ivory. One door lamented the Gauls cast from the summit of Parnassus, the other the death of Niobe, and the deaths mourned by Niobe,
Tantalus's daughter. Then, between his mother and his sister, the Py-
thian god sounded songs, in a flowing garment.

Appropriately for an elegiac poet, Propertius's account of the temple is
softened in a number of ways.[44] First he repeatedly feminizes the scene:
the Danaids appear neither as avengers nor as criminals but simply as a
female throng filling the portico;[45] so too, the cult statue itself, dressed in
effeminate eastern style, stands "between his mother and sister."[46] The one
attempt the poet makes at interpreting narrative elements of the temple's
program, the twin paneled doors that depicted the defeat of the Gallic attack on Delphi and the punishment of the Tantalids, reveals the adoption
of a characteristically sympathetic perspective. Rather than see examples
of divine punishments against human transgressors, Propertius describes
the images as expressing pity not only for the dead children of Niobe but,
through a striking enjambment, for the barbarian desecrators of Apollo's
shrine. A final distinctive element of Propertius's response to the temple is
his emphasis on the creative power of art. Apollo himself is preeminently
a poet, the god who holds the lyre and ends the poem by beginning his
own song; no mention here of the purifying libations the cult statue pours
with one hand. The description of the statue as more beautiful than the
god himself, coupled with the emphasis on the deceptive reality of the
"living statues" of Myron's cows, help make of the temple a celebration

[44] Cf. Gurval 1995.129–31.

[45] Though line 26 of the subsequent poem, about the punishment of beautiful women
becoming a fable, combined with the reference to Phoebus, perhaps gains more point when
read with the Danaids in mind.

[46] As Propertius has sandwiched the poetic representation of the temple between two
poems explicitly addressed to his elegiac mistress? The arrangement and, crucially, poem
divisions are, however, especially uncertain here.

of the powers of artifice.[47] But far from allowing an absorption into the depicted scenes that might, as I suggested before, signify an acquiescence to the powers of the temple's imperial maker, here the creators of wonders remain specifically artists, and even the god himself, rather than being assimilated to the victor of Actium, appears as a figure for the poet.[48]

Propertius's implicit assimilation of the Augustan Apollo to the image of the elegiac poet points to another facet of the complex politics of artistic representation in the new empire. As the viewers themselves become "authors" or producers of images, like Propertius here crafting his own text out of the temple's iconography, what we had previously imagined as a bipolar dialogue between author and observer becomes but the first step in a chain of representations that extend outward and downward through Roman society. If we turn from thinking of 2.31 merely as Propertius's public reading of the emperor's program to consider the role of his own reader in making sense of that text, the relationship between the emperor and poet comes to look different again. Mutual dependence takes the place of a potentially adversarial encounter. Propertius himself now has a stake in broadcasting and glorifying the imagery of the temple even as he projects his own claims about its meaning. Duncan Kennedy had pointed out in connection with verbal "propaganda" how even the regime's opponents are co-opted into disseminating the language of power,[49] and this phenomenon occurs even more clearly in the realm of visual imagery.

Ovid himself in the *Metamorphoses* uses a portrayal of the same god, Apollo, and references to the same monument, in an episode that suggests the complex relationship between his own epic and this imperial poiesis. Whereas in chapter 1 I discussed the Daphne and Apollo episode (1.452–567) as an example of how the concluding metamorphic image perpetuates the thematic tensions within a narrative, here I look specifically at the relation between poetic and imperial authority in the passage, how the poet's reading interferes in the reception of the temple's imagery even as the poet becomes notably someone other than his generic self when he speaks as the emperor's god. Following right after Apollo's defeat of the monstrous serpent Python, an event that had already been employed as a mythological symbol for the victory at Actium,[50] the sudden deflection of the narrative toward amatory pursuits has been taken as a programmatic rejection of the bloated matter of high epic in favor of a typically Ovidian fusion.[51] Apollo's chastening of Cupid for usurping his weapons

---

[47] So too Welch 2005.91–93.
[48] See Gurval 1995.265–66.
[49] Kennedy 1992.
[50] Buchheit 1966.91–92; Nicoll 1980.181.
[51] The conclusion of Nicoll 1980.

and that god's demonstration of his power over the conqueror of Python by wounding him with love's arrow recall the initial scene in Ovid's first collection of poetry, the *Amores*. There Ovid himself was embarking on an epic only to be diverted toward amatory elegy by the arrogant love god who, shooting the poet with his arrow, makes him fall in love.[52] That episode, in turn, varied the prototypical scene of turning away from extended narrative on lofty themes in the prologue to Callimachus's *Aitia*, where it was Apollo himself who appeared to the ambitious poet and warned him to "feed his sheep fat but keep his muse slender."

But the recurrence of such a scene here does not necessarily imply the same abrupt generic shift. Rather than simplifying interpretation of the Daphne episode by asserting the poet's own allegiance to a particular set of aesthetic and ideological preferences and so preparing the reader to see in the origins of the laurel an obtrusion of erotic concerns that debunk its imperial associations, the competition between Apollo and Cupid crystallizes a contrast between different points of view on what follows.[53] And if Cupid wins the battle of the bow, it is not quite so clear that he takes the laurel as well. In fact, as the episode progresses, the programmatic implications of the *Amores* passage are themselves called into question. There it was a formal property of the poetry that above all testified to love's victory, the short pentameter that serves continually to distinguish elegiac from epic meter. But here of course the poem continues in hexameters. More important, it is Apollo himself who is given the last word in the episode. Initially love's triumph alienates the figure of Apollo from his typical attributes: he is the god of prophecy but cannot foresee the outcome of the chase; he is the god of medicine, but there is no cure for love. But Apollo's final account of the laurel's future shows him returning to full prophetic form. Indeed, Apollo makes the laurel a celebration of precisely those aspects of his godhead that both his defeat by Cupid and Daphne's rejection of him had called into question: his beauty, his skill as a poet,[54] and his archery! By associating the laurel emphatically with victory, like his victory over Python, he restores the narrative and ideological trajectory that had been almost shut down by his defeat at the hands of Love.

We of course may resist smoothing over the elegiac seam—the fresh start at the words *primus amor Phoebi* (1.452) that decouples the laurel from the Python story and so breaks the epic sweep from primeval myth to imperial present. Yet Apollo's reepicization of the elegiac opening offers an alternative point of view, one made more attractive by the fact

---

[52] *Am.* 1.1, the parallels between this poem and the episode in the *Met.* are further developed by Nicoll 1980.

[53] For the political implications of generic "polyphony" as an act of rebellion against the monologic code of epic, see the important article of Farrell 1992.

[54] Daphne is notably unmoved by the hymn Apollo addresses to her in lines 1.514–24.

that he does accurately prophesy the laurel's future symbolic functions. And as is not the case in its models, where the poet himself is a character in the *recusatio* drama (cf. Callim. *Aet.* 1 fr.1.21–24; Verg. *Ecl.* 6.3–5; *Amores* 1.1), Ovid's position here remains unclear, and this avoidance of the subjective in turn helps characterize the passage as epic. The traditional function of the scene as marking a decisive generic break combined with his own elegiac origins ought to put Ovid on the side of Cupid. But it is Apollo who takes on the role of the warned and defeated figure usually played by the poet in a first-person *recusatio* narrative.[55] At one level then, this hermeneutic battle pits the god who has presided over Ovid's own prior poetic accomplishments against the established symbol of Augustus's military supremacy. On another, though, as in Propertius's reconstruction of the Palatine temple, it is the significance of Apollo himself that is at stake. Will his cult associations with victory remain in control of the narrative or will his lyre be stolen by the once elegiac poet?

The explicit evocation of a specific point in the visual landscape of Ovid's readers makes it all the more appropriate that the poetological debate about which god will govern the episode's interpretation should be developed through an emphasis on interpreting visual images. We saw before that the interpretation of the metamorphic sign, the laurel tree, depended on how much the reader was able to accept the subjective perspective of Daphne herself, even at the moment when access to that perspective vanishes. If one focus for dissenting interpretations of actual monuments was similarly the imagined subjectivity of the very figure represented, then the visual dynamics that Ovid constructs within the episode reproduce the tensions on which the political interpretation of actual monuments depended.

The question of through whose eyes images and events are seen, what Mieke Bal in her account of narrative calls focalization, emerges most explicitly in the text in the account of Daphne's request for eternal virginity. And perhaps it is no accident that the imagery of and attitudes toward marriage it evokes so closely approximate those we may imagine for the sculpted Danaids as well:

> *illa velut crimen taedas exosa iugales*
> *pulchra verecundo subfuderat ora rubore ...*
> (1.483–84)

She, hating wedding torches as if they were a crime, had colored her lovely face with a modest blush.

---

[55] Knox 1986.14–15.

The first of these lines, while still told from the external perspective of the narrator who reports her emotions, nevertheless makes Daphne's own point of view available to the reader: she hates marriage "as if it were a *crimen*." The beginning of the next line, however, marks a sudden shift; its first word, *pulchra*, by emphasizing an external quality of Daphne (as does the other word that frames the line, *rubore*) makes clear that we are now looking at her from without, and the desirability of this appearance of course establishes the tension between what the viewer who responds to the erotic suggestions of the blush wants of Daphne and what she wants for herself, even as the blush itself masks her face. The word *verecundo*, which reintroduces Daphne as "a character focalizor,"[56] makes this all the more poignant by clarifying that the very physical effect that invites desire springs from the impulse to avoid such desire. In all of these lines we see the narratological working out of a point the poet will make explicit a few lines later: *sed te decor iste, quod optas, esse vetat, votoque tuo tua forma repugnat* (but your own beauty forbids you to be what you choose, and your form fights back against your prayer, 1.488–9). To define Daphne by what she seems to be is to construct for her an identity antithetical to the one that she attempts to realize for herself. And this contradiction foreshadows the crucially different ways in which the laurel itself can be read, as a symbol of Apollonian conquest or as a manifestation of the (absent) victim.

The scene as a whole then leads to an investigation of what, using Galinsky's terms, we might think of as Apollo's authority, his ability to project meaning, which in this case is also to interpose his own powerful presence, through symbolic language. Yet, as in our imagined readings of the visual program of the Palatine temple, his intended meaning exists in competition with other perspectives, the generic and ideological perspective that despite Apollo's claims frames the entire story as the triumph of the erotic figure Cupid, and the recognition in the visual signs Apollo "interprets" of another represented figure whose own point of view can only be uncertainly reconciled to that of the god. But not only does Ovid's text here offer an image that approximates for its readers the tensions animating the act of viewing the actual visual signs in contemporary Rome that result from his tale; the poet correspondingly places himself in an ambiguous relationship with his divine speaker that looks back to his curious redeployment of the *recusatio* scene. There, as we saw, both Cupid and Apollo offer potential figures for the poet. So throughout the episode, Apollo himself hovers between being a speaker who takes over from the poem's narrator even as his distinctive point of view governs the reader's

---

[56] For the term, see Bal 1985.102–6.

expectations and desires and being a character who, as framed by the larger narrative, loses his dignity and power.

To start again with the question of point of view, Apollo himself plays the role of spectator at important points in the narrative (cf. 1.498ff.). This repeated use of *videt* constitutes what Bal refers to as a "hinge":[57] it still counts as a component of an externally focalized narrative (the poet is after all the one who tells us that Apollo saw), but it also makes available a new perspective (what Apollo saw). Whenever the poet lingers over eroticized descriptions of Daphne, as in the account of how the winds strip her flesh, he invites the reader in every sense to see her as Apollo does. On the other hand, an awareness of Apollo himself as a figure in the chase makes a humorous spectacle of the god. Thus, his impassioned plea to Daphne—itself an ungainly mix of the tired conventions of love poetry and lofty autohymnography—becomes all the more ridiculous when Ovid broadens the lens to remind us that the words are delivered in the context of the nymph's flight.[58]

Apollo's own motives are curiously mixed. Even as a lover, he never ceases to be an artist himself;[59] the elegiac role he is forced to play does not suit a god of order. His compositional impulse appears not just in his impromptu hymn but also in his treatment of Daphne, whose disheveled and flowing hair he wishes to comb.[60] It is also responsible for a curious dichotomy in the god's aims in chasing the nymph. As a lover, his intentions are clear, and the satisfaction of his erotic desire depends on his speeding up the narrative to reach the "climax" as quickly as possible. Yet the god as artist seems to stand apart from the god as character, to act as it were as the external focalizer of his own story. In this sense, what the god wants is above all to slow the nymph down, to freeze her motion and his pursuit into a timeless scene. Thus, when the god promises to "pursue more slowly" if the nymph herself will slow her pace, we should regard it perhaps not only as a ruse, and one that makes the god himself look ridiculous, but as an indication of an essential component of the poetic process, one detectable also in the luxuriating similes with which Ovid himself prolongs the account of the pursuit.

---

[57] Bal 1985.114.

[58] For Apollo's speech as a hymn to himself, see Fuhrer 1999.357–59.

[59] For a fuller account of Apollo as artist in the episode, see the discussion of Bretzigheimer 1994.518–24 who, among other themes, reads the episode as a confrontation between Apollonian *ars* and a Diana-like "raw nature." The "imitative" quality Bretzigheimer finds in Daphne herself as *aemula Phoebes* (1.476) would make it interesting to develop her own artistic aspects in relation to Apollo's.

[60] A gesture that would simultaneously further fit her to the role of elegiac mistress whose hair was programmatically combed.

Ovid's dual role in representing the god, framing him within a larger narrative whose self-consciously elegiac tendencies signal a divergence from Apollo's own way of depicting himself and, at the same time, allowing the god to make the story his own, puts the poet himself very much in the same position as our imagined spectator. The poet is audience for Apollo, struggling to make his own poem out of the utterances and expressions of the god, and at the same time subject to viewing and interpretation by another audience. A kind of equivalence then emerges between the god, the poet, and the reader, each of whose own acts of poiesis alternatively testifies to a more powerful governing presence (Cupid, Apollo, Ovid himself) and recontextualizes that presence within an image of the world that he controls—until another audience emerges to "read" it.

Given the close association between Apollo and Augustus himself signaled at the end of the god's speech, we can also add the emperor to this equation. The laurel was his distinctive attribute, part of his Apolline self-image, and by imposing this version of the Daphne story as an origin for it, the poet offers a new reading of the Augustan symbol that can either subvert or be transcended by its dominant connotations within imperial iconography, just as Apollo's prophecy may or may not count as the episode's hermeneutic last word. As in the poem's final lines, the relationship between poet and emperor hovers uneasily between simile and synecdoche. The controlling artist spinning out his text resembles the imperial author producing images that challenge and define his audience. Yet if the text sometimes seems to exist as an autonomous entity, reshaping all it touches, at others it seems but part of a larger system controlled by the emperor whose real presence continually peeks through the imagery of the poem and whose voice, like that of Apollo within the poem, can come to control our reading of it.

My positioning of the poet narrator of the Apollo episode as an intermediary between the god and audience, and the opening up of a chain of correspondences in which each artist becomes reader and each reader an artist might first seem necessitated by the logic of modern critical interests in the power of the audience, but it taps into an issue that took on tremendous potency in the development of the principate: the scope allowed for individual self-representation. It was not only the emperor who wanted to leave his mark on the world.[61] The great aristocratic families of the late republic engaged in a competition to produce visible monuments of their authority on a scale that would have astonished even a

[61] See esp. Eck 1984.

nineteenth-century American industrialist. These visual assertions of status extended from the construction of vast palaces and public buildings within the city, to the elaborate tombs outside it, to the erection of statues, temples, and gateways in the famous cities of the empire. The relationship between such claims to prestige and the consolidation of imperial authority involved a long series of negotiations in which we can trace several wrong steps. Notoriously Cornelius Gallus, not a Roman aristocrat but a member of the rising class of Italian knights who had attached themselves to Octavian, fell from favor and took his own life as a result, according to one historian, of the self-aggrandizing inscriptions and statues he put up during his tenure in the vital post of prefect of Egypt.[62] Equally vexed was the kind of display to be allowed triumphing generals, who in the past had left fantastic visual traces of their accomplishments. Under Augustus, the triumph itself became increasingly the prerogative of members of the imperial family. In its place, senatorial generals receive "triumphal decorations" and a statue in the Forum of Augustus. Thus, like Propertius's persona in 2.31 or the Ovidian narrator in the Daphne episode, but via different mechanisms, their individual fame is partly wagered on the prestige of the emperor's monuments.

The emperor's own public imagery constrained personal expression by other means than simply squeezing out the space for rival display. As Paul Zanker has shown, the motifs and decor employed in less public contexts increasingly bear the stamp of imperial imagery.[63] Luxury items like carved tables sport the Sphinx that had become a token of Augustus's Egyptian victory. Even the cheapest terracotta oil lamps featured imperial symbols. Sometimes these borrowings from the language of power seem part of a concerted effort to assert loyalty to the imperial family or to lay claim to the qualities identified with them. This is perhaps the case with the echoes of the styles and gestures of imperial portraiture that appear on the tombs of freedmen.[64] Other examples of this downward flow of Augustan imagery might result simply from the momentum of fashions or even availability. Did the person who bought the lamp with the image

---

[62] Dio 53.23.5; see the discussion in Syme 1960.309–10. Suetonius's account of the incident (*Aug.* 66.2) places the blame on Gallus's "ungrateful and churlish spirit" without specifying the manifestations of this ingratitude. *ILS* 8995, an inscription set up by Gallus himself, contains a boast to have been the first to lead any army, Roman or Egyptian, beyond the cataract of the Nile. This may be an example of Gallus's fatal penchant for self-promotion. Interestingly, and in a way that can tell us much both about the overlap between poetic and political expression and about the double roles of reader and recorder, the one substantial surviving fragment of Gallus's poetry imagines him as spectator rejoicing to read the *spolia* erected for Caesar's triumph (for a fuller account of the episode with bibliography, see Courtney 1993.259–62).

[63] See Zanker 1990.265–74.

[64] See the classic study of Kleiner 1977.

of victory astride the globe choose that design over others,[65] or did he simply take what was on offer?

My point is not the power of style irrespective of the intentions of its viewers and consumers to reflect and transform mentalities; it is rather to show that, whether the motive of those who put such items on display was proud patriotism, irony, or mere convenience, the visual language available to them was itself constrained by status.[66] Thus, their presentation of themselves to those both above and below them was mediated through imagery that underlined their own place in a larger hierarchy and necessarily drew both its viewers and producers into a dialogic relationship with the imperial center. Furthermore, the overlap between the "voice" of each individual deploying such imagery and that of its imperial *auctor* could be read in turn in a number of ways: it could glorify both, like the statues in the Forum of Augustus where the appropriation of the virtues of the individuals commemorated added luster to the whole complex. Or else the specific context of imitation could orient the spectator in a way that caused her to look at the imperial source with new eyes, most obviously in cases of parody, like the depiction of the archetypal scene of Augustan myth—Aeneas carrying his father Anchises from burning Troy—that gives the protagonists the heads of dogs and erect penises.[67] Yet another possibility is for the viewer to read the appropriation against the intentions of the appropriator in a way that exposes him as an unworthy claimant to the prestige he seeks. Pompeii offers a particularly nice example of the complexities of an imperial allusion as it travels down the social scale. In a large public building in the forum there, Eumachia, the powerful patroness of the fullers, placed copies of the statues of Aeneas and Romulus from the Forum of Augustus in Rome. These images were copied in turn on the business signs of a more humble fuller, Fabius Ululutremulus. Someone else has carved nearby a graffito reading "I sing of arms and the man, not of fullers and screech owls [*ululae*]." The reference to the originary context of the image strategically aligns the reader against the fuller, excluding him from precisely the claims to status that his choice of signs implies. Again, however, we may react against this

---

[65] So Zanker 1990.266.

[66] Thus, Zanker 1988.10, in a discussion with a somewhat different emphasis: "People knew what they wanted to say, but without a real pictorial vocabulary didn't have the 'words' to express it. They could only manage a garbled hodge-podge of elements drawn from the official state art."

[67] See Kellum 1997.174–75 for a thorough and imaginative reading of the image. Especially suggestive in this context is her interpretation of the interplay between the figure of the dog (*canis*) and the first line of the *Aeneid* (*cano*). The shift from "I sing" to "you sing" reflects the alienation of the ideal viewer from the point of view of the poet-narrator of the epic glorification of Aeneas. For an imagined etymological connection between *canis* and *cano*, see Varro *LL* 5.99.

reimposition of status distinctions by sympathizing with the fuller against the snob.

It is important, though, to make clear that the "low-mimetic" imitations that seem to demote or reduce the status of what is imitated cannot be simply understood as a transgressive or somehow "anti-Augustan" act. Rather than being inevitably punished, fools and jesters who imitated the emperor became a distinctive hallmark of imperial self-presentation, performing at such seemingly august occasions as imperial funerals.[68] We have, for example, the funerary inscription of a man who seems to have been the slave or freedman of the emperor Tiberius, a figure not otherwise renowned for his ability to take a joke, whose function seems to have been precisely to mimic the emperor in speech and gesture.[69] Similarly, at the funeral of Vespasian a mime portraying the emperor mocked his most famous quality of stinginess by complaining about the cost of the ceremony.[70] There are many ways of accounting for this phenomenon, starting perhaps with the assumption that the emperors had learned the lesson of the modern celebrity that there is no such thing as bad publicity. We can also see how the emperor's own reception of these jokes gave him a context for displaying precisely his tolerance, indeed appreciation, of such humor—a democratic gesture of bonhomie that gave a counterweight to the stern and godlike figure he assumes in other contexts—while making clear that the interpretative ball was very much in his court: it was up to him to tolerate the joke or not.[71] All of this is not to suggest that the transgressive potential of such acts was necessarily neutralized, that any reference to imperial lechery and baldness was somehow improbably welcome because of the mysteries of ancient social practice. On the contrary, I suggest that their institutional force depends on the awareness of all concerned that they are playing with fire. That, after all, is what makes the accounts of imperial tolerance sufficiently noteworthy to be recorded.

There is also perhaps another sense in which these occasions played a dialectical role in defining by opposition what the *princeps* was. Imitation, of course, depends on recognizing not only a likeness to the original but a difference as well. So, in this case, the audience would always know that whatever characteristics of the emperor the jester may highlight

---

[68] See Purcell 1999.

[69] *ILS* 5225. See Purcell 1999.181 and Sumi 2002.

[70] Suet. *Vesp.* 19, with Purcell 1999.182–83.

[71] Thus, Purcell 1999.187, noting convincingly that Augustus's involvement with the theater, a place generally considered anathema to traditional morality, dates from precisely the same period as his marriage legislation. His interpretation draws on the thesis of Wallace-Hadrill 1982 that the "public relations" task facing the first *princeps* was primarily to walk the tightrope between authoritarianism and civility.

through exaggeration, this was not after all Augustus himself. And here we come to a crucial element in this representational system: however popular, influential, or wealthy he may have become, the imitator was always essentially a nobody, an actor who by definition fell outside the status hierarchy of Roman citizen society. We may regard this figure in a sense as offering a zero grade for the process of self-definition through imitation that we saw before. Here is someone who cannot be exposed or demoted, because he has no status whatsoever: he can most easily and most absolutely play the emperor because he has no face of his own. This fact, central both to the humor and to the tolerability of the imitation through exaggeration, was important not only to the emperor because it ensured that the audience knew it was dealing with mere mockery, not invective or emulation, but also to the upper classes themselves, who can in turn define their own relation to the imperial center against the role of the mere clown. Witness above all the literature of friendship in which the *amicus*, a title that whatever the realities brought an essential facade of equity, is continually defined against the mere flatterer, or parasite. Especially significant in the literature of the Augustan period is the battle that Horace stages in his *Satires* to make it clear—to those both above and below him—that he is a true friend of the great, not someone who has compromised his own status by playing the part of the clown, which at the same time his position uncomfortably resembles.[72]

Another Ovidian story featuring the imperial god Apollo addresses the perils and potentials of such imitation in a way that once more highlights the complex interpretative possibilities open to readers of Ovid's own text. For again the poet will position himself inside and outside the story he tells to assert simultaneously his own control over the text he produces and the powerlessness of the author within the economy of reproductions it describes. The narrative will offer the double possibility of taking its mimetic protagonist as a clown and a nobody, functioning only as a sign for the power of the god, or as a figure capable of being identified with in his own right, in which case his fate aligns the audience against the authority of the gods. The episode in question is the brief account of the punishment of the satyr Marsyas, who picked up the flute invented and discarded by Minerva and, having provoked and lost a musical contest with Apollo, was flayed alive by the god:

> *Sic ubi nescio quis Lycia de gente virorum*
> *rettulit exitium, satyri reminiscitur alter,*
> *quem Tritoniaca Latous harundine victum*
> *adfecit poena.""quid me mihi detrahis?" inquit;*

---

[72] See Oliensis 1998.17–63 on how Horace in the *Satires* defines his "face."

"a! piget, a! non est" clamabat "tibia tanti."
clamanti cutis est summos direpta per artus,
nec quicquam nisi vulnus erat; cruor undique manat,
detectique patent nervi, trepidaeque sine ulla
pelle micant venae; salientia viscera possis
et perlucentes numerare in pectore fibras.
illum ruricolae, silvarum numina, fauni
et satyri fratres et tunc quoque carus Olympus
et nymphae flerunt, et quisquis montibus illis
lanigerosque greges armentaque bucera pavit.
fertilis inmaduit madefactaque terra caducas
concepit lacrimas ac venis perbibit imis;
quas ubi fecit aquam, vacuas emisit in auras.
inde petens rapidus ripis declivibus aequor
Marsya nomen habet, Phrygiae liquidissimus amnis.
(6.382–400)

So when someone from the Lycian race recalled the death of men, another made mention of the satyr, whom, beaten in a competition with the pipe of Minerva, the son of Leto punished. "Why do you drag me from myself?" he said. "Ah, I repent! A flute is not worth so much!" But as he cries out, the skin is ripped away from the tips of his limbs, and there is no part of him that is not a wound; blood flows from all sides, the muscles lie exposed, and the pulsing veins shine with no hide over them. You could count the dancing organs and the sinews glittering in his breast. Him the country-dwelling Fauns—woodland powers, and his brother satyrs, and Olympus, beloved even then, and the nymphs lamented. So did whoever grazed wool-bearing sheep or horned herds on those mountains. The fertile earth grew wet and, damp, gathered their fallen tears, and drank them into her own deepest veins. And she shot them, turned to water, into the open air, whence a river, hurrying to the sea through sloping bed, keeps the name Marsya, clearest of Phrygian streams.

Multiple instances of imitation are at work here, both explicitly within the tale and emerging from the formal properties and position of the narrative. First, the lowly satyr appropriates the instrument of one Olympian god and uses it to rival another. But the tale itself is a repetition in a minor key of the three stories that have gone before, those of Arachne, Niobe, and the Lycian peasants, all of which featured the deaths of humans who had challenged the power of the gods. After a trilogy of tragedies about humans done in by their hubris, we come to a kind of "satyr play" repeating the same plot but now enacted by an ambiguous and potentially ludicrous protagonist. Finally the language in which the satyr renounces the flute becomes for Ovid's readers another potential parody of the higher gods. For he employs the same phrase Minerva herself uses when she casts away the flute in another Ovidian version of the same tale: *non es mihi, tibia, tanti* (Flute, you are not worth so much to me, *AA* 3.505).[73] And what prompts the goddess's act there is precisely a disfiguring reflection, the image of her maiden cheeks bloated with air, which she glimpsed in the "clear" waters of a nearby stream. Within the stylistic language of the Augustan poets, a clear stream reflecting a bloated image creates a kind of tension between form and content that is relevant to the issues the episode raises in the *Metamorphoses*. Clear streams connote slight forms and refined treatment to which bloating and swelling are anathema. All the more so because the most famous statement of the poetics of pure water comes from the same poet, Callimachus, who made a similar stylistic point by rejecting another poet's "large lady" (Callim. *Aet.* 1, fr.1.12).

Marsyas's various imitations of gods and humans are subject to the same kinds of multiple interpretative possibilities as the appropriation of elements of Augustan iconography by, for example, freedmen and fullers. The satyr's borrowings in every case potentially lower the tone of the image and provide a distorting mirror of the actions of those above him—if, that is, we view Marsyas from within the global hierarchies that put Apollo and Minerva on the top and the satyr on the bottom. Apollo's punishment here underlines this level of divine control and reasserts the incompetence of Marsyas as an artist. In this perspective, Marsyas is reduced in status to an inadequate *lusor*, and the gods are threatened by the suggestion of parity/parody on the part of their imitator. On the other hand, if we allow the satyr's own words to guide our reading, then the radical differentiation of divine model from "satyric" parody is no longer so easy. Let us take, for example, the satyr's imitation of Minerva in the *Ars*, which is usually taken as another way in which the poet alienates sympathy from him. As the niceties of the satyr's rhetorical figures seem

---

[73] Murgia 1986 argues that the imitation works the other way around and that *Ars* 3 in fact postdates *Met.* 1–6. This redating, based on a method of applying the procedures used in textual criticism to literary imitation, has remained controversial. Even if it is accepted, I would contend that, given Ovid's penchant for a posteriori revision (see Hinds 1985 and Tarrant 2002b.27–29), such imitation essentially amounts to a rewriting of the earlier text as well and so fully justifies our reading the Marsyas episode through the lens of *Ars* 3. The third version of Minerva's outcry, at *Fasti* 6.701, "*ars mihi non tanti est; valeas mea tibia,*" *dixi*, in the context of Minerva's account of the origin of the Quinquatrus festival, with its witty pointing of Ovid's self-citation through Minerva's self-citation (*dixi*), does not directly contribute to my reading of the *Met.* passage, except to the extent that it further highlights the intertextual life of Minerva's expression and plays again on the possibility of hearing it as Ovid's. This last point takes on greater significance if we imagine *Fasti* 6 as a postexilic work and Ovid's *Ars* as responsible for the poet's *relegatio* (as does Barchiesi 1997b.90).

incompatible with the gruesome punishment he is even then suffering,[74] so the fact that he is made to utter words that the goddess spoke when concerned merely about her appearance makes him all the more a figure of laughter—except that, in taking over the goddess's language, he has reapplied it in a context that is more appropriate: Marsyas's anguish over the loss of his skin only reinforces the frivolity of the goddess's concern over her face. Again the episode offers us two incompatible perspectives: In one Marsyas is seen from without as a figure in a cosmic scene controlled by the gods and in a text manipulated by the poet, but in the other the grotesque satyr, as a poet himself, reverses such hierarchies.

In fact, a comparison with the imperial *imitator* instructively clarifies the prominence of Marsyas's authorial independence. Unlike the *imitator* Marsyas refuses to acknowledge the preeminence of the original—this is most immediately apparent in his attempt to rival Apollo but also implicit in the unconsciousness of his imitation of Minerva, whom he has never seen playing the flute and whose speech in the *Ars* he has of course never heard. His is no self-advertising parody; on the contrary, he thinks of himself as an original artist and tries to compete on those terms with a god.

In generating this double perspective on Marsyas, as a transgressor put in his place by his defeat and punishment at the hands of a god, and as a sympathetic figure offering his own organizing view of his experiences, Ovid employs two of the same techniques we saw in the Daphne episode: the manipulation of the reader's position as spectator and play with the traditional imagery of the Callimachean program.[75] The narrator turns Marsyas into a spectacle, not a man but a wound whose bodily vulnerability testifies to the power of Apollo,[76] a procedure that requires Marsyas to lose not only his face but his whole skin and to be seen through, as it were, as opposed to offering a recognizable form to display to the world. Exactly contemporaneous with this loss of control over his form, Marsyas loses control over his voice as well; in place of being able to articulate a subjective view of his experiences, Marsyas can only point out the loss of a self—"Why do you strip me from myself, why do you strip the 'me' from me?" This kind of stripping is made more apparent in what follows by the fact that the narrator (and here it is important to

---

[74] Anderson 1972.202: "Marsyas is talking with most unlikely sophistication here about the fact that his skin is being ripped from his body." Cf. also Bömer ad loc.

[75] For a different view of how Ovid's text creates the possibility for strongly contrasting responses in its audience, see Williams's (1996.82–83) reading of the episode. He presents the voyeuristic delight elicited by the combination of detailed description and neutral detachment as ultimately undercutting any tendency for compassion on the part of the audience.

[76] See Segal 1998.

bear in mind that we are dealing not simply with the poet-narrator but with an internal speaker telling the story for his own purposes) gives him words that are not his own. He can only reproduce the language of the goddess and therefore becomes even more of a parody and less of a person. To the extent that any nonhumorous, sympathetic figure of Marsyas emerges, it is so far only through an awareness of this suppression and the kind of adversarial reading that such an awareness provokes.

Things change when sympathetic spectators enter the picture, the fauns and nymphs who mourn Marsyas's death.[77] The opening out of potential responses to the satyr's death through the introduction of an internal audience coincides with a shift in the generic properties of the story that similarly helps reorient the audience's response to it. Suddenly, instead of seeing a lone satyr in the world of the imperial gods, we have put him back in the context where he belonged, amid a community of nymphs, fauns, and other denizens of the world of bucolic poetry.[78] And their central function here, preserving the memory of Marsyas through mourning, recalls an essential purpose of bucolic poetry as shaped by Vergil's *Eclogues*: the commemoration of friendship.[79] (Interestingly, the friend remembered at the end of the *Eclogues* was himself an unfortunate imitator of "Apollo," Gallus.). This bucolic lament quite literally takes the form of an underground tradition: the tears collected by the earth, which eventually overflow into a fountain and seek the sea as the "purest of Lycian streams," an unmistakable symbol of the poetics of slight forms.[80] At this moment, the pure poetry of the bucolic makes its own little world: like the poem's account of the origins of the world, the account of the stream's genesis manages to touch on the realms of land,

[77] Another avenue for relating the flaying of Marsyas to the problem of authorship is taken by Theodorakopoulos 1999.156–57, who sees the satyr's punishment as a complete loss of form predicting both his loss of the powers of expression and his inability to leave behind any material trace except through the responses of spectators.

[78] See Tissol 1997.127 for more on the precise stylistic imitation of Vergilian pastoral here and its imagined impact on its audience. For the role of commemoration as the key to bucolic as the expression of absent presences, see Hardie 2002c.20–21.

[79] Cf. the discussion by Alpers 1996.92–93 of the pastoral lament as the poetic restoration of a lost world.

[80] This imagery is given particular energy here by the contrast with the muddy lake in which the Lycian farmers splash about as frogs. For the poetological imagery there, see Clauss 1989 and Myers 1994.83–90. An anonymous commentator on an earlier version of this analysis makes the important point that even the "anti-Apolline" connotations of this embrace of Callimachean aesthetics are open to significant revision. For it is, after all, Apollo himself who tells that poet to keep his muse thin, and the specific topos of poetry as a pure stream was most memorably developed by the god Apollo himself in the closing lines of Callimachus's hymn to the god (Call. *Hymn to Apollo* 105–12). Thus, even if we read an endorsement of poetic refinement in the passage as the triumph of Marsyas's memory over his punishment, the poet still ends up speaking the language of the god.

sea, and sky. What is more, this imposition of a bucolic order emerges as a recapitulation of the process that gave rise to that other great enemy of Apollo, the Python: there, the earth became the unwitting mother of a grotesque, chthonic brood after soaking up the waters of the flood (1.416–21).

But our temptation to identify the voice of the poet with the clear stream of poetic memory should not be left unqualified. As in the Daphne episode, the deliberate flagging of the language of a particular genre has the ultimate effect of muddying the waters, of forcing us to realize how carefully Ovid has "dismembered" his own poetic voice in the episode in a way that highlights the conflict between different ways of reading and the pressures that he himself is subject too as a prospective imitator. Who is telling this story and why? It is not Ovid, nor is it even "Ovid," the poet-narrator. Rather, the most immediate narrator is "another," one of those prompted by the fate of Niobe to "fear the manifest wrath of the gods and all the more zealously to honor Latona with a cult." In other words, we might expect the narrator to tell the story from the point of view of the outraged god rather than of the justly punished satyr. And not only does the tale function perfectly as a cultic hymn, recalling the power of the god Apollo, but it also explains the initial focus on Marsyas as a mere wound, a pure symbol of the punishing power of Apollo. As in the case of Daphne, the figure of the victorious god emerges with particular clarity from the body of his victim. For the satyr's exposed organs recall at once the brilliance of the sun (*perlucentes, micant*), the strings of a bow (*nervi*), and the chords of the lyre (*nervi, fibras*).[81] The conversion of the satyr into the god's instrument, continued through the words *salientia* (used of strings quivering under the impact of the pick) and *numerare* ("to put in meter"), hints at the essential participation of the poet in what he describes; singing of Marsyas and punishing Marsyas become analogous acts in the worship of Apollo.[82]

How far one should take this anonymous raconteur as an alter ego for the poet of the *Metamorphoses* must always remain an open question, as do the parameters of his song: does the same narrator tell the whole story, even through the very differently inflected account of the

---

[81] The musical "resonance" of Marsyas's innards was independently observed by Princeton graduate student Sarah Ferrario, to whom I am grateful for discussions of the episode.

[82] On the general role of the Homeric Hymns as intertexts in Ovid's poem, see Barchiesi 1999.

As Philip Hardie points out to me, *per litteras*, this makes it all the more significant that the stream that introduces the contrasting tendency to remember Marsyas's self, rather than his fate, derives here from the tears of the spectators and not from the actual blood of the satyr. In other versions of the myth, this is indeed the case.

mourning, or does the "poet narrator" take over after *fibras*?[83] Another potential poet figure similarly forces the audience to evaluate the position of the author, Marsyas himself. He, like the anonymous speaker, is also a poetic performer and, indeed, a poet whose words can be recognized as those of the "real" Ovid, the poet whose name appears on the *titulus* and who was also the author of the *Ars Amatoria*. Thus, for all Ovid seems to control his text, whether as the actual author, or because he participates with the internal narrator in framing Marsyas as legitimately punished victim, there is also the seed of a subjective authorial presence in the very center of this process of external focalization that places Ovid within the story he tells and so depicts the actual poet as at the mercy of the forces he describes. The multiplication of potential authors here not only helps to make the reader aware of multiple points of view but also allows for various constructions of Ovid's status and how it affects his poetics. By not being Marsyas, the poet avoids the role of the mere *lusor*, or rather of the impotent rival, and becomes a participant in the manifestation and legitimate exercise of power. But the more he does this, and the more his poetry is taken as an exaltation of the cult of Apollo in particular and of the maintenance of hierarchies in general, the more he seems to fall precisely into that role, to flatter the emperor and to mimic the god.

The tendency for the persona of the poet to collapse into the figure he seems to regard from outside recalls a device familiar above all from Horatian satire, where the resemblance of Horace to figures that he seems to depict only to mock, like Davus and Nasidienus, not only becomes disquietingly revealing about the poet himself but also projects a corrosive effect upward through the social hierarchy, as the patrons and readers whom Horace himself resembles are made uncomfortably aware that they themselves are far from the top of the food chain.[84] From the other perspective, if we take Marsyas as a sympathetic figure, whose status as an artist we are prepared to endorse, then Ovid's potential distance from this figure not only lessens the political implications involved in taking on the voice of Apollo's rival but more importantly reveals that even the autonomous artist is caught up in a larger context that inevitably exerts its pressure over the meaning of his words and, indeed, determines the very modes and language available to him. So too, the *nobilis*, or freedman, can increasingly manifest his own position in the world only through the imagery of the emperor. The poet Marsyas comes to merge with the voice of the god—appropriately, because he is being punished for just that.

---

[83] Tissol 1997.126 draws particular emphasis to the dramatic shift in tone at this point.

[84] See esp. Oliensis 1997.

III. Upward Mobility?

So far in this chapter, a close reading of the poem's conclusion has shown how the different ways of construing the priority of Ovidian fiction translate directly into differing views of the authority and status of its poet, especially in relation to that of the supreme author of the Roman imperial cosmos, the emperor Augustus. Then, I offered a broader context for understanding why Ovid should have framed his authorial capacity in this way. The kind of tension between poetic and imperial roles highlighted at the poem's conclusion emerged less as a specifically targeted challenge to the political position of the emperor than as a sign of how the definition of status throughout the Roman social hierarchy was manifested through the borrowing of imperial language and symbols in such a way that both the difference from and similarity to the top of the pyramid emerged from each borrowing. Not only does this speaking through the language of another place each author even more at the mercy of the interpretations of any given reader: it actually breaks down the distinction between reception and authorship, as self-expression becomes inevitably an act of reception and as the reading of the artistic and verbal language of superiors gives scope, in the degree of assent given or refused, for the realization of a social self on the part of the recipient.

Another episode reinforces the radically indeterminate status of the creator in Augustan Rome and also draws a clear link between the social status of makers and the phenomenology of representation: the story of Daedalus and Icarus. Yet Daedalus's story invites reading from below as well as above. Like most studies of how Ovid constructs his social status in the poem, I have started at the top by analyzing the likenesses and differences between poet and emperor. However, the same pattern of overlap and distinction also characterizes Ovid's treatment of his position relative to the figure who stood at the bottom of the social order, the slave.

Tales of transformation and the use of fictions had a particular connection to slaves. I have already suggested in the preceding chapter that the capacity for mutability itself has different implications according to the social status of those to whom it is applied: slaves were by their nature subject to transformation both upward through manumission and downward through a dehumanizing violence that was sometimes figured in images that turned the human slave into a beast. As William Fitzgerald has explored, the slave's mutability and position at the threshold between the human and the bestial make metamorphosis a crucial if sometimes implicit element of the depiction of slavery in Latin literature.[85]

---

[85] Fitzgerald 2000.87–114.

Fitzgerald's work also suggests how slaves themselves functioned hermeneutically in Roman society to raise broader issues of stability and change very like those put in play by Ovidian metamorphoses. The *Metamorphoses*' obsession with change has seemed to critics to point simultaneously in two directions: on the one hand, it suggests a world genuinely in flux, a perspective that undercuts any claims to a permanent order; on the other, because of the terminal role of metamorphosis in so many of the poem's narratives, it has provoked the claim that only the final forms matter. Change takes place in a miraculous and fictional past that contrasts to the stable world in which we live. The negotiation of these alternatives depends very much on how we regard transformation itself, where a focus on real-world products contrasts with the point of view of those human figures who experience transformation as a total and inexplicable rupture of the world they know. Thus, read from the safe perspective of the present, with the sure knowledge that the stories are fictions, the work becomes more reassuring than it does if we enter into those fictions by identifying with the figures it depicts. Slavery too has the capacity both to affirm and to undermine static hierarchies, and this doubleness again springs from how we view the figure of the slave. As foreign, alien, and animal, the slave provides a naturalizing confirmation of the powers that hold him in bondage. But as flesh and blood human beings, defined perhaps by experience of them as individuals rather than by legal and economic definitions, the very existence of slaves provides the most radical challenge to any kind of social order by pointing out that "we" too could undergo a reversal of fortune that would put us in their place. The reverse metamorphosis of slaves to freedmen undermines social categories not only by signifying that, in the words of Ovid's Pythagoras, *omnia mutantur* (15.165) but also because it suggests a disjunction between appearance and reality since freed slaves can acquire so many of the outward signs of status. But the other side of Pythagoras's dictum, that the soul remains the same, recalls how slavery's changeable nature could in fact make it the ultimate confirmation of aristocratic stability: the mind of the truly noble figure, as stoics in particular remind us, can endure even slavery unchanged.

This resemblance between the signifying power of the slave and of the metamorphic *fabula* becomes all the more striking when we remember that the *fabula* was a characteristic discourse of the slave.[86] The Tiberian freedman Phaedrus[87] begins his first book of Aesopic fables with a pro-

---

[86] The thematic connections between fable and slavery in Latin literature, and how they shape the use of the fable in the works of Horace and Petronius, are the subject of an important article by Marchesi 2005.

[87] Or perhaps his upper-class impersonator; see Champlin 2005.

tective disclaimer not so different from Ovid's insistence on the fictionality of the *Metamorphoses* in the poem he addresses to Augustus. "If anyone wishes to abuse me, because not only wild animals, but even trees speak, let him remember that I am merely jesting with made up stories."[88] The lines draw an important connection among the work's transformative subject matter, its self-advertising fictionality, and the status of the author. As elsewhere Phaedrus will claim that slaves invented the *fabula* for self-protection, to express what they wanted to say without attracting reproach (*calumniamque fictis elusit iocis*, 3. prol. 37), so here he escapes abuse by a retreat into the unreal. But the speaking beasts do more than reinforce the standard definition of the fabulous as remote "even from the semblance of reality" (Quint., *Inst.* 2.4.2). As the low form of the narratives to follow becomes a lightning rod for the abuse that might otherwise fall on the low-status author, so the fabulous talking trees and beasts, whose surprising capacity for speech belies their form, figure the otherwise inarticulate slaves to whom they have given the same power. But the obvious point in Phaedrus is that the *fabula* can be read not just as the mark of servility but as the means of escaping its constraints. So while the noble is always at liberty to trivialize Phaedrus's texts, by making explicit the essential duplicity of the fable, the poet also alerts his reader to the serious speech that lurks beneath it.

Ovid was certainly no freedman. But this fact does not lessen the significance for his work of the inheritance of *fabula* as a kind of speech that invites double reading and so draws attention to the relative position of author and audience. On the contrary, as in the poetry of Horace, the use of *fabulae* takes on a new level of complexity here because to be seen as speaking *fabulae*—in Ovid's case, to expose a connection between the learned subject matter and epic form of his poem and the slave's use of *fabulae*—in and of itself reveals the author in an unflattering light.

The most striking connection between slavery and metamorphosis in the poem comes in the unnamed figure of Mestra, daughter of Erysichthon, and her story will serve briefly to introduce the use Ovid makes of slaves in the construction of his own persona as artist (8.843–77). As Erysichthon's insatiable hunger drives him to poverty, he resorts to selling his daughter into slavery. Commanded to meet her new owner by the seashore, "this noble girl refuses to have a master" (*dominum generosa recusat*, 8.848) and seeks help from the god Neptune, who had previously seduced her. Neptune "renews her form" by giving her the appearance of an elderly fisherman. Armed with this new resource, Erysichthon

---

[88] *Calumniari si quis autem voluerit, / quod arbores loquantur, non tantum ferae, / fictis iocari nos meminerit fabulis* (Phaed. 1. *pro.* 5–7). See esp. Bloomer 1997.77–86 on this aspect of Phaedrus's poetry.

"often gave her to masters, but she, now as a horse, now as a bird, now as cow, now as a hind, would get away and so offer unjust nurture to her greedy father." As the only human figure to possess *transformia corpora* (8.871), Mestra is exceptional in the poem.[89]

This personal mutability also applies to the generic registers her tale invokes, for her miraculous ability is appropriately bestowed on her by a god, but she uses it to turn herself into a variety of lesser forms, the stock low-status character of the fisherman, and a succession of wild animals— all in response to a situation drawn from new comedy, a genre of representation distinguished precisely by its verisimilitude. And this ambiguity applies also to her social position. The text is emphatic that Mestra has already been sold—*hanc quoque vendit inops* (8.848)—and is so a slave. But her ability to change shape lets her escape the reality of this state and preserve her own sense of herself as *generosa*. So too, her multiple capacities for disruption—by violating contracts, by assuming the prerogatives of the gods, and by offering, within the context of the narrative, a renewable resource with the potential to thwart Ceres' punishment of Erysichthon[90]—are all held in check. Not only does Mestra explicitly gain her power from a god, but she has herself paid for it with her virginity, the loss of which would have been one of the prime consequences of enslavement. Finally, her rate of gain cannot keep pace with her father's hunger, and so the moral tale of divine vengeance is allowed to reach its end. In this way, Mestra's preservation of her own identity is molded to be perfectly compatible with the maintenance of every kind of order. Her changeable outward form at once provides a camouflage for an undetectable self and divides Mestra into an inner and an outer being that mirrors her hybrid state. Correspondingly, Ovid's audience possesses the potential for a double reading of Mestra, either as a character humbled and contained by circumstances or as the constant *generosa* unchanged by them. Like the fable itself for Phaedrus, miraculous transformation serves both as a device of the slave and as a figure for her. This double vision of course distances the audience from the viewpoint of the master, who cannot recognize Mestra because he is able only to see her *forma*. But our ability to penetrate Mestra's disguise itself has ambivalent consequences; on the one hand, it ensures that we never take her simply for a slave, but on the other, it removes precisely the capacity to trick and deceive that are her own greatest resource against the fact of enslavement.

The multiple ways of construing identity that Mestra's shape changing highlights take on a special significance because they go together with

---

[89] On this and for a valuable account of Ovid's adaptations of previous versions of Erysichthon's tale, see Fantham 1993. Also Hollis 1970.132–34.

[90] Fantham 1993.31.

a particularly transparent self-transformation on the part of the authorial voice as well. After finishing with Erysichthon's tale, the narrator
resumes as follows: "Why do I waste time on strangers? I too have the
power of renewing my body, a power limited in number" (*quid moror
externis? etiam mihi nempe novandi est / corporis, o iuvenis, numero
finita, potestas*, 8.879–80). Even once we remember that the first-person
speaker is in fact the river god Achelous—and this may take a moment
because the god has been speaking for more than 150 lines—an Ovidian
voice may still echo in the phrase *novandi corporis*, recalling as it does
the programmatic beginning of Ovid's poem[91] and also with the pun
finita numero (a power bounded by, or limited to, meter), as though these
transformations stop at the boundaries of the poem. Ovid's shape changing here emerges as the simultaneous impersonation of a slave and a god,
but again with complications. For while the "slave" Mestra maintains
her freeborn status through the gift of transformation that itself reminds
the audience of her possession by a god, the god, although he wields a
power for metamorphosis that is his own, sees that power limited in a
number of ways. He is restricted to two forms, serpent and bull, and,
more important, he resorts to them only in the account of his battle with
Hercules, when his *virtus* fails. If shape changing for the god, in contrast
to the slave, is a sign of weakness and powerlessness, then it is appropriate that he should bear on his countenance a mark of this disgrace that
he cannot conceal. For Hercules defeats Achelous by ripping out one of
his horns while the god sports his bull shape. The loss of that horn, the
contemporary social aspect of which as a loss of status or *capitis dimi-
nutio* emerges from the poet's description of it as a *capitis ... damnum*
(9.99–100), remains but imperfectly disguised by the willow crown he
bears.[92] As Ovid then becomes neither quite servile nor divine, the art
he practices shifts its connotations as he is seen in each figure, signifying
empowerment in the person of the slave but "loss of face" in the person
of the god.

The tale of Daedalus and Icarus occurs near the beginning of the same
book that ends with Mestra. And again we shall find the shape-shifting
capacity of a low-status figure measured against that of the gods. Dae-

---

[91] Even to the enjambment of *corporis*.

[92] Indeed, this is another of the places where Ovid's self-representation comes close to
the techniques exploited by Horace in the *Satires*. In Satire 1.5 the poet and his high-tone
friends on their way to Brundisium are amused by a slanging match between two *scurrae*,
one of whom bears a scar on his brow, which his rival Sarmentus compares to a ripped out
horn. The point, though, is that these two characters who ought to be so different from their
elite audience in fact rather resemble them. Thus, for instance, Sarmentus is derided as a
freedman (as Horace's father was) and tries to conceal this blemish by having been named
a *scriba* (as Horace himself did).

dalus's story also obviously invites reflection on the actual status of the work's author. His two most famous works as a craftsmen are described in ways that recall the poet's art. Thus, the labyrinth he builds in servitude to Minos to conceal the shameful offspring of Pasiphae is likened to the river Maeander,[93] whose poetological genealogy goes all the way back to Homer, and the wings with which he tries to return home to Athens receive a simile comparing them to panpipes. Daedalus is already a figure on whom Ovid has put a personal stamp, having told his story previously in the second book of the *Ars Amatoria*, in a context where his prime characteristic, *ingenium*, resembles the *ars* the author himself needs to chain in love (*Ars* 2.34).[94] But for our purposes the most significant analogy between Daedalus and Ovid is one that will emerge fully only when the last line of the work has been read: the craftsman's literal flight from the realm of Minos predicts the metaphor with which Ovid will figure his artistic triumph, as he flies above the stars.[95]

Above the stars, though, is precisely where Daedalus does not want to go. He warns his son Icarus not to fly too high and not to look up to the stars but to keep his eyes fixed on his father (8.203–8). Whether we take this scene, coming almost halfway through the entire *opus*, as a trial run for the poet's spectacular final takeoff, as an example of the kinds of limiting prescriptions that Ovid as super-Icarus will superbly overcome, or as an all too accurate prediction of the loss of real presence that comes with a purely poetic immortality,[96] the passage's evocation of the work's concluding gesture gives it a special significance for understanding the nature of Ovid's poetic ambitions. My own treatment of this much-studied episode will focus not on the abstract questions of artistic failure and success but on how it addresses the issue of the artist's status in terms that reflect both contemporary mechanisms of social ascent and the poem's concern with the relative priority of imitation and reality. Specifically, I want to highlight the indeterminacy of Daedalus's status and the extent to which evaluations of Daedalus are shown to depend very much on the position from which the reader views him and his creations.

[93] See esp. Pavlock 1998 and Boyd 2006.

[94] The comparison of the two Ovidian versions of Daedalus has been a frequent exercise. For the best and most recent treatment, see Sharrock 1994b.87–195. In the *Ars*, Ovid seems to go to extravagant lengths to avoid explicitly making the obvious comparison of himself to Daedalus. Surprisingly, the figure who serves as the analogy for the poet in the transition into and out of the narrative is Minos, who can neither keep love out, nor restrain even a human winged figure as Ovid tries to wrestle with a winged god (*Ars* 2.21–22 and 97–98). This distancing from the conspicuous poet figure and assumption of the position of the master Minos is an interesting parallel to the partial identification between the poet and Daedalus that I discuss later.

[95] For flight throughout the poem as a figure for creation, see Wise 1977.

[96] See esp. Oliensis 1997.

Many kinds of hierarchy are at work in the story of Daedalus and Icarus, such as the ascendancy of fathers over children and the capacities of human beings in relation to gods. On a literary level, these issues come to involve the scope of epic as opposed to elegiac narrative and, more importantly, the relationship of Ovid's work to its Vergilian predecessor. For Ovid here, Icarus-like, represents precisely what in the *Aeneid* the father Daedalus himself was unable to portray on the dedicatory sculptures Vergil has him construct upon his safe arrival at Cumae, the death of his son (*Aen.* 6.14–33). I start, though, with a hierarchical relationship that has played but a slight part in analyses of the episode but would perhaps have been among the most striking to ancient readers, the ambiguous social status of Daedalus himself. On the one hand, he practices an art that literally and figuratively brings him close to the gods.[97] His skill as a craftsman allows him to imitate them in their transcendence of physical boundaries, in the forging of the crafted cosmos with which the poem began, and in their very capacity for duplicitous imitation. Yet that same ability also marks him out as a *faber* (*ingenio fabrae celeberrimus artis*, 8.159), an un-epic word for craftsman that was also, of course, the designation for a common slave occupation—as indeed the name Daedalus is also attested for slaves.[98] The figure of Daedalus also interestingly features in the décor of a number of freedmen entertainments in the imperial period. He appears in a wall painting in the house of the Vettii in Pompeii, which, as Barbara Kellum has shown, abounds in metaphorical and mythological references to the state of slavery that the Vettii themselves have just escaped.[99] Most famously, the chef at Trimalchio's dinner who can himself produce wonders of illusion by sculpting any food out of pork also bears the name Daedalus.[100] This demotion of craft emerges perhaps in the Daedalus episode itself in the figure of the three low characters who look up at the flying figures, for each of them is identified and characterized by the tool of their trade, which in two cases is a literal means of support: the fisherman has his rod, and the shepherd and farmer lean on their staff and plow.

[97] See Hoefmans 1994.143 on the significance of the word *opifex*, 8.201. By contrast, Leach 1988.448 n. 59, drawing on MacMullen 1974.140, strikingly suggests that the word *opifex* itself bore the stigma of mere craftsmanship and that, far from Daedalus being exalted by comparison to the gods, the gods are tainted by a description they share with Daedalus.

[98] Bömer ad loc.

[99] Kellum forthcoming.

[100] *Sat.* 70.3. It is worth noting here how the passage confers a Daedalic aspect also to the chef's freedman master, for Trimalchio points out with pride that he has named the slave Daedalus out of his own *ingenium*. Because this was itself Daedalus's characteristic attribute, Trimalchio's own fashioning of the slave as Daedalus, while intended to elevate both master and cook, ends by lowering Trimalchio too to the level of his servile swine sculptor.

While neither text insists on this aspect of the figure, read against such a background there is enough in the language of both of Ovid's accounts to bring Daedalus's servile relationship to Minos into play. In the *Ars*, the position of Daedalus appears first focalized through the perspective of Minos as that of a guest, *hospes* (2.21). Yet Daedalus justifies his flight with the claim that "there is no other route for me to flee a master" (*qua fugiam dominum*, 2.40). The *Metamorphoses*' Daedalus does not repeat such a bald claim to have been reduced to servitude,[101] but the poem picks up on the language of possession that accentuates and prepares for it in the earlier text and gives it a special connection to its own concluding negotiation of status. According to Daedalus in the *Ars*, Minos possesses the land and the sea (2.35); in the *Metamorphoses*, this possession receives further rhetorical accentuation, and the king of Crete comes to possess all (*omnia possideat*, 8.187), if only in a hypothetical clause. Yet Augustus, who does indeed attain such world dominion, finds in the poem's final pages his position described in language that again recalls the personal possession of Minos and reintroduces the explicit language of slavery. For Jupiter says of him that the "the entire habitable world will be in his possession [*huius erit*], and the sea will be his slave [*serviet*]" (15.830–31). While not simplistically exposing Ovid as the emperor's slave, the similarity in phrasing does relate the issue of Daedalus's status to the present relationship that Ovid most explicitly uses to define his own.[102]

The doubleness of Daedalus's position in the narrative, as both slave and free exile, as something more than a man in the godlike nature of his craft and something less than a free man in the necessity that drives him to make use of it, emerges too in the contrast between his two great works in the poem, the labyrinth and the wings. The first is itself a device of enclosure and enslavement for a half man and for the captive Athenian youths.[103] The wings too have the effect of modifying human nature, making a monster, like the Minotaur himself, that has the characteristics of man and beast, but here the emphasis is on freedom and elevation, by which men come near to the realm of gods. The language describing

---

[101] This perhaps furthers Sharrock's point that the Daedalus of the later poem generally seems to lack the humility of his elegiac forerunner and not to know his place.

[102] The other similarity between the fates of Ovid and Daedalus is of course the exile that each endures. While the postexilic revision of any passage of the *Metamorphoses* must remain unprovable, whatever the intention of the author, the craftsman's situation in Crete would almost inevitably have intensified for any reader after 8 CE the exercise of seeing Ovid through Daedalus.

[103] Note the presence of *domuit* in line 171, which though it grammatically governs only the Minotaur, also suggests the enslavement of the youths.

both inventions heightens this contrast and relates the opposition between openness and enclosure to the twin themes of freedom and status.
The labyrinth not only imprisons; it conceals what would be a blot on
the reputation of Minos. By contrast, its existence is a product of Minos's
executive will.[104] He proposes, Daedalus disposes. Yet Minos's enclosure of his own disgrace suddenly emerges as the promotion of Minos's
reputation (*celeberrimus*) and the means by which he becomes a *dux*
(*ducit*, 8.161). The wings by contrast are explicitly designed to exploit
the "openings" in Minos's power but bring in images of concealment
and enclosure (*vincula pennarum*, 8.226) that reduce Daedalus himself
to a hapless figure no longer leading another in escape but lost and in
need of guidance (*ubi es? qua te regionem requiram?* 8.232).[105] Daedalus
intended the wings to impose a sort of ring structure on his own career
by bringing him back to the place of his birth, but the effect has been to
define a different origin for him by making the end of his flight recall the
experience not of the maker of the labyrinth but of those trapped inside
it. And, in fact, like the situation of the slave Mestra, for whom metamorphosis as a route out of slavery seems also a condemnation to endless
repetition, Daedalus too, for all his flapping, is doomed to go nowhere by
the structure of Ovid's own narrative. We last see him on another island,
Sicily, again as a fugitive, placing himself in a subordinate position to yet
another king, Cotalus. His end thus recalls the beginnings of his narrative
within the poem, as a slave in Crete, not the beginnings of his own life
story as a free man in Athens.

Three interconnected points result from this analysis of the nature
of Daedalus's creations. First is the transparent relation between social
prominence and narrative prominence. Daedalus's emergence to freedom marks an important transition in the subject of Ovid's poem, which
ceases to be about the king Minos and comes to center around the craftsman. Yet, as we have seen, the beginnings of this transition are made
problematic because the accomplishment of the labyrinth can be read
as testimony either to Minos's authority or to Daedalus's *ars*. The battle

---

[104] *Destinat hunc Minos thalamis removere pudorem / multiplicique domo caecis in-
cludere tectis* (8.156–57).

[105] One subtle way of signaling this reversion to the labyrinth was pointed out to me by
Philip Hardie (*per litteras*). *Met.* 8.232 recalls *Aen.* 9.390, *Euryale infelix, qua te regione
reliqui*. But the imagery of the subsequent lines in turn points back to Vergil's description of
Theseus retracing his steps through Daedalus's labyrinth (Hardie 1994.143–44), a passage
of which Daedalus is himself also arguably the author in that it occurs in the account of the
monument he erects at Cumae. It presents an appropriately intricate network of allusions to
retrace in order merely to return to the labyrinth, along the way returning the language that
describes Nisus to the context in which it first appeared, not a lover in search of his beloved
but a father mourning a son, if we consider the (omitted) climax of Daedalus's memorial.

between ruler and craftsman for preeminence in this portion of the poem thus anticipates the struggle at the poem's conclusion between a focus on Augustus and one on the poetic maker himself. And this fluctuation in the narrative, which will play out in the differing ways in which Daedalus's story is framed within the poem, are reflected by, and in themselves determine, the ambiguities of the figure of Daedalus, especially as they are focused by the question of metamorphosis. To read the story from Minos's point of view is to see Daedalus as violator of his position, an ungrateful guest—relying again on the *Ars* as intertext—or a rebellious slave, while Daedalus presents himself as someone seeking an original freedom and Minos as the hubristic tyrant who violates the boundaries between land and sea. Seeing the master, so to speak, and seeing the slave result in radically different views of the story.

Second, the social spectrum that runs from king to slave mirrors cosmic progressions from beast to god and from the underworld of the labyrinth to the sky. And Daedalus's own creations seem by imitation to transgress both the lowest and the highest bounds of the human position within that universe. The labyrinth is like hell—but not exactly like because you can escape from it. Flight makes men almost gods—except for the consequences of falling. And as the limitations of each resemblance reflect positively and negatively on the human state—positively when it allows man to avoid death, negatively when death marks the ending of flight—so the double hybrids within the book, figures who seem caught in an unending metamorphosis,[106] define the human in relation to animal and god. The fact that these are hybrids, rather than creatures undergoing metamorphosis, further highlights this ambiguity, because they can be fit into narratives moving in either direction. The Minotaur can be a man turning downward to bestiality: Daedalus can be a man reaching for divinity.

The third point to stress is the active capacity that Daedalus's imitations have not just to reflect his own status but to transform others'. For as his labyrinthine *opus* (8.160, and another important lexical link to Ovid's "work") is seen as that of a slave glorifying Minos, it also becomes an instrument of enslavement for others. So too, his attempt at flight involves not just self-transformation but aims to be equally uplifting for a second double, Icarus, whose ultimate fall in turn imposes a limit on his father's skill. In just the same way, Ovid's self-definition through this episode is bound up with offering the readers a chance to realize and rethink their own social status by measuring likeness and difference to the various figures in the text.

---

[106] For the relationship between hybrids and metamorphosis, see Sharrock 1996.

One place where the universal mythical order traced by Daedalus's journey comes most closely into contact with a very specific social order is in the justification and account of Daedalus's invention of wings. The narrator prefaces Daedalus's act of creation with the comment that "he set his mind [*animum*] toward unknown arts and renewed nature [*naturam novat*]" (8.188–89). Besides the further equation between Ovid's work and Daedalus's that comes from the collocation of *animus* with the idea of newness (*in nova fert animus …*), the final phrase bears an important double signification. Daedalus's flight simultaneously transforms his own specific nature and revolutionizes the entire natural order.[107] Both aspects of the phrase, which itself links personal status to cosmic stability, can impose a negative reading on Daedalus's activity as hubristic transgression. Yet such a view stands in contrast to the inventor's own conception of his natural place. For Daedalus, flight offers not so much reinvention as a return to his *loci natalis* (8.184), a word whose obvious etymology connects it closely to *natura*. By contrast, as we have seen, Minos's obstruction of land and sea bears a close resemblance to the contemporary criticism of the Roman upper classes for violating nature by building over the boundary between land and sea.[108] Is Daedalus unnatural in his desire to escape his position at Minos's court, or is Minos's imposition of limits itself transgressive? When put in such terms, the different views of nature that animate these contradictory readings resemble the alternative uses of the same term, *natura*, in discussions of ancient slavery. On the one hand, slavery could be seen as itself a natural condition,[109] while on the other it was imposed on the slave contrary to the conditions of his birth.[110] The figure of the slave as a "hybrid" both like and unlike its masters thus raises the same questions about order as Daedalus's flight does and gives those questions a new bearing for the reader as a member of Roman society.

If Daedalus and his works bear this unsettling capacity to collapse differences between high and low, it stands in stark contrast to the artist's own idealization of his flight and its effects. For Daedalus's instructions to his son Icarus prescribe a middle course as a safe road to his destination. This emphasis on moderation, whose poetological aspects have been thoroughly explored, is also characteristic of the upwardly mobile

---

[107] See Hollis 1970.59 for the latter meaning.

[108] Most famously in Horace *Odes* 3.1.33–34. See, for the whole conceit, Edwards 1993.143–49.

[109] Arist. *Pol.* 1.2.15.

[110] *Dig.* 1.5.4.1. For the whole debate and its history at Rome, see conveniently Bradley 1994.132–53.

ex-slave.[111] Phaedrus similarly both advocates and aims for a style of speech that will not attract the scorn of those above by seeming to over-reach one's station.[112] Yet one of his darker fables, that of the ape and the lion king, points out how the nonnegotiable absolutes of power relations allow for no middle ground. The moral is: "There is the same punish-ment for those who speak and those who keep silent."[113] So in the case of Daedalus, there is not any middle between being looked up to and looked down on. The metaphor of the road itself will be undone precisely by the devices that he has built into the labyrinth, whose deceptions re-sult from the indistinguishability of roads heading in different directions (8.166–67). This emerges especially from the simile invoking the river Maeander, who "mocks us in his clear waves and with an ambiguous gliding—or fall, *lapsu*—flows forward and backward and meeting him-self sees his future waves and drives his uncertain waters now toward his sources and now toward the open sea" (8.162–66).[114] This image antici-pates Daedalus's tale in the river's apparent deception by its own devices and traces the alternative paths of Daedalus's narrative, which begins as a return to his source but ends on the open sea,[115] but it also points out the essential interpretative paradox of the episode that more than any other imprisons Daedalus: the middle road disappears because from dif-ferent points of view every road looks the same. The moment when the fisher and herdsmen catch sight of Daedalus and Icarus and believe that they are gods is interesting not only as a warning to the alert reader of imminent disaster but also because of its emphasis on perspective—literal and social. The spectators looking up at these flying figures themselves occupy low-status, frequently servile occupations: it is only when viewed from "below" that the maker appears as a god.

But it is not only within the narrative that contrasting perspectives lit-erally offer different ways of reading Daedalus. Ovid has himself "nested" the story between two others, those of Ariadne and Perdix, that make his own audience adopt different points of view, which are again rep-resented through the metaphors of altitude. The truly miraculous flight

---

[111] Hoefmans 1994.145, by contrast, argues that making such a transgressive figure as Daedalus a spokesman for the virtues of moderation is simply an example of Ovidian irony. Her analysis does not take account of those aspects of Daedalus's situation, in particular his enslavement to Minos, that make him seem an appropriately humble figure to deliver such advice. She goes on to argue that the contrast helps reveal Daedalus's Lucretian perspective, since to an Epicurean there is no danger of hubris.

[112] See esp. the analysis of Bloomer 1997.73–109.

[113] *Una enim est poena loquentis et non loquentis*, Phaedrus 4.14.

[114] For further discussion of the Maeander simile and its role in the episode, see Pavlock 1998.143–47.

[115] For the narratological significance of this river, see Boyd 2006.180–84.

of Ariadne's crown will take it above the stars (8.176–82), precisely the signpost Daedalus uses to warn Icarus of the heights to avoid. If Ariadne keeps us from the error of the fisherman by marking off the truly divine, the ground-nesting partridge, Perdix, the revelation of whose murder has led many readers to see the transgressive side of Daedalus,[116] provides a contrast (8.236–59). In comparison to him, Daedalus is guilty of a jealous preservation of status, looking down on Perdix with *invidia* and, appropriately for the symbolic geography of the episode, casting him down from a great height, Minerva's acropolis. But the presence of Minerva, who forms a contrast to the fisherman by allowing us to see Daedalus from the top down, brings another twist. While Minerva's easy gift of wings to the falling Perdix distances her from the human craftsman Daedalus, the reader of Ovid's poem may be reminded more of likeness than of difference. For Daedalus's envy of a younger rival recalls nothing so much as the Minerva's own punishment of Ariadne at the beginning of book 6. So while Minerva gives us a godlike view of Daedalus, the resemblance between the figures makes us see her with different eyes, revealing the unattractively human visage the gods themselves can wear. The stability of a fixed perspective crumbles in the face of a resemblance that reverses the place of higher and lower. As in the Marsyas episode, the goddess who more than almost any other in the poem aims to establish an absolute divine scale for measuring the cosmos is herself undone by an unwonted similarity to an inferior.

We have already seen this mirroring effect at work in the symmetries between the two inventions of Daedalus, but its consequences extend outward to include even the viewer-audience. The opposition I have set up between the godlike Daedalus and the overreaching Daedalus destined to fail reminds us that the narrative itself has given us a pair of flying men, one of whom stays aloft, while the other, Icarus, falls precisely for refusing to follow in the path of his father and leader. If one accepts the authenticity of line 216, this split also initially casts Daedalus himself in a double role, as both actor and spectator of another's efforts: *Et movet ipse suas et nati respicit alas* (8.216).[117] Whether or not this spectatorial role is present at the beginning of the flight as well, the fall of the other at its conclusion provides Daedalus with a moment of self-recognition as he now has the opportunity of looking down on himself and recognizing the limitations of his art, which he curses in a verb that itself conveys a downward momentum (*devovit*, 234). At the same time

---

[116] See esp. Faber 1998.

[117] Tarrant's (1982.360) argument that the line, which exactly reproduces *AA* 2.73, sits awkwardly in its context within the *Met.* and is therefore a post-Ovidian assertion carries conviction.

it makes the figures of the one who falls and of the one who stays aloft identical to the outside viewer. When Daedalus realizes the death of Icarus, Ovid says, dramatically, that "he saw feathers in the water." These feathers would be simultaneously those Icarus has lost and his own reflected from below.[118] Again we may notice that the mirroring of high in low overlaps with a narrative circularity that takes Daedalus back to his original place. For the gesture of "hiding" the body of a deformed son in a tomb looks uncannily like the service performed for Minos in building the labyrinth. And as that moment marked a transition of fame, when concealing Minos's shame became a sign of Daedalus's celebrity, so here Daedalus's own failure goes together with the immortalization of the "lower" successor, Icarus, who reproduces Minos's authority as he gives his name to both land and sea.

But what kind of model does the triangular relationship between *opus*, artist, and viewer sketched within the Daedalus story provide for how Ovid's text works to define both author and audience? I earlier suggested that Daedalus's works, as the products alternately of subservience and liberation, also imposed this state on others: the labyrinth is itself a prison, the wings a source of freedom for Icarus and, to the extent that Ovid in the *Ars Amatoria* does establish a parallel with his own art, for the poet himself. In the case of the bucolic trio that looks up at the flying Icarus, the sight at once gives them a glimpse of and belief in the existence of higher beings, while it confirms the lowness of their actual status. The fisherman, the shepherd, and the farmer look at Daedalus and Icarus that way precisely because of who they are, and the act of gazing affirms that position both for themselves—in the distance they perceive between themselves and the "gods"—and for the literary audience that watches them watching. We might imagine that social status would similarly function to determine perspective in the case of Ovid's historical audience. Perhaps the slave or freedman might have been more inclined to sympathy for a figure whose own craft, as many of theirs did, provides his means of freedom, and whose punishment is to lose the son who, in the case of Roman freedmen, would have consolidated ascent to the ranks

---

[118] A possible objection to this reading is that seawater is not, in fact, a good reflective medium: hence a discussion among Latinists about the plausibility of Corydon's seeing his image in the Ocean at *Ecl.* 2.26–27 that goes back at least as far as Servius and is summarized in Clausen 1994.73, who intimates that in this case the poet's imagination is not limited by physical realities. In support of this position I might note that Joseph Conrad, who had more firsthand experience of the sea than any Vergilian commentator, nevertheless entitled his memoir *The Mirror of the Sea*. For another possible case of Ovid's referring to a reflection appearing on the sea's surface, cf. the discussion of 4.713, in chapter 7, section 2. In the latter case the reference could be simply to a shadow, and perhaps that might be an acceptable compromise here as well.

of citizens. Or perhaps they more than any other would have been alert to the transgressive nature of Daedalus's flight. The masters, by contrast, might have been secretly pleased to discover in the tale of Perdix a justification for rejoicing in Daedalus's failure and an affirmation of his guilt.

While social perspective may indeed have played such a role in the tale's reception, it is important to remember that, within the narrative, the point of view of the fisherman is obviously shown to be wrong.[119] The reason for this is that he and his fellows recognize only difference, not, as Daedalus himself would do in the case of Icarus, similarity— hence, another model of reading suggested by the passage that has the opposite effect from putting each audience member in her place. Not only does it make it possible for each reader to try on different roles, but it challenges any stable assumptions about social difference by pointing out an identity among figures at different levels, encouraging the high to see themselves lowered and the low exalted. In this way again, Ovid's techniques recall the use of servile characters in genres like satire, where the assumptions of a radical separation based on rank is undercut by figures like the slave Davus who sounds too much like his master.

How the text can act on its audience in this way is a subject that occupies us more fully in the next two chapters. Here, though, I want to conclude by asking what picture the Daedalus story gives of the position of its own author. As in the poem's final movement, here too the poet's authority depends on the success and nature of his work as imitation.[120] In fact, the same imagery of high and low that we have seen energize issues of status within the episode also gives a map for different kinds of creation. The gods make reality, the craftsman copies. This ontological hierarchy takes us from the crown of Ariadne, which really becomes a constellation that only resembles a crown in appearance, to the good craftsman Perdix, whose imitations derive from looking down at fishes, not up at birds, and are themselves free from deception. You would not be mistaken to think that Ariadne's crown was a constellation—it is, and you would never confuse a saw with a sawfish, but Daedalus's wings do blur the bounds between representation and reality. This alternative between viewing imitation as real and its maker as a god and viewing imitation as an artifact and its maker as a craftsman parallels and reaffirms the distinctions we have been describing within the story and suggests how to transfer them to the figure of the poet himself, who is at once a godlike maker of fictions and, when we become conscious of his *ars*, merely pretending to be. Thus, not only is mimesis itself graded according to its

---

[119] See Hoefmans 1994 on how this error mirrors a classic Epicurean theological mistake.

[120] A similar evaluation of Daedalus's failings as imitator will be found in the stimulating analysis of Barkan 1986.74–75.

approximation to reality, but how we view the resulting products determines where we place their maker on the scale the text establishes.

We have seen that this connection between imitation and status is not simply a product of Ovid's text but a crucial feature of the construction and evaluation of identity in Augustan Rome. Throughout the social spectrum, upward mobility could be conveyed by assuming the names (in the case of newly liberated freedmen), clothing, hairstyles, and artistic imagery of those above, and it made the acceptance of this refashioned identity dependent on the recognition of similarity rather than difference on the part of others, whose acquiescence in this recognition would itself be conditioned in part by their own positions. Such a point of view also gives a special poignancy to the failure of imitation ever to be what Daedalus's imagery and the episode's emphasis on instruction (*exempla*, 8.245; *praecepta*, 8.208, 243) suggest that it might be, a steady and reliable means of perpetuating sameness without inviting *invidia*, or contempt.

Ovid's own imitation puts him in competition with a host of superiors: with the gods, if we view it from inside the bounds of its own fictions; with epic predecessors like Vergil, if we view it within the literary historical tradition, but also, from an extratextual, social perspective, with the emperor himself. And within the text of the Daedalus episode a flickering resemblance between the poet and a succession of different characters help to sketch the variety of ways in which the poet himself can be seen. It was, after all, Minos whom the poet had chosen in the *Ars* to figure the difficulties of his poetic task; Icarus, whose playfulness (*lusus*, 8.199) obstructs the completion of his father's work (*opus*, 8.200) and whose ambition prevents him from merely following in the path of another, enacts a whole set of cherished artistic principles that also provide a partial picture of Ovid's authorial stance. [121] And to the unstable figure of Daedalus too, Ovid is both like and unlike. The most telling moment of differentiation comes when Ovid compares the anxious Daedalus at the beginning of his flight to a bird teaching its offspring to fly (8.213–14). All Daedalus's labor to make wings seems grotesquely ineffective in comparison to the poet's mimesis, which turns man into bird with a few strokes of the pen.

But Ovid cannot so easily get himself free from the labyrinth of resemblances that he has created. The simile comparing to musical instruments the crafted wings, which at once accentuate order through the placement of feathers arranged from long to short and violate this order by them-

---

[121] On Ovid's cultivation of puerility as a defining quality of his poetic persona, see Morgan 2003, esp. 77–79.

selves rising (*clivo crevisse ... surgit*, 8.191–92),[122] show Ovid himself as a craftsman forging his own means of ascent. But in this image of the text as Ovid's wings, it is perhaps significant that he has chosen to emphasize the panpipes, a figure for a type of poetry, bucolic, that was rather below epic in literary status. If Ovid's poem is itself set for an upward flight through the genres, perhaps we can try to look down on it as well to see what it is trying not to look like. With its clearly pointed moral, its cautions about overreaching, and its own imperfect transformation of protagonists to animals, this epic *fabula* comes to earth as a narrative not unlike that in which the slave according to Phaedrus masks and reveals himself. And, indeed, the second story in Phaedrus's collection tells of a jackdaw who disguises himself as a peacock, only to face social ostracism when his false feathers fall off. Horace had applied precisely the same fable to a case of literary imitation, when he warns the aptly named high-flier Celsus away from making his reputation by imitating writings "which Palatine Apollo has already received," "lest the crow be laughed at when stripped of his stolen colors."[123]

---

[122] The wing's delineation of and violation of order is particularly interesting in light of the textual crux in 8.190: *nam ponit in ordine pennas / a minima coeptas, longam breviore sequenti*. In the first half of the line the feathers seem to get progressively longer, in the second, shorter ("with the shorter following the long"). Anderson 1972, who does print the line, suggests the possibility of deleting it, following Merkel and Hollis. Tarrant 1982.359–60, who brackets the line in his OCT as an interpolation, adds to a concern with the logic, which within the context of the reading I propose would make sense, an objection to the Latinity of *coeptas* describing the feathers as opposed to the crafted wings.

[123] Horace *Epist*. 1.3.15–20. I am grateful to Ellen Oliensis for reminding me of the applicability of this passage. Cf. too the avian imagery representing literary imitation in *Odes* 4.2.

PART TWO

Spectacle

CHAPTER 3

Homo Spectator: Sacrifice and the Making of Man

As we saw in the preceding chapter, the multiplicity of points of view available on Daedalus's flight also conveys the instability of the poet's own status. At times, his creative abilities make us look up to him as a god; at other times, we see him as a servile craftsman whose skills at best allow him to imitate his betters. But the uncertain, intermediate position occupied by Daedalus, and through a further "imitation" by Ovid himself, mimics in turn the originary position of all human beings within the cosmic order. So too does the poet's double role as a maker of images and as someone who is subject to scrutiny in the very process of doing so. The next three chapters will broaden the focus from Ovid's reflections on his own role as creator to consider the wider mythical and social implications of the "double vision" constructed by Ovidian fiction. I begin with Ovid's account(s) of human creation to demonstrate how the poem presents the human form itself as subject to the same pattern of contrasting readings as the miraculously transformed beings who populate the rest of its pages and how Ovid's account privileges vision as the index of the human condition: men at once are measured and evaluated by how they are seen and measure their own ambiguous place in the cosmos by means of their gaze. This emphasis on visual cognition as the mode for human appraisal of themselves and their world lends a new importance to the poem's construction of its narrative as a series of hermeneutic challenges based on contrasting perspectives. For the most frivolous of ancient epics from such a point of view acquires a uniquely powerful ability to reproduce those experiences and judgments that define the human. Its narrative becomes the ideal vehicle for transmitting the full power of myth. After such general considerations, the next two chapters return us to the specific historical context of the poem's first audience to ask how Ovid's translation of religious and social experience into sight allows us to relate his poem to contemporary uses of spectacle as a means of representing and enacting Roman conceptions of the world.

I. Creations

As Ovid's poem repeatedly confronts us with miraculous and unbelievable changes of shape, the human appearance can come to define the normal and recognizable, what Daphne loses when she becomes a tree. Yet Ovid's presentation of human origins invests even the most identifiable of forms with uncertain and contrasting meanings. By including even one account of human creation, Ovid would ensure the human shape its place among the *nova corpora*, the "unfamiliar bodies" he claims as his subject. But Ovid gives no less than three such stories (1.76–87, 1.156–61, and 1.395–415), and thanks to the complex interrelationship between these different alternatives, the human body prompts the same questions as the poem's more fabulous phenomena: What does "form" reveal about identity? What narratives give it meaning? What connects, and what separates, the resulting physical form from the marvelous history of its origins?[1]

Let us begin by looking more closely at these three accounts of the creation of human beings and the very different implications of each for understanding the nature of man; for the narrative presents each story as an etiology explaining what man is. Thus, after the flood, Deucalion and Pyrrha recreate the race of men out of stones: "From this cause we are a hard race, having experience of labor [*experiensque laborum*], and we give proof [*documenta damus*] of our origin" (1.414–15). The prior account of human origins, to which this final one is linked by reference to earth as the "great mother," is the most alarming of all: Earth covered with the bodies and drenched with the blood of her offspring, the rebellious giants, animates this blood and transforms it into human shape.

On one level, the contradiction between these two accounts of human origins is easily reconciled. The terrible humans created from giants' blood were wiped out by Jupiter in the flood, and "we" are the hard-working descendants of the stones. But this simple solution based on the order of cosmic history cannot so easily separate "us" (and note how Ovid uses the first person only of the later race, 1.415) from the victims of Jupiter's wrath. Elements both in the surface of Ovid's text and correspondingly in the phenomenal world bind the two races of man. As we have seen, the description of earth as our *magna parens* in the final creation story stresses its connection to what went before. More important, both races share the same human form. Thus, to one looking at the

---

[1] For another view of the contrasting origins of the human race as a programmatic introduction to the poem's anthropology, with a fuller account of the intellectual background of the concepts presented in the poem, see Schmidt 1991.25–36. Schmidt includes each of the ages of man as a new origin, and so comes up with eight different accounts, which together offer "a treasure house of human history, his encyclopedic-narrative anthropology" (30), in which each resulting impression of mankind illustrates a part of the story he will tell. Cf. also Tarrant's (2002a) programmatic reading of Ovid's creation story as predicting the continual reemergence of a chaos of collapsing distinctions in the human narratives that follow.

surviving traces of both these primeval acts of generation—that is, to an audience whose perspective is anchored in the present—the "content" of our human "form" remains an open question. And if Deucalion and Pyrrha ensure that our shape is a proof of our harsh origins, so in that earlier creation Earth gives a contrasting significance to our human appearance (*faciem ... hominum*, 1.160), making it "a memorial" of the race of giants she created (*ne nulla suae stirpis monimenta manerent*, 1.159).[2]

When we turn to Ovid's account of the creation of the human form itself, we find a similar set of contradictory possibilities. For Ovid again offers two alternatives for the first creation of man, and the choice between them raises questions about man's relationship to the gods above and the beasts below like those we met in the Daedalus story. Mimicking the later struggle between Earth and the flood survivors over what our appearance recalls, this first creation again juxtaposes two different readings of the human form, each of which can be allied with the intentions of an alternative "creator":

> *Sanctius his animal mentisque capacius altae*
> *deerat adhuc et quod dominari in cetera posset.*
> *natus homo est, sive hunc divino semine fecit*
> *ille opifex rerum, mundi melioris origo,*
> *sive recens tellus seductaque nuper ab alto*
> *aethere cognati retinebat semina caeli,*
> *quam satus Iapeto mixtam pluvialibus undis,*
> *finxit in effigiem moderantum cuncta deorum,*
> *pronaque cum spectent animalia cetera terram,*
> *os homini sublime dedit caelumque videre*
> *iussit et erectos ad sidera tollere vultus.*
> *sic, modo quae fuerat rudis et sine imagine, tellus*
> *induit ignotas hominum conversa figuras.*
>
> (1.76–88)

A more sacred creature than these and one more receptive of a lofty mind was still lacking, and one that could be lord over the others. Man was born, whether that craftsman of the universe, origin of a better world, molded him of divine seed, or the earth still new and just separated from the lofty aether still retained the seeds of her kin, the sky, and the son of Iapetus molded that earth, mixed with rain water, into the form of the gods who temper all things. And though the other creatures are prone and look upon the earth, he gave man a face looking up and ordered him to see the sky and to lift his upright

---

[2] For a complementary reading of the multiple creations of man, see Wheeler 2000.33–35.

countenance towards the stars. Thus, what had been rude and form-less earth was transformed and put on the unknown shapes of men.

The *sive ... sive* construction articulates the two possibilities Ovid offers: we were created either by the "first maker of things" or by Prometheus, son of Iapetus. The first version makes man an integral part of the plan of the cosmos and consubstantial with the gods themselves—born from divine seed. The very differentiation of the maker of the world from those gods enhances this sense of parity: we are not the creations of the gods but creations like the gods. The second, though, relegates human origins to chance, and to the actions of a suspect, and inferior, maker. Ovid's account of creation has stressed above all the discrimination and ordering of the elements, the separation of air from earth and of earth from sea. From this perspective man appears not as the next stage in a process of forming a better world but as the residue of chaos that has escaped the ordering hand of the creator. Rather than relating us to the gods, this second alternative stresses the resemblance between "most divine of ani-mate beings" and "all the other animals" (*sanctius animal*, 1.76 ~ *cetera animalia*, 1.416).[3] They too percolate upward from a mixture of elements within the earth after the flood sent by Jupiter has erased the differentia-tion first imposed on chaos.[4] These offspring of earth are not only alien from the gods but literal rivals to them. The climax of this account of natural history is the generation of the chthonic serpent Python, which Phoebus must defeat to win the oracle of Delphi. The transforming crafts-man that shapes man from earth in this second version bears a mythical history that only reduplicates those questions raised about the position of man. For Prometheus himself can be described as born from the divine seed because he was a Titan and therefore a cousin of the Olympian gods. And despite other more positive views of his role as a benefactor of man fulfilling the instructions of Zeus (e.g., Plato *Prot.* 320c–322d), he more commonly appears as the rival and victim of the highest god (e.g., Hes. *Theog.* 536).

The nature of this second maker, then, is as ambiguous as the very uncertainty about who did in fact create us renders our own. And this is appropriate because Ovid's account makes man at once a crafted prod-uct[5] and himself a craftsman, resembling both of his possible creators. Thus, the case of the phrase *mundi melioris origo* renders it just possible

[3] Cf. Barchiesi 2005.164: "D'altra parte la differenza assoluta fissata tra uomo e animale … è un presupposto carico di ironia tragica, in un poema in cui la frontiera tra animale e uomo si rivelerà così permeabile alla violenza trasfigurante della metamorfosi."

[4] So too Wheeler 2000.21–23.

[5] For the significance of man as the product first of pottery (*finxit*, 1.83), then of sculp-ture (*simillima signis*, 1.406), see Barchiesi 2005.164.

that the words refer not to the numinous *artifex* but to man himself, the grammatical subject of the main clause. The second creation shows man as an image, *effigiem*, but an image of those who themselves order and regulate others.[6] So in the last two lines of the description, it is unclear whether the earth "once rude and formless" being "transformed by put[ting] on the unknown shapes of men" refers to the creation of man or the creation wrought by man changing the appearance of the land through distinctive human arts like agriculture. Both passages similarly point the resemblance between the human animal and his poetic creator Ovid: the verb used of Prometheus, *finxit*, also gives us the word fiction, and the references to transformation belong to the standard language of metamorphosis in the poem.[7]

If man then appears as transformer, and transformed, he occupies a similar double position in relation to the visual processes that become increasingly more prominent as the passage progresses. Man appears as both subject and object of sight, as distinctive for what he looks at as what he looks like. We differ from other animals because of our resemblance to the gods and because we look up at the sky rather than down at the ground.[8] The intermediacy implied by being at once gazers and subject to the gaze of others emerges again from both aspects of vision. Man's resemblance to the gods contributes to his own status in relation to animals, but it throws into relief his subordination to the gods, whom he can merely imitate. He himself becomes a kind of visual puzzle, like another metamorphic product, Daphne, whose form can represent either Apollo or herself. This description of man made in the image of the gods, though, might have recalled to an ancient reader an alternative prioritization of man and god: as we have seen, Xenophanes (fr. 15 DK), had argued that gods resemble men only because they are made by them. If horses had hands, they would show the gods as horses. And so this point of view again exposes the human creator, Ovid, whose own exaggerated anthropomorphization of the divine will be especially evident in his virtuoso presentation of the houses of the better sort of god clustered "on Heaven's Palatine" (1.176).

Man may look like the gods, but he does not look as the gods look, down from the heavens onto earth. In this sense, to make man, as viewing subject himself, the object of an external gaze erases that first sense of likeness to the gods and stresses the difference, again highly marked in all metamorphoses, between how the transformed looks to others and

---

[6] On the Platonic history of this idea, see Robinson 1968.258–59.

[7] Anderson 1996.160.

[8] Schmidt 1991.29 claims that this passage represents the first attestation of the connection between man's resemblance to the gods and his erect posture.

his own point of view. Ovid's account of man looking at the sky opens yet more possibilities for understanding man's place in the cosmos. Does he look up at the sky in wonder and awe or with a Promethean sense of rivalry? And the command that the maker (Prometheus or the *opifex*?)[9] gives man to "raise his countenance to the stars" bears a similar double edge: to look up at the stars from below—compare the similar command Daedalus gives to Icarus—or to raise his visage up to the heavens, so that he is seen as a god himself, as Caesar in the poem's final metamorphosis will be set among the stars. The language of the last line and the situation it describes take us back to the very first element in the description of Chaos itself, which consisted of "one *face* in the whole circle of the cosmos" (*unus toto naturae vultus in orbe*, 1.6). The blurrings of identity that come about because man shares his countenance with the gods result in an epistemological confusion that gives special point to making him the physical product of chaos.

Ovid was not the first to employ vision in this way to diagnose the position of man. Cicero in the *de legibus* uses very similar language, including the same essential contrast between man's sight and appearance, to clarify our purpose.

> *Nam cum ceteras animantes abiecisset ad pastum, solum hominem erexit et ad caeli quasi cognationis domiciliique pristini conspectum excitauit, tum speciem ita formauit oris, ut in ea penitus reconditos mores effingeret.* (*leg.* 1.26)

> For when [nature] had cast all other animals down to seek food, she raised up man alone and roused him to gaze upon the sky as upon his ancient origin and dwelling place, then she formed the appearance of his face in such a way that she might mold in it his concealed character.

Humans here exist both to see and to be seen. We look upon the sky as a sign that our motives are not limited to the physical sustenance of our bodies, and while Cicero does not here spell out the similarity of our appearance in this regard to the gods, he does take our upward gaze as a proof of divine origins. He is therefore defining us by looking at us looking, and this process leads strikingly into his next point, which is precisely that nature made the face to be an index of who we are. That Cicero

---

[9] Fantham 2004.25 suggests that Ovid with *iussit* in line 86 has returned to his first account of human creation and made the *opifex rerum* the source of this command. If so, it is very suggestive that he has left so open the possibility of reading the much less authoritative Prometheus as the source of this injunction. In support of attributing the command to *natura* is the passage of Cicero's *de legibus* (1.26) discussed below, where our erect posture is part of nature's design (Lee 1953.80).

segues so easily from the appearance of man in general to the physiog-
nomic decipherment of face and deportment that played so large a part in
Roman invective links grand philosophic speculation to the very practical
use of appearance as a determinant of status and character in Roman
public life, a connection we also find operative in Ovid's programmatic
account of the loss of human form.

Because the act of gazing and the interpretation of appearances from
outside play such a pivotal role in fixing man's place in the hierarchy of
the cosmos, it is appropriate that the first of the poem's myths of metamorphosis should narrativize these processes by making man's primal
encounter with the divine a tale of misperception and mistaken identity.
We have already discussed the Lycaon story as an example of how Ovid
charges the visual aspects of metamorphosis with an uncertainty that
in turn carries the reader toward the investigation of political questions
on the grandest scale. Here I want to stress the importance of problems
of reading appearances within the narrative and to argue that the story
continues a pattern set up in the account of human origins that places vision at the center of man's relations with his superiors and inferiors. J.-P.
Vernant famously analyzed the complex of myths that Hesiod tells about
Prometheus in his own portrait of the origins of the human condition to
demonstrate that binary oppositions within the narrative between giving
and not giving and between revelation and concealment bind together essential human practices like fire, sacrifice, sexual reproduction, and feasting.[10] The Lycaon story, I suggest, can be read in similar terms as Ovid's
equivalent to the Prometheus story.[11] It mobilizes the same constellation
of actions—feasting, sacrifice, and even fire—to depict the interactions
of gods and men in a way that can, as much as anything in the poem, be
called normative for the events that follow. But the special emphasis Ovid
places on problems of recognition within the encounter between Jupiter
and Lycaon creates a parallel between deciphering the hierarchies of the
cosmos and discovering the "truth" in the appearances presented by his
poem. And if the creation story opposes the visual appearance man offers
others to his own role as gazer, so here we find the human Lycaon in the
same double situation: he tries actively to penetrate the disguise of others
while his own visual contrivances are tested by the king of the gods and
his appearance is put on display as a proof of who he really is.

The similarities between this tale and the accounts of Prometheus in
the Hesiodic poems derive from the structural and thematic positions the
narratives occupy in their respective poems, but they are also—to adopt
the terms used by Vernant—syntactic and sociocultural. Both narratives

---

[10] Vernant 1988.183–202.

[11] A Vernantian reading of the Lycaon episode was anticipated by Feeney 1991.194–95.

operate through establishing a similar pattern of oppositions between parallel actions, and both ultimately function to differentiate man from beasts and gods.

Hesiod divides his account of Prometheus's rivalry with Zeus and its consequences for mankind between his two didactic poems. Thus, the *Theogony* (509–72) tells how, at the assembly of gods and men at Mekone, Prometheus set two deceptive portions of a sacrificed ox before Zeus. A tempting layer of fat concealed only bones while the flesh was wrapped in the meager looking stomach. Zeus accepts the first portion and, in his anger at Prometheus's deception, takes away from mankind the gift of fire. Prometheus steals fire back concealed in a fennel stalk, and Zeus gives an equally deceptive evil in place of the good that has been stolen. That evil is woman, who conceals a "dog's mind" within an attractive form to which all of the gods have contributed enchantments. As the *Theogony* focuses on the choice Zeus makes at Mekone and presents the evil gift he gives to man as the narrative coda, the *Works and Days* (66–125) merely refers to the division of sacrifice and concentrates on the bad choice Epimetheus makes in accepting the gift from Zeus. In the *Theogony*, the stories are presented from a divine perspective, as a proof of Zeus's power, specifically to show that "it is not possible to deceive the mind of Zeus." By contrast in the *Works and Days* the emphasis falls on the consequences for man: Prometheus's trick is the reason that the gods have hidden our livelihood. As such, the Pandora story parallels "another myth" that Hesiod gives as a description of the condition of man, the myth of the ages.

Ovid's Lycaon narrative combines aspects of both Hesiodic stories; indeed, the difference between how the story fits into human history and the uses the gods make of it animates Ovid's tale. Like the Prometheus narrative in the *Theogony*, Lycaon's is a story of crime and punishment deployed by its Jovian narrator with heavy-handed didacticism: "I shall teach what the crime was, and what the vengeance" (*quod tamen admissum, quae sit vindicta docebo*, 1.210). When the king of the gods arrives in human disguise, Lycaon tries to prove his guest's mortality by killing him and his lack of divine omniscience by serving him the flesh of a slaughtered hostage. But Jupiter, at least in the hindsight his position as omniscient narrator allows, was not fooled for an instant. Lycaon's punishment also marks an epoch in human experience—the total destruction of the race. So the presence of destructive evils as an integral element of the cosmos, albeit in the slow-acting form of toil and disease, is the essential message of the Pandora story in the *Works and Days* (101–4). And like the Pandora story, Lycaon's is paired with the account of the ages of man, though placed after rather than before it. Other significant Hesiodic themes in the Lycaon episode are the role of justice—as a Greek king punished by a present Jupiter, Lycaon would be a good warning for the corrupt *basileîs* in the *Works and Days*—and the emphasis on concealment. The first word of the Pandora story is *krupsantes*, the gods have concealed from men the means of life, whereas the god here hides himself. Finally, the fate of Lycaon, fleeing from the house to wander in the wilderness deprived of the power of speech bears some resemblance to the conclusion of the Pandora story, as the evils released from Pandora's jar wander abroad in silence "for Zeus in his wisdom took away their voice" (104). Even the account of Jupiter's destruction of Lycaon's house forms a variation on a Hesiodic theme: Zeus had punished man by depriving him of the gift of fire; Jupiter retaliates against Lycaon by giving him fire in its most destructive guise, as a punishment (*vindice flamma*, 1.230).

The mythical history of Lycaon also well fits him to take on the role of a Prometheus in setting deceptive meats before the king of the gods, and within Ovid's tale the essential symmetry between the protagonists matches the one Vernant has found in the Hesiodic myth. Like Prometheus, Lycaon was renowned as the inventor of sacrificial practices. In the precivilized world of Arcadia, a place that in Augustan literature takes on many of the characteristics of the Hesiodic golden age through its absence of agriculture and meat eating, Lycaon founded the first city, Lycosura, and established the important cult of Zeus Lykaios.[12] Forbes-Irving describes him as a "founder and creator of the present order of human culture" and specifically likens him to Prometheus in the ambiguity with which his innovations are regarded.[13] For as in the case of Prometheus, mythical traditions preserve diametrically opposed accounts of this king as, on the one hand, one who is singled out for his justice and, on the other, one whose desecration of the table of the gods through cannibalism reenacts the separation of gods from men.

But the central point of rivalry in Ovid's account, and the one that brings it closest to the Hesiodic emphasis on concealment and the discrepancies between appearance and substance, is that both the human king and the king of the gods act to distinguish truth from falsehood and to disseminate the resulting truth among their audience. As in the Hesiodic story, the two protagonists play both active and passive roles in relation to appearances, at once acting as creators of illusion and as the audience for the productions of others. Ovid's casting of this opposition between appearance and reality in terms of truth and falsehood, though, relates this mythic theme closely to the problems raised by his own narrative. Jupiter comes to earth because he has heard a terrible report about

---

[12] For the contrasting traditions relating to this ambiguous figure, see Forbes-Irving 1990.90–95 and Piccaluga 1968.31–38.

[13] Forbes-Irving 1990.90.

the age (Ovid's own account of the Iron Age?), which he hopes will prove false (1.212). But not only was the account true; it was less than the truth (1.215). Jupiter's method of proof involves creating a fiction of his own. He will wander the earth in human disguise—*humana ... sub imagine* (1.213).[14] As a result of his experiences, Jupiter claims to have fixed the truth about mortals and requires the assent of the divine audience to the tale that he is even now putting forth. Yet his own use of disguise, or rather of a combination of truth and falsehood (for at the same time that he has disguised himself he also produces signs of his true identity, *signa*, 1.220),[15] inspires a process of testing and proclamation of "truth" on the part of his human audience. Lycaon, who is inspired by a faith in appearances, determines to prove (*experiar*) that the god really is what he appears to be, that Jupiter's own fiction is true.[16] And he will also make what he discovers believable to his subjects: the proof will be clear and public (*aperto*) so that "the truth will not be doubtful" (1.222–23). Again this act, which Jupiter presents as at once impious skepticism about divine communications and a testing of reality through deceptions to rival his own, from a human perspective looks a lot like the way we might expect a pious reader to respond to Ovidian fictions, with the knowledge that they are such because the representation of the gods in human form, as Xenophanes and others insisted, only proves that human workers created them in their own likeness. The importance of this rivalry for Jupiter is signaled by his ironic repetition of the crucial words of the king, *experientia veri*, in describing his impious preparations (1.225). These twin processes of learning and teaching anticipate precisely the language that will be used to interpret the nature of human appearances in the account of the men created by Deucalion and Pyrrha. Derived from the hard realities of rock, we are *experiens laborum*, and we give proof (*documenta damus*) of our origin, 1.414–15. Lycaon's attempt to gain experience of the truth will lead ironically to humanity's unwelcome experience of labors, which confirms their essential condition in the Hesiodic world, and the teaching that the human race will do comes not from the specific publication of what they themselves have learned about divine reality but from furnishing *documenta* to those who look at them. Thus, even as Lycaon attempts to produce his clear proofs, he is being used as a lesson in human impiety by a divine observer.

It has been argued that the presence of such elements as cannibalism, feasting, and sacrifice in Ovid's tale of Lycaon are mere narrative surviv-

---

[14] Note again the "metamorphic" term *imago*; Anderson 1996.173.

[15] A contradiction noted by Due 1974.106.

[16] *experiar deus hic, discrimine aperto, / an sit mortalis; nec erit dubitabile verum.* 1.22–23: "I shall test, with a public proof, whether this is a god or mortal; and the truth will be beyond doubt."

als. In some archaic period, the Greeks may have used myths like those of Lycaon and Prometheus to explore and describe how vital practices like feasting and sacrifice affirm and define relations between man and the gods. But Ovid, however many details of these myths his learning might recover for us, treats such stories above all as a literary phenomena, or morality tales, or psychological case studies, rather than as a complement to a living tradition of ritual. Thus, Forbes-Irving remarks that Ovid's Lycaon story, like his account of Lyncus, has simplistically replaced the ambiguity inherent in Greek accounts of "culture heroes" with morally clear-cut accounts of villainy.[17] But a second look at the Lycaon story can help close this gap by pointing out that Ovid's narrative does indeed demonstrate an interest in the social practices that give such tales a role in defining the very nature of human civilization. And not only does the *Metamorphoses* here reproduce the ambiguity looked for in myths that grapple with man's separation from the gods; the Lycaon myth illustrates precisely how the poet has transferred the ambiguity inherent in practices like sacrifice to the specific phenomena that complicate a reader's response to his own text: the visual uncertainties produced by metamorphosis and the questions of credibility raised by his literary account of it.

As Vernant describes, a fundamental effect of sacrifice, as of the various culinary and reproductive practices Hesiodic myth relates to it, is to "provide the frame of reference within which the human condition is defined in its distinctive characteristics insofar as man differs from the gods and from the beasts."[18] Sacrificial ritual and the meal that follows are thus to be distinguished from the "omophagy and allelophagy of the beasts that devour each other,"[19] as well as from the appetites of gods whose share of the sacrificial meal retains no trace of its fleshliness but has been reduced by fire to pure essence. The sacrificial process thus inevitably makes the definition of man an uncertain and relative one, superior to the beasts but inferior to the gods, and continually invokes this ambiguity through the pattern of partial resemblances that make man at once look like the victims and honorands of the ritual. Like the gods, man shares in profit from the killing of the animal. The extent to which he shares in the responsibility for killing has been a key issue in a variety of modern studies of sacrifice. The god may be said to order the killing and man to be his agent; the animal may itself seem to ask for death by violating some divine injunction.[20] On the other hand, however the killing may be mitigated or justified, the act itself, performed by human agents

---

[17] Forbes-Irving 1990.95. Cf., though, his comments on Ovid's narrative skill at 1990.37.
[18] Vernant 1988.197.
[19] Vernant 1988.198.
[20] Burkert 1983.1–12, e.g.

on a being that despite its differences nevertheless shares our essential presence in the flesh, forms the focus of sacrificial ritual.[21] Hence, an important aspect of sacrificial ambiguity: the ritual establishes differences between the participants only via potential confusion. As many theorists, especially Rene Girard, have stressed, the ordering violence of sacrifice is always shadowed by the possibility of a corrupt sacrifice that erases the set of distinctions that make human civilization possible.[22] These shifting identifications between man, beasts, and gods help to explain why such divergent traditions cluster around the figures, like Prometheus and Lycaon, who are associated with the foundation of sacrifice. The ritual seems to reinforce all the qualities and practices that elevate human life from bestial indiscriminacy but that also keep us from ever attaining the state of the immortals. And, of course, many of the cultural practices that make man unlike beasts, such as the avoidance of incest, are also sources of difference from the gods. In historical terms, sacrifice may provide an essential means of communion with the immortals in the Iron Age present, but it also marks off that present from an ideal golden age—at once a time of divine happiness and bestial simplicity—in which man lived in much closer connection with the gods and in a way that more closely resembled their own mode of existence. Hence, figures like Prometheus and Lycaon are made responsible in myth both for the very institutions that make mortal life possible and for the initial ruptures that separated man from the gods.

This highly schematic overview of what sacrifice might have signified to an ancient participant will already have recalled a number of the central concerns in Ovid's own treatment of man's place in the cosmos. There too we found an interest in establishing the human condition in contradistinction to both gods and beasts, and there too a fundamental ambiguity emerged in the double depiction of humans as kin and agents of the divinities and, alternatively, as their Promethean rivals. These themes also punctuate the Lycaon story, as the king's dangerous resemblance to the gods at the beginning of the narrative gives way to his unequivocal designation as a beast at its conclusion—with the important caveat that both the impiety of his rivalry and the semantic clarity of his transformation emerge from the highly partisan narrative of his divine opponent: if the social and theological function of sacrifice depends on the partici-

---

[21] For the idea of "the comedy of innocence" designed to pretend that human sacrificers bear no guilt for the victim's death, see Meuli 1946.

[22] Girard 1977.36–38; the ambiguities in Girard's interpretation of sacrifice involve the social roles of the participants, specifically the difficulty of fully excluding the sacrificial victim from membership in the community constituted when its violent impulses are united against him, and so of socially constructive violence being distinguished chaotic and indiscriminate violence. See the further discussion in the following chapter.

pants' perception of it, we already see how narrative's capacity to influence its audience's view of its own relationship to the events described can determine their alignment within the hierarchies sacrifice puts in play, and Ovid shows us this by making us so supremely conscious of Jupiter's status as narrator.

Lycaon's attempts to locate his visitor in relation to the community of men also involve the two central acts of sacrificial ritual—killing and eating. Both the king's plots, to kill his divine visitor and to make him the participant at a cannibal banquet, work to the same end of convincing the humans that make up his audience of the stranger's essential likeness to themselves. And yet, if pointing a resemblance to the divine is always available as a positive interpretation of sacrificial ritual, here in the corrupted sacrifice that results from the slaying of an innocent, indeed a human, victim, the arrows are all made to point in the opposite direction. Rather than mortals becoming more like divinities, Lycaon tries to prove that divinities are after all like mortals, and the result is to reduce mortals themselves to the level of beasts. An appropriate result for an action that in its application of the traditional sacrificial procedures of boiling and roasting to the very unsacrificial killing of a human victim not only confuses the tripartite boundaries that legitimate sacrifice reinforces but also erases the distinction between killing and eating in a sacrificial context and mere violence.

But if Lycaon's actions emerge as violations of essential sacrificial prescriptions for establishing the legitimacy of the victim, Jupiter himself deploys two strategies recognized as important to the logic of sacrifice to ensure that the audience views the violence inflicted on Lycaon as justified. By violating the rites of hospitality, Lycaon, like the ox who was made to eat grain at the altar during the Athenian Bouphonia, has earned the wrath of the divinity.[23] At the same time, though, Jupiter downplays his own instrumentality in inflicting violence on the king. Solodow has noted that Jupiter is at pains to present Lycaon's metamorphosis as the spontaneous result of his character, a natural process that provides independent confirmation of Jupiter's judgment of his actions.[24] But the rhetorical effectiveness of the ploy goes hand in hand with its role in justifying sacrifice by making the victim himself responsible for his own death. Jupiter, then, tailors his account of Lycaon's transformation to make us

[23] Interestingly, more positive accounts of Lycaon as a Numa-like inventor of religious institutions makes him responsible for the very conception of the "truce" (Plin. *NH* 7.202: see Piccaluga 1968.34.). The justification of sacrifice through the guilt of the victim, most famously exemplified by the Athenian Bouphonia (see, e.g. Meuli 1946, Burkert 1983.36–38), also figures in the explicit account of sacrificial origins offered by Pythagoras toward the poem's conclusion (15.111–15, *et prima putatur hostia sus meruisse mori ...*).

[24] Solodow 1988.168–69.

respond to it with neither sympathy for the "beast" Lycaon nor blame for his own actions, which we hear as part of an audience of gods.

Such manipulation of perspective becomes all the more striking when we consider the story not within the frame of Jupiter's argument for cosmic destruction but within the larger one of Ovid's presentation of the gods. For here we meet a glaring contradiction of one of the tenets of sacrifice most frequently affirmed in the Roman epic tradition, that of substitution. In the *Aeneid*'s account of the foundation of the Roman state, the logic of sacrifice allows a single victim to absorb the vengeance that a divinity would otherwise visit on the entire community. Thus, Palinurus, and—ironically—many others, becomes the "one" whose life is claimed in place of the many.[25] But Ovid's Jupiter does not make Lycaon into a scapegoat. He does the exact opposite by treating him as an *exemplum* whose individual conduct demands the death of many: *occidit una domus, sed non domus una perire / digna fuit* (1.240–41). And this occurs despite the fact that according to Jupiter's own narrative the populace did not share in the king's impiety but rather properly recognized the divinity and performed *pia vota*. We may also note that if the god's own view of what Lycaon has done stresses the bestial aspects of Lycaon's actions as a sign and corollary of his perversion of sacrificial ritual, Ovid's account of the god's speech effects a similar boundary crossing by lowering gods to the status of men. Nowhere are the gods more ruthlessly anthropomorphized than in this opening scene, and no more problematic human characteristic emerges from Ovid's depiction of them than the very human passion that inspires Jupiter's revenge plot, which as we have seen is also the point where his own observance of sacrificial principles breaks down. One objection that the minority raises to Jupiter's plan is that it will lead to a cessation of (bloodless) sacrifice: *quis sit laturus in aras tura* (1.248–49), a question that is as relevant outside the frame of its narrative context as within. If these are the gods, why do we worship them?

My analysis has so far shown that references to ritual practices, especially to sacrifice, within the Lycaon narrative are more than inert survivals. Considering the whole of Jupiter's narrative in light of the sacrificial patterns alluded to within the story helps to clarify both the god's rhetorical strategies and their weaknesses. But the relationship between sacrifice and narrative proves even more profound. A larger interdependence and, indeed, equivalence emerges between the acts of representation and the performance of sacrifice. Within the frame of Jupiter's own tale, accounts of sacrificial violation serve to depict Lycaon as Jupiter wants him to

---

[25] *Aen.* 5.815, *unum pro multis dabitur caput.* On the theme of sacrificial substitution in Roman epic, see Hardie 1993.19–56.

appear. But to recognize such a device at work is also to recognize its reversibility. Lycaon's sacrifice is corrupt only if we accept the god's depiction of it. Assenting to the truth of the god's representation of Lycaon as a wolf necessitates and reinforces the coloring that Lycaon's actions take on when viewed in the light of sacrificial practice. On the other hand, to adopt Lycaon's point of view and see Jupiter as a man—and the contrivances of the human narrator and Ovid themselves abet such a reading—levels the playing field between them and reduces sacrifice to mere rivalry. The truth of Jupiter's account is thus bound up also with a reading of the image that concludes it, of seeing the fantastical metamorphosis of Lycaon as not only factually true but also telling the truth about Lycaon. Earlier I observed that Ovid particularly highlighted the credible representation of reality as a point of overlap between divine and human capacities and hence at once a point of resemblance and rivalry between god and man. Within the Lycaon story, our uncertainty about how to judge Lycaon's *experientia veri* offers another essential parallel between this process of constructing truth and the ambiguous Promethean practices that at once bring us closer to and mark us off from the divinity. All the more so since Lycaon's *experientia veri* consists in the plan to kill one man and the actual sacrificial treatment of another. Ovid's narrative framework here shows yet another way in which the very process of representation assumes a sacrificial dimension, for while beasts are present as neither narrators nor narratees, the overlap between Jupiter's divine audience and Ovid's human one raises the possibility of hearing Jupiter's account as a god or of supplying the very different human perspective that an awareness of Ovid's own narrative role promotes.

But if the act of balancing the different available narrative perspectives on Lycaon—Ovid's, Jupiter's, and indeed Lycaon's own—requires a working out of the likenesses and differences between man and gods resembling that at the center of sacrificial ritual, precisely the same procedure is required in the case of the different visual perspectives whose narratives make available the spectacle of Lycaon's metamorphosis. The greatest "proof" Jupiter offers of the bestiality of man is in fact the transformation of Lycaon. Believing that Jupiter's story is true requires believing that Lycaon is a true wolf, that his new visual appearance, like the *humana imago* Jupiter takes on as a disguise, nevertheless exposes *signa* that confirm his essential identity. That this view of Lycaon in turn requires the shutting out of other ways of perceiving his appearance, as well as of other points of view for telling his story, shows the reversibility of the relationship between seeing and believing here, anticipating the mutual implication of interpreting image and interpreting narrative to be developed in the Io story (see chapter 1). If you do not believe Jupiter, you are less likely to see Lycaon as really a wolf; if you see Lycaon as something other than really a wolf, you are less likely to endorse Jupiter's view of the necessity of a universal cataclysm to wipe out the human species. Thus, not only does this first example of the most common metamorphic pattern in the book, where divine action imposes an irreversible transformation on mortals, signal the essential contrast between subjective and objective perspectives on the images that result from metamorphoses, but its juxtaposition with the various accounts of the creation of man connects this contrast with the uncertain nature of the human condition itself and identifies the viewing of metamorphosis—which is bound together with the acceptance of fictions—as the poem's distinctive means of addressing the larger issue of man's place in the cosmos. In the account of the creation of the human form—and note again how much this account is focused precisely on external appearance—we observed the essential difference between looking at man and looking as man and traced the different implications each perspective possessed for seeing humanity. This double perspective, of course, easily translates to the experience of Ovid's readers who are—with the possible exception of the imperial family!—all human, and who will also be reading about humans. And if, as I suggested in the previous chapter, the reception of such external images becomes itself an act of creation and construction, then the similar double role of man as both created object and, by extension, a creator and transformer of the world, whose own maker Prometheus is in turn simultaneously divine maker and victim, adds a further connection between the reception of Ovid's poem and the processes he has singled out as essentially human.

The seemingly abstract parallels I suggested between the functioning of sacrificial ritual and the reception of Ovidian narrative can also be seen in action in Lycaon's transformation. Indeed, the visual process we have defined as crucial to reading metamorphosis was also a potentially important determinant of the participant's response to sacrifice. I say potentially because we have no real first hand Roman accounts of what being at a sacrifice was like and must therefore rely on theoretical deductions from the nature of the ritual itself, which can also be supplemented by fictional narratives of mythical sacrifices. The very appearance of the victim in sacrifice comprises elements that blur the distinction between bestial victim, divine honorand, and human celebrant. As domestic animals, the victims occupy an intermediate category between truly wild and unmodified nature and the humans whom they aid in transforming nature through agriculture. Their decorations, such as fillets and crowns, also echoed the visual differentiation that set apart the very religious officials who would preside over their death and consumption. At the same time, basic elements in the victim's appearance, like its sex, age, and color, recalled the form of the divinity to whom it was offered. Sacrificial ritual, like Ovidian metamorphosis, also drew attention in a more literal fashion to the relationship between outer appearance and inner substance. Walter Burkert's suggestion that the exposed viscera of the victim resemble those of man creates another visual bridge between the human and the bestial.[26] The killing of the victim inevitably fosters a similar identification because it affirms that the animal shares the essential characteristic that defines humanity in relation to the gods, mortality. The inner form of the victim, however, also provides the most explicitly hermeneutic moment of the ritual, for the appearance of its organs is read by the *haruspices* as a sign of the state of relations between gods and man. Looks alone could be deceiving: an unblemished heifer might bear a diseased liver. Thus, this glimpse within, even as it potentially unites spectator and victim, affirms the truth about the human community and its standing in respect to the gods.

What Ovid's audience sees in Lycaon similarly unites visual experience with religious understanding. To affirm the essential bestiality of Lycaon, that his outer form reflects his inner form, consolidates solidarity between man and the gods—who are appearing in their own most human guise. Lycaon was fundamentally cut off from the very category of the human even when he looked like one: his genesis from the blood of giants and the destruction of virtually the entire race in consequence of his crime further insulate us from him. Indeed, like many a sacrificial victim, Lycaon in this regard bears comparison to the scapegoat figure that, by being made responsible for the pollution afflicting the community, purifies it by his death. His very punishment and the results that follow exempt us from accepting his cannibalism and hubris as tendencies that all humans share. Except, as always, Ovid has complicated things, for Lycaon is also the polar opposite of a scapegoat. Not only will his crimes recur among generations after the flood, but, more important, he does not die on behalf of the many. Rather his crime leads to the destruction of his entire society. The recognition of Lycaon, by contrast, as still fundamentally human despite his shape, like the overidentification with the sacrificial victim, has the effect of realigning the human reader's sympathies by exposing the bestiality of the gods. Indeed, Jupiter's last words highlight the phenomenon of bestiality itself in a way that makes it uncertain whose "face" manifests it. In describing how Lycaon's behavior indicates the character of the entire human species, he exclaims, "as far as the earth extends, the fierce Erinys holds sway" (*fera regnat Erinys*, 1.241). This attempt further to put a bestial face on humanity can do so, however, only by creating a "wild" divinity. And because the Erinys herself appears as a representative not only of mad criminality but

---

[26] Burkert 1983.20.

of revenge, and specifically of revenge that repays crime with crime, the characterization seems to reflect back on the god who produces it, inviting us to ask how far the civilizing "justice of Zeus," whereby punishment sanctioned by the highest divinity preserves the rules and distinctions of the human community and the cosmos, stands from the wild justice of vengeance that erases the lines between victim and killer.

The attempt that I have made to show Ovid's creative engagement not just with the narrative details of myth but with its theological dimensions and the ritual practices that inform them stands in contrast to much recent work on the mythical aspects of the *Metamorphoses*. It may seem to many readers to pull against the tone of the poem by freighting with seriousness a work that in these very passages questions whether it can ever be taken seriously. At the same time, the readings of sacrifice that I have put forward may seem doubly remote from Ovid's world, first, because they were originally developed to interpret the practices of archaic Greece and, second, because of the great gulf that is felt to divide the Roman experience of myth, whose narratives and human actors were overwhelmingly Greek, from any cult practices. For Ovid, myths were "texts,"[27] not only because he acquired them from his reading or because they were perceived as elements that relate his work to literary predecessors but more fundamentally because the very edifice of myth as a discourse about the gods was perceived to belong intrinsically to the realm of reading and performance.[28] Thus, Varro in his influentially systematic treatment of Roman theology famously broke his subject down into three theologies: the gods of the state (the focus of cult), the gods of nature (the allegorical use of the gods to describe the cosmos), and the gods of the stage (the representation of the gods familiar from poetic and dramatic representations of myth). Varro's approach to the gods stands behind an important modern assumption about how the ancients organized their religious experience, which has come to be known as "brain balkanization." This attractive term, first developed by Paul Veyne and influentially applied to Roman literary experience by Denis Feeney, assumes a radical separation between the ways the Romans conceptualized the gods on the basis of discursive context. Thus, a Roman who was philosophically skeptical about the existence of the gods could nevertheless participate actively in cult or enjoy—and think seriously about—the representation of the gods in tragedy. The model of the "balkanized brain," while very productive for the study of Roman literature in

---

[27] A definition that must be expanded to include "images," as we discuss in the next chapter.

[28] Graf 2002.110.

general,[29] has nevertheless served to reinforce a preexisting *relegatio* of Ovid to the shores of the literary. Thus, while Ovid's use of myth is often viewed as nothing short of revolutionary, his accomplishment, however differently defined, always consists in reestablishing myth within a new system of meaning to compensate for its separation from cult. Ovidian myth becomes a medium for anthropological description, manifesting a compendium of human behaviors that provide a new and culturally free-floating source of value for myth, but one directed above all at human experience and relying on essentially narrative properties.[30]

However, there are limits to how absolute such intellectual segregation can be, and Ovid's treatment of the gods does not restrict itself to the territory of the mythical. On the contrary, throughout his poem he invites readers to measure very different conceptualizations of the gods against one another. Jupiter as the sky god, as the head god of the state religion, and as the rambunctious rapist of Greek myth may well all exist in different spheres of experience, but the very fact that they share the same name necessarily problematizes their relationship to one another. All provide competing answers to the question of who or what Jupiter is. I have already looked at how Ovid's exaggeration of the problem of the "split divinity" provokes theological speculation within the text. And the first book of the poem abounds in similarly striking juxtapositions of the philosophical, cultic, and "mythic": the very council meeting where Jupiter recounts Lycaon's crimes raises precisely these issues by its relentless imposition of contemporary social and political fashions on the Olympians. Such hyper-anthropomorphization might at first seem precisely to establish Ovid's works within the realm of the "fabulous" and deflect serious theological speculation even as it seems to turn aside a political reading of Jupiter. But I would argue that the effect of this description is precisely to put the Greek gods in the center of contemporary Rome, to foreground questions not only about how Greek myth describes imperial Rome but also about the connections between literary descriptions of the gods and immediate human experience. The whole phenomenon of divine metamorphosis, which throughout the poem forms an essential complement to the metamorphosis of humans, programmatically addresses this issue, for in taking on human form, the divinities are also moving precisely into the sphere of the mythical. And the error that leads to Lycaon's destruction comes from his unwillingness to recognize the possibility of such divine boundary crossing. Thus, while Ovid certainly

---

[29] Especially with the qualifying recognition that these discursive spheres can never operate in isolation from one another, see Feeney 1998.21. For the concept itself, see Veyne 1988.41–57 and Feeney 1998.14–21.

[30] See Feeney 1998.70–74, citing Schmidt 1991.70–78.

expands the relevance of myth as a means of describing human action, as Feeney and Schmidt describe, he does not also strip it of its theological significance or of its relation to cult.

On the contrary, I find Ovid's most striking transformation of myth is precisely his use of metamorphosis to reproduce the open-ended and immediate experience of the divine offered by sacrifice through purely narrative means. Ovid's treatment of the gods, then, rather than making the best of the cultural isolation of myth from other forms of religious experience, actively challenges such absolute distinctions and ultimately appropriates for his own literary representation the issues and very modalities of cult. Indeed, the traditional decoupling of myth from religion only gives greater power to the effect Ovid achieves. For the preconception that mythical gods cannot be "real" at once contributes the alternative perspective that lends complexity to Ovid's mimesis and, at the same time, makes the emergence of some element of divine power in a fictional context all the more astonishing.

But what might the significance of this move be for a Roman audience? How relevant are Vernantian and Girardian readings of Greek sacrifice for understanding its role five hundred years later in a different society? Put in even larger terms, what precisely is it that ritual might contribute to the reading of Ovid? In terms of the central moments of sacrifice, there are no essential differences between Roman practice and Greek.[31] There were, of course, infinite ritual variations within as well as between each culture, and it is probably fair to say that, from the point of view of the individual participant, every single experience of sacrifice was different. But the essential modes of participation, as spectators, consumers, and beneficiaries of the accord with the gods bought through the victim's life, were the same at Rome as at Greece, and so too were the three essential actors, the human sacrificers, the animal victim, and the divine honorand. Of course, these similarities do not imply that sacrifice "meant" the same thing in every circumstance.[32] It almost certainly did not have the same effect on any two participants at any given sacrifice, and recent anthropological studies of ritual have stressed not its conservatism but its extraordinary adaptability to changing historical contexts.[33] Nevertheless, what I might call the syntax of sacrificial practice, the process of balancing identification with and difference from victim and honorand through which the participant interprets the experience, remains essentially the same.

[31] "In structure, though not in detail, the ritual was closely related to the Greek ritual of sacrifice": Beard, North, and Price 1998.1.36.

[32] See Feeney 1998.120.

[33] Bloch 1986.

Nor is it the case that sacrifice played a less important role in the more "sophisticated" culture of Augustan Rome with its complex systems of religious thinking than it had in Hesiod's Ascra. The imagery of the new principate abounded in representations of sacrifice, making this ritual process an essential component of how Augustus defined his own position in the community.[34] And lest we think that these images were aimed at a very different audience from the cultural elite addressed by epic poetry, sacrificial imagery figures largely throughout Vergil's *Aeneid*. How one makes sense of that epic's final act, the killing of Turnus, will depend in large measure on the response generated by these sacrificial patterns.[35]

Recent attempts to interpret the function of representations of religious ritual in Latin poetry have met with criticism from a number of perspectives. Scholars who make such arguments are accused of overlooking both the representational aspect of literature and, even more crucially, the ancient authors' awareness of the distance that separates text from reality.[36] Thus, even passages that seem to locate their reader at an actual ritual performance can do no such thing and make their failure as apparent as they make their ambition. More fundamentally, the very impetus to develop such arguments has come under attack as a diminution of the power of literature itself, which, especially to scholars dazzled by the results of anthropological approaches and dissatisfied with the strongly formalist bent of Latin literary studies in the middle years of the past century, can be redeemed only by embedding it in other cultural practices that seem somehow more real.[37]

In light of these challenges, let me be more precise about the role I am claiming for sacrificial imagery in Ovid's poem. It does not consist in the subordination of the reading experience to some direct encounter with reality. There is no master sacrifice that will function as touchstone for understanding Ovid's effects properly, or that will clarify the poem's ambiguities. It is, however, important not to overstate the limits to the mimetic powers of the poem. Of course, when a poet asks his audience to "behold" a ritual procession, the injunction can always remind his audience that such direct visual experience is just what a poem cannot offer. But to concentrate only on the "absence" of the represented strips all mimesis, not only textual and not only of rituals, of its power. A museum visitor standing before a Vermeer will hardly thank a cicerone for reminding her that the people in the painting are not actually there. And no artist was more interested in the simultaneous affirmation and denial

---

[34] See esp. Zanker 1990.102–35 and Elsner 1991a.
[35] E.g., Hardie 1993.19–56 and Bandera 1981.
[36] See esp. Feeney 2004.4–5.
[37] E.g., Feeney 1998.116.

of the magic of mimesis than was Ovid. It is precisely the tension between acceptance of and resistance to the represented world that energizes all of the interpretations I have and will offer throughout this book. The impetus to move through the text into a "real" world beyond is not a historical accident of our contemporary intellectual climate but a response that Roman literature itself invites, even as it invites interrogation of it.

What I am arguing here is not for the erasure of literary illusion to recover some fundamental and explanatory authenticity but for the mobilization of references to this experience to create a dialogue between reading and ritual through which the responses generated by each are at once transformed and delineated. The reader of the Lycaon story would never confuse what the narrative describes with any ritual she had witnessed. The transformation of a human being into a wolf cannot happen in reality; wild animals were excluded from the list of sacrificial victims, nor are there any ritual preparations that would help locate what Lycaon suffers as part of a sacrifice. There are, however, internal allusions to elements of sacrificial practice—the *pia vota* of the crowd, the combined boiling and roasting of the Molossian hostage, the shared feast between Jupiter and Lycaon, and the equivalences between Ovid's Lycaon and his Hesiodic counterpart Prometheus further underline the significance of these references. This in turn prepares the reader to recognize both how questions potentially generated by sacrifice—for example, the guilt of the victim, the legitimacy of the killing—are reproduced from such literary devices as the introduction of a highly partisan internal narrator (Jupiter) and, crucially, the combination of distance and identification allowed by contrasting visual perspectives on transformation.

The deployment of the sacrificial dynamic as a comparand for what Ovid achieves through these literary strategies, however, gives them a distinctive importance, and this is not simply because of some innate glamour of ritual experience. Precisely because a recognition of sacrificial experience within this highly different scene represents such a dramatic crossing of boundaries, it helps to ensure that we do not read the transformation of Lycaon as an unbelievable *fabula*. It makes clear, in purely literary terms, that Ovid's problematic epic can also address the themes of a Hesiod and, like its Vergilian predecessor, invite reflection on the relationship between the individual and community through depictions of ambiguous victims. At the same time, it also becomes a demonstration of the capacities of literary representation—and of its incapacities as well—in relation to other contemporary modes of display and performance. For, as we consider more fully later in this chapter, sacrificial ritual functioned not only to define the hierarchical position of humanity but also to delineate hierarchical relations within human society. The boundary crossing at work in reading literary representations of metamorphoses as comparable to sacrificial ritual thus also relates to a claim to social authority on the part of its author. In the following chapters, we will look more at how Ovid generates a dialogue between what his text can make a reader see and other forms of ritual that operate largely through vision, such as theatrical performances, triumphs, and gladiatorial displays. But to recognize the importance of such a dialogue within the Ovidian corpus as a whole, there is no need to look farther than the *Fasti*. One important result of the interpretation that I offer here will be to recover a new element of complementarity between Ovid's twin poetic encounters with myth and with ritual. Briefly, if the *Fasti* textualizes ritual, transforming the significance of actual ritual practices by embedding them in a complex and open-ended nexus of explanatory narratives, the *Metamorphoses* ritualizes texts, by making clear that the very phenomenon of literary representation can inspire in its audience the same kinds of social and theological speculation as ritual.

But if the means by which sacrificial ritual poses questions remain fairly constant, at least within the scope of Greco-Roman culture, the questions themselves, together with the answers provoked and even the interest in addressing them at all, vary with time and circumstance.[38] Thus, beyond registering an alertness to the deep structures of sacrifice, Ovid brings his own distinctive emphases to its representation and embeds it in the very contemporary thematic interests of his poem. Two interrelated issues emerge in connection with sacrifice in the episodes we have just examined that in turn clarify their significance for the work's larger political concerns. The first is an analogy with sensory and cognitive perception. Within the Lycaon narrative, the king's ritual innovations all have a heuristic aim; he wants to affirm something about the place of man in the world and at the same time demonstrate it to others. So too in the rival demonstration Jupiter offers to his audience, the meticulously cataloged phenomenology of Lycaon's transformation has a similar function of revealing a truth that his own audience will accept as true. Because Ovid's audience would not be able to taste the meat at a sacrificial feast, can come closer to realizing a visual description, and closest of all to sharing in evaluating the plausibility of a narrative, this centering of sacrifice on what is seen and what is described, in place of, for example, what is consumed, enhances his own audience's potential participation in the event. But such an emphasis on the visual is more than a matter of authorial convenience. Through sculptural representations like the Ara Pacis, as well as literary ones like the bougonia at the end of the *Georgics*, and Livy's account of the fetial sacrifice, mediated depictions of sacrifice became focal points of Augustan culture, all the more valuable perhaps

---

[38] A point repeatedly stressed by Feeney, e.g., 2004.11.

because their potential audience surpassed the limits of space and time that bound even the grandest and most frequently repeated ritual. In highlighting the overlaps between sacrificial experience and the reception of representations, Ovid thus draws attention to an important aspect, even transformation, in the means by which ritual reached its community.

This leads into the second of our larger themes: Ovid's emphasis on the role of art in both human creation and the creation of humans and the consequent designation of artistic representation as a sphere of rivalry between man and the gods. Obviously, this is not an Ovidian invention—think only of the role of mimetic technai in Hesiodic accounts of the struggle between gods and man, or the Aeschylean Prometheus's invention of all the arts by which man modifies nature. But from the beginning of Ovid's account of human origins, the fundamental nature of human identity is approached through questions about the identity of our creator and what we ourselves are meant to create. Equally significant is our simultaneous adoption of an active and passive creative role; human beings' intermediate cosmic status finds a mirror in the indeterminacy of their position as something made by others and something that constructs its own images. As we have seen, this introduces a fundamental competition in perspectives both within Ovid's poem—between the perspectives of human characters and the perspectives adopted by the narrative on human characters—and in our evaluation of the status of the poem itself—between an acceptance of Ovid's representation as the truth about the world and an awareness of it as a highly personal poetic construct. But again it would be misleading to deduce from this that Ovid has simply made his poem about poetic creation. For, as we saw in the preceding chapter, the figure of the craftsman becomes in Ovid's hands an essential tool for describing the conditions of identity in Augustan Rome. Not only has the simultaneous reception and reprojection of images become itself an important means by which each individual conveys who he is. In metaphorical terms as well, the extreme hierarchization of levels of creation within the poem, where no figure can escape contextualization in someone else's story and everyone, even Augustus, is liable to be judged a mere imitation of his betters, also links problems of representation to contemporary status anxieties. That Ovidian man should encounter the gods only through a mutual struggle to establish the truth of images thus seems a very Augustan updating of archaic creation myth.

Here, however, it is again important not to impose restrictive limits on the poem's scope by reading its theological dimension simply as a projection of the political. That the terms in which Ovid defines god and man are conditioned by circumstances of history and class does not mean that they are not legitimate attempts to investigate the categories of god and man. Characteristically, Ovid combines in this very section of his poem his most overt attempt to address "timeless" questions of human identity with the narrowest and most topical political allegory. Thus, the first appearance of the Olympian gods in the poem, the very assembly at which Jupiter presents his tale of Lycaon, introduces the gods tricked out with all the manifestations of political status in the new empire. They dwell on heaven's Palatine, they conduct business according to the procedures of the Senate, and they display an exaggerated horror at Jupiter's personal endangerment that calls to mind the public displays of outrage after attempts on the life of Caesar. This is not the place to offer a prolonged analysis of the scene, but its role in energizing a number of the poem's central narrative strategies should be clear. Again the contemporary frame of reference draws attention to Ovid's role in fashioning his gods at the very moment when his Jupiter most demands acceptance of his own "truth." At the same time, this investigation of the authority of the Ovidian narrator has implications outside the frame of the poem as well. For the diminution of the gods to pale imitations of the imperial Senate also offers a way of responding to the actual uses of Olympian divinities in self-glorifying depictions of the new imperial order. However, the narratological and political implications of how we read these gods form a piece with the creation as a whole. As we have seen, the problems of accepting gods who look too human again forms a bridge between the response generated by Ovid's poem and the problem facing a Lycaon. And our own inclinations simply to dismiss this Jupiter on the Palatine as the most secondary and derivative of any conceivable "gods" powerfully demonstrate larger questions about the possibility that man has never done anything other than invent gods after his own image and that human beings can never achieve any apprehension of the divine through human craft. Here as well, to catch some trace of religious experience in Ovid's poem illustrates another dimension of the marvelous paradox of finding truth in fiction.

II. Pythagoras

The most explicit presentation of "sacrificial theory" in the *Metamorphoses*, indeed anywhere in extant Latin poetry, comes as part of Pythagoras's four-hundred-plus line attack on meat eating. Here I want to show first how closely this passage engages with the themes and images developed in the poem's opening presentation of the origins of man and the transgressions of Lycaon. Again, contrasting focalizations articulate the radically different alternatives that sacrificial ritual makes available for "reading" the place of man in the cosmos. Finally, I consider how the use of Pythagoras as an internal narrator affects our understanding of the relation between Ovid's text and real ritual performance.

However one understands the relationship between the character of Pythagoras, the *Metamorphoses'* narrator, and Ovid's authorial perspective, there is no doubting the structural importance of the speech within the work.[39] Taking up the entire first half of book 15, Pythagoras's speech bridges an essential transition between Greek legendary material and Roman history and, within itself, recapitulates the movement of the entire poem from the first beginnings of humanity to the poet's own present. Pythagoras's very identity and his mystical subject matter link Ovid's work to key moments in the Roman epic tradition that focus specifically on the authority of the poet.[40] Thus, Ennius evokes Pythagorean eschatology to justify his writing of epic as the reincarnation of Homer. Critical response to the passage has been as varied as its own contents and stylistic registers and ranges between those who regard it as Ovid's exposition of a theory of nature that gives new seriousness to his theme of transformations and those for whom the parody of philosophical epic by one of the weirdest figures in ancient philosophy provides a final deflationary move. A full assessment of Pythagoras's credibility and its impact on Ovid's construction of his own poetic voice would go well beyond the scope of this argument. What I would assert here, though, is that Ovid's Pythagoras offers a comprehensive reading of the poem, and the act of assessing that reading allows each member of the poet's audience to retrace in turn her own experience of the work.

Pythagoras intends his instruction to have an impact on two practices, dining and sacrifice. His notorious insistence on abstinence from animal food made Pythagoras seem something of a crank, and the prominence of this motif here has been cited as evidence that Ovid presents him from the outset as a figure not to be taken seriously.[41] Yet it is important to remember that meat eating signified much more than a life choice or wellness regimen. It was intimately connected with the ritual of sacrifice in two important senses. First, "metonymically" the consumption of victims formed an important element in Roman public sacrifice, and one that, as John Scheid in particular has emphasized,[42] acted especially to establish social solidarity within the community of sacrificers. These sacrificers became "participants" in the sense that they literally received a part of the victim for consumption. Second, the Roman use of meat eat-

---

[39] On this subject, see esp. Segal 2001 and Myers 1994.136–66.
[40] Hardie 1995.
[41] Solodow 1988.163–68.
[42] Scheid 1984.

ing to establish the boundaries between insider and outsider corresponds to a conceptual and "metaphoric" connection between sacrifice and meat eating traceable in Greek literature and thought. Like sacrifice, humans' consumption of cooked meat marks their intermediate position between gods and beasts. And Pythagoras's argument against meat eating makes as much of this distinction as any Vernantian student of ancient religion might wish. To consume flesh is potentially to consume not "another" but a member of the same species as you. It means therefore to take on the characteristics of wild beasts. Similarly, using the gods as justification for sacrifice collapses the divine into the human by attributing our own (bestial) emotions to them. The result of meat eating, then, becomes a conceptual chaos mirroring the physical one produced by the very process of ingesting animal flesh.

And this alternative view of the "proper" rituals of ancient and religious and social practice is rooted in turn in a more fundamental set of assumptions about one of the central epistemological questions raised by the poem, the relationship between appearance and identity. Thus, one could argue, against Pythagoras's practical teaching, that it is merely his own distinctive and "antisocial" assumption of an essential sameness—where, if one accepts appearance as a valid index of reality, only difference appears—that brings such moral confusion to practices that would otherwise offer a clear map of the hierarchies both within the cosmos and within Roman society. And here it is important to note that the exiled Pythagoras brings the same perspective to appearances as the rebel Arachne. Things are not what they seem, and very different beings can look out from the forms that they bear. Where Arachne placed divine subjects in wolf's clothing and preserved human identity by presenting victims as unchanging, Pythagoras goes a step closer to Ovid by embedding human consciousnesses in nonhuman forms, and a step closer to "us" by insisting that human identities potentially look out not only from the specific cows figured in the myth of Io, for example, but from "real" cows like the ones lowing on their way to the altar.

This transition from the mythical, specific, and fictional to the present, general, and real corresponds with many other structural features of Pythagoras's discourse. As we have seen, the speech comes at the moment when the poem's focus shifts notably from Greek myth to Roman history. And as Pythagoras himself moves from the distant origins of sacrifice and the nature of man to predict Rome's future, he provides one possible model for how the reader might understand her own historical context in light of what she has so far read in Ovid—a notoriously problematic model as we have seen, because it presents Roman power as paradoxically unchanging in a world where everything is transformed. The passage's generic nature comes into play as well, for didactic poetry insists more explicitly than any other genre on the connection between text and practice. The reader having received instruction from the poem must then go out and apply it in the conduct of his life and the performance of his work. Pythagoras's particular insistence on the practical consequences of his teachings, the avoidance of animal food, receives an additional didactic immediacy through the intermittent presence of an addressee, Numa, who like the high-status Memmius in Lucretius's epic, comes in and out of focus as a possible reference for the second-person pronouns in the teacher's speech—an indeterminacy fully appropriate to Numa's own quasi-fictional status.

Thus, both the form and content of Pythagoras's speech invite attention to the relation between text and context, and this has a particular importance for understanding the representation of sacrificial ritual in the passage. As part of his effort to recontextualize literary production in ancient Rome, Thomas Habinek has recently suggested that sacrificial ritual was an important area of mastery for the poet (*vates*) within archaic culture.[43] If so, the poet or singer was significantly present at the performance of public rites in a way that, with the possible exception of Horace's role at the secular games, cannot be matched in any better-attested period. Here I suggest that within Pythagoras's speech Ovid creates analogies between the visual dynamics of sacrificial practice and the ambiguities of his own narratives of metamorphosis that allow his own vatic utterance to be recentered in the religious life of the larger community.[44] In presenting sacrifice, as we shall see, from the visual perspective of the victim, Ovid's Pythagoras on the one hand demonstrates how to write sacrifice, by concentrating on an aspect of actual ritual experience that can be reproduced in literature, as opposed again to the consumption of sacrificial meat that is Pythagoras's actual subject. At the same time, he allows for authentic sacrificial practice to be seen as an extension of the metamorphic theme of the poem and so to echo and reinforce its own negotiations of the place of the individual within the physical and political worlds.

Ovid relates the ambiguous narratology of metamorphosis to ritual experience in Pythagoras's account of the sacrificial act itself, which concludes the opening indictment of meat eating:

> *nec satis est, quod tale nefas committitur: ipsos*
> *inscripsere deos sceleri numenque supernum*

---

[43] Habinek 2005.226–33.

[44] Though I would not go so far as to argue that this recentering derives from a desire to reclaim a vatic role that was actually known to have existed at an earlier phase of Roman history.

caede laboriferi credunt gaudere iuvenci!
victima labe carens et praestantissima forma
(nam placuisse nocet) vittis insignis et auro
sistitur ante aras auditque ignara precantem
inponique suae videt inter cornua fronti,
quas coluit, fruges percussaque sanguine cultros
inficit in liquida praevisos forsitan unda.
protinus ereptas viventi pectore fibras
inspiciunt mentesque deum scrutantur in illis;
inde (fames homini vetitorum tanta ciborum)
audetis vesci, genus o mortale! quod, oro,
ne facite, et monitis animos advertite nostris!
cumque boum dabitis caesorum membra palato,
mandere vos vestros scite et sentite colonos.
(15.127–42)

Worse than the commission of such a sin, the gods themselves are enlisted in the crime, and they believe that the heavenly power rejoices in the death of a labor-producing bullock. A victim without a blemish, of surpassing beauty (for it works harm to have pleased), decorated in fillets and gold, halts at the altar and, unknowing, hears the priest praying and sees placed on her own forehead, between her horns, the very grain that she cultivated, and struck, she stains with blood the knives already seen, perhaps, reflected in the clear water. Straightway, they inspect the organs wrenched from her living breast and examine within them the intentions of the gods. And thence (so great a hunger do men have of forbidden food) you dare to eat, o mortal race! Don't do this, I beg you, and turn your minds to my warnings! And when you put your mouth to the limbs of slaughtered oxen, know and perceive that you are chewing your own co-farmers.

Here, in discussing the very same outward form with which in book 1's account of Io Ovid produces one of his most elaborate exercises in shifting focalization, we find an equivalent sudden shift from looking at the cow's remarkable *forma* to seeing what the cow sees, the knife reflected in the water—the context in which Io saw her own bovine image and so became aware of her transformation. Or, rather, what takes over from the view of the cow is a kind of double vision, allowing the reader to see with the cow or to see the cow seeing. The connection between this passage and the programmatic metamorphosis of Io becomes even closer when the sacrificial victim is described in terms of her beauty in language also used when females attract the erotic interest of the gods (*placuisse nocebat*). Conversely, Io herself, like the victim, was presented as a gift to the goddess Juno (*munus*). And, as in that earlier passage, the visual shift at the center of the account goes together with an encouragement to identify more broadly with the female victim by attributing human motives to her—subtly anticipating the didactic point of the scene, which is precisely to perceive (*sentite*) the victim as human. Thus, the description of her as *ignara*, while literally connoting the befuddlement of a brute beast—what does a cow know about sacrifice?—nevertheless creates a sympathy for her ignorance by inviting the reader to anticipate a poignant human anagnorisis. Similarly, the phrase *quas coluit* hovers delicately between Pythagorean editorializing and mimesis of the cow's own developing awareness.

This reverse metamorphosis that makes a maiden of a cow also takes place through a clever intertextual gesture; for Ovid's cow sacrifice recalls Lucretius's description of the maiden Iphigeneia, who was herself ruthlessly undeceived about her fate, when, before the altar (*ante aras*), she sees her weeping father and concealed knives (*DRN* 1.84–101).[45] Iphigeneia too had been described previously in terms of her external decoration (*infula virgineos circumdata comptus*, 1.87); it is again at the moment of sacrifice that the poet suddenly makes her the subject of a verb of perceiving (*sensit*, 1.90). Where Lucretius takes sacrifice with a human in place of an animal as victim as a measure of the horrors of *religio*, Ovid's Pythagoras trumps him by transforming the maiden Iphigeneia into a cow, or, better, lets us recognize the human antecedent lurking beneath the victim in a sacrificial act not by itself marked out as extraordinary or monstrous—making the Lucretian sacrifice at once more "fabulous" (cow turns into girl) and more "everyday" (happens all the time, not just at Aulis).[46] At the same time, the doubling of Io and Iphigeneia as the maidens within the cow further connects and complicates both episodes in Ovid's poem: the reference to water as the medium through which the cow sees the knives reflected also now summons up a "paternal" presence, because Io's father is the very river in which she saw her own reflection, and his immediate concern that his daughter has now lost the chance of a marriage recalls the nature of Agamemnon's deception of his own daughter.[47] And if Pythagoras here uses intertextuality

---

[45] Segal 2001.73 calls the account of sacrifice "highly Lucretian" but does not pursue the specific comparison.

[46] Ovid also reintroduces the metamorphosis that Lucretius leaves out of his account by not mentioning the climactic substitution of a deer for Iphigeneia, but the effect of reinserting metamorphosis into the story is not to lessen the horror of a fictional sacrifice but to increase the horror of "real" sacrifice.

[47] Ovid deploys another Lucretian intermediary in making this link between the human Iphigeneia and the bovine Io. In *DRN* 2.350–66, Lucretius, having argued that animals can recognize one another as individuals, develops the example of a mother cow seeking a

to prove his point about humans reborn as cattle, he also compels the shift in focalization that Lucretius opens up for his own readers. Lucretius lets his audience share the victim's viewpoint with the emphatically placed *sensit*. Pythagoras makes the same verb, here transformed to an imperative, his final injunction to his audience: "Perceive, *sentite*, that you are chewing your fellow *coloni*," as though we have completed the metamorphosis hinted at when we see and hear what the victim sees by now becoming Lucretius's Iphigeneia, whom we have simultaneously transformed into a cow. See these cows as yourselves, he tells his hearers, even as he transforms them by making them see as Lucretius's victim while they see cows.

The consequences of Pythagoras's effort to transform the way we see sacrifice by literally introducing a new visual perspective on the act extend beyond the sympathy it mobilizes for the animal victims in the ritual and the analogy it suggests with the transformed victims of divine power within the poem. Another question of equal importance to Ovid's text and Pythagorean philosophy is also at stake: the representation of the gods. Pythagorean teaching was as noted for its rejection of anthropomorphized divinities as it was for vegetarianism, and according to Plutarch's life of Numa, the originally aniconic nature of religion at Rome was a legacy of his teaching.[48] So in our passage Pythagoras describes the divinity simply as a *numen supernum*, suggesting a single, formless, divine power that is physically above us.

This is another way in which the philosopher imposes contrasting visions on the sacrificial experience. Not only does the death of the victim become a double spectacle when we see both the visual effects of her

---

calf that has been slaughtered at the altar. The combination of the description of sacrifice with the presence of a parent—though here with the genders precisely reversed, even as the emotion of loss so strikingly absent on the part of the human father emerges poignantly in the cow mother—recalls Lucretius's earlier treatment of Iphigeneia. Ovid's earlier account of Io in turn contains some echoes of this second Lucretian scene. The "complaints" of Lucretius's mother are specifically re-"edited" to moos in the case of Io (*querellis, DRN* 2.358 ~ *conata queri mugitus edidit*, 1.637); the situation of foiled contact between parent and child is the same in the two scenes, as is the riverbank setting. Indeed, Ovid's allusion almost certainly plays on a recognition that Lucretius himself adapts a previous Io narrative here, having converted the erotic language and the imagery of wandering torment to the situation of a mother deprived of her calf. I owe the suggestion to look at this second Lucretian passage in these terms to an unknown audience member when I presented an earlier version of this argument in a lecture at the University of Leeds.

We should also observe that Ovid elsewhere adapts this Lucretian simile in a context that links it to the erotic preoccupations of his Io scene: Apollo laments his own destruction of the unfaithful Coronis like a heifer watching her son being slain by the sacrificial hammer (2.623–25).

[48] Plut. *Numa* 8.7.

death (*inficit*) and her own vision flickering out (*praevisos forsitan*), but the gods too become something we can see in different forms. We watch the ritual authorities literally seeking out the minds of the gods by looking down and into the organs of the victim (*scrutantur, inspiciunt*). Here Pythagoras, though, sees only human folly and hubris (*audetis ... o genus mortale!*), for the *numen* is above. In this sense, too, Pythagoras's representation of sacrifice contrasts directly with the revelations offered by its practitioners. The latters' misguided sense of cosmic direction has led them to conflate god and beast in a transgression of boundaries precisely complementing what occurs when humans behave like animals by eating a cow that is really human. In ritual terms, then, Pythagoras's viewpoint alienates his audience from two fundamental ways in which sacrifice offers the possibility of communion between human society and its divine benefactors, by physically consuming the victim together and by looking on the victim as different from the assumption of a superior position.

Yet it is important to remember that this game of looking up or looking down is not one that Pythagoras can ultimately control. For, especially if we recall the language of human creation at the poem's inception, to look at things as a beast seems essentially to violate divine injunctions to men to raise their gaze. The philosopher may blame sacrificial participants for reducing humanity to bestiality, but he does so by means of an even more radical and, if we keep our own perspective anchored in the real world of Roman opinions, harder-to-accept assertion of an essential identity between the human and the animal.

But it is not only the *haruspices*' view of the gods that is at stake. Their cow-dwelling divinities mirror another mistaken way of seeing the gods that Pythagoras makes responsible for the very existence of sacrifice, the presentation of the gods as driven by human motives. And if the diviner's perspective recalls real-world ritual practice, it is now paired with a "poetic" strategy everywhere at work in Ovid's poem. In lines 15.127–29, the justification for sacrifice depends on viewing gods as rejoicing at the death of the victim, so that we have "enlisted" them in our crime. To press the metaphor of *inscripsere*, the human gods who validate sacrificial ritual recall the all-too-human "written" gods we meet in book 1 of the poem. The sacrificial lesson of Pythagoras then, reechoes the tendencies of Ovid's excessive anthropomorphization of the divinities and underlines how distant such literary divinities are from philosophical conceptions. Io's divine suitor, caught as he is between the twin compulsions of shame and love, seems from this perspective even more a parody, and the narrator of such a *fabula* an equivalent to the misguided instigators of sacrifice in his criminal misunderstanding of the nature of the gods. The lovestruck king of the gods needs a Platonic philosopher to remind him that the divinity, being perfect, can desire nothing; a schoolboy could have told him and Juno that the gods have nothing to fear.

This latest element in our analysis suggests an important way in which the character of Pythagoras acts as a mediating figure to help us understand the poem's larger negotiations with external reality. As a man who has left his own state, whose prescriptions are also alien from the Roman practices they are supposed to inform, and whose message of political mutability inevitably bears troubling consequences for the prospects of Roma Aeterna, Pythagoras can seem a very "anti-Augustan" figure. And this position seems confirmed by his explicit attack on a practice, sacrifice, crucial to the new principate's self-representation in ritual and iconography. We have also seen that the techniques Pythagoras applies to revealing sacrifice resemble those deployed by another Ovidian rebel, Arachne, in the sphere of visual arts—showing the human faces of the victims of the gods. But the reference to Arachne reminds us how hostile Pythagoras would be to her own misrepresentation of the divinities as criminals—*ipsos inscripsere deos sceleri*. Of course, as the fate of Arachne's tapestry shows, artistic forms are as impermanent as any others. For Pythagoras's perspective is emphatically not that of a poetic outsider to the rituals of the state. On the contrary, his speech here symbolically equates a poetic "theology" like Ovid's, which shows the gods as human, with the ritual practices of extispicy, which, again like Arachne, imagines the gods as beasts. His philosophical perspective can also make Ovid's fiction seem very "politically correct" in the Augustan sense especially because the first context in which we see humanized divinities makes them transparently figures of political authority. All of this should remind us that Varro's "three theologies," the theory obviously in play here, never exist in their pure states. Rather the "public theology" always borrows from both the "poetic" and the "philosophical." Here, to see with Pythagoras, poetry can align itself with philosophy to reveal the anthropomorphic fictions of religious practice or, on the contrary, can appear as the ally of ritual and exile the philosopher from the fabric of the poem as he has been exiled from his native polis.

Finally, it is important to remember how Pythagoras's position as internal narrator can have a similar triangulating effect, making Ovid's narrative by contrast potentially seem more real, or conversely highlighting Ovid's own exile, as just another storyteller, from contemporary reality. We have seen the many ways in which Pythagoras does not resemble the author of the poem—his own unwillingness to represent the gods and, as strikingly, his own obvious presence as a narrator directly addressing an audience and guiding its interpretation of his words. Indeed, Ovid seems to hold the philosopher at narratological arm's length by never explicitly naming him, so that the most famous ventriloquist and shape changer in Latin literary history never quite emerges in the poem or becomes Ovid. But perhaps the absence of naming makes the point that this "soul" has abandoned only the name of Pythagoras to achieve a literary metempsychosis in Ovid's representation of his words; in this sense, so completely has he become Ovid that he can no longer be called Pythagoras. The paradox generated by the absent name of Pythagoras reminds us that throughout the poem Ovid has complemented both the awareness of his narrative's fictionality and the double vision his text generates on scenes of transformation, through the use of internal narrators. Thus, in the case of Marsyas, we have seen an explicitly didactic narrator slanting his audience's response to the event away from sympathy with the victim. Pythagoras's account of sacrifice offers another didactic reading that pulls in the opposite direction. In both examples, accepting the lesson offered by the internal narrator means seeing precisely half of what Ovid's text has to show. And the recognition of their partiality can reveal by contrast the wholeness of Ovid's poetic representation and suggest its closeness to an objective reality rather than a contingent and limited human representation of that reality. But, of course, the alternative to this reality effect is to remember that Ovid is human too and to recall the similarities he often stresses between his internal narrators and his own historical persona. Like Orpheus, for example, he tells metamorphosis stories after turning away from love. And, if we imagine the postexilic composition, or at least reception, of the poem, Pythagoras's own status as exile—the first thing we learn about him—cannot but recall the *relegatio* of the poem's own author.

But if Pythagoras's narratological impact on the poem's audience resembles those of earlier narrators, the scale and the stakes of the dilemma he poses have escalated. Pythagoras offers a complete *Metamorphoses*, from the beginning of time to the present, and the reader who takes this as the *Metamorphoses*, and Pythagoras as a mouthpiece for Ovid, will need to unread a great deal of what has gone before. This involves at once an alienation from the earlier part of the poem and a positioning of Ovid as an outsider to his own society. Witness the many times that an acceptance of Pythagoras as a mouthpiece for Ovid's philosophy of change has gone together with an anti-Augustan interpretation of his work. Correspondingly in prophesying the Ovidian present, and perhaps in claiming as his subject not what happened in the mythical past but how the world always is, Pythagoras's speech claims to write the author's and audience's own experience in a way that no other speech in the poem does so explicitly. The remedy, though, to allowing Pythagoras into history and letting him write Ovid for us is, as always, to remember that he is embedded in a fictional poem. Ovid's own language in his account of the creation of man condemns him as someone who rejects the human duty of looking up by adopting the point of view of prone animals. Thus, on the one hand, seeing Ovid's gods as gods and his poem as the world helps keep Pythagoras in his place, while following Pythagoras's bovine gaze keeps Ovid's own historical status before our eyes by showing us an unexpected human self "reflected" at the center of multiple levels of representation, all of which contribute to affirm the otherness of their object.

CHAPTER 4

Poets in the Arena

One of Ovid's most sophisticated devices for explicitly positioning his prestige as author within the Roman economy of political power comes through his interweaving of poetry with public ritual and spectacle. In his great appeal to Augustus from exile, the poet gives his participation in public festivals of thanksgiving as material proof of his personal loyalty to the emperor (*Trist.* 2.57–60). But beyond contrasting such sure and tangible signs of Ovid's place in the Roman community with an *animus* and *mens* that are invisible and thus, like the products of his genius, subject to misinterpretation (cf. 2.77–80), Ovid takes over for his poetry the language of public festival. His *Metamorphoses* becomes the most functional and least prestigious of public utterances—the voice of the crier proclaiming the name of Caesar (*vestri praeconia nominis*, 2.65), and so too offers proofs of his own mind even as it seems to speak nothing but "Caesar." From the literal incense that Ovid offered as a small "part" of the crowd, his reports of Caesar's deeds become metaphorical incense; his greater work (*maius opus*, 2.63) becomes the smallest offering (*minimo honore*, 2.76) by which even great gods are won over. At the same time that Ovid seems to place festival performance in a different epistemological category from poetic composition, he reminds the reader that the transformative power of words can make poetry into a kind of worship.

Another measuring of the capacities of poetry and spectacle adds new dimensions to this paradox and at the same time offers a strikingly new venue for seeing *Metamorphoses* in action. The first poem of the fourth book of *Tristia* traces one kind of reception, as Ovid invokes the favor and protection of Rome for his written work, which makes the return that he cannot. The second makes the poet the recipient of an oral report of Tiberius's triumph in the capital, from which the poet's exile physically separates him, but to which he gives an impressively verisimilar substance in the opening verses. A transformation similar to the one we saw in *Tristia* 2 happens again as the poet looking at Rome positions himself at both ends of the telescope: when he was physically at Rome, he was once again small, a *parva pars* of the rejoicing crowd (*Trist.* 4.2.16 ~ *Trist.* 2.58). Now, though, only a small report (*fama ... non nisi parva*, 4.2.18) of the great procession gets as far as Tomi. And if his physical presence as a small part of the crowd becomes politically symbolic of his subordination to Caesar, who can view him and judge his sincerity, now it is the insubstantial report whose accuracy Ovid must scrutinize and embellish lest it deceive him (*fallunt*, 4.2.17—both "escape" and "deceive"). Indeed, Ovid's accomplishment in lending reality to *fama* is all the more striking here because the report did deceive him: the triumph never really took place.

In the center of this Wonderland of shifting sizes comes a subtle reminder of the poetic products through which Ovid's own *fama* tries to maintain some objective stability: as the people gaze on the captives in Tiberius's triumph, they will meet with two kinds of faces, some changed according to the circumstances (*et cernet vultus aliis pro tempore versos*, 4.2.23), others still fierce and with no perception of their actual status (*terribiles aliis inmemoresque sui*, 4.2. 24). The first of these lines recalls both of Ovid's greatest works. In the midst of the similar festival described in *Tristia* 2, the *Metamorphoses* was described as *corpora ... versa* (2.64), and here the same adjective applies to the faces of the captives (indeed, *vultus* often in the *Metamorphoses* itself describes the appearance altered by transformation). The primary meaning of *versos* here is not "transformed" but "turned away," in a gesture of shame befitting the Germans' captive state. But this averting of the gaze itself becomes another transformation of appearance, especially because it generates a physical difference between some of the captives and those who retain their initial ferocity. In fact the faces that are turned away are perhaps not "changed" at all, because such a gesture shows a pride in self inappropriate to one who has truly been brought low by conquest. Between the different versions of these faces comes "time" (*tempore*), whose plural was the first word of, and thus a shorthand designation for, the *Fasti*.[1]

But if what the populace sees when they look at Tiberius's triumph is nothing other than Ovid's poetry, what does that mean for the poem? At the most obvious level, it turns imperial victory into another battleground for pitting poet against prince, reality against textuality. After all, Tiberius's victory at the moment of reading coexists with Ovid's word picture of it—and conversely, as the poem reveals, the triumph itself relies on reading as the audience is confronted by a series of written inscriptions identifying the depicted scenes.[2] But beyond this further explora-

---

[1] Here the word seems simply to mean "circumstances," but precisely the same surface meaning concealed a pretty transparent allusion to the literary work just at the end of the previous poem (4.1.105). When Ovid there asks Rome's aid for a song "no better than my circumstances" (*non melius quam sunt mea tempora carmen*), he is also describing the *Tristia* in relation to his *Fasti*.

[2] See Hardie 2002c.309, and for another complementary interpretation of the poem, Oliensis 2004.

tion of the political dynamics of representation, in this chapter I reflect the metaphor of "poem as spectacle" back on the *Metamorphoses* itself to show how the problems of recognition posed by metamorphosis resemble those at the center of crucial civic spectacles like sacrificial ritual, dramatic performance, and, as here, the triumph. The "visual" aspect of Ovid's poetry, so frequently noted by recent criticism, thus becomes more than an aesthetic problem, a reflex, as it has sometimes been treated, of contemporary taste for spectacle. Rather, I want to explore the possibility that the poem's emphases on the problems of seeing and the simulation of a visual image for its readers appropriate for the text the same potential to realize and refigure the position of audiences in relation to the public rites of the new empire, where, as we saw in chapter 2's discussion of Augustan visual monuments, who you were was determined by what and how you saw. Obviously a text's power to evoke the visual is one of its supreme fictions. To imagine that one sees what is so evidently not there provides an asymptote for the reader's accession to the poem's deceptions. But this tension between acquiescence in and resistance to the poem as something to be seen itself mimics the very issues of recognition raised by the visual images it constructs. Like the presence of Io within the guise of the cow, the elevation of the fictive to the same experiential plane as an actual spectacle can seem real or purely imaginary.

To give a clearer sense of how such literary "spectacles" can describe questions of civic identity and prompt reflection on the nature of the state, let us look more closely at Tiberius's—or Ovid's—triumph in *Tristia* 4.2. This passage provides an excellent starting place because the very language with which the spectacle is described seems so explicitly to invite comparison between the sights offered in a triumph and Ovid's text. Also the spectacle within which that text is inscribed is incontrovertibly political, whereas the political nature of sacrificial and dramatic rituals that provide the focus of later discussions needs to be demonstrated. The "changed faces" of the captives recall not only the *Metamorphoses* as a literary composition but also the central hermeneutic problem it raises, the recognition of a stable subject within a changed form. For the very fact of transformation in the case of the triumph is made problematic: some faces are changed, others are not. And how can one be sure of the difference? To return to a similar problem raised at the beginning of the *Metamorphoses*, Jupiter presents homicidal king Lycaon's new wolf's face not in terms of change but of a clarification of the very identity that justifies his punishment. The first adjective used to describe Germania, *fera* (4.2.1), which equally applies to untamed races and wild animals, perhaps smoothes the transition between the bestial countenances we meet in Ovid's epic and the fierce captives. The first line of the poem raises a similar question about the change or sameness of Germany through a linguistic "transformation" that recalls the initial line of the *Metamorphoses*:

> *Iam fera Caesaribus Germania, totus ut orbis,*
> *victa potest flexo succubuisse genu.*

At first glance, Germany seems "fierce to the Caesars," a characterization that changes from predictable to profoundly disconcerting with the last three words, *totus ut orbis* (like the rest of the world!). But a change in syntax as we move on to the second line tames this cosmic disorder. We realize that Germany is no longer fierce to the Caesars, but that, like the rest of the world, she has bent her knee to the Caesars. However, such a comforting conclusion relies on our accepting that Germany as a personification, and as a grammatical subject, is susceptible to change and does not retain her essential quality of hostility even after her subjection. And this, after all, is the question raised by the captive faces beheld in the triumph.

The problem of mutability raised by the captives relates directly to the viewer's understanding of Rome herself and its effect on the world. To see the German as tamed becomes a sign of the transformative capacity of the state—its ultimate potential to make the entire world bend the knee to its power. On the other hand, the very persistence of Germany and the Germans in ferocity has an equal but opposite benefit for the reading of Roman power. For the ferocity of the Germans legitimates their subjection and demands the civilizing force of Rome, whose violence in turn can be differentiated from the arrogance and indiscriminacy of her foes. Also, the magnitude of Tiberius's accomplishment demands that the German be seen in all his might. Too humbled a foe threatens to remove the triumphant aspect of the triumph. Attested scenes where the populace reacted with horror and pity to the sight of dejected captives show that this danger was a very real one for the triumphator.[3]

But if the metamorphosis of the Germans takes on shifting and contrasting meanings that derive value at once from the captives' sameness and their difference from what they were, the beginnings of the poem present a similarly complex picture of Rome itself as resistant and subject to change. This will be the first of many hints that one of the dangers of mutability—indeed the one stressed by Pythagoras in the context of what we might call the imperialism of consumption—is that enemies will change into one another. The very celebration of victory changes the face of the city. The lofty Palatine is "veiled" with garlands (4.2.3), as if it were the head of a personified Rome matching the allegorical figure of Germany brought low, and the smoke of incense "dyes" the sky (4.2.4).

---

[3] Cf. the pity aroused at the sight of Arsinoe in Caesar's triumph of 46 (Dio 43.19).

While here Rome's changeability suggests the capacity to put on the face of the victor, another kind of transformation affects the youths growing up in the home of Caesar and the mothers and daughters-in-law whose fertility makes possible the rise of a new generation. Yet the aim of this process of natural renewal is precisely stability. The imperial youth grow up so that the house of Caesar "may rule the earth perpetually (4.2.10)." Livia's gesture of honoring the gods is one that she will repeat frequently (*saepe datura*, 4.2.12). Most revealing of the contrasting impulses toward celebrating Rome's eternity as the result of replacement and renewal and as an unchanging sameness exempt from natural processes is the juxtaposition of mothers with the Vestal Virgins who preserve the sacred fire "with perpetual virginity" (4.2.13–14).

These contradictory views of whether Rome herself changes and how it changes others develop directly from the physical sight of "changed faces" in the triumph. But not only does the text raise the question of whether and how the faces of the captives have changed; they seem to change in the very process of being viewed, as visual elements recorded in the description of the triumph generate new similarities among the participants. This second dimension of change is as important for the political reading of metamorphosis as the first, for it reminds us that not only is the issue of changeability significant—and changeable—in the abstract, but the very recognition of change depends on the active participation of a viewer whose way of construing the scene is, importantly, independent of any objective truth. Hence, Ovid's emphasis on the fact that the spectator whose impressions, recounted in direct speech, become Ovid's description of the triumph, himself does not know what he is talking about but makes up a story to suit the images (4.2.25–26).

One significant visual link that elides the differences between the figures in the triumph comes above all from the color purple, which first describes the blood with which the gleaming white sacrificial victims "beat" the ground (4.2.6). The first of the German captives, the leader in war, conquered (*victum*) if not an actual *victima*, begins the conversion of the image. He too gleams (*fulget*, 4.2.27 ~ *candida*, 4.2.5) with a purple that signifies not blood but the essentially foreign rank of king. That the purple dye is defined as Sidonian at once stresses the foreignness of his garb and further assimilates him to another female victim, Vergil's Dido. The sacrificial pattern is activated again to reestablish a sense of national difference that justifies conquest, as a subsequent German captive is said to be guilty of a hideous violation of the law of nations by performing human sacrifice of Roman victims (4.2.35–36). How just, then, that such a captive should now enter into the victim's role! Unless of course we really do make him a victim, in which case the sense of our own difference as Romans vanishes. The sacrificial victim next appears in the visual image of the river god, the Rhine, whose crown of sedge cannot conceal that his horns have been broken (4.2.41). This figure, whose ill-disguised broken horns seemed to have plucked him from book 8 of the *Metamorphoses*, where the river god Achelous bears the same deformity for the same reason and tries to hide it in the same way, also changes color like a sacrificial victim as we refocus our attention from the deceptive green crown to the native blood (*suo sanguine*, 4.2.42) that infects his waters. Above these images appears the triumphing Caesar.[4] This distinction between high and low takes us back to the opening distinction made in the poem, as the lofty Palatine will be covered in garlands to celebrate Germany being brought low. But that glance at the first lines becomes less straightforward with the mention of the color of the imperial cloak, *purpureus*, purple, like the blood of the victim (4.2.48).[5] If it is valuable to the iconography of victory that the faces of the Germans reveal an unchanged ferocity, it is perhaps even more essential that Caesar maintain a stable countenance that shows no signs of changing into that of the defeated, by taking over their regal insignia, their abominable sacrificial practices, or even the stain of defeat manifested by the blood in the Rhine. Yet that is precisely the transformation the text suggests, with the help of some pointers back to the *Metamorphoses*. The flowers that cloak Tiberius's path (*tegente*, 4.2.50) recall the garlands that mask the Rhine's defeat. Garlands themselves appear in the next line as the emperor binds his brow with Phoebus's laurel. The laurel's associations both with victory and with ritual purity are equally relevant here, as the conqueror also stresses his own exemption from pollution. Yet is this too simply a mask for violence and vulnerability? The imperial laurel is a sign we are familiar with, and any reader of the first book of the *Metamorphoses* would know how many differences in perspective lie behind the simple assertion that the laurel belongs to Phoebus. With these associations in mind, the time when the emperor seems most to have put on the form of the victim comes when he utters the conqueror's cry, *io!* (4.2.51).

In one of the most striking transformations enacted in *Tristia* 4.2, the poet Ovid becomes an audience for the reports of the triumph, and yet that very report exists only when audience members themselves become "poets," narrating the events of the spectacle, here, conveniently, in elegiac distichs. This idea of how every reception of imperial images becomes an act of creation—one that we explored at length in chapter 2—reemerges here at the fullest level of political significance as the various

---

[4] With what follows, cf. the important comment of Hardie 2002.310 on the figure of the emperor in this poem: "In *Tristia* 4.2 the triumphant Caesar is placed on the same level of reality or unreality as the conquered personification of Germania."

[5] Oliensis 2004.310 notes that in *Tristia* 1.1.5–6, the same color adorns the cover of books of poetry.

guises that Ovid himself takes on in narrating the triumph figure different positions in relation to the power of the state. Ovid appears as its imperial center, and someone whose remoteness from events takes the form of a flight into fiction and imagination. He bears a likeness to the spectators, whose Romanness consists in reading the triumph, and to the captives, whose current state testifies only to the forces that have defeated them.[6] The spectator's report of things he does not know puts him in a position of likeness to Ovid, who is simultaneously reporting the same things, in a state of at least equal or greater ignorance.[7] His later description of this process as fiction links it more directly to the poetic modes of the *Metamorphoses*, whose images we have seen emerge from the description itself. If we accept that reading the images of the triumph becomes a way of "performing civic identity," then Ovid's poem refutes the alterations of exile, ensuring that he is still a *parva pars plebis*.

And yet the written text that results assimilates the poet to the role of Caesar whose triumph contains not only images to be viewed but texts to be read (cf. *leget*, 4.2.20).[8] Indeed, the images of the triumph render a cosmos as comprehensive as that assembled at the beginning of the *Metamorphoses* and through similar means. We have already seen the substance of the triumph glossed in words that recall how Ovid designates his poem, *corpora versa*. The passage in lines 37–38, describing the geographic images presented in the triumph, "this lake, these mountains, these many fortifications and rivers, were full of cruel destruction, full of blood," provides an equally apt shorthand for the landscape of the *Metamorphoses*. And how does one depict a river?[9] Caesar's Rhine, as we saw, seems to have stepped out of book 8 of the *Metamorphoses*, where the very nature of anthropomorphized gods was itself at issue. Ovid, then, occupies the position simultaneously of subject and spectator. Removed by the emperor's edict from the empowering real presences of imperial display, he exerts his own power in relation both to the emperor, by recasting his truth as fiction and giving the fiction that the triumph occurred the ring of truth, and to his own audience-spectators, in imposing on them another written image of the cosmos. Thus, one might say that the changeable face of the victim, who starts off by looking like an emperor and makes the emperor look like him, most resembles Ovid's own. That Ovid's face has changed "according to the time" is after all a con-

---

[6] Cf. also the interpretation of Oliensis 2004.310.

[7] See the perceptive comments of Hardie 2002c.309.

[8] Though there is an important difference: Caesar's *tituli* give each captive a precise and stable identity reflecting reality, just what they do not have in Ovid's report. For, except for the Rhine, he gives no proper names to people or places, and the identity of all figures correspondingly remains anything but stable.

[9] Hinds 2001b.130–36.

stant refrain of the exile poetry.[10] If in reality the emperor has been able to remove the poet from the state, fiction allows him back in. More precisely, Ovid's power comes from the ability of the figures in the triumph seemingly to change their identities, whereas the emperor has everything invested in keeping them always the same.

This reading of *Tristia* 4.2 has so far shown how Ovid's conjuring of imperial spectacle gives him another means for presenting the political consequences of metamorphosis, as described in chapter 1, and for creating his own poetic persona as a model for the imperial subject whose response to the representations of imperial power becomes in turn a form of art. In this chapter, I want to expand the discussion by adding a new dimension to the likeness between Ovidian poetry and public spectacle. Rather than see the poetry merely as evoking and appropriating actual spectacles, as Ovid claims to do here in the case of Tiberius' triumph, we can also read the poetry as offering its own visualizations of the past that, without any reference to the events of the forum or circus, take over the political dynamics present there to construct a civic dimension to the act of reading and provide a new sphere to measure the powers of the poet.

This shift away from reading real spectacle as the model for Ovidian spectacle, however difficult it would have been for a Roman reader who had the emperor's monuments inevitably before her eyes, is doubly appropriate for the *Metamorphoses*. First, that poem seems deliberately to avoid doing what the *Tristia* does in describing specific historical events. Most of the scenes to be visualized in the poem take place in a mythological past far removed from contemporary history. And when actual events are described, like the assassination of Julius Caesar, the poet deliberately creates a very different spectacle from what any real viewer could possibly have seen by showing the action from the perspective of mythical characters, the gods Venus and Jupiter. Yet the distance between past and present cannot be absolute. From the gladiatorial spectacles now known to scholars as "fatal charades" to theatrical performances like Varius's *Thyestes*, performed at the Actian games of 29 BCE, to the artistic "spectacles" of the temples of Apollo on the Palatine, imperial self-presentation recasts Greek myth to define the present. At the same time, converting the fabulous and far-off to the real and immediate by, for example, showing Actaeon torn apart by dogs conveyed the wondrous perhaps even godlike magic of Roman imperial power, however "playfully." This overlap in subject matter inevitably contaminates the two aesthetic experiences of reading and viewing and brings me to the second reason why the juxtaposition of the two suits this poem distinctively among all Ovid's works: a tension between visualizing Ovid's myths in terms of spectacle and re-

---

[10] Most tellingly, in relation to the *Metamorphoses*, cf. the *vultus* of *Tristia* 1.7.1.

reading spectacle through the lens of the narratives the poet tells becomes in itself yet another kind of visual doubling that allows the reader to think about the relative pressure imperial reality and poetic fantasy exert on one another. One sign of this relates to the etiological character of Ovid's transformations. Ovid's stories may be locked in the distant past, and they may reach a reader through the comparatively remote and paradigmatically unreliable idiom of the reported tale. But for all that, their fictions promise to take us back to *the* Actaeon, or *the* Niobe, whom artistic depictions and imperial games can evoke only through representations. If we did not have the Actaeon story as a paradigm, the sight of a man torn apart by dogs would take on a different cultural meaning. More precisely, the battle between reality and fiction involved in seeing the gladiator as Actaeon or, in Ovid's case, seeing Actaeon as a gladiator reproduces and brings into focus similar issues to those evoked by the violence of the spectacle in isolation.

In making this argument about the reciprocity between Ovidian visualization and contemporary Roman spectacle, I aim to unite two modern approaches to the poem. The first, we might say, gives priority to Ovid, by focusing on the descriptive elements that provoke a visual response to his work. The second, in turn, attributes this interest to extratextual influences. It is commonly assumed that the "graphic" elements of Ovid's work respond to the greater popularity of spectacle, especially violent spectacle, in imperial Roman culture. Ovid by including such scenes as the flaying of Marsyas was either catering to his audience's taste for such spectacles or indulging his own.[11]

Gianpiero Rosati provides the fullest and most influential example of the first approach, detailing how Ovid's techniques of description provoke a visual response from his readers through such devices as particularization of details, the inclusion of internal spectators, and the imagined presence of the reader herself as "viewer" through such narrative statements as "you could have seen...." Another important contribution of Rosati's study was to recognize the correlation between problems of seeing and the phenomenon of metamorphosis, as something experienced visually from a number of contrasting perspectives. In explaining Ovid's interest in the contradictory aspects of appearance, Rosati bases it on the poet's perception of the nature of reality itself as bearing the uncertainties of artifice; he speaks of the "spettacolo del mondo" where nothing is ever as it seems.[12] Thus, he is using spectacle at once in its most general sense

---

[11] See the discussion in Tissol 1997.125, citing Wilkinson 1955.162 and Galinsky 1975.63.

[12] Rosati 1983.95–173, esp. 169–70.

as something to be seen and with a more specific and particularly modern meaning of "artifice," "deception." Ovid's illusionism for him derives from a theory about the nature of all reality, not the specific representations of his historical period. He too recognizes the connection between Ovid's text and staged spectacles, as well as the omnipresent visual representations of mythological scenes in works of art.[13] But for Rosati, these images are important for Ovid primarily because they make it easier for him to elicit visual responses to his poem from an audience that would already be habituated to "see" the scenes he describes.

If Rosati's work leaves room for more analysis of the importance of Roman *spectacula* in understanding Ovid's use of the visual, those approaches that explain his interest in constructing visual scenes simply as the product of an imperial Zeitgeist are limited both by their vagueness about the effects of such generalized influence and by their failure to connect Ovid's emulations of actual spectacles with the importance of visual response as a thematic interest within the poem. Such comparisons were often developed before recent interest in Roman spectacles, particularly gladiatorial competitions, has revealed their political and, indeed, aesthetic complexity. Thus, Galinsky, writing in 1975 about the effect of Roman taste on Ovid's focus on violence, claims, "Quite in contrast to its treatment in Greek literary poetry, the horror of myth is transmuted into a non-spiritual, non-intellectual, and external affair which corresponds to Roman realities."[14] Fuller consideration of the cultural significance of violent spectacle in Roman culture makes Ovid's textual evocations much more than an index of his participation in Roman cruelty.

My approach here tries to work both outward from the text and inward from the cultural phenomena it refers to. Specifically, I argue that Ovid's stagings of episodes as gladiatorial, ritual, or theatrical spectacle are most fully explained as more than simple borrowings that add vividness to the distant and unfamiliar episode and contextualize it in the here and now. Rather, as has emerged from the analysis of literary intertexts, the evocations of extraliterary "sources" as well invites reflection on the differences and resemblances between their manifestations "on the stage and on the page." At one level, the competition between imitation and reality involved in seeing stories as spectacles offers another way of defining the position of the poet, but consideration of the significance of vision within the text, especially the important role of seeing as a trigger for exploring the multivalence of metamorphosis itself, suggests a more focused, and ambitious, claim: the problems of recognition that emerge from seeing within the poem resemble different forms of visual

---

[13] On shows and games, see Rosati 1983.143–44, and 137–38 on the visual arts.

[14] Galinsky 1975.139.

ambiguity present in actual spectacle. In both cases, reconciling different possible points of view energizes the response to the sight and demands reflection on the position—speaking politically as well as literally—of the viewer. Thus, perception of an overlap between the audience's experience of Ovid's work and the spectator's attendance at civic spectacles shows at once what is at stake in the reading of Ovid by pointing up its relation to issues of community and identity and, at the same time, clarifies and comments on the processes of spectacle itself.

Two important precedents for reading Ovidian spectacle as in dialogue with, rather than as reflections of, actual spectacles provide our starting point. Stephen Hinds, writing in 1987, made an observation similar to Rosati's on Ovid's evocation of theater and arena as stages for climactic events in his poem. The self-consciously described pastoral landscape on Mount Enna, where Proserpina plays before her abduction by Pluto, consists of an open glade surrounded by trees that "deflect the sun's beams with their leaves, as if with an awning." (5.388–89). That last comparison, as Hinds points out, relates the shady grove typical of poetic "pleasant places" to the circular space of the amphitheater, where awnings would protect spectators from the sun. So too, Ovid explicitly likens the killing of Orpheus by Thracian Maenads to the sight of a deer killed by dogs in a *venatio* (11.26–27). Again, the simile alerts the reader to the spectacular configuration of Ovid's setting: the Maenads first see the poet as spectators (*cernunt*) as he performs for a very different audience of tamed beasts, which are in turn described as a theatrical audience (*theatri*, 11.22). But where Rosati saw allusions to spectacle as a device to alert the reader to the visual qualities of Ovid's own work, Hinds sees a deliberate blurring of literary landscapes and the contemporary settings of the stage. And this blurring at once changes the character of the scene, in this case again Proserpina's abduction, by highlighting the audience's expectation of violence: "The familiar 'stage' of pastoral is here an amphitheatrical arena, and the performance … no bucolic song recital, but a cruel spectacle of which the maiden Persephone is destined to be the unwilling star."[15]

The overlap Ovid constructs between the fictional landscape of his poetry and the all-too-real urban settings of the actual spectacle takes on a broader significance in the recent work of Philip Hardie. For Hardie, the evocation of spectacle points forward to the literature of the later first century in confusing the categories of "spectacle" and reality.[16] As spectacle replaces reality in the self-presentation of the emperors, Ovid's appropriation of that realm within his own poetry—and Hardie here is

[15] Hinds 1987a.35.
[16] Hardie 2002c.316.

speaking primarily of the representations of specific Roman spectacles in the exile poetry—both points up the fictional aspects of imperial display and, in so doing, elevates his own fictions to the same level of authority. This last move becomes a typically Ovidian refraction of an established Augustan interest in asserting equivalences between literary and imperial display well exemplified in the works of Vergil and Livy. Thus, in *Georgics* 3, Vergil promises to construct a temple for the new emperor that bears comparison with the actual temple of Palatine Apollo even then being built. And Livy's portrayal of historical events as spectacles belongs in the context of Augustan reenactments of the Roman past. Ovid's distinctive technique of putting imperial images on the same representational plane as his own both emphasizes and reflects "a decisive shift in the relationship between 'show' and 'reality' as principate replaced Republic."[17]

For Hardie, then, Ovid's unmasking of the fictive in imperial spectacle stands at an opposite pole from writers who try to enhance the authority of the text by assimilating its own images to actual public display. As his interpretations reveal, however, either relationship is very much in the eyes of a reader who can make the arrows of priority point in either direction. My own dissent from the position Hardie's last quote suggests springs from a different conception of the function of the world of "show." Ovid's reproductions of spectacle may indeed implicate triumph and ritual in a fictional nexus where reality can emerge only from representations, or the poetry may gain a purchase in the real present by describing staged events that, even if they offer their audience the Rhine River only in the guise of a man with horns and garlands, nevertheless can be perceived with the eyes as opposed to the mind. But my position will be that this play of fictionality is not something that the poetry alone exposes about these representations. On the contrary, like the architectural programs we considered in chapter 2, even spectacles like the triumph present a variety of claims about the world, and the audience must always work out for itself what to accept or reject. Nor does this process imply disloyal skepticism or resistance; rather, it is how the spectator participates in the event. The negotiation of truth and fiction in public spectacle helps determine the audience's response to the ritual elements at the core of sacrifice, gladiatorial spectacle, and, in represented form, the triumph. From this perspective, Ovid's emphasis on the representational aspects of these scenes, far from undermining their civic function, enhances one of its essential effects and at the same time makes it clear that this effect is also one that his own poetry strives to reproduce. The more he seems to oppose the perspectives generated by his own representations to those of the emperor, the closer he draws his work to the experience of imperial spectacle.

[17] Hardie 2002c.317.

To back up this claim, I want to examine the kind of spectacle that comes closest in subject matter and perhaps in aesthetic effect to certain episodes of the *Metamorphoses*: the reenactments of mythical events in the gladiatorial arena, which Kathleen Coleman has called "fatal charades."[18] The staged execution of condemned criminals provides the context for these "performances." We hear, for example, of a certain Meniscus offering "a great spectacle to all" by being burned alive like Hercules, after having been made to steal the Golden Apples of the Hesperides. Another criminal perished in a reenactment of the death of Orpheus, and there are also accounts of a Daedalus and a Pasiphae. The attested examples of this kind of execution cluster in the reigns of Nero and the Flavian emperors and thus postdate Ovid's poem by more than half a century. What justification, then, is there for using them to understand the interaction between the *Metamorphoses* and the performances of its own era? First of all, my reading does not assume that Ovid's poetry responds to or reproduces specific enactments of the myths he describes as "fatal charades," although the possibility cannot be ruled out.[19] When Ovid invites us to see the death of Orpheus played out as a *venatio*, he is not simply evoking something he had seen (indeed, his Orpheus is simultaneously likened to a deer!). However, to understand in what way precisely this imaginary setting would transform the significance of the scene, it is very revealing to see how one Roman responded when Orpheus actually did meet his fate in the "morning show." Closer examination of accounts of "fatal charades" indicates that the realms of myth and imperial spectacle are not so far apart. The use of amphitheatrical spectacle to represent the realm of myth, and vice versa, reproducing the same kind of contextual overlapping as Ovid's similes, puts questions of fiction like those we have encountered in the *Metamorphoses* at the center of public spectacle and connects these questions to other dimensions of the event as well. Thus, the thought exercise of imagining some responsivity between Ovid's depiction of the death of Orpheus, for example, and the enactment of the same event in the arena, even if we cannot be sure that it is one that

[18] Coleman 1990.

[19] Our evidence is not in itself sufficient to establish a sure starting point for the practice. The fullest accounts come from a very unique source, the *liber spectaculorum* written by Martial collecting epigrammatic mementos of the unprecedented series of games with which Titus inaugurated the Colosseum. We have no such detailed accounts of specific *munera* earlier in the imperial period. But there is evidence for adding an element of role-playing to violent spectacles already in the reigns of Caesar and Augustus: a large-scale naval battle in 46 BCE showed "Tyrians" battling "Egyptians"; another under Augustus in 2 BCE reenacted Salamis, with "Athenians" against "Persians" (Coleman 1990.70–71). (The evidence for the first spectacle comes from Suet. *Jul.* 39.4, for Augustus's from Dio 55.10.7.) The death of the bandit Selurus in the mid-thirties BCE shows that both the taste and the technology for elaborate executions were already in place (see below, n.25).

would actually have been available to Ovid's original audience, nevertheless throws into relief a number of important similarities between the two modes of representation and can help explain the significance of Ovid's simile.

Comparison to Livy, another author, of an earlier generation, who also uses the production of visual scenes to define the political position of his work, can help reveal what is distinctive in Ovid's evocations of spectacle in the *Metamorphoses*. Livy's "spectacles" took the form of historical scenes focused through the perceptions of viewers within the narrative, helping his own audience to "see" as they read. The visualization of the past was also an important element in the displays of the emperor, whether this took the form of reviving archaic rituals, constructing his own actions as imitations of past ones, or integrating statues of exemplary figures from the past into the design of his forum. But one striking aspect of Livy's use of spectacle is its autonomy. While his reader may compare his own description of the fetial ritual, for example, with its actual reperformance, Livy's visualizations of events are not staged as contemporary ritual but approximate it by putting the past directly on display. In showing these historical scenes to his readers, Livy may be implicitly rivaling Augustus, but the figures he explicitly follows in directing the gaze of his readers are the kings and consuls summoned up by his own narrative. The "self-generating" aspect of Livian spectacle is also closely bound up with the question of genre. While, as recent scholarship has stressed, Livy's discussions of historical methods reveal all reconstructions of past events as just that,[20] nevertheless he also relies on the audience's expectation that what a historical narrative offers is the truth. The battle of Aquilonia, for example, belongs to the realm of fact, not fiction. Livy's narrative then, to speak in very general terms, derives its authority from the ability vividly to convey "real" events from the past by means of the narrative alone, without needing to evoke contemporary scenes to lend them impact.

Ovid's comparisons of mythical events to contemporary scenes, like those of the arena, are almost diametrically different in respect both to expectations about the "reality" of what he describes and to the relation between his text and contemporary spectacle. In inviting his readers to visualize the death of Orpheus as a *venatio*, he has taken an episode that is both miraculous and mythical and set it in a context immediately apprehensible from the lived experience of his readers. A fundamental tension arises from the projection of the utterly fictional into the empirically real. In a similar way, the first representation of Ovidian gods at their most fabulous, that is, as the personifications familiar from epic poetry,

[20] See Miles 1995.8–74.

simultaneously makes them wear the masks of contemporary prestige. They dwell on a Palatine, they meet in a Senate, and they regard their leader as the Romans do Caesar. Thus, whereas Livy's visualizations of the past by virtue of the essential reality of what he put on display could transport the reader out of the present, Ovid summons up the visual aspects of the present to create a tension between present and past that at once makes the fabulous impossibly real and, in doing so, implicates reality in his own fictions. A spectator of the staged death of Orpheus who knew Ovid's text might have experienced all the more keenly a reciprocal tension between a representation that was undeniably real of an event that could never have happened. Indeed, it would perhaps complete the Ovidian miracle in a way that no textual image ever could, thus exposing at once the powers and the limits of his poetry.

An emphasis on the fictionality of what spectacle represents has an obviously different political charge in the case of a "fatal charade" than of the scenes depicted in a triumph—although even there we have seen that the superimposition of the fictional characters of the *Metamorphoses* onto the historical actors of the triumph emphasizes issues that the viewing of that event perhaps ought to raise for its Roman spectators. Everyone in the audience at a mythological charade—if they were capable of recognizing the allusion in the first place—knew that the man they saw being torn apart was not Orpheus, and probably the majority of those who did would have recognized that, whatever the historicity of Orpheus as a poet, the figure with the power to charm inanimate objects who was torn apart by Maenads belonged to the realm of fable rather than literary history. Far from spoiling the fun, the reification of fiction was the point of the display. To assent to this belief and, at the same time, to realize the impossibility of such an assent were perhaps key to the aesthetic experience involved in such displays. As the poet Martial says of a reenactment of Pasiphae's mating with a bull, *accepit fabula prisca fidem* ("the old story has become believable," *Spect.* 5.2), a comment that not only evokes precisely Ovid's language of fiction but also demonstrates the importance of an awareness of the fabulous nature of the story at the very moment it is being made real.[21] So Kathleen Coleman has suggested the reality of such performances stood in contrast to their fictional imitation on the theatrical stage and also showed the emperor "work[ing] a miracle."[22] In this context, if Ovid's restaging of the event in purely fictional terms is taken to highlight the fictionality of what is depicted, this only amplifies the miraculous effect of an actual reenactment and makes

---

[21] Coleman 1990.67.

[22] Coleman 1990.68 and 73 (quote). See also Bartsch 1994.50–51 with the comments of Auguet 1972.103 and Dupont 1985.398 cited there.

the miracle all the more vivid. By contrast, his own poem offers its mimesis of reality without any actual visual images and thus stands at a further remove; indeed, the very flimsiness of its own illusionism would seem all the more exposed by comparison to the such performances. Yet another way of interpreting the absence of a present manifestation of Ovid's Orpheus, though, is that by doing more with less, Ovid's fiction, if it succeeds in making the reader accept it, has performed the greater miracle. At the same time such an acceptance exposes the gladiatorial Orpheus as nothing but a slave, his poem describes the authentic, legendary Orpheus.

Thus, the juxtaposition of the two representations of Orpheus in the arena, rather than manifesting the superiority of poetic making over imperial display, creates a far more complex effect because there is no sure way of assigning priority to present reality or to the myth it illustrates. The poet's restaging of the imperial reification of his story may be seen as enhancing the effect of actual imperial display in contrast with his own or as beating the emperor at his own game. And if we think not of how a reading of Ovid affects interpretation of the amphitheater but of how knowing about the amphitheater changes one's reading of Ovid, then whatever enhancement Ovid gave the emperor in the former case, the emperor now returns to the poet, for without projecting the amphitheatrical paradigm onto Ovid's narrative, its full ambition and power would not emerge so clearly. Ovid has perhaps relocated the site for experiencing the effects of this miraculous conversion of fiction to reality from the arena to the text, but in doing so he reveals the debt his poetic accomplishment owes to the model of actual imperial display.

Another aspect of Coleman's discussion of mythological charades complements this analysis by demonstrating that "fatal charades" themselves raised the question of the relative priority of the here-and-now performance and the myth it enacted. The performance of myth in the present and without the artificiality of the stage, where you knew that what you were seeing was make-believe, could make its miracles "credible" in a way they never had been before. This is particularly true in the gruesome case of an impersonation of Pasiphae where a female prisoner seems actually to be mated with a bull. Here the fantastic process of metamorphosis—albeit a metamorphosis that even in myth was the product of artifice rather than miracle—becomes all too real. But on the other hand, whenever mythical representation was transferred from the meticulously controlled world of the text or the fabrications of the stage to the reality of the arena, anything could happen. The best-known stories can be transformed when enacted by real protagonists fighting for their lives, and it is revealing about what interested a Roman audience in these performances that our accounts of "fatal charades" note such variations. Thus, two of Martial's epigrams describe stories that came out differently in the arena: "Orpheus," of course, fails to charm with his lyre the wild animals sent to kill him and is done in by a bear (*Spect.* 24–25). Another bear dispatches a Daedalus, who cannot escape with his wings.[23]

Not only did these performances provoke speculation on whether such realization affirmed the power of myth or triumphed over it by demonstrating its essential falsity. Penetration of the illusion by a focus on what was actually happening rather than on the represented story shows another aspect of the battle between truth and fiction in the reception of these events. The most telling example of this comes from another of Martial's epigrams (10.25), this one describing the reenactment not of a Greek myth but of a quasi-legendary event from the early days of the Roman republic, when Q. Mucius Scaevola endures having his right hand burned off as a demonstration of Roman *fides* and *virtus*. Here the performance seems to have gone exactly according to plan. The "Mucius," almost unbelievably, succeeded in seeming *patiens*, *durus*, and *fortis* throughout the ordeal. But Martial himself steps in to detonate the audience's admiration for this feat by differentiating it from legend: "For when, under threat of torture, he was commanded: 'Burn your hand!' it was a braver thing to answer 'No.'" An awareness of the realities of the arena, specifically that this is a slave who, far from resisting torture, only succeeds in his impersonation under the threat of torture, turns on its head the very point of the story.

Martial's comments reveal another point of contact between the poetics of these performances, if such brutality should be dignified with that expression, and Ovidian fictionality: both potentially involve issues of status. Martial's exposure of the constraints placed upon the performer in this case deftly transform physical torture from the demonstration of Roman *libertas*, which it was for Scaevola, to the paradigmatic mark of servitude in the case of the real performer. Perhaps one motive for stripping the scene of its verisimilitude is that its very persuasiveness might have blurred the difference between the two and suggested that such fortitude, far from being the prerogative of a Roman master race, which was what Mucius wanted to show, could be equaled even by the lowest of the low, a *damnatus*. The nature of the performance allows one to see the actor at either the top or the bottom of the social scale, depending on whether he is viewed from inside or outside the drama he enacts, with significant consequences in turn for how that drama is interpreted. In a similar way, Ovid's own position, as we saw in the preceding chapter, shifts

---

[23] *Spect.* 10. I am less convinced than Coleman that this was a staging of the Daedalus myth as a fatal charade. Rather, but equally significantly, I think it is Martial who has staged the execution as myth by playing on the name of the victim.

as we construe him as like and unlike the poetic makers described within his poem. In this respect again, conflicting class associations of *fabula* as a rhetorical form come into play. We have already seen how according to Phaedrus *fabulae*, particularly those in which humans mask their voices as those of animals—and it is interesting to note here the role of animal disguise in the "charades" involving Pasiphae and perhaps Daedalus, become a potentially subversive genre through which the low can speak a language incomprehensible to their masters. Does the trumping of *fabulae* by reality here matter in part because it unmasks the slave disguised as something else?[24] While we have evidence for only a tiny fraction of what may have been a much broader repertoire of myths to be enacted in the tortures of the amphitheater, it is interesting that both Orpheus and Daedalus are attested as subjects. For these are not simply figures from myth, but characters who themselves produce representations through song or the mechanical imitation of nature. Because both artists offer their own images of reality, their appearance within the spectacles of the emperor further heightens an awareness of the contrast between truth and fiction. The presentation of both characters in the amphitheater would thus be of a piece with Ovid's deployment of them in his poetry, where the autonomy of the world created by each—as we have seen demonstrated in the analysis of the Daedalus passage—becomes an issue through which Ovid can pose the question of the status of his own poetry. The death of Orpheus in the arena may then represent in the crudest possible terms the ultimate victory of the *princeps* over the *poeta*.

There is in fact some evidence that staged deaths could indeed be used to subvert the "fictions" of the victim: thus, the bandit Selurus, who boasted that he was son of Etna, was executed by being thrown to the beasts when a collapsible model of the volcano dropped him into their cages. Augustus was not simply hoisting the bandit on his own petard; he was demonstrating precisely through the flimsy staginess of his props that Selurus's boasts were mere fictions and that the power of life and, in this case, death belonged to the emperor.[25]

[24] Another way of reading the *fabulae* performed in the arena, though, works in the other direction. The *fabulae* of myth, when viewed from lower down in the social hierarchy, offered a mark of social status to those who learned them—hence the eagerness of Petronius's upwardly mobile Trimalchio to demonstrate his command of myth, and his high-status creator's emphasis on the spectacular errors he makes. In the context of the arena, the bears who undermine the glamour of myth by devouring the poet Orpheus may perhaps have cheered those who regarded such mythological references as the mark of a status from which they were excluded, and so enhanced the common touch of the emperor who produced the show.

[25] Strabo 6.273. See the discussion of Coleman 1990.53, who proposes a date in the mid-thirties BCE.

This last example stresses the way that death provides a "moment of truth" for the fictions enacted in such shows, compelling spectators to make decisions about what is real and what is artifice. We can imagine this process as a stripping away of disguises to remind spectators either of the real identity of all participants or of the point when they succumb to fictions so completely as to accept them as real. We may also imagine that such complex revelations become difficult for any author of spectacles to control. One can readily conceive of a sympathetic account of Selurus that would stress precisely his humanity and convert the stage props and papier-mâché Etna into the hubristic cruelties of a tyrant. In a very similar way, we have seen how Pythagoras's representation of sacrifice replaces what would be the moment of death at an actual ritual performance with two divergent ways of reading the victim, either unmasking her as a human beneath false appearances or transforming a real cow into a tragic Iphigeneia through a poetic sleight of hand, depending on the reader's preferences and predispositions.

As the last example shows, the relation between questions of fiction and reality and responses to violence influence one another reciprocally in complex ways. If we assent to Pythagoras's view of what the cow really is, then "we" potentially cross the boundaries of the spectacle by identifying with the victim against the society that profits from her death. If we keep our eyes on bovine appearances, it helps us to watch her death as that of an "other." In the arena, masking violence as the enactment of a mythical plot can help distance spectators from its all too real effects. But it can also heroize and raise the status of a servile or even animal victim—the danger, perhaps, that Martial senses in the slave's too successful impersonation of Scaevola. Conversely, too great an awareness of the suffering of the victim can make it impossible to sustain the dramatic illusion and cast an unwelcome attention on the artificer himself.

Helen Morales has documented a very similar process at work in the reception of visual arts. She examines a *controversia*, an imaginary court case, recorded by the Elder Seneca (10.5),[26] centered on a famous painting by Parrhasius on display in the temple of Minerva. The painting depicted Prometheus in bondage, and Parrhasius had tortured a slave to death to observe the effects of such torment in the flesh. The case to be argued is the prosecution of Parrhasius for harming the state by this action, and the various rhetoricians who take it on are forced to consider the question of what it is that one sees when one looks at the painting. If it is the Titan hero, the artist's fiction is accepted as reality, and the "real" context of the painting, to honor the chief god of Athens, rebuts the charge of harm-

---

[26] And therefore from a milieu in which we can document Ovid himself participating as a young man. Morales 1996.

ing the state. But if we see the reality behind the realistic fiction, and it is of course the realism of the painting that creates this dilemma, then the artist becomes merely a torturer who has defiled the temple rather than adorning it. Another equally important issue in this debate, teased out by Morales, is the audience's potential absorption into both the fiction and the creative process. The recognition of "Prometheus" as a slave disintegrates fictionality not only from within, by restoring the absent model, but from without, by creating a sympathy that puts the spectator himself in pain through identification with the victim. More precisely, Morales demonstrates that the viewers' absorption potentially involves taking on either a passive role (Parrhasius "tortures"—*torquet*, 10.5.3—the eyes of the spectators as he tortured the slave) or an active one, making them complicit in the punishment they see inflicted (they view as the artist and so as the performer of torture). We have repeatedly seen this process at work in Ovidian fiction, as absorption in a story subjects internal audiences to metamorphosis or conversely puts them in the role of the agent of transformation.

Morales' analysis helps us perceive the problems of fictionality raised by Ovid's text as part of a broader response to representative arts in the early imperial period, one clearly shaped by responses to contemporary arena spectacle. Although the fictional case is set in Athens, it has been translated to Rome by more than the simple act of being made the subject of a Latin declamation; the rhetor's imaginary exhortation of Parrhasius to "burn, whip, torture" his slave model echoes the famous gladiator's oath to undergo precisely these punishments. The construction of viewing as a collective act, benefiting or harming the entire community, the conflation of representation with violence, and the emphasis on the participatory nature of spectation all find important analogues in responses to gladiatorial spectacle. What is the relevance of this discussion for a reading of Ovid? It is not simply that all roads lead back to the arena and that Ovidian conceptions of fiction find their origins in or primarily address those spectacles. Rather I want to demonstrate the readiness with which questions of reality and fiction manifest themselves in aspects of Roman practice including the arena shows, sacrificial ritual, and theatrical performance. Thus, in the context of Augustan culture—and Ovid in various ways encourages us to recognize this overlap—a topic that we may think of as primarily a formal, narratological question possesses an unexpected utility as a map of responses to phenomena powerfully and directly connected with the construction of each reader's identity as a member of Roman society. Not only, then, does Ovid train the gaze of his audience by exploring the limits of fiction, but he potentially transfers such a civic context to the reception of otherwise very remote events. The *Metamorphoses*' fictions energize and are energized by a dialogue with the spectacular emanations of imperial power. The poet moving from the realm of fantasy and fiction gives solid flesh to his creations, while the emperor competes with the poet in realizing myth. The aim of the rest of this chapter is to show how such a dialogue emerges from another episode in the poem where the acceptance of fictions receives explicit attention, the encounter between Pentheus and Dionysus.

The story, so familiar from Euripides' *Bacchae*, forms the climax of the third book at the conclusion of a set of tales about the origins of Thebes, many of which share a number of motifs in common. First, like Argus from book 1, three of the central characters in this book, Cadmus, Actaeon, and Pentheus, find themselves suddenly thrust from the role of audience or spectator into that of participant—or, indeed, victim. For again, as in the Argus episode, the transition from spectator to spectacle coincides with the moment when each story reaches its violent climax. The pattern is first articulated at the instant when Cadmus has killed the monstrous serpent that has devoured his companions. While Cadmus inspects the monster's size, he hears a mysterious voice ask him why he is staring at the serpent, "since [he] too will be gazed upon as a serpent" (*quid, Agenore nate, peremptum / serpentem spectas? et tu spectabere serpens*, 3.97–98).

The last line points to a second significant theme in these episodes: the sudden shift from the active to passive role in the act of gazing accentuates a dramatic disjunction between outward form and a perceiving self. This receives extensive treatment at the center of the book in the story of Echo and Narcissus, where the youth has the, to him, incomprehensible experience of viewing his appearance from outside.[27] The role of metamorphosis in signifying such a split receives extended treatment in the story of Actaeon, changed to a deer for glimpsing the naked Diana and then torn apart by his own hounds. As his companions watch his gruesome death, they wish that Actaeon himself could be present as a spectator, a wish that figures him as a "mirror image" of Narcissus who cannot stand apart from his form to view it: "They complain that he is absent and that, slow, he does not perceive the spectacle of this fortuitous prey. He would indeed wish to be absent, but he is present, and he would rather watch than feel the cruel deeds of his dogs" (3.245–48).

Finally, the text offers many stimuli for translating the dilemmas of viewing it explores to the contexts of contemporary Roman spectacle.

---

[27] For the thematic centrality of this seemingly divergent story to Ovid's Theban cycle, see the important analysis of Gildenhard and Zissos 2000b who convincingly read it as a stand-in for the omitted story of Oedipus.

The first of these invitations comes just after the issue of shifting spectacular roles has been signaled by the mysterious warning to Cadmus that he too will be gazed at. After Cadmus sows the dragon's teeth, a simile compares the crop of earthborn warriors to figures (*signa*) on a theater curtain being raised:

> sic ubi tolluntur festis aulaea theatris
> surgere signa solent primumque ostendere vultus
> cetera paulatim, placidoque educta tenore
> tota patent imoque pedes in margine ponunt.
> (3.111–14)

As, when curtains are raised at the theater on festival days, images are wont to rise and show forth first the faces and then the rest little by little, and are exposed, drawn up in a gentle motion, and set their feet on the lowest edge.

This simile has been taken to mark the beginning of a series of episodes drawn from tragedy, but such an explicit "staging" of the narrative forms an important step in a developing interest in the unstable position of the spectator.[28] For the simile does more than simply invoke stage machinery; it also enacts its own theatrical illusion by bringing depicted *signa* to life. This effect emerges most clearly in the simile's final line, when the images, which have so far been described in language more or less appropriate to their real status as curtains, now seem to set their own feet on the "threshold" as though they were real people. The actors on the stage? Or the people that they in turn represent? As if to signify how these images have suddenly crossed the line, Ovid omits any transition back from the vehicle of the simile to its tenor, the sown men. But these efforts to bring the reader into the illusionary space created—a move made easier by staging it in terms familiar from contemporary spectacle—are answered within the narrative by a warning issued by one of these actor-warriors to the internal spectator Cadmus, not to "insert himself" among them (3.117). Doing this would mean entering a cycle of civil war in which killer and victim immediately change places, again precisely the import of the warning voice at the serpent's death. Appropriately, then, just as the scene takes on a contemporary Roman flavor that seems potentially to envelope the poem's historical audience, the reader is forcibly pulled back into the role of mere observer. Yet, of course, this injunction doubly implies her absorption, because on the one hand it means identifying with Cadmus and on the other it closely connects the experience of reading to

---

[28] Hardie 1990.226. See also Gildenhard and Zissos 1999a.172.

that, for example, of a gladiatorial competition, where it was precisely by maintaining such distance even in the face of gripping identification with the combatants that the spectator underlined his distance as a Roman from the servile fighters below.

The death of Actaeon too may be compared to a *venatio*, the hunting shows of the arena, though here Actaeon has fallen out of stands to become the victim. And the process culminates in the death of Pentheus himself, who is suddenly seen even as he goes to see the rites of the Maenads (*hic oculis illum cernentem sacra profanes / prima videt ...*, 3.710–11). Euripides, of course, had "staged" Pentheus's death by casting the king as a spectator who is seen as he himself tries to gain a better vantage by mounting to the top of a fir tree. But Ovid updates the scene to the Roman arena, setting it in a plain, *campus*, that is clear of trees and, for that reason, easy to see or good for seeing (*spectabilis*, 3.714), and set off by the forests that surround it.

But these reminders of settings where a contemporary audience might have seen events like the death of Actaeon played out visually do not simply make Ovid's narrative more "spectacular." On the contrary, they create a tense dialogue between the two mimetic modes, which, far from blending into one another, can also appear as adversaries pulling their audiences toward opposite responses and understandings of what they represent. We have earlier encountered viewers within the narrative who facilitate the audience's own imagined visual participation in the scene. Here, though, we meet spectators whose understanding of events veers dramatically from that of Ovid's own audience, and again the phenomenon of changed appearance provides the gauge for this difference. The audience that thrills to the action of Actaeon's death can do so because it remains in ignorance of the story Ovid has told and sees only a deer. Pentheus's own death signals the split even more dramatically. His violent dismemberment at the hands of his mother and aunts has sometimes appeared as an anomalous appendix to the tale of the prisoner "Acoetes," which features precisely the kind of metamorphosis missing in the account of Pentheus. Yet here more than anywhere else, metamorphosis emerges as a question of perspective. Agave and Ino in their madness do perceive that Pentheus has an animal form, that of a wild boar,[29] whereas the reader of Ovid's narrative will acknowledge no such change. The double vision of metamorphosis has here been split neatly in half between these audiences, one of which sees only a boar, the other only a man, and neither a man becoming a boar. The narrative drives a further wedge between its audience and these internal spectators with a moment of self-reference. When Pentheus fails to make his aunt recognize him, he appeals to her recollec-

---

[29] Also Otis 1970.140.

tion of the dead Actaeon. But she "does not know who Actaeon is" (*illa quis Actaeon nescit*, 3.721). Her ignorance at once assimilates her to her son's killers and separates her from readers who "witnessed" Actaeon's transformation through the medium of Ovid's narrative.[30]

The tension between reading and seeing that plays out in Pentheus's final moments emerges appropriately from an agon between two combatants that in several ways symbolizes the competition between fiction and imperial spectacle as a mode for perceiving what is happening. The idea of Dionysus as a practitioner of the same kind of art as the author of the text that represents him will be familiar to anyone who approached Ovid's text with Euripides' metatheatrical *Bacchae* in mind. However, by replacing the "palace miracle" of that play with a retelling of the Homeric Hymn to Dionysus, Ovid substitutes for the dramaturgical god working through *opsis* to hint at his identity an "epic" divinity who uses a narrative about metamorphosis to prove that he is who he is not (i.e., Acoetes). Pentheus's response to the narrative also couples its deceptive, riddling nature with its status as something heard rather than seen (*"Praebuimus longis" Pentheus, "ambagibus aures,"* 3.692).[31] And instead of emerging in visible form, as the god did at the end of the *Bacchae*, Bacchus's final mention here has him slipping away from the "solid" chains in which the king sought to bind him into the more nebulous world of narrative, for his miraculous escape is merely something reported (*fama est*, 3.700).

Pentheus's role, by contrast, is throughout the narrative to impose "real" physical compulsion on speakers of words by his presence. He "casts forth" (*proturbat*, 3.526) the prophet Teiresias, in the midst of his speech (*talia dicentem*, 3.526), and, in a frenzy of imperatives, gives orders for the god himself to be brought in bound (*"ite citi"—famulis hoc imperat—"ite ducemque/ attrahite huc vinctum! Iussis mora segnis abesto,"* 3.563–64). The Pentheus who considers listening to stories a waste of time and had begun his "reception" of the god with his eyes rather than his ears (*adspicit hunc oculis*, 7.577) has similarly been trans-

---

[30] The very words of Pentheus enact another division between internal spectators and the witnesses of metamorphosis. For the reader, Pentheus's appeal will look very much like Shakespeare's Lavinia citing Philomela as a way of telling her own story. Actaeon was seen as a deer but was really not, so don't you bacchantes make the same mistake now. But I doubt whether this can be taken as Pentheus's intention. First of all, there is no sign that Actaeon ever was "recognized" in the guise of a deer by a human audience, and it is equally unclear that Pentheus perceives that the bacchantes see him as a beast. In such circumstances, Pentheus's appeal to Actaeon's shade need be nothing other than a rhetorically familiar appeal for pity by making the potential perpetrator of violence see a resemblance between the victim and a near relation (human, of course). When Pentheus invokes the "specter" of Actaeon, then, he expects his audience to see a human image, while the poet's audience will be more likely to see a deer's.

[31] Can one even hear "hearing" in the Greek name Akoetes?

lated into a very Roman in figure in the way he combines violent spectacle with the projection of his own authority. His final shift from watcher to victim not only shatters the conventional image of the spectator's distance from events but also more subtly inverts a paradox of Roman power, that an emperor was never more conspicuously powerful than when he adopted the role of spectator. For another striking feature of Pentheus's first glimpse of the disguised god comes when the narrative focuses attention on the king's eyes less as instruments of vision then as objects of vision that themselves convey his own fury (*oculis quos ira tremendos fecerat*, 7.577). Far from being weakened when seen as opposed to seeing, his very act of viewing his victim reveals his own might.[32] A corresponding emphasis on visual manifestations of power emerges from Pentheus's first address to his captive, as someone "about to perish and furnish by your death an example to others," 3.579–80. Pentheus's reliance on Bacchus's death as evidence of the folly of violating his own authority not only recalls the general Roman language of exemplarity but more specifically resembles the violent death of a figure like Selurus, himself a brigand, as direct visible proof of what legitimate imperial authority looks like. Pentheus's victim must be witnessed to affirm his authority, or if it is merely recorded, it must be believed as something true, not something made up.

A more direct link to contemporary Roman ideologies of power comes in the content of Pentheus's exhortation to his fellow Thebans to resist physically the imposition of the new cult. Philip Hardie has pointed out the many similarities between the Theban heritage Pentheus invokes here and the foundation legends that, in the words of Livy (*praef.* 7), add majesty to the Romans' own account of their origins.[33] The Thebans are children of Mars (3.531—called by his old Roman name, *Mavors*).[34] Their ancestry, somewhat incongruously, combines a divinely led band from an eastern city (Tyre, 3.539), and the vigor of a native stock, the Sown Men born from the dragon's teeth. Pentheus exhorts his hearers to live up to the reputation won by their ancestors in the past by demonstrating manliness against a stereotypical characterization of an effeminate easterner, "locks dripping with myrrh, soft [*molles*] crowns, and clothing embroi-

[32] This moment in the downfall of Pentheus echoes his own (mis)interpretation of his descent from the dragon slain by Cadmus. Cadmus assumes that this implies his own assumption of the place of his victim and thus responds with terror. But the combination in that earlier scene of the words *serpens* and *specto* suggests the Greek name for the beast, *drakon*, the gazer. And the terror that Cadmus experienced in looking at the snake was appropriate to a creature whose power came precisely from its gaze.

[33] On the Roman overtones of Pentheus's speech, see esp. Janan 2004. For the similarities between Theban and Roman origins in general, see Hardie 1990, Galinsky 1975.221.

[34] Also noted by Anderson 1996.391, who throughout his commentary on the passage astutely observes important parallels with contemporary political rhetoric, and especially with the vision(s) of the Roman past developed in the *Aeneid*.

dered with purple and gold" (3.555–56), who, rather problematically, recalls their own origins in the East. Interestingly, his concern is less with the physical survival of Thebes than with the preservation and projection of a true image of hard Theban manliness. References to shame and disgrace punctuate his exhortation. If Thebes must fall, let it fall by war so that its fate will compel lamentation rather than concealment (3.548–52). It befits the youth of Thebes to adorn themselves with arms and helmets, rather than bacchic garlands (3.541–42). And the Thebans will affirm their strength and power by proving the falsehood of the story that the "other" tells about himself. "I will force [the youthful Bacchus] to confess that his 'father' is falsely claimed and that his rights are fictions" (3.558).

Again, the proof of Pentheus's own power comes through a demonstration of the reality of appearances. Pentheus will show that his opponent is exactly what he seems to be, an effeminate eastern boy, in part by demonstrating the actual emptiness of his own divine paraphernalia. Not only are the god's forces physically weak; they are illusory. Bacchus is a *vanum numen* (3.559–60), an empty divinity who relies on deceptions, *magicae fraudes* (3.534). The dancing and music to which he devotes himself appear in Pentheus's words not only as effeminate but also as materially insubstantial in comparison to the too solid weaponry of the Theban soldiers. Thus, the musical instruments of the god are described as "mere bronze beaten with bronze" (*aera tantum aere repulsa*, 3.532–33) and are said to be without strength. This concept too recalls a characteristic topos of Roman military rhetoric. When for example, in Livy's book 10, the Romans encounter a Samnite legion that has been outfitted with a particularly splendid and distinctive costume, the Roman commander Papirius Cursor exhorts his troops not to fear what he describes as empty finery. Roman iron will prove the ineffectuality of Samnite gold (10.39.12).

Before looking at how "Acoetes'" narrative responds to the issues raised by the king's rhetoric precisely by demonstrating the potency of fictions, it is important to note that Pentheus's claims about the real Theban past, like the ignorance of the bacchants who kill him, potentially set him apart from the actual audience for Ovid's narrative of Thebes's origins. Most strikingly, Pentheus's rejection of the story of Bacchus's birth requires the rejection of the Semele story, which has been told directly by the narrator. So too, his account of Thebes's own history, itself full of inconsistencies, shows, at best, divergent interpretations of the events Ovid's narrative records. Other than Cadmus, what old men of Tyrian stock survived the dragons' attack?[35] And while Cadmus experiences the warning that he

---

[35] Ovid never says that all the Tyrians were killed, although he does not mention any other survivors. And if Cadmus still had surviving companions, then there would seem to be no need to sow the dragon's teeth to restore the lost population.

will become a serpent as a terrifying reminder of the impermanence of victory at the very moment he wins it, Pentheus, identified throughout as the son of the serpent,[36] rejoices in that heritage and actually urges the Thebans to imitate the serpent in their defense of their native land. For him, "becoming the serpent," far from suggesting that all victors will take on the position of victims, provides only a guarantee of future success. The serpent won once, and if they can only continue to be serpents, the Thebans will win in the future. Similarly, Pentheus initially addresses his audiences as the offspring of Mars, recalling that the serpent was itself *Martius* (3.32). However, Ovid earlier says not that the Sown Men were the children of Mars but rather that they died from Mars as a metonym for war (*Marte cadunt*, 3.123).

These discrepancies may at first suggest that the narrative simply sets Pentheus apart from the community of the audience, as, for example, it does those internal spectators who cannot see that the hunter Actaeon has now become the quarry. This kind of reading would also easily assume a contemporary ideological slant: Pentheus's misunderstanding, or willful misreading, of his nation's legendary past to cement his own authority could have found some important parallels in contemporary manipulations of Rome's own history.[37] Yet to read Pentheus's speech exclusively in this way is in another sense to underestimate the power of Ovid's portrayal of him not just as a figure of the present but indeed as a figure who assumes an independent reality apart from Ovid's representation. If we expect that Ovid's audience might resist Pentheus's rhetoric, that is actually the situation in which Pentheus finds himself in addressing the Thebans under the spell of Bacchus (note "you just stand back!" *modo vos abstite*, 3.557), so that fictional narrative here represents the actual circumstances of its reception. Ovid also strikingly adopts the first person in a simile that describes the king's wrath by comparing it to a raging river, "as I myself have seen" (*sic ego ... vidi*, 3.568–69), at once intruding his own presence into the internal audience, and suggesting that Pentheus is to be figured only by things that can really be seen.[38] If we accept this invitation to move the king into the contemporary present,

---

[36] The literal meaning of the name of his father Echion, who was one of the five surviving offspring of the dragon's teeth.

[37] See Janan 2004.

[38] This desire to be present, which importantly goes together with the need to manifest authority, plays a pivotal role in precipitating Pentheus's death. In the *Bacchae*, of course, Pentheus is lured to destruction by a secret desire to see the lubricious mysteries of the god. But such a motif does not drive Ovid's Pentheus. Rather his trip to the mountain appears as the next stage in a process of giving commands. "Pentheus persists and now no longer simply orders others to go, but goes himself" (*nec iam iubet ire, sed ipse / vadit*, 3.701–2), as though his physical presence were a way of imposing his *imperium* ever more directly.

as the familiarity of his patriotic topoi would have made it easy for an Augustan audience to do, then his claims appear as something more than misreading. He becomes the voice of history whose version of the events of Roman prehistory has been borne out by the distinctiveness of its own accomplishments.

This emphasis on Pentheus as a present figure can perhaps be tracked by the frequency with which he is named in the narrative, and the uses he makes of the patronymic Echionides to advance claims about his own identity on the basis of inheritance. But his name occurs for the last time in the story at the moment when he is first struck by his mother's weapon (3.712). From then on, as his own kin fail to know him, in place of a name he seeks to be recognized by claiming likeness to a figure in a story, one that his addressees either do not know or do not believe. And as his identity disappears, so his physical presence literally dissolves as the parts of his body are stripped away. Appropriately, Ovid omits anything like the final scenes of the *Bacchae*, where the identity of the victim is finally recognized in gazing at his severed head.

The figure who confronts the king is altogether more difficult to get a hold of. If Pentheus moves from presence to absence by becoming like the character in a metamorphosis narrative, it is only as a figure in fiction that his opponent assumes any identity at all. The narrative parallels to Euripides' play strongly suggest that we take Acoetes to be the god in disguise, but he is never identified as such directly.[39] There are hints in this direction, but by leaving out an epiphany and keeping his god firmly offstage, Ovid ensures that we recognize Bacchus only when he appears as what he is not, as a character who recedes ever further back into the realm of miraculous narrative. This lack of identifiable substance goes together with a further play on appearances on the part of "Acoetes." As his opponent trusts so much in the power of presence, believing that things are what they seem and discounting illusions, like the hollow bronze of the god's instruments, by reducing them to what they really are, so the god appears in precisely the vulnerable guise that his opponents assume to be his real identity. The guards who capture Dionysus present him not as a god but as a mere servant (*comitem famulumque sacrorum*, 3.574), assimilating him to the class of people that the king himself orders about (cf. *famulis*, 3.562). This is also what the pirates within Acoetes' narrative make of the god, thinking that his vulnerable appearance makes him sim-

---

[39] The figure of Acoetes himself is not referred to anywhere in extant earlier Greek literature but first appears in the *Pentheus* of Pacuvius (synopsis in Serv. Auct. *ad Aen.* 4.469). For background and a discussion of the "oft ventilierte Frage" of whether Acoetes is to be regarded as a figure in his own right or simply as an alias for Dionysus, see Bömer 1969–86.2.588–89. Hardie 1990.231, n. 41, suggests that Ovid's Acoetes may have been influenced by Vergil's Sinon.

ply something to be plundered (*praeda*, 3.606). So here the god tricks his opponent by seeming to be what he is seen as. Pentheus accuses Bacchus of lying when he claims to be the son of Jupiter; Acoetes makes just the opposite claim, identifying his status as that of a humble fisherman and stressing that this *ars* is his sole inheritance.

Let us now look more closely at the narrative with which Acoetes attempts to persuade Pentheus to believe the unbelievable in order to see precisely how it enacts the power of fiction. The stranger claims to be a fisherman who has learned the skills of navigation. When the ship on which he is helmsman puts in at Chios, the sailors find a mysterious somnolent youth, whom they wish to kidnap and hold for ransom but whom he alone recognizes as a god. As they make off with him, the ship suddenly halts; tendrils of ivy and bunches of grapes encase the oars and sails. The god appears surrounded by the *simulacra inania* of lynxes and the "fierce bodies of painted panthers," and all the men, except the narrator himself, are transformed into dolphins (3.668–75). The vivid, exotic, and fantastical elements of the narrative directly answer Pentheus's earlier splenetic rejection of the foreign and the unbelievable. Yet the strategy of the poet and the god is not quite a simple insistence that the miraculous story is literally true. Rather, the story emphasizes the potency even of mere appearances, stressing that the god is most emphatically there when he seems to be someone else. Thus, for "Acoetes" the form that deceives the sailors provides a sign of their victim's divinity. "I behold his dress, his appearance, and his gait; nothing I saw could be considered mortal" (3.609–10). So too the epiphany of the god aboard the ship is heralded by apparitions that are explicitly identified as false: "empty images" of lynxes and "fierce bodies of painted panthers."[40] And, to move out one fictional level from the story that Acoetes tells to the circumstances of the telling, the same paradox appears when the disguised god swears by himself. "I swear by the god himself [and no god is more present, *praesentior*] that what I am recounting is as much true as it surpasses credibility [*tam vera … quam veri maiora fide*, 3.658–60]." The narrator's attempt to swear by the god, of course, further enhances the fiction that he is not Dionysus himself and thus constitutes another deception.[41] But the claim that no god is *praesentior* is an absolutely true statement—if we read Acoetes as the god, of course. Notice correspond-

---

[40] The description refers most directly to the markings on the hides of real leopards, but it can also suggest that the leopards themselves are merely painted images.

[41] This pattern of gods swearing by themselves in disguise is particularly familiar from comedy. In this way, for example, in Plautus's *Amphitryo* the disguised Mercury tricks Sosia, a scene that bears many other resemblances to this one, not least the god's assumption of a low-status identity.

ingly that what Acoetes claims is that the story is true *in proportion* to its apparent unbelievability.

Various kinds of transformation accompany the god's epiphany. We have noticed before that the *simulacra* of lynxes surrounding the god seem to highlight the emptiness of the appearances the divinity produces. Yet at the moment of transformation, the sailors physically experience such *miracula* in their own bodies; like so many Actaeons, they feel rather than see their destruction. And as we have identified such a shift in perspective as a moment when the effects of metamorphosis spread outward to include its audience, so we become aware at the instant when the unbelievable happens that the narrative being told to Pentheus describes the situation in which he finds himself—disbelieving a god who appears before him—and predicts his own destiny. For the transformation of the sailors' bodies in this false narrative closely anticipates the actual dismemberment of the unmetamorphosed body of Pentheus. One of the sailors attempts to stretch his arms toward the ropes of the ship to save himself only to discover that his arms have turned to fins. In the same way, Pentheus will discover that he has "no arms with which to supplicate his mother" (3.723 ~ 3.679–80).

But as an unbelievable story begins to control reality both for the sailors and for Pentheus, a similar process may well be at work for Ovid's audience, thanks, again, to the evocation of the experience of contemporary spectacle. As the first stage in the miracle, the ship stands still, as if the dry shipyard held it (3.661), an expression that may hint at Ovid's own transportation of the ship to the terrestrial realm of his audience, and perhaps of the similar transformation of elements effected by imperial power thematically important in circus spectacle among others. Lest this last suggestion seem too fantastical, the word Ovid uses of the dry dock, *navale*, was also applied to the *stagnum navale*, the term for the artificial lake on which emperors would stage sham sea battles.[42] And if there is a fleeting hint of such contemporary events in Acoetes' simile, it sets the stage for an initial transformation of the god's victims into spectators. Although busily engaged in trying to get the frozen ship under way, the sailors are first described as looking on in wonder (*admirantes*, 3.662). At the same time their activities seem to transform them into stagehands who can only put the finishing touches on the conversion of the scene to a spectacle. The sailors keep trying to ply their oars and unfurl the sail; the word used for sails, *vela*, can also be applied to the awnings that shaded the audience at a spectacle. But the oars are frozen as ivy winds around the vessel. Beyond symbolizing Dionysus's power, ivy was used in artistic

---

[42] See Coleman 1993.

representations as a border or frame; Arachne will similarly use it to frame her own catalog of gods in disguise. The possibility of seeing the stilling of the ship as its conversion to a representation of itself becomes greater when the ivy reaches the *vela* and "marks them" (*distingunt*, 3.665) with its berries.[43] And it is on the stage that has been so constructed that the sailors, converted from *admirantes* to *miracula* (*in quae miracula verteris*, 3.673–74)—an exclamation appropriately put in the mouth of one of the sailors at the instant when he himself turns from watcher to miraculous dolphin—conclude their performance. Their rhythmic swimming comes to look more and more like dancing (*saltus*), as they "play" in the manner of a chorus (*inque chori ludunt speciem*, 3.685). Thus, as the characters within the narrative see their reality suddenly transformed in unbelievable ways, the external audience, as it sees the boat transformed into a painted or staged vessel, sees the miracle come true in the sense that it sees the ship converted into the sort of image in which such a myth might really be enacted. The final moment of the miracle becomes the least miraculous of all, a mere stage illusion. And to one looking back from this scene, it is easy to see simple theatrical expertise revealed as the real secret of the *ars* the character Acoetes claimed at the start. For that art involved deception (*decipere*) of "dancing" fishes (*salientes pisces*) as a substitute for flocks (of actors? *greges*, 3.585–87). So when "Acoetes" lands on Chios, he again dances (*saltus*) on the sand (of the arena? *harena*, 3.599). By this reading, the god does seem indeed reduced to what, like fishing, was a typically low-status and foreign occupation.

Before moving on to a concluding analysis of how this episode construes the relationship between fictional and historical spectacles, I want to highlight another motif that structures both the plot and imagery of the Theban narratives and must also be integrated into any political reading of them. That motif is sacrifice. The previous chapter argued that in Pythagoras's representation of sacrifice, metamorphosis, which allows the audience to "become" the victim in the sense of seeing from her perspective, functions as a narrative equivalent to the experience of witnessing the killing at an actual ritual. The Theban sequence, perhaps more intensely than anywhere else in the poem, concentrates stories that link the moment of transformation at once with the infliction of violence and with the contrast in perspectives between victim and onlooker. At the same time, the very fact that these stories do form a sequence helps to illustrate what one might call the commutative property of metamorphosis, that each metamorphosis engenders further transformations and that those who witness, and even hear accounts of, metamorphosis are liable to experience their own transformations in turn. Here, too, we will

---

[43] For painted *vela*, see Bieber 1961.179.

find that invocations of sacrificial ritual help add a political dimension to these narrative effects. For Pythagoras, sympathetically viewed metamorphosis provides a narrative substitute for the climax of sacrifice; so within the Theban story, the sequence of metamorphoses opens out from an attempt at sacrifice.[44] After arriving at the site of Thebes, Cadmus prepares to sacrifice to Jupiter, and it is on their way to fetch water for this ritual that his companions meet the deadly serpent who initiates the theme of spectator becoming spectacle. There is no mention in the text of this sacrifice ever being completed, and perhaps the narratives that follow all compensate for this ritual lapse until the final lines of the book close the sequence with Bacchus's propagation of new *sacra* (3.732).

The very difficulty of imposing any ending on the sequence that leads from Cadmus to Actaeon to Pentheus takes on a special significance in light of this sacrificial precedent. According to Rene Girard's theory of sacrifice, every successful sacrifice results from a kind of substitution.[45] The animal victim in a sacrifice serves as a stand-in for an actual member of the community, against whom the violence of the group can be directed but whose actual death would provoke reprisals and thus precipitate further violence. Thus, at the moment of its death the victim takes on the double role of insider and outsider; while its animal shape obviously differentiates it from the human spectators; nevertheless these spectators' capacity to recognize a resemblance to themselves in the victim is essential for the success of the sacrifice.[46] Each sacrifice therefore

---

[44] The probable victim of this sacrifice, the cow that led the Tyrians to Thebes, offers another anticipation of Pythagoras's staging of sacrifice. Of course it also presents a number of ironic and suggestive links to the story of Europa that motivates Cadmus's quest. She had failed to recognize the presence of an alien consciousness, here divine, in a bull. Now her brother prepares to sacrifice a cow that shares her own defining traits of virginity (here symbolized by the absence of any "mark of servitude," 3.16) and beauty (*speciosam*, 3.20—the sensual double entendres of the moment when she reclines on the site of Thebes, 3.22–23, heighten the parallels with Ovidian rape narratives). And the recipient of this sacrifice is to be none other than the god who abducted her. (In most other versions of the story the heifer is sacrificed to a chthonic deity, either the earth or, more commonly, Pallas Onka; cf., e.g., Apollodorus *Bibl.* 3.4.1. See Vian 1963.109–10 for discussion and citations.) These recollections alternatively suggest an identification between the sacrificer and his victim, who would here be a kind of substitute for his own lost sister, and between the sacrificer and the god, who similarly victimized Europa. And the reassignment of a bovine countenance from the male divine pursuer to the female mortal victim anticipates already the reciprocity between victor and victim that will be the explicit theme of the following narratives.

[45] Girard 1977.1–38.

[46] Girard 1977.5: "Sacrificial substitution implies a degree of misunderstanding. Its vitality as an institution depends on its ability to conceal the displacement on which the rite is based. It must never lose sight entirely, however, of the original object, or cease to be aware of the act of transference from that object to the surrogate victim: without that awareness no substitution can take place and the sacrifice loses all efficacy."

simultaneously actualizes two possible conceptions of violence, one in which the collective use of violence against an outsider confirms and unites the community, and another in which the violence of the community appears directed against a member of the group or indeed the spectator himself. In the latter case, a cycle of pointless and unstoppable violence results, Girard's "sacrificial crisis," which can be resolved only by channeling all the antagonistic impulses within a society against a single individual who must be replaced in turn by a ritually acceptable (nonhuman) victim. The imagery of sacrificial crisis has been frequently discovered in the Romans' accounts of their own indiscriminate, and dangerously recurring, civil wars.[47] And within the Theban narrative we see a similar image of the war of all against all at the very inception of Theban society, in the Sown Men who substitute for the original Tyrians after they became victims instead of sacrificers. Both the impiety of the process and its immediate reciprocity are highlighted: these are brothers killing brothers, as Cadmus's victim would perhaps have substituted for his own sister, and the instant that one brother kills another he himself becomes a victim.

The new Thebans thus seem the collective embodiment of a society where sacrificial substitution has broken down and of the narrative principle of victor becoming victim. As we have seen, for Cadmus the sight of this warfare almost compels him to include himself in it: "Terrified by this new [strange] enemy, Cadmus was preparing to take up arms when one of the people whom the earth had created shouts, 'Don't take them. Don't involve yourself in civil wars'"(3.115–17). Because Cadmus's danger approximates that of the spectator so deceived by theatrical representation that he takes it as real, falling into the scene means losing sight of the distinctness not just of the recent history of Rome, which has so definitively moved out of its period of indiscriminate and unstoppable violence, but also of the distinctness of Rome in the larger schema of world history as the place where the fluctuations of identity caused by metamorphosis stop. Thebes famously played the role of defining other in Athenian drama.[48] And as Hardie points out, in Pythagoras's prediction of the immortality of Roman *imperium*, Thebes again assumes a contrastive function, as one of the cities whose power has vanished and who survive only as a *nomen* (15.429).[49] In the crudest terms, the loss of boundaries and distinctions between reality and fiction, and between beast, man, and god, that the Dionysiac presence in the narrative puts in play, imposes a

---

[47] Bandera 1981, Hardie 1993, e.g., and for this episode now esp. Janan 2004.
[48] See esp. Zeitlin 1986.
[49] See Hardie 1990.225–26.

"Girardian" sacrificial crisis as punishment for a too rigid view of difference, like that adopted and urged by Pentheus, and this crisis projects outward to affect Ovid's own audience via a poetics of allusion in which the Romans' victorious past merges with those of its victims, those whom their own history would make "other." Only a Pentheus, with his insistence on difference, can save them from such deception, as indeed he does in sacrificial terms by emerging as the "one" victim who establishes himself as legitimate. But that is only in a story about other people.

The link between attitudes toward fictionality and the reception of the sacrificial experience as either beneficial or destructive for a society structures many facets of the alternative narratives presented by Pentheus and Bacchus. Pentheus, as we saw, reads the deadly origins of Thebes as a source of strength and life. His narrative of both the encounter with the dragon and the men born from his teeth reveal an identification only with the victors and not with the victims. The serpent alone slew many, with no recognition that it was slain in turn, and the Sown Men themselves are simply those born of Mars, with no mention of precisely the killing of kin that Pentheus himself urges them to enact in the defeat of his cousin Bacchus. This reading of the past gains a sacrificial coloring through the description of the serpent as the one who alone slew many, an inversion of the traditional role of the victim as the one whose death provides salvation for the multitude (*qui multos perdidit unus*, 3.544). Pentheus's own death will illustrate the opposite sacrificial principle, when the "whole crowd rushes against him alone" (*ruit omnis in unum*, 3.715).

The ability of the one to slay many, which Pentheus uses to urge the many to slay one (Bacchus), is undone precisely by the capacity of this "one" to assume a multiplicity of forms. And the language of Acoetes' reply also deploys the motif of the one for many, but to demonstrate the power of the single god against a society that does not recognize him. The narrative of Thebes's foundation as a whole may well constitute an anti-*Aeneid*, but within the encounter of Pentheus and Bacchus, two contrasting readings of the *Aeneid* emerge, refracted largely through different views of its sacrificial moments. Thus, Pentheus's praise of the Tyrian old men as those "who borne through long seas sea voyages have founded a Tyre here, and here settled exiled Penates" (3.538–39) is shot through with the language of the *Aeneid*'s prologue (ironically reapplied to the Tyrians, ancestors also of Rome's arch enemy Carthage). But if Pentheus figuratively claims the mantle of a descendant of Aeneas for those whom the real *Aeneadae* defeat, Acoetes offers his own anti-*Aeneid* in turn, featuring a disastrous voyage where the many are all destroyed on account of their impiety, not simply pursued despite their piety, and in which the narrator plays the pivotal role of anti-Palinurus, a steersman who, rather than being the one victim guaranteeing the salvation of many, becomes the only survivor.[50]

These reminiscences of the successful voyage of the *Aeneid* help to sketch a complex vision of the balance between the individual and the social answering those of Pentheus and his reading of the *Aeneid*. On the simplest level, Acoetes' tale points out the destruction of a collective enterprise—and notice how the many named sailors summon up the same sense of a social group as the catalog of Actaeon's hounds—balanced against the salvation of the one individual. As opposed to Pentheus's attempt to rouse the many Thebans against the one, here the original group's destination, like the sailors themselves, vanishes as the single sailor finally arrives, appropriately, at the new *sacra* of Bacchus.

The play with the role of Palinurus also helps relate this transformation to an overturning of sacrificial roles. The men themselves attempt to ensure the success of their own enterprise, the abduction of Bacchus, by killing the one who resists it—literally trying to cast him overboard as Neptune does Palinurus. One of the villainous crew members, Aethalion, ironically recalls the sacrificial function of Palinurus, as he, again unknowingly aping Neptune, drives Acoetes from the tiller: "Doubtless our whole salvation rests on you alone" (*te scilicet omnis in uno / nostra salus posita est*, 3.647–48). As Pentheus, while focusing on the victory of the single dragon, refuses to see that the one against whom he leads the Thebans may have the same power, so here the men, only too aware of the vulnerability of the individual, fail to recognize his power to benefit them collectively by standing in for all of them. Indeed, rather than seeing him as a metonym for them all, one of the sailors thinks he can simply take the place of Acoetes at the helm.

From the moment in which Bacchus is taken, the voyage moves from the attempt to kill the one on behalf of the many to a true bacchic sacrifice, blurring the boundaries between human and animal so as to combine the destructive and salvific powers of the god. And to guide the audience's own perspective in the same direction, Ovid makes the intended victim himself the narrator,[51] as if to ensure that we see the crewman's

---

[50] *de modo viginti ... / restabam solus*, 3.687–88. It is also significant that the sailors who so explicitly fail to recognize the god Bacchus are aiming at Delos, the spot where the Trojans will receive the advice from Apollo that they themselves misinterpret. Indeed, Bacchus himself will become an impersonation of the very Trojan Penates who reveal this mistake to Aeneas, when he cries out to his abductors *non haec mihi litora, nautae, / promisistis* (3.652–53; cf. *Aeneid* 3.161–62: *non haec tibi litora suasit / Delius aut Cretae iussit considere Apollo*).

[51] More precisely, if we assume that the "fictional" Acoetes is really the god in disguise, then the same figure emerges both as the intended victim within the fiction and as the actual killer for those who recognize him.

attempt as murder, as he sees it, and then witness the bacchic rituals as a participant. The importance of this narratological perspective emerges again in the account Acoetes gives of the sailors' metamorphosis, which drains them simultaneously of individuality and subjectivity. Rather than staging this transformation as instantaneous for all, Acoetes creates a chain of individual events highlighting, as we have seen, the transformation of each viewer into a *miraculum*: Medon starts to change; Lycabas addresses him and becomes a dolphin at the same moment; then Libys sees his own body change, as does an unnamed "other" (*alter*). At this point the perspectives of individual sailors vanish, as the many, who now share but a single appearance, take on plural verbs and the collective identity of a chorus (3.671–86).[52]

If we read the death of Pentheus as an invitation to think about the interaction between Ovidian fiction and imperial spectacle, what conclusions can we draw from it? Initially the relationship between the two modes of representation seems an agonistic one, as Pentheus, a figure readily transposed with a Roman *imperator*, disbelieves and disregards a narrator of metamorphoses. We have also seen how the battle between the two involves specific strategies of responding to the spectacle of violence. Pentheus's attempt to convert Bacchus's punishment into a *documentum* confirms a powerfully hierarchical view of both external and internal relations. The Thebans as a nation are superior to easterners, and the individual king is superior to the multitude of servants, *famuli*, whom he commands and punishes at will.[53] This perspective both reinforces and depends upon accepting things for what they seem to be, that is, judging appearances from an exclusively external perspective perhaps corresponding to the safe position of spectators who watch a gladiatorial combat secure that they will not themselves be tossed into the ring. By contrast, Bacchus insists on just such a possibility and reduces the king who seemed unique in his power to the unique victim of the god's devotees. Believing in *miracula* means precisely losing that sense of isolating externality from what you see and correspondingly surrendering a sure

---

[52] The idea that Acoetes has escaped from an impious attempt at "sacrifice" leads to another connection with the use of that motif in the *Aeneid*: Hardie 1990.231, n.41 has compared Acoetes to Sinon, the figure who deceives the Trojans by pretending to have escaped from the plot of his fellow Greeks to sacrifice him to ensure the success of their expedition. If we read Acoetes as Sinon, it provides yet another perspective on Acoetes. The knowledge of the prior text thus resists its transformation and offers a narrative that by also fitting Acoetes' situation encourages us to disbelieve him. Here the *Aeneid* cooperates with Pentheus in framing our view of the stranger.

[53] What Actaeon would have said, if he had a voice, is "Know your master" (*dominum cognoscite vestrum*, 3.230).

sense of social identity and position within the group. Thus, an initial impression powerfully suggests that a reading of the *Metamorphoses* equips its audience with other eyes through which to watch sacrifice and gladiatorial spectacle and so strikes at a fundamental mechanism for generating Roman and imperial ideology.

But other elements of the narrative complicate that picture. First, accepting fictions and identifying "selves" within them have consequences for the audiences inside the narrative that may well have spoken to the anxieties of a contemporary reader. In the case of Cadmus, losing awareness of the theatrical conventions that separate a Roman audience from what it saw brings him very close to entering an antisocial world of endless rivalry between equals all too like the period of civil war. The easy recognition of a self in the other that comes, for example, from seeing sacrifice, as Pythagoras will, is undoubtedly a much easier move for a twenty-first-century academic than it would have been for a member of the Roman upper classes where questions of stable succession and the ultimate permanence of Roman power had become acute. Bacchus was always a terrifying god.

In addition to this demonstration of the social dangers of an oppositional reading of spectacle, the very distinctness of these dialectically opposed poles of viewing begins to dissolve, and as a result mapping the figures in the narrative onto contemporary social roles becomes less straightforward. Initially, Pentheus seems to fit the model of the bad reader of fictions, resembling Argus before him and anticipating the skeptical Pirithous of book 8. And yet it is not the king but his bacchic killers whose perspective stands in sharpest contrast to that of Ovid's audience. They are the ones who do not recognize Actaeon. One way of understanding this is simply as an example of poetic justice, punishing Pentheus's blindness through an equivalent blindness on the part of his murderers. Perhaps in this sense the comment serves as a final test for the Ovidian audience, ensuring our own ability to recognize the identity of two such seemingly disparate figures. But if so, then the door opened by such recognition makes it difficult to maintain a sense of the distinctness of Ovid's own bacchic victor. And indeed at the very moment of his triumph Bacchus himself comes most closely to resemble the imperial figure he defeats. The encounter began with Pentheus promising that Bacchus's death would be a proof (*documentum*); the final interpretation of Pentheus's death gives it a virtually identical admonitory and exemplary function, but this time affirming the power of the god as opposed to the king: "Warned by such examples, the women of Thebes throng the new rites and make offerings of incense and cultivate the sacred altars" (*talibus exemplis monitae nova sacra frequentant / turaque dant sanctasque colunt Ismenides aras*, 3.732–33). The bacchic perspective, if we may call it that, has led not to the destruction of sacrifice but to its institution. Our crude identification of Pentheus with the emperor and Bacchus with the poet gives way before a different recognition of the similarities between this triumphant figure and Augustus himself.[54] For the *princeps* too claimed to be the son of a god and imposed a new religious order after vanquishing the self-promoting jingoism of a hereditary aristocracy.

Acoetes' metamorphic life story highlights a moment when he himself turned from *ars*, the fishing skill left him by his father, to "rule," *regimen* (3.593). The next stage in our line of reading would be to uncover in the creator of fictions the true voice of a hidden god by showing how Bacchus's own conflation with Pentheus parallels a move on the poet's part to highlight his fiction not as an alternative to public spectacle but as its equivalent. For as we have seen, Bacchus's final framing of Pentheus as a negative example mirrors the stopping point of Acoetes' own metamorphosis narrative, which ends when the weird and miraculous dolphins take on the familiar form of a spectacle, specifically a choral dance. So far we have concentrated on how the text accommodates different views of the emperor, but now we must turn the tables and recognize again how the approximation to imperial performance articulates alternative views of poetic fiction itself. For if the end of fiction is to become as real as spectacle, this is at once the performance of a true miracle, in the sense that these creatures of myth have taken on the form that makes them part of the material world of a Roman audience, and the destruction of its miraculous capacity, because the reality it achieves is only that of a stage illusion. So we have seen that in actual spectacle, the mythical story behind "fatal charades" contributes luster to the imperial achievement of staging the impossible and at the same time always potentially shows how far the death of a slave in fancy dress falls short of bringing legend to life. Here too the ability to maintain the priority of either fiction or reality becomes as difficult as distinguishing Pentheus and Bacchus, and the real emphasis of their encounter comes to fall more on the process of dialectic they set in motion than on its resolution.

And the conclusion of the episode contains powerful pointers toward the difficulty of any final closure. Within the sequence of book 3, we saw how the reactions to earlier *miracula*, the death of Actaeon and the birth of Dionysus in particular, generate new narratives as audiences' perspectives diverge on what they have seen and heard and what it means. The formal unit of the third book seems to end by imposing unanimity in

---

[54] Indeed, Wheeler's (1999.172–81) study of the shaping of audience response within Ovid's narrative presents the fictions audiences are punished for not believing as precisely the claims of the new emperor. For Augustus as Bacchus, cf. the presentation of Bacchus, a mortal made divine, as a forerunner for Augustus's own apotheosis in Horace's *Odes*, e.g., C. 3.3.13.

reading, as the final couplet offers Bacchus's view of Pentheus's death as an *exemplum* and closes the narrative arc that began with failed sacrifice by imposing new *sacra*. But the fourth book begins with the opening up of a new set of divergent readings as the daughters of Minyas refuse to participate in these *sacra* and deny the truth of the story that Bacchus is the son of Jupiter. The processes at work to sustain the momentum of the poem's own narrative themselves have a bearing on the issue of Ovid's appropriation of spectacle. In our earlier discussion of fatal charades, we saw that poetic representation came not only before the event but after it as well; Martial's literary representations of staged representations of legendary events mobilize different ways of responding to those experiences. In simpler terms we may easily imagine that so complex a visual experience as the death of Selurus could have produced neither a unitary response among its audience nor even an unequivocal one on the part of an individual spectator. Thus, the ideological work of such spectacles depends on the story that is told about them, and that story in turn invites revision and reexamination. We have seen how both imperial spectacle and Ovidian fiction can demand consideration of the most fundamental questions of individual and national identity. A synchronic reading of the two highlights the breadth of the questions asked by both and the multiplicity of answers they allow. The uncertain and reciprocal question of which comes first provides a further prism through which these issues are at once intensified and multiplied.

CHAPTER 5

Philomela Again?

The story of Procne, Philomela, and Tereus at first seems to lack the kind of links to contemporary Roman ideology and spectacular praxis that formed the starting points for our reading of the Pentheus tale. Yet it is in part the deliberate turning aside of such recognizably Roman features within the narrative that gives it its programmatic importance for understanding the dialogue Ovid creates between the visual experience of metamorphosis his text offers and the world of civic ritual and spectacular performance. The tale's obviously tragic parallels, even as they confirm its status as a Greek, as opposed to Roman, story will draw our attention from the arena to the theater, another mode of spectacle that enmeshed the spectator in a complex fixing of the borders between reality and representation. I begin by arguing that Ovid's treatment of ethnicity and gender in the episode recalls anxieties that recur specifically in discussions of the effects of theatrical performance and that, as we saw in the preceding chapter's treatment of the Pentheus episode, focusing these anxieties through the phenomenon of metamorphosis "textualizes" them, allowing his poem to comment on the theatrical experience and to reproduce it. One factor that accentuated the potential seams between what happened on a Roman stage and the real-world experience of its spectators was precisely that these foreign performances were so carefully integrated into the civic life of the Roman state. As the next stage in my argument, I try to demonstrate that Ovid creates a similar effect within his narrative by correlating a tragic view of the narrated events with other discursive frameworks: in particular, the rape of Philomela is read against the foundational historical episode of Lucretia and also embedded within the Roman ritual calendar. This last perspective emerges from the intertextual relationship between the *Metamorphoses* and the contemporary *Fasti* and further reinforces their complementarity as two sides of Ovid's great cultural project.

Let us begin with a brief sequence at one of the crucial turning points of the story that brings to the fore the entire episode's complex construction of the cognitive and emotional effects of looking. Procne, having just recovered her mutilated sister Philomela, deliberates on a course of revenge against the husband who raped her. At just this moment, her son Itys arrives.

> Peragit dum talia Procne,
> ad matrem veniebat Itys; quid possit, ab illo
> admonita est oculisque tuens inmitibus "a! quam
> es similis patri!" dixit nec plura locuta
> triste parat facinus tacitaque exaestuat ira.
> ut tamen accessit natus matrique salutem
> attulit et parvis adduxit colla lacertis
> mixtaque blanditiis puerilibus oscula iunxit,
> mota quidem est genetrix, infractaque constitit ira
> invitique oculi lacrimis maduere coactis;
> sed simul ex nimia mentem pietate labare
> sensit, ab hoc iterum est ad vultus versa sororis
> inque vicem spectans ambos "cur admovet" inquit
> "alter blanditias, rapta silet altera lingua?
> quam vocat hic matrem, cur non vocat illa sororem?
> cui sis nupta, vide, Pandione nata, marito!
> degeneras! scelus est pietas in coniuge Tereo."
> nec mora, traxit Ityn, veluti Gangetica cervae
> lactentem fetum per silvas tigris opacas,
> utque domus altae partem tenuere remotam,
> tendentemque manus et iam sua fata videntem
> et "mater! mater!" clamantem et colla petentem
> ense ferit Procne, lateri qua pectus adhaeret,
> nec vultum vertit.

$$(6.619–42)$$

While Procne was deliberating, Itys came to his mother. She was reminded by his presence what power she had and, regarding him with cruel eyes, said, "Ah, how like your father!" Speaking no more, she prepares her terrible crime and boils with silent rage. But as her son approaches her and wraps her neck in his small arms and joins kisses to a child's endearments, the mother indeed is moved and hesitates, her anger broken. And her eyes grow damp despite themselves with involuntary tears. But as soon as she senses that her mind stumbles from excessive piety, she turns again from him to the countenance of her sister. And, gazing at them both in turn she says, "Why can the one use endearments while the other is silent with her tongue ripped out? When he calls me mother, why can she not call me sister? See, daughter of Pandion, to what husband you are married. You fall off from your birth! In the case of a husband like Tereus, piety is crime." Straightway she dragged off Itys, as a tiger of the Ganges drags the nursing offspring of a deer through the dark forests. And when they reached the secluded part of that lofty palace, while Itys stretches out his hands and, now seeing his doom, calls out "mother! mother!" and seeks to embrace her neck, Procne cuts him down with a sword, where the breast and side meet, and she does not turn away her face.

Procne here faces the familiar tragic dilemma of deciding who she is, mother or sister.[1] Not only does the conflict between family roles and the emotions they inspire, anger and love, appear in her own eyes, alternately cruel and tearful, but the very question of which figure Procne will become seems to result from where she directs them. However, the emphasis on vision testifies to much more than its power to stir the emotions. Procne channels the effective demands made by the sight of each figure through a complex measuring of likeness and difference between them.[2] Itys is unlike Philomela, largely because, being articulate, he need not rely simply on the visual impression he presents. Most important, in looking at the figure of her son, she stresses a seen likeness to his father against the likeness to herself on which her son's audible appeals to her as mother insist. The recognition of Itys as his father overlaps with an intellectual recognition of what sort of man Tereus is, which is itself expressed in visual terms (*vide*) as if to stress its indistinguishability from the visual stimulus of Itys' countenance. Gazing at Itys becomes a process of objectification: Procne looks on him as increasingly alien to the point where he comes to signify someone who is not there and loses his power to express his subjectivity through speech by calling her *mater*.

But if Procne comes to regard Itys as a sign of the otherness of her husband, her language stresses the equally unnatural identity she takes on with her sister, the other object of her gaze, whose speech she must supply rather than disregard. In fact, the very line in which she recognizes her husband in her son makes her indistinguishable from her sister. The

[1] Cf. Tarrant 2002a.353–54, who sees the collapse of distinct family relationships in the episode as a recollection of Ovid's Chaos. The importance of what I here treat as a doubling of family roles was, as "boundary violation," highlighted as a major theme in the episode by Barbara Pavlock 1991. Pavlock stresses how such violation of category boundaries colors Tereus as a tyrant, comparable to the Roman Tarquins responsible for the native analogue of this crime, the rape of Lucretia. As her term "violation" implies, she sees Tereus very much as the agent whose crimes set these distortions in motion; the deformation of Procne that leads to her revenge offers a vision of the ultimate consequences of tyrannical cruelty. My own emphasis by contrast is on the role of representation in effecting change, and while not presenting Tereus as a victim, I stress his own role as spectator transformed by what he sees. In relating our two positions, I would also like to point out that for the Romans the tyrant was already a tragic role. Cf. Livy's presentation of the anomalies and transgressions that characterize the reign of Tarquin as "tragic." See Feldherr 1997.

[2] Cf. Hardie 2002c.269: "Procne ... is strengthened by the difference that she perceives between Itys and his aunt Philomela, the difference between speech and speechlessness."

vocative "daughter of Pandion" that seems to mark the expression as a soliloquy, points out that her sister Philomela could be described in precisely the same terms, and both have united sexually with Tereus.[3] Thus, Procne's role as mother of Itys is the only one that distinguishes her from Philomela, and in rejecting her child as "other" she takes another step toward becoming her sister, looking as she would look and speaking as she would speak. This climactic moment, therefore, juxtaposes the two opposed ways of viewing we have been tracing throughout the poem, an objectification that decouples appearance from identity versus a powerful identification with a seen presence that unites spectator and spectacle and allows her to take on the voice of the silent image.

Procne seems to have fulfilled Cadmus's destiny in turning into what she sees. Yet that disturbing prophecy also depended on the gazer taking on a form alien from himself and being gazed upon in turn. So here, having seemingly positioned herself as viewer in a way that reestablishes her integrally as what she was, a daughter of Pandion, by looking at someone like her, Procne together with Philomela is suddenly seen to have changed her fundamental identities. Philomela becomes anomalous precisely because of her too close similarity to her sister. Both have shared the bed of the same man, so that neither has a single role in relation to the other, or, to accentuate Philomela's own view of the situation, she has become her own sister's "other woman" (6.606). Procne, far from returning to an original state of virginal innocence as an Athenian princess, will be figured in the text as Indian tigresses as a direct result of her identification with Philomela.[4] More important, it is just at this moment that the wife begins to resemble her husband most closely: if seeing a sister appears to establish an identity between viewer and viewed, simultaneously restoring the viewer to an original identity, a characteristic modus operandi for Tereus was a deceit that made things different from what they seem, so that what gave the appearance of piety was in fact crime. Here, though, the sisters themselves are about to devise their own trap of false appearances, concealing the presence of Itys in the meal, and pretending that the father's act of consuming it will be the performance of a cult ritual (*pietas*) rather than criminality (*scelus*). A trace of this paradox, that the affirmation of identity through gazing has the power to transform the self into its own antithesis, emerges when Procne's apostrophe to the daughter of Pandion

---

[3] As Anderson 1972.217–18 points out, variants of the story survive that actually have Tereus wed Philomela under the pretense that Procne has died (Apollodorus 3.14.8, Hyginus *Fab*. 45).

[4] It was in fact just this desire to see Philomela that sets the tragedy in motion in the first place, as the echoes of the language of Procne's first conversation with Tereus poignantly remind the reader.

is followed by the cry *degeneras,* which in different ways describes all four protagonists of the episode with equal aptness: the raped Philomela; Procne, whose hesitation seems to her a sign of baseness; Itys, who too clearly shows the traces of his descent from Tereus; and Tereus himself, who has fallen away from the ideal husband he appeared to be.[5]

The multiple identities Procne simultaneously assumes in this short passage give her experience, for all the text's emphasis on ethnic difference, some powerful resonances for Ovid's Roman audience. First of all, her situation well describes the paradoxical place of the Roman wife in the structure of the family, for in most Roman marriages the wife always remained legally a member of her own birth family and therefore a stranger within her husband's home and in this respect alien even to her own children. Yet the tensions Procne enacts here also bear comparison to a more general experience we have come to see as shared by all genders in Ovid's audience: the issue of who Procne is at once depends on and determines whom she sees and how she sees them, whether she identifies with Itys or Philomela. Her decision thus magnifies that crucial aspect of the reception of fiction brought into focus by metamorphosis, the choice between the objectifying and the sympathetic point of view. But beyond figuring this hermeneutic choice, Procne's performance here once again projects it onto a recognizable component of Roman public life, the theater. Her speech reproduces one of the best-known, indeed archetypal, moments in ancient drama, Medea's monologue debating whether to punish Jason's adultery by murdering their children.[6] And the dramatic representation that seems to emerge from the text at this

[5] Cf. also the comment of Gildenhard and Zissos 1999a.169: "With her redefinition of central moral signifiers, Procne abandons the world of *pietas*, of Athenian family values, in which she grew up and where words had standard meanings and ethical value. Instead she acknowledges her presence in a universe which lacks any moral dimension."

[6] The intertext has been frequently recognized. See esp. the comments of Anderson 1972.230–31, Pavlock 1991.43, Curley 1997 and Larmour 1990. Indeed, the entire episode weaves together the central elements of the two most famous tragedies of the Augustan age, Varius's *Thyestes* (so Tarrant 2002a), describing the other mythological banquet when a father eats his sons, and Ovid's own *Medea*. Of course, the real Medea is waiting in the wings at this point in the *Metamorphoses* to appear at the beginning of the subsequent book. For a fuller discussion of the thematic links between the narratives of Procne and Medea, see Newlands 1997.192–95.

Pavlock 1991.46 introduces another very apt tragic parallel, Agave from the Bacchae: "Like Agave, [Procne] becomes carried away by her participation in the Bacchic rites and then cannot perceive her child for what he really is, but instead dissolves the distinction between father and son." If we consider that from an Ovidian perspective playing the role of a bacchant could also mean acting as one from Euripides' *Bacchae*, the conflation between the fiction Procne has contrived and the institution of drama develops an even greater intensity.

moment is also, importantly, a spectator. Thus, Procne's own transformations, as she looks from one character to another, invite the audience to investigate similarities to what they experience when they look at her. She is at once playing a part in a drama and enacting what happens when we watch such a performance.

To understand the significance of the explicit theatricalization of this episode, we must first examine more closely Roman conceptualizations of what watching a play could do to its audience. Ruth Webb's discussion of late antique responses to the theater provides an especially suggestive summary of some of the issues involved. Although she treats a later period in the history of the Roman stage, the concerns she illustrates about the effects of dramatic performance draw on ideas going back at least as far as Plato and amply demonstrated for early imperial Rome. Webb sees in the early Christian polemic that paints the theater as a snare of immorality haunted by pagan demons a reflection "of the experience of the theatre audience, an idea of the theatre as a domain outside normal experience where the spectator is caught up in something Other at a certain risk of alteration to him or herself."[7] To understand the terms of this alteration, Webb goes back to Platonic conceptions of mimesis developed in *Republic* 3 (esp. *Rep.* 3.393–96). There Plato worries that (male) actors themselves are assimilated to what they represent, becoming habituated to extreme and debilitating emotion by imitating those who suffer from it. This idea of the alienation of the actor from himself through mimesis emerges in the miracles of imitation chronicled in texts like Lucian's *On the Dance* (19), where pantomime performers astonish even the most skeptical spectators by seeming really to become such different characters as Ares and Aphrodite. But the moral dangers of imitation apply not only to the performers; Christian writers in particular express the fear that merely by watching men portray women, the male members of the audience themselves will be effeminized.[8] Thus, the situation of Procne, as she becomes different from herself, enraged and "degenerate," in the act of looking reproduces anxieties about the effect of theatrical performance on its spectators. More dangerously still, Procne at that moment in which she is both spectator and visualized as a performer enacting "Procne" suggests the communicability of this effect to those who watch her even as she herself crosses the barrier that ideally separates spectator from actor.

---

[7] Webb 2005.3.

[8] Webb 2005.6–9, citing esp. Gregory Nazianzen *Carmina* 2.2.8, 2.2.94–97, and the counterarguments of Libanios to such a position, *Orat.* 64.70. See also now Lada-Richards 2007.64–78.

In Rome anxieties about the theater especially involved questions of gender and ethnicity, as is revealed in Juvenal's discussion of Greek actors' ability to portray women:

> an melior cum Thaida sustinet aut cum
> uxorem comoedus agit uel Dorida nullo
> cultam palliolo? mulier nempe ipsa uidetur,
> non persona, loqui: uacua et plana omnia dicas
> infra uentriculum et tenui distantia rima.
>
> (Sat. 3.93–97)

Is anyone better when he plays the part of Thais or when the actor takes the part of the wife or of Doris, adorned with no cloak? The woman herself seems to speak, not an actor. And you would say everything below the belly was smooth and void, parted by a slender crack.

I introduce this passage in particular into the discussion because its description of the moment when the audience accepts the fiction of the performance, when the actor seems to become what he imitates, so vividly recalls the language of Ovidian metamorphosis, with its catalog of transformed body parts and the introduction of an imaginary spectator (even the rhythm of that final half line, tenui distantia rima, has an Ovidian flavor).[9] For Juvenal, the excellence of the actor lies in a mimesis so perfect that he appears actually to turn into what he plays. At one level the ease with which Greek actors seem to lose their male genitalia can be easily parsed as an attack on their masculinity—especially if one bears in mind the Greek Plato's fear that actors become like what they imitate. But Juvenal's explicit concern is a much more insidious danger to Roman society. Because the Greeks are such good mimics, they make excellent parasites, deceiving their hosts through flattery and taking on a variety of deceptive roles not on the stage but in actual social interactions. While Romans marvel at the Greeks' ability to confuse reality and illusion on

---

[9] The phrase tenui rima itself has an Ovidian precedent at Met. 4.65, describing the crack in the wall separating Pyramus and Thisbe, and Ovid four times in the Metamorphoses makes up the second half of the hexameter with tenui + a tri- or quadrisyllabic adjective ending in –a + the disyllabic noun modified by tenui (1.549, 3.161, 6.127, 11.735), a pattern whose precedent perhaps occurs in Catullus 64.113, tenui vestigia filo. Vergil, by contrast, never uses this pattern: his preferred position for tenui is at the start of the second half of the second foot.

Earlier in the passage as well, Greek skill at role-playing is likened specifically to metamorphosis: in summa non Maurus erat neque Sarmata nec Thrax / qui sumpsit pinnas, mediis sed natus Athenis (3.79–80). While the most obvious referent of the allusion is of course Daedalus, the lines could indeed be read as the moral of the Procne and Philomela story.

stage, they miss their ability to transform the real space of the Roman city into a world of playacting that ultimately dissolves its ethnic identity and creates a "Greek Rome" (3.61). Juvenal's purpose here, then, is to draw the curtain and expose the fraudulent illusionism that threatens Rome's own integrity—making you not believe in the fictions that the Greeks try so hard to produce. As this invective reminds us, the Greeks do not lack male genitals; on the contrary, their lust threatens every member of the Roman *familia*, the wife, the virgin daughter, the son who was once chaste, even the old grandmother (3.109–12).

The mechanism for Rome's ethnic transformation as Juvenal describes it is admittedly less direct than the one Webb finds in the fear that looking at someone playing a woman effeminizes the spectator.[10] This difference makes sense given that the satirist here aims to alert his audience to the infiltration that is happening offstage rather than on. But the result is similar: the spectator society loses its ethnic distinctiveness, and at the same time its individual members are stripped of the sexual roles that give them status as members of the freeborn community of citizens. But Juvenal's re-creation of the theatrical experience also helps point out the other side of its sociopolitical potency. Of course, dramatic performances would never have played an important role in Roman public life if they posed such a threat to the integrity of the *populus Romanus*. Because the theater itself was so strongly marked off as Greek, it also allowed Roman audience members a wonderful opportunity to remind themselves of how different they were from both the Greek scenes that were set before them in tragedy and comedy and the actual Greek actors who played them.[11] The Roman theater, I suggest, offers a double potential for either cata- lyzing an awareness of who the audience member really is or blurring the distinctness of that identity through recognition of a likeness to the figures on stage, or perhaps simply through acceding to the fictions pro- duced there. Far from enforcing a simple message about the nature of the audience's Romanness, I imagine the theatrical experience derived its civic power from the dynamic tension between these possible readings. Again, Juvenal's strategy[12] in the third satire suggests how an awareness of difference between Greece and Rome comes from a view of the theater that stresses the reality of the performance as opposed to the reality it

[10] A position reconstructed from the response in Libanios, *Orat.* 64.70.

[11] One favorite example of how theatrical spectacle offered a context for making display of distinctively Roman virtue comes in Valerius Maximus's (2.4.2) explanation of why the Romans originally provided no seats for watching plays: it was to put on display their own masculine ability to endure standing up.

[12] Or rather the strategy of the character Umbricius, for the whole satire is itself a "dra- matic" monologue.

imitates, showing that the Greek actors are not what they seem. But I doubt whether matters were quite so simple. For merely to enter the fiction on stage strips the actors of what Webb sees as their uncanny power to seem to be one thing *while* being another. In this way, the focus on the realities of performance that appear to insulate the spectator from the performers' deception may serve also to highlight the true miracle of their achievement, which appears only when we keep the actors' bodily presence fully before our eyes. Seeing a male actor as a woman is less weird than seeing a male actor become a woman.

After suggesting that Procne's soliloquy mobilizes theater as well as a "spectacular" analogue to deciphering the hermeneutic options offered by the poem, I want first to illustrate how often motifs of acting and performance appear in the entire episode and how they suggest transformations in sexual and ethnic identity. It is not that Ovid presents the Philomela story as a drama—though one should remember that the story begins in Athens, the very epicenter of dramatic production—but that he makes it unclear where acting begins and ends, as appearances, words, and actions mask, invert, and also reveal the real intentions of characters and outcomes of the "drama." Ovid's manner of portraying the narrative focuses on moments, like the brief speech with which we began the chapter, where being and seeming overlap, and correspondingly when the positions of actor and spectator are doubled—just those moments, in other words, where the social dangers posed by actors become most intense. After that, I move beyond the argument about theater per se to show that Ovid's Philomela narrative in the *Metamorphoses*, when taken together with the treatment of the same myth in the *Fasti*, draws attention precisely to the possibilities for the reception of Greek mythic fictions in the context of the official rhythms of the Roman religious calendar. Ovid's two poetic narratives thus combine to interweave fiction and reality.

The first device to makes us think about the relationship of appearance and reality, while it has nothing to do with performances on the part of human actors, is itself a distinctive feature of the tragic drama, and its very presence helps to frame the characters in the story as distanced from the audience's perception of things, as if on stage. The device is dramatic irony: because of the dramatic situations in which characters find themselves, their words and actions bear a significance opposite to what they understand and intend. Tereus and Procne marry one another, but as so often in tragedy, this is a wedding that is no wedding.[13] Hymenaeus, the god of marriage, is absent, Gratia is absent. But the Eumenides are

---

[13] A tragic allusion also discussed by Hardie 2002c.260.

there, and their presence, in Athens, alone makes one think of tragic models.[14]

Procne's first speech points up the characters' own misunderstanding of their condition and recalls another of the Athenian drama's classic deployments of irony.

> ... *blandita viro Procne "'si gratia" dixit*
> *"ulla mea est, vel me visendae mitte sorori,*
> *vel soror huc veniat: redituram tempore parvo*
> *promittes socero; magni mihi muneris instar*
> *germanam vidisse dabis."*
>
> (6.440–44)

Procne sweet-talked her husband with these words: "If I have any charm, either send me to see my sister, or let my sister come here; promise your father-in-law that she will come back in a short time; you will give me something like a great gift (the image of a great gift) to have seen my sister."

Procne begins with an invocation of her *gratia*, yet the poet has just re-marked that she has none (*non illi gratia*, 6.429). Present, though, is a divinity who is almost the diametric opposite of Gratia, but whose name on the page looks suspiciously like Gratia's, Gradivus, the male god of war who is Tereus's father. That this verbal icon, *gratia*, should summon up a reality at odds with it points up the disjunction between seeming and reality throughout her speech. Seeing her sister looks like a great favor, but it will be a disaster instead. Furthermore, this emphasis on seeing, the first time the motif occurs in the episode, perhaps connects Procne's misconception of her situation to the position of Sophocles' Oedipus, who thinks he sees when he is blind, and in fact blinds himself in part

---

[14] An owl turns up as well sitting on the rooftop of the home, "and by this bird (with such an omen) they are married" (6.432). The last line for those with foreknowledge of the trans-formation that will end, or eternalize, this fatal union, produces unbearable comic irony (Anderson 1972.210). It thus opens a chasm between the external and internal audience, but beyond its focalizing effect, it bears a more serious thematic importance. The owl itself hovers between the literal and the figurative—really there, but also a transparent poetic de-vice for designating a doomed marriage. When the bride Procne becomes a swallow, she flies up to the roof of the palace, the same vantage from which the owl watches her wedding. If we see this owl as real—as an indication of the real circumstances of her wedding to which she is blind at the time—then her metamorphosis provides an apt closure to the story: the metaphorical bird that begins her story becomes the reality it predicts, and at the same time the illusions and deceptions that characterize every event of her marriage are at an end. Or, if we see the owl as a figurative one, a stock poetic device, then her metamorphosis marks her own reincorporation into the world of fictional literary representation, as though she blended into the pages of a book. I explore the consequences of these two strategies of read-ing the final metamorphoses at a later stage in the discussion.

to avoid the terror of seeing a sister who is also a daughter. In Procne's case as well, family roles will redouble one another in horrifying ways. Her language here already suggests a reciprocity between herself and her sister ("either send me to her, or her to me," 6.441–42) that anticipates the moment when Philomela's rape by Tereus makes her at once a sister and a rival to Procne. And as we have seen, the last viewing of Philomela mentioned in the text makes both sisters like one another as murderesses but most unlike the people that they would want to be.

The speech that predicts the dark consequences of seeing and the divergent realities that lurk under identical signs also puts in motion a set of performances that in turn transform those who watch them and, brilliantly, forms the Aristotelian first action in a plot that will lead from Procne's blind wish to see through a series of moments of vision to the final catastrophe when Tereus realizes too that he is what he sees, that he has consumed the body of the son whose head Procne shows him. This fusion of the spectator and the object of his gaze, who is often in some important sense an actor, bears comparison with that ideal moment in the Roman theater when the spectator becomes permeable to the representation he watches.

Before fleshing out my suggestion by looking more closely at some of the links in this chain of spectacles and performances, let me sketch the sequence as a whole. The first speech of Procne is also the first presentation of direct discourse in the episode, the first moment when we move to the unmediated "dramatic" mimesis of action from mere epic narrative. As a result of watching Procne, Tereus goes to Athens, where he at once sees Philomela, and though having immediately fallen in love with her, simultaneously pretends to be fulfilling Procne's orders as he speaks to the king (6.444–510). The sight of Philomela, constantly renewed on the voyage back to Thrace, leads to rape and in turn to another false speech on the part of Tereus, when he pretends to Procne that Philomela has died (6.511–570). Meanwhile the mutilated and now dumb Philomela weaves a visual representation of what occurred, a *carmen miserabile* (6.582)—a tragedy—which, when her sister sees it, she recognizes as her own "*fortuna*" and, being struck dumb, takes on the characteristic of the sister she sees represented there (6.571–86).[15] Procne responds to

---

[15] *evolvit vestes saevi matrona tyranni / fortunaeque suae carmen miserabile legit* (6.581–82). The text of line 582, an important one for my argument, is not entirely certain. I follow throughout the reading given by the oldest surviving manuscripts and printed in Anderson's Teubner edition. The language is doubly striking: first, a genitive is only very rarely used in Latin to express the subject of a song (it much more commonly refers to its author, and occurs once as a defining or appositional genitive, "the song of the *Thebaid*"), and, second, the word *carmen*, "song," seems at odds with the emphasis on the purely visual aspect of Philomela's tapestry. Readings attested in later manuscripts have offered solutions to both

the sight of this woven tragedy by performing as a bacchant, in order to get from the palace to the woods. When she arrives there, she brings her sister into the performance by costuming her too as a worshiper of Dionysus (6.587–600). Back at the palace, Procne strips herself of her costume, but her sister refuses to look at her "seeming to herself the rival of her sister" (6.606). At this point, Philomela, the nonspectator, becomes a performer,[16] acting out the tragedy whose script she had previously sent her sister (6.601–9). After the resulting reconciliation comes the viewing of Philomela that makes Procne a murderess, as well as a deceiver in turn, feigning the ancestral festival, which would of course be an Athenian (dramatic?) festival, at which Tereus "takes his own innards into his belly" (6.609–51). Philomela then jumps out holding the head of Itys. This unmistakably theatrical revelation brings Tereus full circle, back to

---

difficulties, presenting *germanae* for *fortunae* and *fatum* for *carmen*. In the second case, I believe there are strong literary reasons for retaining *carmen*. First, the very strangeness of describing Procne here as "reading a song" helps alert Ovid's readers to the contrast between written and aural, which plays a thematically crucial role at the episode's conclusion, where marks or letters (*notae*) are substituted for song as the distinctive characteristic of the birds the sisters become. Second, the expression *carmen miserabile* already subtly anticipates the moment of transformation that, I suggest, reveals its special significance. For the phrase *miserabile carmen* is used precisely of the nightingale's song by Vergil (G. 4.514). It is unlikely that a copyist simply inserted a reminiscence of Vergil here for a number of reasons: the phrase appears in reverse order and in a different metrical position, and, as yet, there are no nightingales present in Ovid's text.

The reading *fortunae* seems less certain, and indeed the most recent edition, Tarrant's OCT, opts for *germanae*. The genitive is odd, but the syntactical oddness would correspond to the shock of its meaning—in reading Procne is said to discover neither the story of what happened to Philomela nor even the crime of her husband, which is what Philomela wanted to show, but a revelation of her own circumstances. *Germanae*, on the other hand, seems initially banal but does form a pointed contrast, heightened by assonance and chiasmus, with the *saevi tyranni* whose wife Procne also is. In the end, I prefer *fortunae*: it is certainly the *lectio difficilior*, and while unusual, not difficult to understand, especially in the environment of a phrase like *indicium sceleris*, used four lines previously to describe the very same tapestry. In both phrases, what the object shows appears in the same case, and this parallel in turn highlights the significant discrepancy between the intentions of the author at the moment of the work's creation (a revelation of crime done to her) and the meaning it takes on for its reader at the moment of its reception (a description of her own circumstances).

[16] Philomela's voicelessness, as well as the separation of gesture from words, in fact recalls a striking and modern theatrical innovation of Augustan Rome. She resembles a pantomime dancer, for whom gesture, especially hand gesture, takes the place of voice—*pro voce manus fuit*, 6.609—while the text was performed by a reciter. On the "corporeal eloquence" of the pantomime dancer, see Lada-Richards 2007.44–55. I note in particular her likening of the dancer's performance to witnessing a metamorphosis (53–54). If one can connect the "lamentable song" of Philomela's tapestry with her own silent dramatics and in turn with Ovid's poetic representation of them, with *notae* again taking the place of speaking presences, then each medium in its different way struggles to manifest—to transform itself into—voiced drama via its own silent semantic system.

his Aeschylean beginnings, invoking the Eumenides who have been there all along[17] and employing a well-known metaphor with many tragic parallels: calling himself the tomb of his own son, Tereus applies to himself the topos often used to describe the vultures who feed on corpses.[18] At this point Tereus, like Procne, enters this figurative world through metamorphosis into a bird (6.652–74).

One of the most straightforward examples of theatrical contagion, by which the act of performing violates the integrity of both performer and spectator comes when Tereus, returning to Athens at his wife's command, seeks permission for Philomela's visit. Recall that even Procne's own first speech signals her blindness to her circumstances and to the consequences of her request and was less the sincere expression of her desires than a piece of rhetoric crafted to influence her husband, the necessary agent of her "plot." She speaks "wheedlingly to her husband" (*blandita viro*, 6.440), and he immediately puts her plan into action with another, contrasting, speech act as he "orders" the ships that will take him from his native Thrace to her native Athens (6.444). No sooner, though, had Tereus begun to perform his wife's commands than Philomela's arrival makes him a spectator in his own right, setting up a new complication in the relationship between who Tereus is and who he seems to be. Ovid ensures that we, like Tereus, see this event as a spectacle, beginning with the exclamation *ecce*, and emphasizing the external appearance of Philomela, her *forma, paratus,* and *cultus.*

Tereus's reaction to this sight, in its objectification of Philomela and the possibility it offers the audience of sharing his enjoyment, stands as a textbook example of the "scopophilic" gaze made famous in film studies and well applied to this passage by Segal.[19] But two further observations help us place the scene within the episode's treatment of issues of theatricality and identity. First, like Procne in response to Itys, Tereus is carried away by a point of view that reduces its object to externals—Philomela's adornment and *forma* trigger his infatuation. And, second, such externalized viewing, with its focus on a display of wealth and costume that perhaps recalls the material opulence of theatrical performance so often castigated by Roman moralists like Pliny the Elder,[20] leads here too toward a regression into barbarism, though of course barbarousness has a

---

[17] On the role of the Eumenides in the episode, see now Gildenhard and Zissos 2007.

[18] *flet modo seque vocat bustum miserabile nati,* 6.665. The most outlandish version comes from Gorgias, where the vultures are simply glossed as "living tombs" (82 B5a D–K): tragic examples are Aesch. *Septem* 1020–21, Soph. *El.* 1487. Bömer 1976.117 argues that the line has its source in Accius's *Atreus* (*natis sepulchro ipse est parens,* fr. 226 Ribbeck), but see contra Liapis 2006.229, with further bibliography.

[19] Segal 1994.260.

[20] Cf., e.g., *NH* 36.113–15, with the discussion of Edwards 1993.143.

rather different relation to identity for a Thracian than for an Athenian. Whereas for Procne seeing Itys as other turned her into a being alien from herself, for Tereus this watching activates his own distinctive ethnic identity—at least from the perspective introduced by the narrator (6.458–60). And in this respect his response to the sight of Grecian splendors recalls a very distinctly Roman attitude.[21] He sees the wealth of Greece as *praeda* to be seized and is captured (*captus*, 6.465) by captive Greece like the fierce victor in Horace's tag (*Ep.* 2.1.156). Indeed, his nationalist response recalls in many ways the rape of the Sabine women, which Ovid himself set as a primitive theatrical performance and uses as an *exemplum* to persuade present-day Romans not to miss out on the *cultissimae* women coming to the theater to be seen themselves (*Ars* 1.97). After all, Tereus, like Romulus, is a son of Mars (6.427).[22]

But as we look back with our inner Roman to these foundational moments in our own cultural history, another, different spectacle takes shape that elicits quite a different response from the audience within the narrative. For the captive king now himself becomes a producer of images, both as an actor and as a creator of fictions. "He returns with lustful countenance to the orders of Procne *and performs his own vows with her as a pretext.*"[23] His desire generates a discrepancy between seeming and reality in his own appearance, and the Athenian audience, with a theatrical sophistication completely different from the barbarous Thracian, looks past the physical presence of the actor whose *cupido ore* actually reveals his own intentions, to hear words and accept the fiction that the desires they express are those of the absent Procne. Accustomed, of course, to seeing men play women on the stage, they assume that is what is happening here. They need a Juvenal to remind them of the sexual danger posed in real life by this barbarian actor. It goes without saying that the sophisticated Romans of Ovid's own day, who in the *Ars Amatoria* have to be reminded of the primitive conditions in early Rome, might more naturally identify their own perspective with the cultivated Athenians, and the narrator gives them a further push in this direction by explicitly pointing out Tereus's barbarity even as he exposes his words as a performance.

The scene, then, anticipates Procne's encounter with Itys by contrasting a manner of viewing that "sees" only *formae* and seems to imagine a spectator "self" distant from and in control of the object of his gaze with

---

[21] Cf. especially the warning about the effects of the *spolia* from Syracuse in a speech Livy composes for Cato the Elder, 34.4.3–4.

[22] With the ambiguous presentation of Athens here, cf. the argument of Gildenhard and Zissos 2004 that Ovidian references to Athens over the course of the poem chronicle its displacement by Rome as the world city.

[23] *cupidoque revertitur ora / ad mandata Procnes et agit sua vota sub illa* (6.467–68). On the importance of theatricality in this scene, see Hardie 2002c.263–64.

another that accepts dramatic illusions, that hears voices, and so allows for the construction of a subjectivity within what one sees. Here though, these two responses become strongly associated with divergent ethnic identities, the first as "barbarian," the second as Greek. And while we have not yet identified the "subjectivizing" response as feminine, we can certainly say that Tereus's mode of seeing activates and is motivated by a very masculine desire.

Ultimately, both modes of viewing bear different threats to the spectators' own integrity, their ability to maintain a difference between self and other. Tereus, even as he plots the rape of Philomela, is already captured, *captus*. And this initial glimpse of Philomela begins a "plot" that will end in another act of viewing through which the king will learn all about the dangers of spectatorship. A key point in Tereus's erotic combustion comes when Philomela embraces her father to persuade him to assent to Tereus's plea. "Beholding kisses and arms wrapped around necks, he receives all these impressions as goads and torches and as food for his madness, and as often as she embraces her father, he would wish to be that father, nor would it be less impious," (6.479–82). The imagery of food[24] and of fathers embracing their children anticipates none too subtly the moment when Tereus will experience this metaphor as reality by literally engulfing his son, Itys. Here the desire to become what he sees, the father of Philomela, may seem to be an example of empathic watching, but as the narrator's ironic comment reminds us, it is nothing of the kind. When Tereus wishes that he were Pandion, the desire shows his complete absorption in outward signs; he wants to be doing physically what Pandion is doing; he certainly does not want to be doing it *as* Pandion. So too when Tereus becomes a maker of fictions, "*fingit*," what his imagination creates is not a subjective Philomela but simply a more intimate exterior; he imagines what she looks like naked (*qualia vult fingit quae nondum vidit*, 6.492). His own role as producer of fictions throughout the episode continues the tendencies of this first scene: he uses lies, false appearances like the *fictos gemitus* (6.565) with which he convinces Procne that her sister has died, to impose a barrier to the expression of Philomela's perspective. His lies, like the *inane sepulcrum* he contrives (6.568), are intended to be mere signs that make it impossible to recover a living presence within what they signify. Correspondingly, his physical transformation of Philomela herself, in ways that eerily anticipate her final metamorphosis, strip her of a voice and force her to rely on visual signs, the woven *carmen miserabile* she sends to her sister, even as her tongue becomes something to see rather than to hear.

---

[24] Hardie 2002c.263, n.10, nicely observes an allusion to the Lucretian characterization of love as appearance without substance.

In support of my earlier claim that Ovid stresses the resemblance between the phenomenology of performance and that of narrative fiction, notice that the extended consequences of Tereus's seeing Philomela are also expressed in the language of fiction and credibility. Tereus, playing Procne's loyal husband, "is believed to be *pius*" (6.474). Later, Tereus's obsessive recollection of what he saw, his imprisonment in the spectacle of Philomela, extends to the imagination of what he did not (yet) see (*fingit quae nondum vidit*, 6.492). Here Tereus appears simultaneously as the creator of fictions and as their audience; he fashions for himself the rest of Philomela. Later he assumes the active role of "author" for both his female victims.[25] To Procne he narrates a false tale of Philomela's death, also dramatizing it with feigned laments (*dat gemitus fictos commentaque funera narrat*, 6.565). In the case of Philomela, instead of playing a new part he unmasks the brutal reality of his desires, but the result is to make his fictions real by imprisoning the living Philomela in the fantasies he has created.[26] Ovid had described Philomela to his audience as "like the dryads and naiads we are accustomed to hearing about walking in the midst of the forest" (6.452–53). The real circumstances in which Tereus traps his victim resemble the nightmarish realization of such a storybook world of bucolic fancy. From the cultivated city, he drags her to the deep, dark woods of Thrace.

So far we have seen in the Tereus story a realization of the darkest potentialities of tragedy, a virtual anthology of the genre extending from the *Oresteia* through the *Oedipus* and *Medea* to the *Bacchae*, dramatizing how the act of watching draws spectators toward union, literal and figurative, with the figures they see until social roles that must be kept distinct—mother and killer, for example—collapse together and all protagonists find themselves trapped in a recognizably tragic scene. But what is at stake for Ovid's poem in articulating this process as he does?[27] Is he simply exploring the dynamics of a mimetic form that played a role in Roman civic life which we tend to underestimate? Or, if, as I have suggested, Ovid's commentary on tragedy sets up a model to compare and contrast with the workings of his own fiction, what would be the results of such a comparison? What model of the psychological and civic effects of the *Metamorphoses* emerges? Does he share the Platonic anxiety that the mimesis of Procne will turn his audience into unbalanced, murderous

[25] Cf. the observation of Segal 1994.262 that Ovid's own disbelief that Tereus rapes the mutilated Philomela repeatedly (6.561) "refocus[es] the story on belief and evidence."

[26] The epic expression "painted ship" again potentially signals the threshold of illusion (6.511), as the ship that had first brought Tereus onto the foreign stage, where he enacts Procne's request, now carries Philomela back to the world of Tereus's fantasy.

[27] An important precedent for this line of inquiry, which nevertheless comes up with rather different answers, is offered by Gildenhard and Zissos 1999a.

swallows? If not, what are the terms in which it matters for his audience to become like or realize its difference from the figures in a story? This question strikes at the heart of my larger argument that Ovid overlays models of representation possessing the greatest immediacy in his own culture on mythical, foreign, and fantastic material. Some answers can be found by turning from the metapoetic aspects of the Tereus story to its thematic content to point out ways in which the issue of how to see a mythical character like Philomela relates to an audience's sense of itself in civic terms, of the distinctness of the Roman. My argument makes use of another Ovidian text, the *Fasti*, which more explicitly addresses the place of Greek narratives in the ritual life of the Roman state, and specifically of the suggestive references to Philomela within the account of the rape of Lucretia at the end of book 2. These references have benefited from much critical attention, but more of it has focused on what Philomela says about Lucretia than what Lucretia says about Philomela.[28] Here, I turn the tables by using the *Fasti* passage as a lesson on what it means to read Greek myths as Roman, and as a Roman.

My argument that Ovid's Tereus story was a narrativization of a dramatic performance and, in that medium, also provided a palimpsest for reading Roman concerns through and against a Greek plot recalls an earlier moment in the myth's reception at Rome: I have suggested allusions to a multitude of Greek tragedies in the episode, but a Roman audience would not have needed reminders of the *Medea* or *Oresteia* to see Ovid's plot filtered through tragedy. The *Tereus* was itself a tragic subject, treated in a lost work of Sophocles and in Latin by the late second-century BCE playwright Accius. The best-known event in the reception history of Accius's play came in 44 BCE when it was revived at the Apollonian games, four months after the assassination of Julius Caesar. The urban praetor for that year, who thus bore responsibility for the program at this festival, was none other than M. Junius Brutus, and his first choice was a play that aimed transparently at molding the public reception of his own deed: Accius's *Brutus*, a dramatization of the events that led his namesake to drive the Tarquins from Rome and establish the republic. But Brutus was away from Rome at the time of the games, and another tribune, C. Antonius, brother of the future triumvir, substituted another that he thought would be less inflammatory, the *Tereus*. Whatever Antonius's intentions, Cicero (*Att.* 16.2.3) reports that Brutus was pleased with the reception of the *Tereus*, which seems also to have mobilized public opinion in his favor. We cannot know, of course, what the audience saw in *Tereus* that helped galvanize its reaction, although most have speculated that that play itself portrayed Tereus as a stereotypical

[28] See esp. Newlands 1995 and Joplin 1984; an important exception is Pavlock 1991.

tyrant punished for his excesses.[29] It may also be that this effect was amplified by a recognition of the similarity Tereus's rape of Philomela offers to the plot of the Roman play for which it was perhaps known to be substituted, that they were thus reading Lucretia through Philomela.[30] In any case, the aspect of this affair important for my analysis is the audience's perception that contemporary Roman events could be read through the dramatization of Tereus's deeds, perhaps via an intermediary evocation of a Roman "drama" that comes nearer to a direct allusion to the present. And yet the substitutional quality of the *Tereus* will also be significant for my argument; the *Tereus* may resemble a Roman story but is not one, and the absence, for example, of a main character called "Brutus" was presumably what made it tolerable to Antonius where the other play was not.

Ovid's Tereus, too, contains many pointers toward historical events and cultural practices that distinguished Romans from barbarians, but it also allows for a focus on difference as well, and so provides Roman readers with an alternative to recognizing themselves among the play's protagonists. In fact, the narrative is remarkable not only for how often it evokes questions of ethnic identity but also for the variety of perspectives and criteria it presents for measuring who is a barbarian. The tale first seems to make an issue of its Roman reception precisely because it is so obviously foreign. Its main characters are two Athenian maidens abused by a figure decisively identified as a *barbarus* (6.515, 533, 576) and who bears the most un-Roman offices of *rex* (6.463, 490, 520, 614) and *tyrannus* (6.436,[31] 549, 581). The plot depends on a secret conspiracy among women of precisely the sort that a reader of Livy's account of the fall of the Tarquins, or of the bacchanalian conspiracy, would recognize as interrupting the continuities of Roman public life. And the women's plot achieves its end in a banqueting scene explicitly described as an imitation of Greek practice: Procne has invited Tereus to this solitary feast—a perversion already of the communality that was especially valued in the Roman *convivium*—under the pretense of an Athenian ritual.

---

[29] Lana 1958–59.357, n. 3; Erasmo 2004.99. Bilinski 1958.44 argues that the *Tereus* possessed a direct political message at the time of its first performance, as an attack on the demagogic tribune Saturninus in 103 BCE.

[30] See Degl'Innocenti Pierini 2002.134–36.

[31] This example—describing Procne as "daughter of Pandion given in marriage to the famous [evident?] tyrant," *claro Pandione nata tyranno*—is particularly interesting. Although the bracketing word order eventually makes clear that the tyrant is Tereus, grammatically it could also refer to the Athenian king Pandion. And indeed this ruler is just as much a *rex* as the Thracian (cf. 6.488 of the *regales epulae* that form the darkest anticipation to Tereus's later acts).

But Ovid's narrative does not simply offer his Roman audience another self-congratulatory confrontation with monstrous "others." For the dynamic of cultural opposition I have been tracing is itself dramatized within the text in a way that immediately complicates the strategy of Romanizing the Tereus story through an emphasis on ethnic difference. When the raped Philomela addresses Tereus as "proven a barbarian by polluted deeds" (*o diris barbare factis*, 6.533), we are reminded that the identification of the king as barbarian is in part focalized through the perspective of an Athenian, a member of a citizenry marked out for its wealth, social organization, and above all *cultus*, in whose eyes the Thracians were historically the barbarians' barbarians. And yet, just at this moment, Philomela adds a new element in the categorization of barbarians. The assumption that birth and race determine character, one that the narrator evoked at the moment when lust for Philomela overcame Tereus (6.459–60), seems to her demonstrated by Tereus's hideous actions. But if it is deeds that define the barbarian, then her own slaughter of Itys at least levels the playing field, as the much-noted simile likening these two blue-blooded Athenians to Ganges tigresses more than suggests. This textual emphasis on the instability of the category of the barbarian "other" becomes all the more complex for a Roman audience because the Ovidian story makes clear that the distinction between civilization and barbarism is itself a foreign import. It may be possible to read with an Athenian ethnic perspective, taking the archetypal *urbs* Athens—as it is arguably depicted on Minerva's tapestry at the start of book 6—as a stand-in for Rome. But repeated Roman anxieties about Greek culture, of the sort eloquently expressed by Juvenal, keep this elision of national identities from being automatic—especially in a case where the barbarian Tereus is the son of Mars or, to make the link to Romulus even closer, is "perhaps" the son of Mars (6.427).[32] This triangulation of different viewpoints on what defines a barbarian, making it possible to read Roman as Thracian or as Athenian, recalls the dramatization of contrasting perspectives on family roles when Procne chooses whether to be a mother to Tereus or a sister to Philomela, and ends up being neither.

That Ovid should engage his audience in questions about what it means to be a Roman and that these questions should mirror and arise from a character's anguished redefinition of family roles make perfect sense if we view Philomela's drama through the narrative for which the *Tereus* was substituted in 44 BCE, the rape of Lucretia. Much more than

[32] *Forte* here is perhaps "perhaps," or perhaps "fortuitously," or perhaps the neuter of *fortis* ("strong") modifying *genus*. In the latter case the word helps to affirm rather than cast doubt on his divine parentage: mighty descendants befit the god of war.

a lurid, outrageous, and "polarizing" episode from Roman legend, the Lucretia story led to a decisive transition in Roman history, the foundation of the distinctively Roman political structure that was the republic. And this transition, whose importance is fully described by Livy, had as its prerequisite the growth of affection toward wives and children that settled and united the scruffy shepherds and asylum seekers who made up Rome's first population:

> *neque ambigitur quin Brutus idem qui tantum gloriae superbo exacto rege meruit pessimo publico id facturus fuerit, si libertatis immaturae cupidine priorum regum alicui regnum extorsisset. quid enim futurum fuit, si illa pastorum conuenarumque plebs, transfuga ex suis populis, sub tutela inuiolati templi aut libertatem aut certe impunitatem adepta, soluta regio metu agitari coepta esset tribuniciis procellis, et in aliena urbe cum patribus serere certamina, priusquam pignera coniugum ac liberorum caritasque ipsius soli, cui longo tempore adsuescitur, animos eorum consociasset?* (2.1.3–5)

There is no doubt but that Brutus, who earned such glory for the expulsion of a proud king, would have wrought a disaster for the state, if from his desire for a liberty still unripe he had wrested power from any of the earlier kings. For what would have happened if that riff-raff of shepherds and immigrants, exiled from its own peoples, having gained under the sanctuary of some inviolable temple if not liberty at least impunity, and released from the fear of kings, began to be stirred by the storms of demagoguery and, in a city still strange, to sow dissensions with the nobility before affection for wives and children and love of the land itself, to which they had grown accustomed over a long time, had bound together their spirits?

Ovid's Philomela provides an answer to Livy's rhetorical question, showing what happens when two immigrant women, loosed from fear of a tyrannical king and unmoored from the affections that bind them toward spouses and children, "sow quarrels with fathers." I have previously argued that Livy correlates the "metamorphosis" that produces the distinctively Roman state with a generic shift from drama to history. The public history of the Roman state extending over time frames and incorporates the overprivileging of personal passions that deforms family relations on the tragic stage.[33] While it would be simplistic to conclude that Ovid here complements Livy's narration by presenting the "tragic" disintegration of a foreign family as an implicit foil to the Roman response to rape as a symptom of tyranny, such a perspective provides a useful start-

---

[33] Feldherr 1997.

ing point for thinking about how Ovid raises the issue of Romanness in his narrative and parallels the way that Ovid's own Lucretia story, in the *Fasti*, encourages us to frame the Tereus story.

To better lay the groundwork for reading Philomela against the Lucretia of both annalistic history and etiological poetry, it is important to notice the particular emphasis Ovid places on the structuring of time in this portion of the *Metamorphoses*.[34] Livy had contrasted the self-renewing rhythms of the republic, when the magistrates are new every year, with the "long time" of the *regnum*, which can really be measured only at its end[35] but is the essential seedtime, so to speak, for the coming of *libertas*. Ovid begins the account of Philomela within an undifferentiated and amorphous time structure typical of this portion of his poem, where events are often temporally related to each other by casual synchronicity: Tereus enters the poem as the ally who helps the Athenians win the war that had kept their king from attending the funeral of Amphion, whose wife Niobe had been the subject of the poem's most recent narrative (6.424–25). But within the account of his marriage, an emphasis on annual repetitions clearly articulates the temporal relation of events: the beginning of the dramatic chain, Procne's appeal to Tereus (6.440–44), happens "after Titan had led the seasons of the cyclical year through five autumns" (*iam tempora Titan / quinque per autumnos repetiti duxerat annos*, 6.438–39). After Tereus has abandoned Philomela in the woods and returned to the palace, another annual cycle passes, marking a major break in the narrative: "The god had traversed twice six cycles with the year completed" (*signa deus bis sex acto lustraverat anno*, 6.571). Then, after Procne's "reading" of Philomela's tapestry sets events on course toward the final revenge, "it was time" (*tempus erat*, 6.587), or, more precisely, it was "the time when Sithonian daughters-in-law are accustomed to hold the triennial rites of Bacchus."

This emphasis on time has a number of important functions. First, it provides another context for highlighting the tragic cast of events. The ideas that all things come to light with time and that time has the power to overturn all human expectations underpin much Greek tragedy. Here the anticipations of sameness and regularity connoted by the annual cycle of the seasons emerge in Procne's own first assumption that Philomela's visit will form a short temporal interlude at the end of which things will return to the way they are: she bids Tereus promise Pandion that "Philomela will return in a short time," *tempore parvo*, 6.442, where the

---

[34] For a different interpretation of this pattern, see Segal 1994.269–71.

[35] Cf. the emphasis on reckoning up time as a marker of change in the last sentence of Livy's first book: *L. Tarquinius Superbus regnauit annos quinque et uiginti. regnatum Romae ab condita urbe ad liberatam annos ducentos quadraginta quattuor. duo consules inde comitiis centuriatis a praefecto urbis ex commentariis Ser. Tulli creati sunt, L. Iunius Brutus et L. Tarquinius Collatinus* (1.60.3–4).

word *tempore* "rolls around" in the same metrical position *tempora* had occupied four lines before to describe the passage of five years (6.438).[36] But this short time will never come to an end, and as a result Pandion will die "before reaching the final time of a long old age" (*ante diem longaeque extrema senectae / tempora*, 6.675–76).[37] Second, from a broader historical perspective the question of the repeatability of events becomes a significant issue in the narrative and recalls the language that designated these temporal transitions. But such temporal markers also summon up the dimensions of Roman time that give their essential structure to the two literary forms that provide crucial intertexts for his story: they recall both the annalistic model of history that records the sequence of events throughout the *longue durée* of Roman history and the annual cycle of festivals according to which those distant events are regularly remembered in the present—the subject of Ovid's own *Fasti*.

If we look first at the "diachronic" elements of Roman history, the rape of Lucretia that marks the beginning of the annual round of historical Roman time is not the only defining moment from the Roman past to appear in the episode. In each of the three main sections of the Tereus narrative (the "prologue" describing Procne's marriage, the abduction and rape of Philomela, and Procne's discovery of the crime and punishment of Tereus), this Greek myth recalls three important foundations of Rome, by Aeneas, Romulus, and Brutus. One measures the Romanness of the episode, then, by contrasting these events against those that originally gave a distinctive future to the Roman state: the doomed marriage of Aeneas and Dido, Romulus's rape of the Sabine women, and the foundation of the republic.

It is important to note, too, that in all of these Roman narratives the long-term historical consequences go together with, indeed depend upon, the proper interpretation of potential disruptions in the "timeless" phenomenon of Roman marriage.[38] In the case of Aeneas and Dido, the very sterility of their union, noted by Dido, helps mark it off from the fundamental aim of Roman marriage, the production of offspring—in a circu-

---

[36] Counting inclusively in the Roman fashion, *tempore*, recurs after five lines so that the metrical cycles precisely parallel those of the seasons.

[37] If time mocks all human expectations, the characters in turn compensate by falsifying time, or by transforming its recurring moments into the means to their own ends. Thus, Philomela makes use of the Thracian bacchic ritual to disguise her recovery of her sister, and later concocts an Athenian festival as a pretext for her terrible banquet. Tereus by contrast had not only told the false story of Philomela's death but commemorated it by bringing offerings to her tomb, a phrase that to a Roman ear might have evoked the annual rituals of Parentalia.

[38] I am, of course, arguing not that Roman marriage practices do not change over time but that, like many Roman social customs, they were validated by being perceived as timeless.

lar fashion, Aeneas and Dido have no future literally because they have no future. With the Sabine women, it is precisely the presence of such a future, guaranteed by offspring, that in their own eyes legitimates the violence which separated them from their families. Lucretia's violation by Sextus Tarquinius can never look like a marriage, for its victim is already a *matrona*; but the point here is to throw the blame for the destruction of the family unit on the tyrannical and soon-to-be-expelled Tarquin. In reading the Tereus narrative against these episodes that at once instantiate and depend upon particular views of the Roman family, we find again a double possibility for its interpretation. On the one hand, the otherness of this Thracian family chronicle helps to define the particular elements of the Roman stories that make the difference. And yet contrast can never be completely divorced from comparison. All three Roman narratives describe controversial, even shocking actions, whose foundational value comes from the adoption of a particular perspective on these potential crimes. Ovid's Tereus disembeds these tales of rape and violated marriage from the Roman historical context that shapes their reception. In doing so, he hints at what such stories might look when viewed within the "timelessness" of myth; for, as we shall see, Tereus's family is at once far away and long ago, and always present. When we turn our attention to the *Fasti*, we again discover that making their story Roman depends on keeping them out of the synchronic cycle that every year reinstantiates Romanness.

To give some substance to these rather abstract claims, let us look more closely at how Ovid's Tereus evokes and differs from these Roman narratives. The motif of the polluted marriage to a foreign princess looks back to the marriage of Aeneas and Dido. As Hardie has suggested,[39] Philomela's first apparition itself draws on the initial glimpse Aeneas catches of Dido in Vergil's poem. The second "marriage" between Roman and foreigner, the rape of the Sabine women, is suggested by Ovid's emphasis on the relationship between father-in-law and son-in-law in the long middle panel, the use of deception and performance to lure the victim, and the shared Martial ancestry of Tereus and Romulus. (The similarities with the Lucretia story, which I take as a given, are explicitly made by Ovid in the *Fasti*.)

Already it stands out that the accursed marriage Aeneas rejects provides the model for Tereus's legitimate marriage to Procne, while the Sabine marriage that will provide for Rome's future here parallels the sterile rape of Philomela. This reveals in turn a whole set of crucial differences that seem to keep Tereus off the path to Romanness. The foreign, urban, cultivated Dido whom Aeneas does not take with him to his new/old native land, herself fights shy of her threat to slaughter Ascanius and feed

---

[39] Hardie 2002c.260–62.

him to his father (*Aen.* 4. 602); Tereus loses a human future because Procne does not.[40] The sense of marital roads not taken accelerates as we move forward to the rape of the Sabine women. There the rape itself was motivated by a scarcity of women (Livy 1.9.1); Tereus by contrast already possesses a wife and has no motive other than the sexual desire that is never allowed to surface in the case of the Romans. Correspondingly, the aftermath of that rape led to the union of peoples precisely through the articulate intervention of the victims themselves. Here there are no such possibilities: the victim has been permanently silenced by her attacker. And, in the last of these parallels, Lucretia explicitly renounces any attempt to revenge herself on Tarquin, leaving that up to her male relations, whose actions in turn are what translate her sufferings from a personal to a political tragedy; Philomela lacks just those kinds of assistants. As her rape, unlike the story of the Sabine women, had merely separated her from her birth family without establishing her in a new *domus*, she can call on neither a husband nor a father to act on her behalf. Rather, she possesses only the *germana soror* of a Dido, a sister whose very similarity to her picks up on another of the major preoccupations of the episode, an endless return to likeness. By contrast the three Roman stories all decisively transform the state.

When we turn from the diachronic Roman backdrop of Ovid's Tereus story to the synchronic one suggested by treating the *Fasti* as an intertext, many of the same issues emerge, particularly the problematic repeatability of these mythical crimes. Ovid explicitly mentions Tereus and Procne just at the conclusion of his treatment of Lucretia, whose story is made the etiology for the *regifugium*, a ritual performed on February 28 that was associated with the expulsion of the Tarquins:

> *Fallimur, an veris praenuntia venit hirundo,*
> *nec metuit ne qua versa recurrat hiems?*
> *saepe tamen, Procne, nimium properasse quereris,*
> *virque tuo Tereus frigore laetus erit.*
> (*Fasti* 2.853–56)

Am I mistaken or has the swallow, herald of the spring, arrived, and did she not fear lest winter, reversing his tracks, should somehow return? For often, Procne, you will complain that you were in too much of a hurry, and your husband Tereus will take pleasure at the chill you feel.

This however is the second of two closely correlated references to the myth that together give unity to an important series of festivals clustering

---

[40] See Hardie 2002c.262–69 on the allusions to Dido's perceptions of Ascanius throughout the episode.

at the end of February.[41] If the later passage welcomes Procne back into the poem, the first had chased her out: this occurs in the account of the Caristia, on the twenty-second, a celebration for the living members of the family focused on offerings to the Lares and contrasting with the celebration of the dead, the Parentalia, which had ended the day before. From this Roman festival of family unity the notorious bad guys of Greek myth, including the child-murderer Procne and her relations, are bid to keep off:

> *Tantalidae fratres absint et Iasonis uxor*
> *et quae ruricolis semina tosta dedit*
> *et soror et Procne Tereusque duabus iniquus*
> *et quicumque suas per scelus auget opes.*
> *(Fasti 2.627–30)*

Let the brothers descended from Tantalus [Atreus and Thyestes] be absent, and the wife of Jason, and she who gave scorched seeds to the farmers [Ino] and Procne with her sister, and Tereus unjust to both, and whoever increases his wealth through crime.

The expulsion of Procne at this point becomes especially significant because it follows just after another episode with many parallels to Philomela's, that of the nymph Lara, the mute goddess, whose tongue is ripped out by Jupiter because she warns off Juturna whom the king of the gods plans to rape. Lara, though, suffers rape as well at the hands of Jupiter's son Mercury as he completes his father's punishment by escorting her to the underworld—hence, the Lares, twins sons of Lara, who feature in the festival of the Caristia.

One important effect of the double reference to Procne here is to enmesh the historical event of Lucretia's rape in a repetitive, synchronic structure. We have already seen how in Livy's account, the tale of Lucretia offered a foil to the normative family values that anchor the Roman state. As there the bonds of parent and child lead to *libertas*, so here the rituals that reinforce those bonds form an almost immediate prelude to the account of the fall of the Tarquins. The *Fasti* reinscribes this momentum from family to state within the annual calendar, and we see, again thanks to Procne, that it does so at what was originally the new year, a moment of vernal rebirth, giving an air of natural rightness and cosmic inevitability to the process. In both of these contexts—the cultural reinforcement of family ties and the natural coming of spring—a very positive model of synchronic repetition is at work: annual reenactments affirm Roman identity, expelling the foreign and making the members of the community closer to one another and their past.

---

[41] This structural function has been well studied by Newlands 1995.155–62.

What the ritual expels is the symbolic *rex*; what the text first expels is Procne and her ilk. Just as much as it offers a negative foil to legendary events in the Roman past that lead up to the establishment of *libertas*, so too the tale of Procne and Philomela as Ovid tells it in the *Metamorphoses* seems tailored to contrast with key stages in the newly narrativized set of ritual processes that lead up to the *regifugium* in the *Fasti*. The Caristia marks the end of the *dies parentales*, during which marriage was forbidden: "Hide your torches, Hymenaeus and carry them away from the black fires. Sad tombs have other torches" (*Fasti* 2.561). The marriage of Procne and Tereus was characterized by a wedding shown as disastrous precisely by the confusion of marriage and funereal torches. Procne herself makes offerings to the dead like those of the Parentalia, but these rites too are misdirected within the narrative: they are given to the empty tomb of a false ghost "not thus to be mourned" (6.570). More striking still is the way the end of Procne's story undermines the ritual of the Caristia itself, which ends the Parentalia. Ovid's account of this festival focuses on vision and feasting as the ritual instruments of family unity:

> *Scilicet a tumulis et qui periere propinquis*
> *protinus ad vivos ora referre iuvat,*
> *postque tot amissos, quicquid de sanguine restat*
> *aspicere et generis dinumerare gradus.*
> (*Fasti* 2.619–22)

It is pleasing to turn one's face away from the tombs and relatives who have died, and after so many have been lost look upon what remains of the line.

Procne finds no such pleasure in turning away from tombs, or in looking upon her offspring. And phrases like *ad vivos ora referre* (to carry back faces to the living) and *quicquid restat de sanguine* (whatever is left over of the blood) become almost unreadable unless one can indeed expel the images of Tereus's feast, and particularly his looking upon his own progeny, from the occasion the *Fasti* summons up.[42]

But if it is indeed so important that Roman rituals not invoke the myth of Procne, why then does the poet herald the return of the swallow at the moment commemorating the rebirth of the Roman state? The answer to this question takes us back to the semantic problems raised both in the "dramatic" scenes where characters assess the "likeness" of appearance to reality and, more pragmatically, in sorting out the similarities and differences between Thracian tragedy and Roman history. I suggest

---

[42] Seneca uses a very similar expression to describe the leftovers at his own Thyestean feast: *Quidquid e natis tuis superest habes, quodcumque non superest habes* (*Thy.* 1030–31).

that Procne can be brought back into Roman etiology only when she can be seen as uniquely signifying difference and that the *Fasti* connects her becoming such a sign with the processes of metamorphosis and textualization. And here is the most significant payoff from reading Ovid's two Philomelas together: Procne can be readmitted to the *Fasti* only once she has become a character in the *Metamorphoses*.

To begin this argument, let us return to the motifs of renaming and semantic confusion. Earlier I pointed to examples from early in the *Metamorphoses*' Procne narrative where Ovid's puns drew attention to characters' misperceptions: Procne appeals to *gratia* in a marriage where there is no *gratia*, but there is a Gradivus. A similar kind of wordplay in the *Fasti*, where near homophones take the place of one another, figures in the narrative that itself "conceals" the story of Philomela: the tale of Lara. Lara, who was originally called Lala, a name whose redoubled form alludes precisely to the character's crime of "repeating" things she should not,[43] enters the *Fasti* as the "silent goddess," another euphemistic substitute for her original name, worshiped by a witch whose aim is to bind up hostile mouths, *inimica ora* (*Fasti* 2.581). Lara or Lala thus comes into the story as a figure whose own silencing by Mercury leads to the silencing of others and the obscuring of the very verbal signifier that defines her.[44] But at the end of the narrative this unspeaking and unspeakable goddess emerges as the mother of two gods who are very visible in what follows, the Lares themselves. Thus, Lara can only reappear with a difference; we turn from the mother whose silence was one of the emblematic qualities of the Roman dead to gaze upon the eternally present, living male offspring, the twin Lares, who are not only distinguished by their own watchfulness but were even then becoming iconographically conspicuous at Roman crossroads.[45] I suggest that this rebirth of the Lara myth in terms of visible symbols ideally disembodied from their narratives parallels what happens to Procne. Her transformation from the figure who does precisely what Romans should not to the sign that projects the cosmic cycle of the year onto the history of the Roman state happens only after her metamorphosis. She is driven out as a woman to reemerge as a swallow.

But thanks to the strong emphasis Lara's story places on the shift from aural to visible signs, the metamorphosis described by Ovid's epic poem coalesces with the transformation wrought by that poem: Procne's be-

---

[43] *prima sed illi / dicta bis antiquum syllaba nomen erat / ex vitio positum* (*Fasti* 2.599–601). Note that Ovid alludes to, but never uses, this ancient form of the name.

[44] We may remember the similar incantatory power that Philomela's *carmen miserabile* has on its reader/viewer Procne, making her the image of her silent sister.

[45] *Fitque gravis geminosque parit, qui compita servan t/ et vigilant nostra semper in urbe, Lares* (*Fasti* 2.615–16). For examples of this iconography, see Hano 1986.

coming a swallow goes together with her inscription as a written "character" in the text. For the *Metamorphoses* too has made a significant transformation in the final form Procne takes on, one that itself substitutes what is seen for what is heard. Traditionally in Greek myth, where Procne was the nightingale and Philomela the swallow, the story of the birds' origins appeared in the nightingale's song, which repeated the name of Itys.[46] Ovid, though, has made the sign that links the timeless forms of the swallow and nightingale to the myth of Procne and Philomela the markings on the birds' breasts, which he describes as *notae* (6.670), a word that can also mean simply "letters."[47] Notice too that in making this switch he makes the birds that Procne and Philomela become recall only their crime: the suggestion of repentance in the lamentation for Itys disappears. So too does the potential for the spoken name to reanimate both the lost child and the mother whose articulate, human voice would thus survive her transformation. (Contrast again the case of Lara, where the surviving sons compensate for their mother's disappearance: these characters emphatically have no sons.) Indeed, Ovid seems to go out of his way not to name any of his protagonists once the metamorphosis begins, making them as unspeakable as Lara.

Another manifestation of this same shift comes in the description of Philomela's tapestry, which she produces because she has been stripped of her voice, as a *carmen miserabile*, a song that induces pity. Whatever her tapestry may be, a text or a visual image, it is certainly not a literal song. At best it is a prompt for one to be articulated by someone reading aloud; yet even here it fails, for it renders Procne too miraculously silent (*et—mirum potuisse—silet*, 6.583). The link between the miracle of silent reading here and the transformative silence of the swallow and nightingale is clearly signaled. The same word, *notae,* we have seen used of the birds' markings describes the marks Philomela makes on the tapestry (6.577), and they have the same function, a revelation of crime (*indicium sceleris,* 6.578), though now the victim has become the criminal. And even the phrase *carmen miserabile* seems a perfect description of the song that Ovid's nightingale has lost, a song that sympathetically repeated always the same word, the name of the lost son.[48]

The lost song of the nightingale represents in clearest form how the verbal slippage we once identified as simply a marker of tragic irony

[46] See Forbes-Irving 1990.248–49. Eustathius's commentary on the famous Odyssean refers to Procne's song as a lament for Itylos (19.518–23) and so makes the story explicitly an aetion for the songs of nightingale and swallow. On the Itys cry in Greek poetry, see Curley 1997.

[47] The "textuality" of this episode is a much-treated theme. See esp. Pavlock 1991.41–42 and Segal 1994.262–66.

[48] Cf. Pavlock's (1991.42) contrast between the graphic tapestry of Philomela, which moves only anger and the traditional association between the nightingale's song and pity.

comes to symbolize the silencing of voices Ovid effects through metamorphosis. Procne's near pun, evoking an absent *gratia* from the son of
Gradivus, eerily predicts the final utterances made by any character in
the episode. The frightened king cries out for his son: *Ityn huc accersite*
(6.652): "Bring Itys here." Procne, as though mockingly misunderstanding her husband, begins with a deformation of the absent name, turning
Ityn into the Latin adverb *intus* (6.555): "You have within whom you
seek." Her linguistic substitution seems to give her the upper hand, even
as she prepares to dispel his ignorance of the terrible truth she knows.
And yet it is Ovid who takes the last word in this terrible game of verbal mutilation. No direct discourse appears again, and as if to make the
point, Ovid describes how much the voiceless Philomela wishes to express her joy in words. But he does describe Tereus speaking, seeking his
son and calling out for him "again and again." The Latin word used is
iterum (6.656), so that, as the characters' own voices fade to silence, we
can actually hear the Greek name disappearing into its Latin allomorph.

Two important points about the effects of Ovid's verbal metamorphosis emerge from this stunning wordplay. The first is the reassignment of
roles: Ovid leaves ambiguous which sister becomes the nightingale, but
that bird's song, which was after all *Itys* repeated, has been taken over
by the most unlikely character of all, Tereus. So too, as we have seen, the
visual, scripted image that closes Ovid's narrative presents no victims
but only a series of criminals. This is the nightmarish final stage in the
process of assimilation through looking with which we began the discussion, as each character takes on the role of the other by gazing at him or
her. It appears not only in the exchange of roles among the participants
as they undergo transformation but also in the transcription of the *notae*
with which Philomela had accused Tereus onto her own guilty breast.
Indeed, the very description of what precisely made those "notes" is itself ambiguous. They are marks of slaughter, cutting (*caedis*, 6.669); her
feathers are "signed" by blood (6.670). Is this the blood she shed when
Tereus cut out her tongue, or when she slew Itys? So too the hoopoe's
protruding beak takes the place of a long blade. Is this the blade/phallus
with which he first attacked Philomela, or that with which she revenged
herself? In the final trace left by the episode, the two referents have been
confusingly united in a single signifier. But the image of the birds' indeci-
sive pursuit is also important for its very repetitive quality.[49] The verbs in
the final lines are present but shift subtly from a "vivid" historical present to a description of qualities that the birds possess to this very day.
Procne flies to the roof of her house, and swallows do habitually dwell

---

[49] Cf. also the comments of Hardie 2002c.272, who interprets the final metamorphosis as
a "mimesis in the natural world of the repetitiveness of mimetic revenge."

there.[50] The chase is never concluded in the myth with the death of the women, and hoopoes chase swallows still. The animal repetition of the myth's conclusion also recalls how the transformation itself reenacts earlier moments: Tereus chasing Philomela with a phallic beak will always recall the rape, a crime made more horrible, as Ovid tells us, because it was repeated (6.561–62). The visualized birds thus come to seem as markers of the very interpretative effects that must be expunged from the story of Procne for it to be Romanized, the assimilation of differences and the resulting perpetuation of crime. But as she becomes emblematic of those fearful transformations of the self, Procne becomes increasingly distant from the human, as though her very form ends the possibility of perpetuating the process by signifying it. Her voice has safely been Romanized by being translated merely to the Latin sign for repetition, *iterum*. So in the *Fasti* the transcendence marked by spring may come for us, but for the swallow, who at line 2.853 becomes Procne again, winter is still lurking in the form of her Thracian husband Tereus, thrilled that she feels the chill blasts.

If the transformation of the protagonists in this story works to relegate them from recognizable human characters to occupants of a distant world of myth, the linguistic transformation of Greek voices to Latin script must always have been an unstable and reversible process. And the very contrast Ovid draws between writing and speech in the episode helps make this clear. For any ancient text is always potentially heard as well as seen. The voices of the characters embedded in the transcription of their words can always bring them back. Indeed, the image that Philomela sends to her sister is paradoxically called a *carmen*, a word that almost inevitably makes one hear the message as song. In any case, the purely visual form of the message acts as an instrument for the further transformation of its audience in the most nightmarish way:

> *evolvit vestes saevi matrona tyranni*
> *fortunaeque suae carmen miserabile legit*
> *et (mirum potuisse) silet: dolor ora repressit,*
> *verbaque quaerenti satis indignantia linguae*
> *defuerunt, nec flere vacat, sed fasque nefasque*
> *confusura ruit poenaeque in imagine tota est.*
> (6.581–86)

---

[50] So too, in terms of smaller-scale narratological problems, the tale's ending overrides the careful articulation of the narrative into stages that the "annalistic" frame evokes. The ending of the story, far from offering any resolution, merely opens the door for a perpetual replaying of the rape described in the central narrative panel.

The wife of the savage tyrant read the piteous song of her fortune and (wonderful that she could!) was silent: grief checked her mouth, and words sufficiently expressive of her outrage were lacking to the tongue that sought them; nor was there time to mourn; rather she rushes, about to confuse lawful and unlawful, and is all absorbed in the image of crime.

The incongruous emergence of a character's "voice" from a written text anticipates an equally striking transformation of the reader who is made voiceless. While many scholars have shown that silent reading was not an unimaginable phenomenon in antiquity, the general expectation that texts were to be read aloud still gives the phrase the flavor of an oxymoron.[51] Thus, the silencing of Procne pairs a reciprocal reversal of the semantics of communication—articulate writing leads to silent reading—with an assumption by the reader of the physical effects of the "metamorphosis" Tereus has inflicted on the message's author, revealed in the not-quite-literal reference to the reader's *lingua*. And both of these transformations figure Procne's recognition that the referent of the tapestry's message is herself. The very close link between textual reception and metamorphosis here—for indeed Procne's "silencing" provides the essential intermediate stage between the episode's two transformations and is linked to both in terms of imagery and theme—should remind us that the interpretation of any metamorphosis in the poem is potentially divergent and change-able as each reader chooses to distance herself from or recognize herself in the transformed figure. In this way it is as hard to keep Philomela a bird as to keep her silent. And as each reader's sympathy may reanimate Philomela and Procne, so too the literal utterance of the graphic signs that "denote" their exclusion can always potentially bring them back: enunciating *iterum*, according to this perspective, makes each Roman reader a new Procne.

The way in which we understand the narrative's own relationship to the different fictional processes it represents proves an equally unstable basis for constructing a response to the issues it raises. For just as both Tereus and the Athenian women offer two competing focalizers within it, so too the Thracian king and his victim Philomela simultaneously offer two competing models for Ovidian authorship. The account of Philome-la's tapestry as a *carmen*, its use of *notae*, and the very fact that it repre-sents the same thing the *Metamorphoses* does—the rape of Philomela by Tereus—have often made this image attractive as a *mise en abyme*, figur-ing, like Arachne's tapestry at the beginning of this book, Ovid's poem as preserving the voices of silenced victims. But if we ally Ovid too closely

[51] Esp. now Gavrilov 1997 and Burnyeat 1997.

with the revelation of the truth in Philomela's tapestry, equally troubling conclusions follow, because this perpetuates the endless "transformation" of identities that erases all difference by making Athenians bestial barbarians and making victims murderers. Another alternative for construing the nature of Ovidian narrative can be gained from the equally self-referential language that clusters around Philomela's attacker: his imagination is stirred by his self-created fictions, as he first mentally "molds as he wishes" (*fingit*) the parts of her body he has not seen (6.492); and he conceals his crime by producing "made-up groans " (*gemitus fictos*, 6.565–66) and "telling" (*narrat*, 6.565) "false funerals" until his tears win "belief" (*fidem*, 6.566).

That Procne and Philomela's revenge also requires them to practice deceptions has sometimes appeared as a further blurring of difference in the episode.[52] But one might equally stress that their deployment of representation depends equally on recognition, on achieving the sign's identity with what it represents. Their tales possess a doubleness much like Ovid's, but it is a doubleness that can seem to entrap its authors as much as empower them, depending on Ovid's readers' consciousness of their status as representations. Again different ways of viewing the episode as drama sketch out two poles of response to Ovid's narrative. Procne's recognition of her sister through the written signs she receives begins two contradictory processes that anticipate precisely her later transformation into her sister. As the text becomes a song, a *carmen*, Procne perceives it as a song about herself, the *carmen suae fortunae*. At the same time that she sees herself in what she reads, though, we watch her from without and see her changed into Philomela precisely by losing the capacity to speak, by becoming an image herself (*poenaeque in imagine tota est*). Again at the moment when Procne views Itys as Philomela would, we see her in the very different form of an Indian tigress. But Procne's becoming an image, or rather our recognition of that "transformation" as a loss of her "self," ironically contrasts with the intention of the women as authors to impose a unity between appearance and reality. For Procne and Philomela's own plot uses dramatic fictions fundamentally to reveal what has been shut up inside as much as to conceal or imprison. From the moment when she crafts her *carmen miserabile*, the person that Philomela represents is herself. Her triumph comes as she again appears as herself brandishing the head of Itys and so exposing rather than concealing her crime.

That final moment of recognition, Philomela's emergence with Itys' head, brings to a climax the tension between these two modes of seeing and prepares for the final transformation that reveals what is at stake for Ovid in the contrasting responses he generates for his narrative. For

---

[52] As done by Hardie 2002c.267–72.

Procne, this marks the end of dissimulation (*dissimulare nequit*, 6.653) and the moment when Philomela wants most to give voice to her own pleasures. And yet Ovid simultaneously heightens the pressure on his audience to see both sisters as actors in a theatrical performance: Procne wants to deliver a messenger speech (*nuntia cladis*, 654), the only way such a scene could be presented in a tragedy. And Philomela, who had been dressed as a bacchant to effect her escape from the stable (6.598–59), now continues performing the *Bacchae*, as an Agave figure holding the head of a dismembered son. The scene indeed alludes to a moment of meta-theatricality in that play, when the actor playing Pentheus, having been dressed as a bacchant by Dionysus, returns as Agave—that is, as a man dressed as a woman.[53] And if we continue to superimpose a tragic performance onto Ovid's scene, then the head of Itys becomes the mask that would have represented the head of Pentheus. Imagining the scene literally enacted in this way draws attention to those two alternative ways of seeing drama. On the one hand we see a tragic character emerging inseparably as the performer, Philomela as Agave, on the other the mask, a mere theatrical sign, representing someone, Itys, who no longer has a body and so can never be there. For Tereus this is the ideal punishment for the time when he dreamed of playing the father and fed his madness only with the costume and form of Philomela. In place of being a foreign spectator, with the possibility of merely enjoying, appropriating, and manipulating the spectacle—a position that I would argue approximates an ideal "Romanizing" view of the foreign theater—he is revealed as himself a character in a drama, less an authentic son of Mars than a figure from the Greek stage.

But if the last step in this reading has seemed to suggest a "sympathetic" Ovidian narrator participating with the wronged Philomela to punish any would-be Tereuses in his own audience, it is important now to insist upon the obvious point that the *Metamorphoses* is not a drama. Indeed, the tragic scene is itself transformed by a phenomenon that could never be represented on the stage, a metamorphosis. Through this device, as was hinted at before in the tiger simile, all of the characters are clothed with forms that conceal human identities and, as opposed to the sequential progression of the drama, freeze them in a final action destined to be infinitely repeated. This transformation also in eerie ways continues the "fictions" of the other Ovidian author within the story, Tereus himself, who takes away the voices of the women he imprisons in his narrative as Ovid strips the birds of their songs. Because, as I have argued, it is

---

[53] Segal 1994.273–79 traces the bacchantic imagery in the episode; his emphasis, however, is less on the effect of allusion to the genre of tragedy per se than on how the slippage from bacchants to Furies affects our interpretation of the moral quality of female revenge.

precisely the dehumanizing of the birds on which a "Roman" reading of the episode depends, it is significant indeed that Ovid should align the most ideologically freighted aspect of the narrative with the actions of a character exposed as a liar whose fictions are believed. This may be another case where the diminution of narrative authority, the exposure of the fictionality of fictions, becomes important precisely as a distancing device—if Ovid's characters are explicitly false, all the more reason not to believe in them.

At first the externalizing, deliberately superficial aspect of the final metamorphosis seems opposed to the sort of internal mutability that Procne experiences in response to her sister's *carmen*. Applying the models of dramatic reception developed through our reading of the Juvenal passage, we might say that recognition of the protagonists of the story as what they have become through metamorphosis goes together with a location of the Ovidian audience as the external spectators of a securely demarcated dramatic spectacle, conscious above all of the barriers between the watchers and what they see—a play and not reality. The loss of human form, together with their imprisonment in textuality, as the letters on the page, especially in a narrative genre so transparently unbelievable as *fabulae*, helps to exaggerate the difference between the characters as subjects and the audience. Paradoxically the desire of the "Roman" reader to interpret the scene in this way becomes another point of similarity with Tereus. Hardie draws attention to the semantic similarity of the two parallel desires of Tereus after he has discovered what he has consumed.[54] He wants at once to call up the Furies to pursue Procne and Philomela, and to "eject the *diras dapes*," which thanks to hyperbaton become briefly synonymous with the contents of his stomach (6.663–64). Adding the emphasis to theatricality implicit in the gesture of calling up the Furies, we can interpret the ambiguity here as a suggestion that dramatization, by making it possible to substitute the outer for the inner, offers Tereus the chance to escape from himself by projecting his situation onto a representation that is fundamentally other—itself a plausible way of reading Roman emphases on the otherness of the theater. And indeed the metamorphosis that follows, which converts the sisters into hybrid females suggestively like and unlike the Furies evoked by the fiction-making Tereus, appears very much as something that results from an act of imagination on the part of the Ovidian audience, "you would think that they were flying, and flying they are." Though to perceive the Tereanness of this gesture means that one has already internalized the perspective of the "stage" figure Tereus, and thus experienced something of the discordant revelation that befalls the king when he looks at the mask of

[54] Hardie 2002c.271.

Itys and recognizes that what this external sign signifies is literally within him.

My argument that the sisters' metamorphosis both figures and facilitates the conversion of Greek myth to Roman *exemplum*, a process that fully emerges only when the *Metamorphoses* and *Fasti* are read together, sheds light on another underanalyzed aspect of the story as it appears in the former poem. For the rape of Philomela is followed by an episode featuring another Thracian *tyrannus*, Boreas, who abducts and violates one of a pair of Athenian sisters, Orithyia.[55] In this story, though, the arrows all point in the other direction: violence, *vis*, which is emphatically the means Boreas employs to gain his desires (6.690), leads not to the destruction of the family and the death of children but to the creation of the family and the birth of twin male children.

This new repetition of the Tereus story is no mere exercise in *variatio* but rather a further "metamorphosis" that reveals yet another possibility for putting Greek myth to ideological use in contemporary Rome and highlights the essential role of audience reception in giving such a different charge to such a similar story. Here the emphases on difference and exclusion that mark the ideal "Roman" reading of the story of Philomela give way to recognition of the present in the past and the translation of the strange and unbelievable into a sign of the transcendence of the here and now. For in addition to the contrast it offers with the barbarism of Thrace's royal family, the tale of Boreas and Orithyia and their upwardly mobile progeny closely evokes some notable elements of imperial iconography, especially those involved in the great imperial mystery of apotheosis.[56] Thus, where the first narrative presented un-Roman activities to be expunged from the public reception of the tale through conversion to a marker of unlikeness, the Boreas episode presents the same story inflected to offer a positive paradigm, predicting and validating Roman practices, provided that "sameness" is recognized. The figure of repetition, which in the first story signified the collapse into a criminally undifferentiated

---

[55] A connection developed in a different way by Segal 1994.277–78. And see Newlands 1997.

[56] My interest here is the central question in the "reception" of representations of apotheosis raised by Beard and Henderson 1998: how precisely does the viewer translate the fantastic mechanism of skyward conveyance used to figure apotheosis (by eagle, winged chariot, or, in the image that visually seems nearest to Calais and Zetes, by winged "angel," as on the Column of Antoninus Pius) into a statement about political reality? Literal upward mobility features already in sculptural images of imperial apotheosis from at least as early as the last decade BCE, with Julius Caesar figured in riding through the heavens in a winged chariot on the Belvedere Altar (whose other faces, interestingly, show the Lares, the figures to whom it was dedicated). On the representation of apotheosis in Augustan poetry and its connection to another sky-bound youth Ganymede, lifted by the agency of an eagle, see Hardie 2002a.

past, now takes on a much more "Roman" look as the terrible Philomela story itself is reenacted in a way that removes its horrific aspects to create a forward-looking *exemplum* in which the audience can see images of the differences that set Rome apart from historical cycles of rise and fall. To use the terminology of Philip Hardie's book, Philomela and her sister enter Rome as absent presences. By contrast, the offspring of Boreas and Orithyia offer real presences, figures whose presentation stresses the continuities between the foreign and the Roman, the verisimilar and the fantastic.

The most obvious way in which the Boreas narrative corrects the emphases of its predecessor is in its treatment of female perspectives, and this was an important ideological issue as well as a narratological one. The crucial difference between Philomela and Lucretia was precisely the absence of male relatives to transform the quality of the revenge enacted for the rape. In this case, Orithyia is never a focalizer in the narrative:[57] there is in consequence no available victim's perspective on which to hang a dissenting point of view—though, of course, the reader may choose to infer one. Not only is Orithyia not a viewer within the narrative; she becomes visible herself only through the male countenance of her sons. Procne could slay Itys because she failed to recognize him as anything but his father. Here this divisive way of seeing—divisive because it perceives patrilineality as exclusion—is shut down. Women, like the Sabine women, become agents in transforming rape to assimilation precisely by acknowledging their status as mothers, and this, as we have seen, becomes for Livy an essential stage in Romanization. Seeing likeness here is as beneficial as Procne's view of difference was destructive. This exclusion of women by the sons who represent and resemble them is enacted within the narrative in a way suggestive of the procedures of Ovid's narrative. For the most significant deed that these two mothers' sons perform will symbolically complete the revenge for Itys' murder. They will chase off the Harpies, another set of flying females—and Ovid refers to them as *volucres virgineas*—who pollute male feasts (7.4).

The second aspect of the Boreas story that invites contrast with its antecedent comes in the account of the metamorphosis itself. In the case of Tereus and the others, metamorphosis becomes a means of distinguishing the traces that these hideous events have left in the present from the events themselves, as well as marking off the whole narrative as something that does not happen every day. Swallows, nightingales, and hoopoes are unremarkable avian phenomena, but murderesses only change into them in myth. On the contrary, in the case of Boreas's sons their

---

[57] This is a focus of Newlands's (1997.203–7) important reading of the episode in relationship to those of Procne and Medea.

final form, winged youths, is that of a miraculous hybrid that cannot be naturalized within the world of experience but is easily glossed from artistic representations in the context, especially, of apotheosis. But if the product is miraculous and artificial, the metamorphosis itself represents no miraculous change in states. Feathers are simply a sign of puberty, like facial hair and pimples, and it is easy to recognize the anthropomorphic Calais and Zetes in their winged form; indeed, they really become themselves only once their wings sprout.

But how do these particular metamorphic processes relate to some of the ideological issues discussed earlier? Let me start with a couple of obvious connections between the Boreas story and Roman foundation myths. We have seen already how the narrative's quick transition from rape to offspring mirrors accounts of the rape of the Sabine women. But other events in the life of Rome's first king are equally present. Again, of course, the focus is on divine twins, and here, as elsewhere, fiction is even better than the real thing because this pair vents their violence only on monstrous feminized others in the course of a foreign naval expedition, without fratricide. That hint at imperial foundations—where the battle of Actium becomes the defeat of Cleopatra rather than of Antony—is also very important, another civil war story rewritten. In these respects, if the Philomela myth makes Roman stories look pretty good by comparison, the Boreas narrative hints at an ideal reading of Romulus's life, with all the troubling ambiguities purged. And while we leave the dynamic duo frozen perpetually in pursuit of Harpies, their very capacity for flight—together perhaps with the omission of any reference to their deaths—hints at the third "rape" that punctuates the career of Romulus, his assumption by his father into the sky.[58] Again the winged form of these youths is especially significant, as they always are what the miraculous imagery of apotheosis insists Romulus became. Finally, the emphasis on a natural continuity between the miraculous and the everyday does not invite speculation only on the specific phenomenon of apotheosis. Rome itself is a natural miracle. Livy's précis of all regal history strikes this note repeatedly, as civic identity grows through natural bonds, so the state itself follows an organic pattern of growth (2.1). When and where this developing organism becomes the stable *telos* of the cosmos is of course a big problem in Augustan thought, and it is significant that this second way of naturalizing Roman power, as a continuation of the effects of cosmic energies, emerges here as well. The *vis* that carries off Orithyia and engenders Calais and Zetes, is the North Wind, who drives the clouds, stirs the seas, makes the aether thunder—another little hint at Romulus's transfiguration, perhaps—and terrifies the dead beneath the earth.

[58] For the importance of rape imagery in Romulus's apotheosis, see Hardie 2002a.

This has been a long and discursive reading and has taken many twists that may have jolted my own audience's *fides*. But the length and importance of the Philomela episode in Ovid's poem warrant such extended analysis, and its explicit focus on problems of reading and interpretation, especially its likening of reading to a visual process, mean that it intersects with a number of phases of my argument. Rather than disembed its various strands, I have chosen to show how they all work together to shape the significance of the episode as a series of models for reading Ovid's text. The first stage of my discussion, the one that justifies its inclusion in a treatment of Ovid and contemporary spectacle, analyzed how the prominent references to drama in the story evoke the experience of being a spectator at a theatrical performance. This experience acutely presented Roman audiences with the alternatives of absorption in a culturally foreign aesthetic product or of a heightened awareness of a distance from the imitations on stage that reinforces membership in the real community of spectators. In this way, the problems of reception posed by the status of drama as mimesis contribute to its civic dimension as a context in which to be a Roman. And so here the explicit dramatization of the story complements a series of allusions to Roman etiological myth. In particular, the *Fasti*'s references to this Greek story allowed me to expand my argument in two directions. First, dramatic performances, which of course occurred in the context of annual rituals, became a synecdoche for all enactments of Greek myth in the here-and-now rhythms of Roman public life. The Philomela story and its sequel, thanks to their embedding in the *Fasti*, explore how the various alternatives for construing likeness and difference offered by the representation of myths translate into a kaleidoscope of possible ideological uses for Greek myth at Rome, while potentially interfering with and destabilizing one another.

This somewhat vague term "representation" points to the second important way that my reading involves the larger arguments of the book: the *Fasti*'s hint that Procne's new form matters to the place she occupies in the Roman calendar led to a demonstration that it is again metamorphosis that energizes within Ovid's narrative the dynamic possibilities for recognition and distance that in other contexts like drama or "fatal charades" give ideological and civic significance to the depiction of these events. On one level, Ovid's narrative comments on and explores how Greek myths can be integrated into the cultural and civic life of the Roman state. But his text is more than a commentary. It offers a representation that allows the reader an array of interpretative options while marking out what the ideological consequences of those options are.

This last point leads me back to the even larger claim with which I began my discussion of sacrifice in chapter 3. For beyond placing the text in dialogue with civic performances that were themselves representations—

often of events generically similar to the ones depicted in the poem—I argued that metamorphosis also translated into literary form the visual dimensions of an even more central ritual act, sacrifice. The coexistence of another Ovidian poem about ritual helped clarify the interactions between literary representation and ritual experience: the two poems between them construct a complementary dynamic for the reception of Greek mythic narrative. The *Fasti* expands the significance of ritual practices by making them refer to a remarkably open and diverse range of narrative "causes." The *Metamorphoses* by contrast offers an abundance of narratives, often lacking specific nonliterary referents in contemporary social and political praxis, and shows how narrative alone can impact its audience's perceptions of issues ranging from theology to cultural identity with the immediacy and complexity of experiences like ritual. Given the importance of my claim about the "ritualization" of the text in the *Metamorphoses*, and because the Philomela story has given us a chance to study at close hand how the *Fasti* can guide our reading of one specific episode, I conclude by looking at the two parts of this final claim, showing briefly how the *Metamorphoses'* narrative of Procne explicitly explores the relationship between narrative, ritual, and fiction in ways that look to the *Fasti*, and then how, without any specific reference to sacrifice per se, the Philomela story too possesses a theological dimension by reconfiguring the relationship between man, beasts, and the gods.

We have already seen the importance of temporal cycles in the structure of the episode, and this emphasis extends to the commemoration of acts described in the poem. Indeed, the plot begins on such an "anniversary." The Thracians, ignorant of their own advantages, proclaim a festival (*festum*, 6.437) for the birth of Itys. Immediately we are told that five annual cycles had passed when Procne asks Tereus to fetch her sister, synchronizing the beginning of the plot proper with the recurrence of this festival. Obviously, it is the work of more than a day for Tereus to sail to Athens and back and imprison the mutilated Philomela in the woods, but again after this event the narrative refers to the passing of another year before the production of the tapestry. Thus, if we cannot say that the turning points of the story all recur in the context of the same annual celebration, we can claim that the cycling of the year significantly marks the interval between the event itself and its "reenactment" as representation.

But if the Ovidian narrative itself is hung on a ritual calendar, and this importantly does ensure that we see each event as a replaying, sometimes in dramatically different ways, of previous stages in the narrative, so too within the story the characters themselves use claims about ritual commemoration to mask their own behavior and drive their own plots. Most important, the festivals they invent are themselves false, so that here, literally, fiction and ritual overlap. Tereus demands mourning at the false tomb of Philomela in a way that looks like a Roman Parentalia. Procne exploits a Thracian bacchic festival to whisk her sister, disguised as a bacchant, from her forest prison. And the sisters "falsely claim [*mentita*] that it is a rite of their ancestral custom [*patrii moris sacrum*], which it is proper [*fas*] that men alone attend" to lure Tereus the banquet where he consumes his own son (6.6.647–49). As the last example shows, the evocations of ritual are accompanied by wordplay that seems to summon up the *Fasti* itself, in juxtaposing fictive festival with the unspeakable acts that will take place there. Thus, when Tereus ceases to dissimulate his lust and reveals his plot, he is said to "confess the unspeakable" (*fassusque nefas*, 6.524). Procne, as she recognizes that crime and prepares her own equally unspeakable revenge, is said to be about to confuse *fas nefasque* (6.585–86), which she will literally do in performing what is *nefas* under the guise of what ritual propriety demands (*fas*). The character that is expelled from the *Fasti*, thus presides over a set of festivals that are themselves fictions, falsehoods that aim only to conceal—another way in which the *Metamorphoses* seems explicitly to offer a foil to its twin, the *Fasti*. For to read the festivals in that poem as based on falsehoods and masking criminality—or, as in the case of the Thracians' celebration of Itys' birthday, on a profound ignorance of what was good for them—would of course dramatically transform one's understanding of it. In this *Nefasti*, all commemoration becomes mere repetition, and the penetration of falsehood, which is the reader's privilege throughout, inoculates Ovid's audience against allowing the two poems to contaminate one another. Unless, of course, the readers locate their own point of view too deeply in the poem's fiction by identifying with a character like Tereus, in which case the festival he celebrates at the end becomes all too true, as it indeed makes the past present for him. Thus, the alternatives Ovid's poem presents for us here are to recognize the overlap between festival and fiction so that we are not allowed to mistake any of the rituals in the narratives as authentic rituals or, by entering the false perspective created by fiction, to experience, as the character within the poem, the mystical moment when Tereus realizes that he is another, that the begetter of his son is his consumer, and that the day that marks the child's birth, if we allow the suggestion of annual recurrence to carry us a little past strict chronology, is also the day of his death.

Tereus's awful banquet takes us back to the poem's first cannibal feast, Lycaon's attempted deception of Jupiter. And we shall indeed find the same "theological" questions raised here, though less directly. The last narratives in book six make no mention of sacrifice but, especially taken together, they do offer contrasting views of the placement of man. The Philomela narrative stands out in Ovid's poem for the almost total absence of the gods.[59] But the circumstances in which they are mentioned are telling. They are explicitly not there at the wedding of Tereus and Procne (6.428–9, the chthonic Eumenides are present, but the mortal characters do not see them); Phoebus aloft in his chariot marks out the times at which the various events take place (6.571); so too Pandion briefly invokes the gods as guarantors of Tereus's pledge to return Philomela (6.499), and Philomela herself after her rape links the existence of the gods with the certainty of Tereus's punishment: "If the gods above see these things, if the powers of the gods are real, if all things have not perished together with me, someday you will pay me penalties" (6.542–4). Philomela's plea makes us ask where the gods are, and a number of interesting answers are possible. Tereus will pay a price, and so perhaps the gods do exist. But since there is no sign that they take any hand at all in Philomela's revenge, one could also claim that her invocation serves all the more fully to point out their absence. Finally the link she makes between the existence of the gods and the question of whether death is the end of all suggests that we answer from an Epicurean perspective. Maybe the gods are watching, but they are merely watching. To enter into the world of the narrative would, then, be to recognize a world where man lives cut off from any gods but is always at risk of becoming a beast. More comfortingly, if the gods merely watch, then we too, who know all the things Philomela asks the gods to see, perhaps watch as gods. For throughout the narrative mentions of the gods help always to differentiate our understanding from that of the embedded characters. Again, the Boreas and Orithyia story helps sharpen these alternative answers to the question of divine presence through the contrast it offers with the preceding story. Here the gods are all too present: one of them as a rapist himself. This suggests the darkest possible answer to Philomela's story—why should gods who themselves rape Athenian maidens avenge an act like Tereus's? But the conclusion provides a more upbeat point of view, stressing that the union with the gods puts human offspring on the path to the skies.

[59] So especially Segal 1994.270.

PART THREE

Ovid and the Visual Arts

CHAPTER 6

Faith in Images

In the first book of his poems from exile, Ovid explicitly compares his *Metamorphoses* to a visual representation, claiming in fact that his poem provides a "greater" image of the poet than any sculptural depiction: *carmina maior imago* (*Tr.* 1.7.11).[1] This is but one of the many connections between Ovid's great work and the arts of painting and sculpture. For not only has the poem provided by far the most significant repository of subjects for artistic representation of any text in the Western tradition other than the Bible, but links have often been perceived between Ovid's highly visualized descriptions and the preexisting masterpieces of classical painting and sculpture. Thus, the final tableau of the second book, as Europa's clothes billow out behind her while the bull on whose back she sits makes for Crete, has seemed to leave the captured maiden in precisely the attitude she will maintain in numerous ancient paintings.[2] Conversely, Ovid's next damsel in distress, Andromeda, first appears in the poem precisely as she was depicted in painting until a viewer,[3] Perseus, literally enters the picture to rescue her from a fate worse than death.

As these last examples already suggest, the relationship between the text and works of painting and sculpture is far more complex than the simple problem of reciprocal influence that originally prompted study of "Ovid and the Visual Arts." Rather, the poet seems explicitly to thematize the visual dimension of the poem, inviting readers to measure the capabilities of verbal and visual representations against one another. Such a procedure per se will hardly be surprising in an ancient text. Comparisons of poetry and painting were a rhetorical commonplace, and any ancient narrator would have learned early in his rhetorical training how to add visual vividness to his account of events. Ecphrases, in its modern meaning of verbal representations of visual artifacts, provided elaborate occasions for epic writers to articulate by comparison and contrast their own artistic aims, as Ovid does with unsurpassed complexity in the account of the tapestry competition in book 6. But the poem's choice of metamorphosis as subject gives a special dimension to its evocation of the visual.

---

[1] On the representation of the *Met.* in *Tristia* 1.7, see esp. Hinds 1985.21–27.

[2] Laslo 1935.424–28; see also Barkan 1986.7–18, Solodow 1988.210, and Wheeler 1999.154.

[3] *Met.* 4.673. Hardie 2002c.183–85.

Rosati's demonstration of the spectacular elements of metamorphosis obviously facilitates the assimilation of Ovidian narrative to works of art, but in an interesting double sense.[4] As recent work on ecphrasis has stressed, the older critical distinction between static ecphrasis, stopping the story even as it portrays an unmoving image, and the dynamic properties of the framing narrative is one that is constantly violated.[5] So Ovid's techniques of visualization both make the reader witness to a narrative process, as change seems to take place before her eyes, and confronts her with the unchanging product of metamorphosis—the tree, the flower, and in many cases the statue—that marks the end of change. These two ways of, literally, seeing metamorphosis open out different perspectives on the poem that introduces these objects to view, perspectives that replicate and intensify the hermeneutic challenges posed by metamorphosis itself. The first stresses the horizons of the narrative, showing the reader a long past event that acquires presence by virtue of being seen. The second by contrast locates the viewer in the familiar world of believable, everyday objects but asks her to see them with new eyes.

If we move from considering the effect of Ovid's techniques of visualization to ask then about the relationship implied between Ovid's texts and the visual arts, another related set of contrasts emerges between a metaphoric connection, which explicates the text while stressing its difference from the world of images, and a metonymic one, where the narrative itself seems to become one of the gallery of visual representations. Statuary and painting function as metaphors for Ovid's poem, as Philip Hardie has described, precisely through their ability to conjure up absent presences while marking that absence. The phenomenon of a literary account of an artistic image doubles the distance between the reader and whatever reality lies behind the description; yet, at the same time, the internal representation of the work of art creating a physically real presence of its vanished model stakes a positive claim for how the literary text can indeed make something out of nothing. Ovid gives an even greater immediacy to this effect by, for the most part, refusing to segregate ecphrastic description from his narrative by introducing a work of art to be described. "We are both stimulated to 'see' the events, and asked to believe in the reality of what we see. Seeing is believing; pictorial illusionism and verbal fictionality are forced into an unusually close symbiosis."[6] The last phrase of Hardie's analysis points to the special, metonymic quality of visual art for Ovid, the sense that the text itself no longer simply

---

[4] Leach 1988.440–66, working independently from Rosati, also draws particular attention to the way in which metamorphosis provides for visualization and makes this the basis of her own comparison between Ovidian narrative technique and the visual arts.

[5] Fowler 2000.64–85.

[6] Hardie 2002c.174.

describes scenes visually but has come to acquire the solidity and reality of artifacts. Its leap into presence reifies not only the events signified but also the very visual images that signify them. Alison Sharrock's discussion of the relationship between metamorphosis and visual representation illuminates another important area of overlap, again brought into focus by the theme of metamorphosis. Every visual work of art possesses the same double dimension of stasis and movement as Ovid's text, and both are complicated by the image of metamorphosis. The visual image, like the product of metamorphosis, is always both what it is—stone, paint, ivory—and what it represents, as the flower is always also Hyacinthus. More important, the material has taken on this double nature precisely through a process of transformation under the creating hand of the artist.[7]

Sharrock's observation that every work of visual art has its own metamorphic qualities, that the viewer mentally initiates a transformation from the material object to what it signifies, is the starting point for my argument here. The suggestion that the poem reproduces for its readers the experience of viewing physically present works of art, as in the preceding chapters I argued it did for ritual performances like drama and sacrifice, provides another crucial link between the poem and the material realities that constituted Augustan culture. For the "real presence" conjured up by Ovid's poem through visual vividness is not merely an abstract ontological paradox but a way in which the poem speaks about, and speaks as, an essential constitutive element of Roman identity. Several of the poem's images, among them the statue of Niobe that is discussed at the beginning of the next chapter, had direct visual equivalents prominently displayed in the public spaces of the Roman city, and even when such images are absent, or undiscovered,[8] the dynamic of viewing that the poem develops and draws on conjures up a response that is not simply an aesthetic one.[9] Rather, as recent research in the Roman reception of art has suggested, the act of viewing potentially brought into play questions of nationality, history, class, and political allegiance, as well as providing a context for religious experience. My aim in this part of the

---

[7] "Raw material becomes a work of art by a process which characterizes the artist as metamorphic worker and makes metamorphosis a powerful signifier of art, indeed a self-reflexive representation of or metaphor for artistic activity. Works of art may be static, but artistry is in a constant state of flux." Sharrock 1996.104. A similar expression of the inevitable connection between metamorphosis and the visual image is found in Barkan 1986.17–18.

[8] Viarre 1964.35: "Il est très rare qu'on puisse établir une entière correspondance entre une oeuvre d'art déterminée et une passage d'Ovide."

[9] Viarre 1964.144 asks a similar question but provides a different answer, one focusing on the magical elements of metamorphosis.

argument is to point to ways in which Ovid's text explicates how visual artifacts can indeed acquire such potency and how his poem both shares in that power and intervenes in the way that images are seen.

Before proceeding, though, I want to make clear that I do indeed know the difference between a text and an image, and that I am aware that Ovid's materialization of his text can take place only in the mind's eye.[10] Those epiphanic moments when image and text appear to merge always happen in counterpoise to a skeptical awareness of the art of words that resists deception. In fact, the opposition between narrative and image contributes as much to Ovid's effect as assimilating one to the other. But the text's ultimate incapacity to undergo physical metamorphosis finds a powerful compensation in its ability to inscribe itself on actual monuments, as, for example, the poet makes the stone Niobes that populate Augustan temples tell his story.

One factor that has until recently slowed appreciation of the dialogue between Ovid's textual images and the Roman visual environment has been, broadly speaking, the emphasis in the study of ancient art on connoisseurial questions of style and identification that have tended to isolate individual works of art from their cultural context. The familiar tendency to read through surviving Roman works to recover lost Greek models has also inevitably detracted attention from the complex reception of such images at Rome. But new shifts in the priorities of art historians have revealed that the act of viewing in Rome involved a network of decisions about how and what to see, affecting and affected by questions of education, class, religion, and politics. I have already given one example, in chapter 2, of how more audience-oriented approaches to understanding the power of images in Augustan Rome can reveal new parallels and exchanges between Ovid's poem and Augustan images on the political level. Now it is time to explore in greater detail some of the many alternatives ways of viewing in Augustan Rome to see how the tensions among them focus on questions very similar to those raised by Ovid's text.

---

[10] Another interesting recent attempt to relate Ovid's poem to the contemporary visual environment is that of Gros 1981. While Gros laudably rejects efforts to find signs of reciprocal influence between the poem and contemporary painting and sculpture, he goes on to imagine a too-impenetrable barrier between literary and visual art. Thus, rather than positing any dialogue between text and image, Gros attributes any similarities of compositional technique to the general aesthetic principles of the age. His final reading of the compositional effect of the *Metamorphoses* as generating a tension between the vividness of the details and the larger narrative impulses of the work (365–66) offers a useful way of reading the poem, and his comparison to the style of the Hellenistic baroque temple design which was even then being replaced by the more message-driven style of Augustan monuments, remains suggestive, even though recent art-historical work has made this opposition in styles less extreme than it once appeared.

One immediate justification for making the connection between Ovidian fictional technique and the reception of the visual arts is that there was no cultural sphere in which the authority and effects of illusionism were more intensely debated. Vitruvius, in a passage well known to art historians, attacks the growing taste for the kind of wall painting that we designate Third Style: earlier painters, though they included mythical subjects (*fabulae*, 7.5.2), had nevertheless produced illusions that gave the appearance of reality. The new painters, by contrast, produce "monsters rather than sure images drawn from definite things" (*monstra potius quam ex rebus finitis imagines certae*, 7.5.3). Such *monstra* not only distort appearances by exaggerating proportions so that columns seem thin as tendrils but also produce hybrids, "slender stalks having half images, some drawn from human heads, others from the heads of beasts." When Vitruvius condemns these paintings on the grounds that "these things neither are nor were nor will be" (7.5.4), he uses exactly the criteria that rhetoricians used to discriminate *fabulae* from other forms of narrative: They represent neither things that are nor things that might have been. In fact, the hybrid forms that exemplify the new style for Vitruvius provide a precise visual corollary to the impossible metamorphosis narratives of Ovid's poem.

But it is more than a similarity in content that links contemporary painting to the *Metamorphoses*. Not only do these visual monsters mix parts of different animals to produce things that never were; they simultaneously make it hard to distinguish where representation ends and begins. Where Second Style painting had offered more easily readable images distinctly framed within an illusionistic décor,[11] here it is impossible not only to find any reality described by the paintings but also to tell where illusion starts and stops. The columns and architectural details that had served as frames now themselves seem to come to life with recognizable animate shapes. This is perhaps what Vitruvius's reference to *certae imagines* implies, certain from the point of view not just of what they represent but also of the boundaries of the represented image. Such paintings complicate the relationship between levels of representation and simultaneously, as Ovid's poem does, question the priority of any external reality, or narrative, over the crafted image itself. Indeed, such a lack of boundaries allows the viewer an enormous freedom to alternate between seeing recognizable verisimilar figures emerge from the image and seeing them reduced to elements in an architectural design. Again Vitruvius's language is suggestive: "Minds darkened by weak judgments

[11] Though see the important reminder of Leach 2004.88 that even here there is no question of actually deceiving the viewer into taking the image as real.

are not strong enough to put to the proof what is able to exist with both authority and reason in decoration" (*iudiciis autem infirmis obscuratae mentes non valent probare quod potest esse cum auctoritate et ratione decoris*, 3.5.4). This complex sentence implies the difficulty of maintaining not only the coexistence of authority and rationality but also, through foregrounding the phrase *quod potest esse*, a leitmotif of part 3, the coexistence of reality with its artistic depiction. The reference to authority here is also telling; by asserting the canon of reality, Vitruvius combats the desire to apportion merit on the basis of art alone. As we have seen in the case of Ovid, so for the visual artist, the creation of fictions can draw attention to the artifact itself and so give a prestige to the craftsman that Vitruvius would deny him.

Jaś Elsner has used Vitruvius's polemic as a tool for understanding the experience of the viewer in the Roman house and to argue that the confrontation with visual illusion itself becomes the locus for the spectator to define a social self. Starting from the connection elsewhere in Vitruvius between visual decorum and social hierarchy, Elsner suggests a link between the subversion of realistic representation and the overturning of political order, which such representations both symbolize and perpetuate. But beyond the association of aesthetic and social control, Elsner's work is especially valuable for suggesting how the process of viewing illusion, irrespective of the content of the image, grants the viewer a new independence from preexisting social positions: because the challenge for the viewer is no longer simply the discovery of a "prior, fixed, and natural reality," a more "complex" act is required, one that engages predominantly viewer and image, without reference to externals.[12] Even Second Style paintings, Elsner suggests, that operate within the accepted rules of verisimilitude, can raise the question of "the 'reality' of the real world itself" and allow the viewer "to see it as merely a set of constructions."[13]

According to this account, the effects of visual illusionism per se in forcing its audience to question the priorities of reality "outside" and "inside" the represented image bear a close similarity to the effects of Ovidian fiction as initially described in the analysis of the Io narrative, which itself depends on the reception of a visual image. Another point of contact between Elsner's understanding of the sociopolitical effect of visual illusions and the reading of *Metamorphoses* we have developed so far is his emphasis on how illusionism deconstructs the very possibility of realism, and indeed of "reality" as a category. So we have seen in the beginning of chapter 2, and this is a point that has also been developed

---

[12] Elsner 1995 (quotes from p. 58).

[13] Elsner 1995.74. See also the development of Elsner's reading of illusionism in Leach 2004, esp. 89.

elsewhere in Ovidian scholarship, that Ovid not only questions the priority of the fictional over the real but also makes a figure like Augustus a metamorphic artist in a way that seems to invite the reader to transfer the strategies developed for interpreting the *Metamorphoses* to other sorts of artistic representations which have more at stake in the claim to offer access to a "real reality."[14]

In the next chapter I return to the act of vision itself to argue through a reading of the Perseus episode that viewing images instantiates the kind of radical identification of the self as social participant that we saw in the sacrificial spectacles of chapter 3. But first I want to turn away from the question of illusionism to draw attention to other "political" aspects of the reception of the visual arts that also find parallels in the ambiguities of Ovid's poem. Specifically I suggest that certain essential properties of the work of art in Roman eyes, above all its innate foreignness, also affect the Roman viewer's experience in ways that explain the tension between poetic narrative and visual image within the poem.

No text has been more important for setting the traditional agenda of Roman art history than Pliny the Elder's treatments of painting and sculpture, virtually the only narrative of art history to survive from antiquity as well as an indispensable guide to the works of Greek art on display in the imperial city. But simply to mine Pliny for such information risks overlooking the fascinating example Pliny offers of how one Roman reads art history. For Pliny embeds details about specific works of art in a larger narrative of Roman cultural history in such a way that to focus on the formal qualities of the works described, as art historians have traditionally done, is already to have taken one side in a larger debate about what matters in a work of art.[15] One place where these alternatives are easiest to observe is in his famous discussion of the Roman house, where Pliny contrasts the display of ancestral monuments like *spolia* and ancestor portraits with the luxurious images merely bought by the wealth of new owners (35.5). The old images gained value as historical markers in a double sense: their very presence commemorated the deeds by which they were won, and as representations they provided reminders of the virtues of the past. By contrast, the new images, made by foreign artists (*externorum artificum*, 35.6), are predominantly material objects (*materiam conspici malunt*, 35.4). But the anxieties here revealed about the social effects of a connoisseurial reading of works of art, in which foreign artistry and imported material occlude the representation of Roman virtues, provide but one aspect of Pliny's own contradictory view of viewing. This tension becomes obvious in the very fact that it is precisely the

---

[14] Especially Hardie 1997 and 2002c.

[15] For a full account of Pliny's motives as art historian, see esp. Isager 1991.

aspects of works of art that he here makes symptomatic of decline that structure his own treatment of them. Painting and sculpture find a place in Pliny's work only because of the materials from which they are made and within each excursus are cataloged according to the artist who has produced them.

The other side to Pliny's view of images appears precisely from consideration of the context where Pliny locates his polemic against modern tastes in home decoration. This emerges in fact from a very formalist perspective on the decline of verisimilitude in portrait painting, the result, Pliny claims, of a general breakdown in the cultivation of the self that makes moderns worthy of and interested in being represented (35.4). The faulty emphasis involved in contemplating works of art only as material objects becomes both a cause and an effect of this phase in the development of art history. This suggests that a reading of works of art that stresses the Roman historical context is not the only frame that can be used to combat the forces of corruption. Rather, Pliny's project involves the "conquest" of art history by making it a metaphor for Roman imperial decline. As the ideal styles of representation, which in turn focus on creating a vivid and lifelike image, constitute a golden age in the history of art corresponding to the historical periods before Rome itself was corrupted by luxury, so the artists themselves become not simply adjuncts to the material value of their products in the modern luxury market but examples in their own right. Their efforts to impose order on natural matter in a way that makes it a signifier of virtue parallel the achievements of the images' Roman conquerors, and perhaps of Pliny himself.

Hence a defense of art history as a scholarly discipline, as well as a pronounced ambiguity that shows itself in a number of Pliny's discussions, depending on whether "actual" Roman history or its reflection within the discipline of art history takes priority. For example, the first foreign paintings are publicly displayed in Rome after the conquest of Corinth, a moment that both marks one of the great triumphs of Roman history and serves as a canonical watershed for the invasion of foreign luxury. Correspondingly, the conqueror Mummius's attitude toward captured paintings enshrines what from one perspective seems a laudable old Roman reluctance to value foreign works of art per se and from another a distant and almost barbarous Philistinism. When a foreigner, Attalus of Pergamon, offers an exorbitant sum for a famous picture of Liber, Mummius calls the picture back and places it in the temple of Ceres, "having suspected that there was some virtue in it of which he was ignorant" (35.24).[16] If the initial reluctance to view the work as anything other

---

[16] Because I am interested here only in recovering imperial attitudes toward the visual arts, the fact that this event is extremely unlikely to have occurred makes no difference to

than booty and the resulting decision to make the work public once its value is known illustrate a traditional ethos,[17] the inability to detect virtue (*virtus*) in the form of a painting seems a defect from the point of view of Pliny's own time, and this defect emerges all the more clearly from a paired anecdote in which a German barbarian shows himself equally ignorant of the worth of painting when, asked what value he would put on a picture of an aged shepherd, he answers that he would not even want the shepherd himself as a gift (35.25). A point of view that sees the value of art only in terms of the social status of the figure it commemorates, just the one that ought to prevail in the Roman house, now defines the barbarian. Another point of conflict comes when Pliny seems to condemn contemporaries not for an excessive interest in foreign works but rather for ignorance of them: "At Rome, the multitude of works of art, and the effacement [of their titles], and especially the huge mass of business and obligations keep all from contemplating them, since such wonderment belongs to men of leisure and requires tranquillity" (36.27). Here the very accumulation that might have been taken as a sign of expansion and splendor has a negative effect on viewing the works of art in their own terms. And the opposition between duty and leisure makes it very unclear whether industry and offices are to be praised or blamed. Is the ideal to have leisure for edifying study or to have something better to spend one's time on?

This brief overview of Pliny's attitudes toward the reception of art thus shows how the contradictory values of "art history" itself, to apply an anachronistic term, depend on the balancing of conflicting framing narratives, one oriented toward the Greek original, the other toward the Roman appropriation of it, with neither ever quite able to escape the other. But his analyses also make clear the striking extent to which the experience of any actual work of art, even prior to the kind of iconographic interpretation discussed in chapter 2, could be complicated by the tension between content and context. Should one see the painting Mummius erects as an adornment of a Roman temple, or as an intrinsically valuable Greek masterpiece whose position in Rome tells the story of her triumph over the East, or as a reminder of Mummius's own public spirit? Or does one concentrate on the qualities of the painting itself, or on the story of Dionysus and Ariadne that it told?[18] The problem is all the more acute in this particular case because the painter in question, Aristides, specialized in conveying the emotional states of his subjects, and indeed one of

my argument. See Gruen 1992.124–29 and Bergmann 1995.88, n. 18.

[17] On the "private" display of art masterpieces as a symptom of *luxuria*, see Bergmann 1995.

[18] Assuming that the painting of Liber mentioned in 35.24 is the same as the Dionysus and Ariadne once on view at the temple of Ceres at 35.99.

the most celebrated of his works showed the horrific image of a baby attempting to suckle its dead mother after the sack of a city.[19] And far from being an inevitable, and accidental, aspect of viewing works of art, the "battle" between Greek and Roman seems to have been deliberately emphasized by contexts of display. Bettina Bergmann has persuasively shown that the opposition between Greek original and Roman imitation has very little value for describing any actual work of art but that Roman contexts of viewing themselves conspired to give the illusion of an appropriated Greek masterpiece. Thus, the décor of the Villa Farnesina creates the impression of a public picture gallery through the elaborate framing of individual panels within the frescoed decoration. As Bergmann suggests, the owners of this luxurious villa could easily have afforded actual ancient paintings.[20] The preference for simply imitating them in part reflected on the status and attitudes of the owner, because the appropriation of works of art in private spaces was symptomatic of excessive grandeur and frequently attracted the attention of moralists. But beyond that, the display doubly makes illusionism the medium that brings such political questions to the fore by making the viewer choose between seeing or not seeing the luxury that would be implied by a real private gallery, as well as between seeing or not seeing the Greek vistas as framed or perhaps overshadowed by the Roman context of display.[21]

The kinds of issues that Roman artistic display seems deliberately designed to generate have an immediate relevance to the "double vision" experienced by the reader of the *Metamorphoses*. In this case too, the overall narrative thrust directed toward the present and the triumph of Rome contrasts with the profusion of individual episodes overwhelmingly devoted to foreign subjects—which inevitably overlap with the content of famous Greek painted panels—to raise the question of whether the poem is indeed an epic celebration of the Roman "now" or a reanimation of a lost past. The connection between assent to illusion and the adoption of the victim's point of view so tellingly developed in Arachne's tapestry would also have several corollaries in the experience of viewing actual works of art. Not only would the framed panels be overwhelmingly Greek in subject matter; they would also have been often portrayed as spoils of conquest. What is more, the capacity to create illusion was precisely what makes the Greek artists themselves masters, according to

[19] Interestingly, Pliny notes that this painting itself was taken as booty by Alexander, the sacker of Aristides' own native city of Thebes, 35.98.

[20] Bergmann 1995.105.

[21] For another important discussion of how viewing Greek objects in the contexts of Roman houses draws attention to issues of social and political hierarchy, see Fredrick 1995, esp. 279.

the veristic standards Pliny adopts (though the exposure of the power to create illusion diminishes the efficacy of that illusion).

These considerations give new significance to Ovid's placement of the visual tableau of Europa at the juncture of books 2 and 3. Beyond emphasizing the contrast in his own work between motion and stillness, the "painting" suggests the thematic content of this opposition and also relates it directly to the experience of the visual arts. On a purely narratological level, this moment in the poem draws particular attention to the tension between the large frame and the individual episode.[22] Europa herself is quintessentially the figure of the refined short poem; the version of the Greek poet Moschus forms a self-contained whole of 165 lines whose narrative is shaped purely by the erotic maturation of Europa, a young girl who in the first line is visited by a dream of the goddess of love and, in the poem's very last word, becomes a mother.[23] But set in the frame of a larger narrative, this Europa-centric view comes into conflict with larger historical forces, as her brother goes off eventually to found a city whose fortunes will occupy Ovid for the next book and a half and which prefigures the foundation of Rome itself.[24] Thus, while Europa's progeny and kin are essential to the development of the poem, Europa herself is not. Indeed, the static image of the tableau offers us our last glimpse of her. The moment when Europa becomes a "painting" then raises precisely the same kinds of interpretive questions that actual paintings of Greek maidens would have done in the context of Roman atria. And like the images that depict her, Europa herself is described as booty (*praedam*, 2. 873).[25] The linkage to visual artifacts thus takes on a special significance because this generic crux comes at a point in the poem that highlights conquest and cultural transmission. The abduction of Europa from Herodotus onward has marked an epoch in the exchange between East and West, and the coming of Cadmus to Greece that it sets in motion not only anticipates the geographic shape of Ovid's epic but brought East-

[22] The word *sinuantur* is itself crucial in pointing to this tension, for while its pictorial dimension highlights the miraculous qualities of painting, because the s-shape which it denotes is the ephemeral product of the winds, it also represents a vice from the point of view of narrative economy. Thus, Quintilian 2.4.3 requires a narrative to be neither arid and starved nor *sinuosa* through recherché descriptions, of which this perhaps is an example.

[23] See the comparison of the two versions in Barkan 1986.12–18. Note also, however, the "cosmic" dimension of Europa's dream in the personification of the two continents who fight for her; Moschus 2.8–9.

[24] This effect is, of course, accentuated by the placement of the narrative at the join between two books, on which see Wheeler 1999.90–93.

[25] In this context, it is important that there were no less than three Greek representations of Europa in Pompey's triumphal portico: statues by Pythagoras and Mikon (Tatian *Graec.* 33) and a painting by Antiphilus (Pliny 35.114). See Kuttner 1999.347, n. 8, and 370.

ern arts, including writing, to the West. Ovid here, among other things, signifies the reshaping of Greek literary "artifacts" into Roman epic in a gesture that collapses the distinction between maiden, image, and text.

This kind of collapse is also evident from the role of Europa as narrative focalizer in this image, and here emerges a second important connection between reading and viewing in the episode. As we saw in chapter 1, the phenomenon of metamorphosis can itself effect a disjunction in point of view between a metamorphosed figure (often a victim) and a spectator (sometimes an amorous pursuer). Here a similar kind of tension emerges but with a telling difference. Within the narrative, Europa has not been changed into anything; it is only Ovid's figuring her as a painting that creates an awareness of different kinds of visual response. And yet this refashioning of Europa as image responds to an emphasis on viewing within the tale. Unlike Io, her natural foil, who having been turned into a cow becomes herself a deceptive image to be read, Europa is presented as the viewer of a work of art. (Ovid's ecphrastic technique, and explicit comment that "you" could compare the bull's horns with things made by hand [2.855], ensures that we see the disguise too in artistic terms.) By functioning as an internal spectator, Europa becomes an available analogue for the reader within the story, a possibility that already complicates the easy treatment of her as "spoils," the perspective that helps code her tale as part of a triumphant march to the West. This capacity of Europa to focalize the victim's point of view typifies her when she emerges again, now explicitly as a visual image, as the first figure on Arachne's tapestry, where, as we saw, her deception by the bull overlaps with Arachne's deception of the viewer and, thanks to the narrator's reuse of the ecphrastic "you," of the reader of the text: "You would think it was a real bull and a real sea" (6.104). Again, Europa offers a conduit for "seeing in" that juxtaposes deception by artistic illusion with adopting a point of view locked within the frame of the representation.

But it is not just that Ovid's technique here accentuates the visual dimension of his own poem, making it like a picture in the responses it evokes and the way it invokes them. By turning Europa into a painting, and by keying the particular "visual" options he makes available closely to recognized ways of viewing actual works of art, he highlights the issue of artistic reception, deconstructing the increasingly charged processes by which his readers interpreted artistic images. This is one aspect of what Ovid gains by explicitly connecting his scenes to works of art, rather than simply relying on the visual disjunctions metamorphosis itself brings with it. Another is to give greater presence to the transformations he described, creating an overlap between image and text that comes perhaps as close as a literary artist can to projecting described objects into the physical space of the speaker.

To show how the Europa narrative exemplifies this double process, let me begin by backing up my claim that the different points of view opened out by the narrative correspond to recognized alternatives for viewing art objects. Europa's response to the bull is precisely the naive reading of images practiced by the barbarian who valued the painting of the ancient shepherd only by the real image represented. She is the spectator so totally absorbed by verisimilitude as to be unaware of the artifice that tricks her. Indeed, she is induced even to suspend her knowledge of the real world by the force of illusion; she knows that "real" bulls are not gentle (2.860), but the monstrous hybrid[26] produced by Jupiter so wins her over that she comes to believe in the mythical bull as gentle lover. Ignoring the strictures of Horace at the beginning of the *Ars Poetica*, Europa is perfectly prepared to allow an artist to place jewel-like horns on a bull's body. One consequence of this way of viewing is that she is so absorbed by the real presence of the bull that she misses the real presence in the bull. As in the case of actual works of art we posited a disjunction between an awareness of the painting as an object in its own right and of the larger social hierarchies its context suggests, so her way of seeing blinds her to the power of Jupiter.

The alternative perspective in this passage comes from the narratorial voice and emerges in the connoisseurial approach his description takes to the crafted bull, praising both its color, and, by implication, the workmanship that went into it.[27] He ensures that we are aware of the process of craft as well as its object, of the real frame that exposes the artist's illusion. And yet before we readers congratulate ourselves too much on not being tricked into taking Jupiter's disguise as a real bull, let us make sure that we are equally cautious about taking it for the art image that it is compared to by the narrator. For the horns, after all, are not made by hand but are real horns, made so by a god. Thus, if Europa's perspective demotes Jupiter to a bull, the "Plinian" narrator reduces him to a man and tempts us to lose the "wonder" in the presence of a miracle that Europa herself feels, if for the wrong reasons (*miratur*, 2.858).

If this suggestion that Ovid uses the Europa episode to deconstruct the contemporary ways of viewing is right, then it is appropriate that her

---

[26] See Barkan 1986.13. For the problems of viewing hybrids in Augustan art, see Elsner 1995.57–58.

[27] There is thus a telling difference between the ecphrastic second-person verbs used in the account of the Arachne tapestry (*verum taurum, freta vera putares*, 6.104) and in the description of the bull (*quae contendere possis / facta manu*, 2.855–56): the first focuses on verisimilitude, and as a result makes the reader not just a viewer of a work of art, but a viewer within a work of art. The second draws attention to craft and keeps the reader aware of the artificiality of the image. Both are equally deceptive, the first suggesting that a crafted bull is real, the second that a real bull is crafted.

deception should have involved the false representation of a bull. For among the most beguiling of those images in which the artist seemed to have surpassed the boundaries of craft, and among the most important subjects for ecphrastic writers of the Hellenistic and Roman periods, was an artificial cow first erected as a votive offering on the Acropolis by the fifth-century BCE sculptor Myron.[28] So lifelike was this cow, according to the epigrams it inspired, that herdsmen tried to drive it off, calves tried to nurse from its bronze udders, gadflies tried to sting it, and bulls tried to mount it. The very act of viewing such a cow prompted meditation on the relative powers of art and nature, expressed in the paradox that nature seemed to have become dead and art to have come to life.[29] So its sculptor emerges alternately as a Prometheus giving new life to statues and, ironically, as a liar who never sculpted the cow at all but simply drove it off from a herd or waited until it turned bronze from age. In another poem, though, the ultimate unreality of the cow points out the artist's own deception in the power of his craft, or, as the poet puts it, art has "raped" him (τέχνη σε βιάζεται, AP 9.798.1). Europa's misprision concerning the bull thus places her in a long tradition of literary viewers. But the tables have been turned in a supremely Ovidian gesture, for this bull is real, or at least it seems so in the world of Ovid's narrative. The deceived viewer here turns out to be right after all, and in place of the sculptor who inevitably falls just short of a divine capacity to create life, the artists are either, in the case of Jupiter, literally divine or a yet more marvelous (or dishonest) craftsman who has produced for the reader an image much more real than Myron's while working with a much less substantial material than bronze. And these reorientations are necessary for a reader himself to move from the static image of a painted Europa to the dynamic world she experiences as a figure within the text.

The hybrid nature of Ovid's account and its doubling of interpretative strategies emerge most clearly in the final tableau itself. For one of the tragic aspects of Ovid's Europa narrative, and a powerful contrast to Moschus's treatment of her, is that she remains trapped within the static image. Europa never reenters the narrative after this final moment. By contrast, Moschus goes on to describe her maternity, as does Ovid in his *Fasti* (5.617). And while the third book begins by describing Jupiter as

---

[28] Steiner 2001.28, n.70. Also Kuttner 1999.363.

[29] See, most clearly the late poet Julian of Egypt:

Πόρτιν τήνδε Μύρωνος ἰδὼν τάχα τοῦτο βοήσεις·
" Ἡ φύσις ἄπνοός ἐστιν, ἢ ἔμπνοος ἔπλετο τέχνη."
(AP 9.793)

shedding his deceptive disguise and admitting his identity, this event occurs in a subordinate clause, merely providing a temporal frame for the start of Cadmus's story, and there is no reference to any response on the part of Europa to his revelation, as though she were now an inanimate image rather than a viewing subject. And just as we have previously described how Europa's point of view offers access to the depicted world, so within that final tableau her own gaze is fixed resolutely backward, toward the Asian shore, girlhood, and book 2. One of her hands, however, holds the horn of the bull. Stephen Wheeler has detected a metatextual pun here: for *cornua* can mean not only horns but the knobs at the end of the book roll.[30] Thus, while as maiden the image looks back, she also mimics the reader in, perhaps, reaching out for the next book roll to continue the narrative (or stressing the end of this one?). This tension between the anticipation of things to come, keyed to the reception of the poem as text, and a desire for regression becomes all the more marked because of the familiar difficulty in rewinding scrolls to go back to an earlier passage. In contrast both to the spatial freedom provided to the viewer by actual visual display and to the backward glance of Europa, reading was an activity that by its nature kept you moving forward. The final image, then, not only echoes the oppositions between context and content, forward-looking narrative and arresting image, but places Ovid's text itself at a moment of transformation, as text engenders image, and that image seems literally to become text. For the horn–book roll equivalence is primarily a verbal pun, an effect that emerges more from reading than from visualizing an image. Thus, the reader hovers between seeing the book as horn or horn as book, as the real presence of the book grotesquely appears in the "painted" image, and reabsorbing the image into the poem's linguistic mode of communication.

I. Pygmalion

The final point of my introduction illustrated how the narrative that ultimately yields the painted Europa disorients the ways in which a Roman viewer might have approached just such an image. The contrasts between absorptive viewing and one alert to the artificiality of the work of art, though, involved more than purely aesthetic priorities. Contrasting conceptualizations of the capacities of the artist like those studied in the second chapter are also at work, as well as the importance of artistic recep-

---

[30] Wheeler 1999.92–93, citing for the Ovidian use of "horns" to suggest the ends of a book roll, Barchiesi 1997a.187. On the book and the bovine in general, see now Ishøy 2006.

tion as a sphere for measuring the relative capacities of man and god, as the craftsman's skill seems at once to represent and to conceal the workings of superhuman forces. This last element of viewing wears a more mundane aspect in the Roman awareness of the power of art to focus attention alternately on the skill of the artist whose hand has wrought the image and on the power and wealth of the patron who has appropriated it. In this next section I want to develop further the political element of artistic reception and its significance for the poem. Using another of Ovid's prominent engagements with the paradoxes of viewing, the Pygmalion episode of book 10, I aim to bring the issues of artistic reception into the same orbit as the accounts of public religious spectacle put forward in part 2. In their different ways, both absorption in mythological scenes and a fascination with the crafts of almost overwhelmingly Greek artists can offer distractions, in the fullest sense, from the contexts in which such works were displayed. They form a bridge to an experience of otherness at the heart of Roman practice that bears comparison to the identifications with actors, captive barbarians, and sacrificial victims potentially set in motion by the triumphs, spectacles, and sacrifices we have met before. My point is not that either the "absorbed" or the connoisseurial responses to images are ipso facto "subversive," but rather that the challenge these works of art raise for the viewer can also be integral to formulating a sense of her place in the community that mounts such a display.

As a link between issues of artistic reception in the abstract and their specific function in a contemporary Roman context, I want to return to the cattle of Myron. If generations of poets found Myron's heifer a good device for thinking about viewing in the abstract, other representations of cattle by the same artist occupied a place of prominence in the social and religious landscape of the city. As Propertius's account of his visit to the Palatine reminds us, four Myronian cows lowed around the altar of Apollo on the Palatine: *atque aram circum steterant armenta Myronis / quattuor artifices, vivida signa, boves* (2.31.7–8). These lines show Propertius's engagement with the poetic tradition surrounding the sculptor's famous heifer: the opposition between the contrasting oxymorons, "artificial cows" and "living statues," mirrors the paradox of animate art and lifeless nature developed, for example, in the later poems of Julian of Egypt.[31] But Propertius's response to the poem also suggests two elements of their placement that charge the cows with additional and more specific significance. First, the poet points out that, as indeed was also the case at Athens, the cows are located around an altar, making them, to those who "recognize" them as real, inevitably also sacrificial victims. Ovid's Pythagoras shows sacrifice as an abomination precisely by

---

[31] See now the discussion in Welch 2005.92–93.

animating a bovine victim "outstanding in form" (*praestantissima forma*, 15.130), imagining her as seeing, not just being seen. Myron's veristic statues by (almost) coming to life potentially acquire a subjectivity that makes them more than simply wonders of art. While it is true that nothing in Propertius's description suggests that the cows become focalizers for the scene in the way that the heifer does in Pythagoras's attack on sacrifice, this presentation of the object as animate enables such a move. More important, there is a parallel between the shift in response generated by the statues and the Pythagorean victim that points to an analogy between the viewing of art objects and the visual dimensions of sacrifice.

The second significant element in Propertius's treatment of the statues involves the way he uses them to define his own reading of the many interpretative possibilities offered by the temple, specifically to give weight to the status of the artist as opposed to the imperial author behind the temple. Indeed, Myron is the only nonmythical mortal individual other than Caesar named in the poem. How much attention do we give to the artist, how much to the emperor? As I suggested before, the tension between Propertius's "elegiac" reading of the monument and its celebration of military victory draws out a tension within the visual program of the temple complex. The god who cast down the Gauls from Parnassus and wrecked Antony's fleet is shown holding the lyre of the poet. The balance between the violent power of Apollo and his connection to the arts of peace—a dichotomy that again affects the reading of Myron's cattle either as celebrating the accomplishments of the sculptor or as victims about to fall on the god's altar—itself bears a resemblance to the questions the bull raised in the mind of Europa. For that maiden too had been particularly troubled by the difficulties of accounting for the bull's own mild and unwarlike nature (2.859). As Ovid puts it, *maiestas* and *amor* do not easily coexist (2.846–47).

One of the passages where Ovid most transparently invokes the parallel between his own literary fictions and the interpretative problems posed by artistic representation comes in the account of the sculptor Pygmalion falling in love with his own statue, a tale that in Ovid's hands has become nothing less than a foundational myth for realism in the visual arts. Here occurs the famous description of "art lying hidden by its own art" (*ars adeo latet arte sua*, 10.252), a phrase that has seemed both to offer a programmatic statement about Ovid's own conceptions of illusionism as an art whose ultimate effect is to disappear in its own fictions and to relate directly to contemporary aesthetic concerns about artistic images.[32] It comes in the description of the statue created by Pygmalion,

[32] Though *ars* in Latin does not connote forms like painting and sculpture as transparently as its English derivative but rather refers to all technical abilities.

so lifelike that "you" would think it real (10.250). And "you" would not be the only one, for the sculptor himself conceives a passion for his statue and in every way treats it as though it really were the maiden it represents. He adorns it in clothes and jewels, lays it in his bed, and whispers endearments to it. Eventually the goddess Venus grants his secret prayer and turns the ivory statue into flesh. When the story is presented in this way, the tale seems almost to provide the fable of which *ars latet arte sua* is the moral: the story of how realistic art transcends its own essential artificiality to become what it represents. And in one of the most important recent readings of the episode, Rosati has argued that this artistic ideal and the narrative that illustrate it reveal Ovid's participation in the cult of artificiality shared with the sophisticated and urbane audiences of the early empire, for whom the highest praise of any work of art was as a superior reality, surpassing the natural world rather than imitating it: "The work of art must not, then, allow deception to appear or betray its artifice. The naturalism Ovid promotes is not that unmediated, naïve and everyday naturalism based on nature, but a second, new naturalism, attained in artificiality and fiction."[33] In contrast to this exaltation of fictions supplanting reality, I argue that both the quote about *ars* and the narrative in which it is embedded enhance the interpretative reciprocity between visual and literary illusionism not by revealing a shared artificiality but by revealing instead how both create the same tension between the epistemological priorities of reality and representation. And in this case Ovid has literally tied the interpretation of his text to the decision the reader makes about whether to accept the reality of a visual illusion.

In context, the line about the deceptive power of art belies its own force. For Ovid, far from simply participating in the capacity to create artificial realities, exposes that capacity, just as he does elsewhere through the self-referential claim to be creating lies and fictions, and thus seems to locate his own reader's perspective outside of the wonderment of the engaged viewer. *Latet* means to lie hidden and can indeed be used of something like a concealed weapon whose danger and force escape notice,[34] and the phrase itself belongs most properly to a "how to" book for the budding artist or speaker.[35] But Ovid has brought art out into the open

---

[33] Rosati 1983.80.

[34] For this sense of *lateo* see the examples in *OLD* s.v. § 1.

[35] Often this expression has been compared to the lover's art of flattery and insinuation described at *Ars Amatoria* 2.313–14: *si latet ars prodest; adfert deprensa pudorem / atque adimit merito tempus in omne fidem* (Rosati 1983.80). This parallel might at first impel us to take the phrase in *Met.* 10.252 at face value. But even in the *Ars* passage, the art is calling attention to itself. *Ars* is after all the title of the poem. So too if we think of the poem

and, by pointing out its own deceptive capacities, done what no speaker should do to the actual audience he wishes to "trap."[36]

The tension between viewing art as art and the possibility of taking art as reality informs both the content and the structure of the Pygmalion story, where the making of the statue symmetrically balances its "deconstruction" or conversion into the reality it seems to be. Nor would it be a fair description to claim simply that Pygmalion is caught up in the reality effect of illusionism; rather he experiences an exquisite tension between wanting life to be like art and wanting art to be alive, between prioritizing an ideal artistic conception and a reality to which it aspires. Pygmalion is famously introduced as a misogynist, who has chosen to live as a bachelor because of his revulsion from the immorality of the Propoetides, a group of women who have been turned to stone through their shamelessness, and his creation of the statue is sometimes connected to his longing for a woman to love. This last assumption is both unsupported by the text[37]—Pygmalion never makes this miraculous sculpture as an ideal surrogate he simply happens to make it while (*interea*, 10.247) living as a bachelor[38]—and misleading in that it already loads the deck in favor of *natura*, implying that a real woman is what Pygmalion wanted all along. On the contrary, Pygmalion's response to "real" women is itself strongly aestheticized from the beginning. What Pygmalion turns away from are not real women but, as the order of the narrative hints, already stone representations of women, and his aversion is explicable as much on artistic as moral grounds: he is offended by *vitia*, a term that connotes not only the vices of women but the flaws of works of art. Indeed, the passion he feels is not for the ideal girl that the statue represents but for the simulated body, the statue

---

as read not only by the men to whom it is ostensibly addressed but by women as well, the whole nature of the seduction described becomes much more complex, with the women appearing less as the duped victims they ought to be than as connoisseurs appraising, as the poet-teacher does, the performance of his pupils.

As Solodow 1988.216 (with 254, n. 31) and Stroh 1968.580, n. 43, observe, the sentiment also resembles a precept used in rhetorical education, that the orator's artifice should never appear (Quint. 1.11.3, 4.2.127). But it is one thing to meet such a statement in rhetorical handbooks yet quite another in works addressed to the very audience toward whom the speaker's *ars* is to be directed.

[36] Cf. Elsner 1991b.161, who notes a complementary problem with taking the phrase as a simple statement of the triumph of art over nature: that art can triumph over nature only by ceasing to be seen as art. "... its very nature as art must be abandoned for it to be recognized as real."

[37] So also Schönbeck 1999.301–2.

[38] Contra Barkan 1986.76 for whom *interea* is "ingenuous," though I agree with his own emphasis on Pygmalion's delight in the artificial per se.

as statue.[39] And the text is rather uncertain, in this earlier phase, about whether he would even want the statue to come to life. What he secretly wishes to ask of Venus is for the statue to be his wife, and the text makes clear that is not at all the same thing: he dares not say *sit coniunx ... eburnea virgo* (10.275), and so he uses the representational capacity of art to hide his real desire and outwardly prays for a wife "like the ivory statue," *similis ... eburnae* (10.276). When he embraces the image, he does not so much want it to come to life as fear its coming to life: "He was afraid lest a bruise appear on the pressed limbs," *metuit pressos ne veniat livor in artus* (10.258). The phrase brilliantly shows the overlap of the tendencies toward reification and aestheticization. For the term *livor*, translated as bruise and suggesting that the statue has assumed the physical susceptibility of real flesh, last appeared as a term describing the personified Envy acting as critic of Arachne's tapestry (6.129–30); a bruise would indeed be a flaw such a critic might well attack (*veniat in*), and the pun between *artus* and *ars* heightens this way of reading. Nor when he dresses the statue, offers it gifts, and even lays it on a couch, does this unequivocally imply personification, because all of these things were done to actual statues in the course of religious worship.[40]

The first scholar to treat the Pygmalion episode primarily as an exploration of the dilemmas of realism was Jaś Elsner. Elsner reacted against the traditional interpretation of Pygmalion as above all a paradigm of the miraculous artist by showing how much more attention is devoted to his role as viewer of the statue he has created. Thus, Pygmalion's experience can tell us at least as much about the audience's response as about the ambitions of Ovid or Orpheus, who is the immediate narrator of the story. Pygmalion's desire for the statue to come to life is an exaggerated description of a potential reaction of all observers of mimetic arts and, for readers of Ovid's narrative, meshes with the desire for the narrative itself to achieve closure—if not with their own infatuation with the ivory maiden.[41] The miraculous fulfillment of Pygmalion's prayer, however, the metamorphosis of the statue into a real woman, changes everything in

[39] Significantly, the statue is described as a representation of a woman only after Pygmalion's prayer to the goddess, where it is described as the *simulacrum suae puellae* (10.280). This is precisely what it is *not* in the first portion of the narrative, where its *forma* differentiates it from real women: it has the form with which no woman could have been born. This is a particularly interesting shift in light of Lively's (1999.212–13) suggestion that the transformation in the statue parallels a similar change in Pygmalion from artist to lover simply by virtue of acting like one.

[40] Schönbeck 1999.307–8 sees them as reflections of Near Eastern rituals that "subliminally" prepare for the goddess's epiphany.

[41] Fränkel 1945.44 provides a notorious example of a reader who comes to share Pygmalion's fantasy (Elsner 1991b.164, Sharrock 1991a.48, n. 62).

Elsner's view. The superhuman nature of this resolution, precisely because it crosses the bounds of realism, brings the reader up short, exposing the desire for the image to become real as pure fantasy. This is also the point where the reader's perspective parts company from that of Pygmalion, who becomes himself a figure of fantasy, left behind in the enjoyment of a fairy tale "happily ever after." Such a reading accords very well with Galinsky's view of Ovid as an ironist, continually exposing the fundamental unbelievability of his stories and shattering the audience's absorption in them. *Ars* may have disappeared for Pygmalion, but for the reader the trap has been sprung, and he is out of danger.

Elsner's examination of the episode in terms of theories of aesthetic response is fundamental to my own reading, but I suggest that Pygmalion and the reader-spectator are at once more distinguishable at the beginning of the episode than Elsner implies and closer together at its conclusion. This makes viewing in the episode a rather more open-ended model for literary reception. It is not quite, as we have seen, that Pygmalion's treatment of the beloved implies a fantasy of art coming to life; it can also imply the much stranger one of its not doing so. The "you" who would believe the statue had come to life until being apprised of the deceptions of art, in such a reading, would not be the artist, who both knows all about art and wants no such thing—who adores his statue because of its difference from the real. In his discussion of the actual metamorphosis, Elsner claims that "in the moment of miracle, Ovid turns the viewer-reader (until then a participant of Pygmalion's desire) into a voyeur—the excluded observer of an imagined world that can never be anything but fantasy." Yet, given that this is a third-person narration and thus the audience is always to some degree externalized, Ovid seems to have worked specifically to make the perspective of Pygmalion available to the reader even at the moment when the statue becomes real. Indeed, her metamorphosis is never explicitly described as a fact by the narrator, who goes out of his way not to say that Venus turned the statue into a real girl. Rather the reader can share Pygmalion's growing awareness that this change has actually taken place. The poet begins his description of her with the word *visa*, "seemed," and the person to whom she seemed to grow warm was Pygmalion. Nor does Pygmalion respond as the inhabitant of a world where these things happen every day. His reaction to the miracle is astonishment and disbelief, just what we would expect of an encounter with the supernatural. Here too Pygmalion can be seen as a surrogate for even a skeptical viewer-reader, suddenly confronted with such an event.[42]

---

[42] The simile comparing the statue as it gradually softens to the wax of Mount Hymettus, warmed by the sun, perhaps suggests how the process involves a change in the viewer's

Of course, the reader's awareness of the criteria of plausibility does not cease to operate either—one can always read this story in the way that Elsner suggests—but the moment of metamorphosis, rather than closing down options and simplifying the reader's position, intensifies the tension between alternative impulses. Both ends of the episode focus on the same contrasts in ways of viewing, between recognizing the artificiality of art and accepting its illusions.

If our acceptance of the miracle is predicated on beholding it through the eyes of Pygmalion, this points to another area of overlap between how one responds to the crafted statue and to Ovid's own text. To make this point, I begin with a simple demonstration of a locus where construing the syntax of the poem raises questions about the extent to which one has accepted the illusions of art. The ecphrasis of the statue begins at line 250 by describing it as the image of a "true" maiden, "which you would believe, if modesty/respect did not stand in the way, to wish to be moved," *quam vivere credas / et, si non obstet reverentia, velle moveri.* As Ovid/ Orpheus slips "you" into the role of the viewer of the statue, the text itself exposes and appropriates the paradoxes of such viewing. "Which" (*quam*) is ambiguous; it can refer to the true maiden, or merely to the "appearance" of a true maiden (*facies*). So too the rest of the sentence can remain a connoisseur's appraisal of the image, or an evaluation of what that image represents. Equally double-edged is the qualifying conditional. Who experiences reverence? The viewer, who knows that the statue cannot really come to life, and so does not allow himself really to believe that it has? Or the maiden, who is kept by her modesty from desiring motion, a word that can have a strongly sexual connotation? The question of the statue's motion has thus become a problem of perspective: what was once an objective description of the properties of miraculous statues has moved very much into the eye of the beholder.

A complementary transformation takes place in the treatment of the statue's sight. As the sentence we have just looked at makes clear, what is involved in the viewer's establishment of the statue as real is possession of its own subjective attitudes. If you are speculating about the modesty of the maiden represented, you have already crossed the line. So too in the description of the miracle itself, the moment when the statue comes

---

perceptions as much as in the material reality of the image. The primary point of the simile is to describe the statue's ability to take on new shapes in response to the pressure of the artist-lover's hands. But the image of soft wax also figures in philosophical descriptions of how the mind comes to accept and retain sense perceptions (see esp. Plato *Tht.* 191c–d). The mind is like a block of wax and images are impressed on it. The expression *ipsoque fit utilis usu* (10.286) also suggests the procedures by which the mind comes to decide which impressions are true, by comparing them with previous experiences.

to life, described as I have suggested in terms of the perceptions of the viewer, focuses on the transition from being seen to seeing. At 281, the statue seems to grow warm (*visa est*); at 294, when the change is complete, she sees (*vidit*: the expression describing her raising her "light" [i.e., eyes, *lumen*] to the "lights" [*lumina*] similarly accentuated the transition from active to passive).[43]

The emphasis on the statue's ability to see as the culmination of the miracle helps make her metamorphosis the axis on which the entire narrative structure of the episode turns. Here we must remember the implications of watching this change through the eyes of a figure, Pygmalion, whose experience is described not by the main narrator of the poem but by Orpheus, whose song makes up the bulk of the tenth book. Each of these intervening interpreters contributes a discernible color to the way the story is told.[44] Not only can Pygmalion function as a surrogate viewer, whose possible desire for the transformation is available to the audience, but his own particular reactions to women, his hatred of what he perceives as the vice of the Propoetides, also inform the narrative's emphasis on the statue maiden's purity. This in turn recalls the didactic program of Orpheus's song: "Let us sing of boys beloved of the gods and of how girls, baffled by illicit desires, have earned punishment through pleasure" (10.152–54). Orpheus's rejection of women as erotic objects derives in turn from his tragic loss of Eurydice, and it is not hard to see in the tale of the artist whose prayers are answered and whose gaze brings life rather than condemning the beloved to death the happy resolution that was denied his quest for Eurydice. The strong motives of each of these "focalizers" may help encourage the reader's distance from, and skepticism toward, the miracle. And in fact Pygmalion's perspective, far from providing greater immediacy to the account of the transformation, has increasingly become a focus of critical attention.[45] But if the coming to life of fictional creations depends on a recognition of their own

[43] Still problematic is the question of whether any real subjectivity can emerge from the ivory maiden other than the projection of the viewer/maker's fantasy. In this connection, it is interesting to note Ovid's treatment of the third traditional element in the animation of statues, speech. The ivory maiden remains mute throughout; as Pygmalion's creation, she never gets the chance to speak, but at the very moment of the change, Pygmalion himself suddenly begins to speak, an act "pregnantly" described as "conceiving words" (*concipit I verba*, 290–91—emphasized by enjambment). In addition to highlighting for Ovid's audience the incompleteness of the statue's coming to life, the words may also place Pygmalion in the role of the statue, that is, they remind the reader that he himself is no more than a representation, crafted by Orpheus, who was crafted by Ovid, come to life.

[44] For the importance of these levels of narration in the poem, with special reference to the Pygmalion story, see Wheeler 1999.154–61.

[45] See esp. Sharrock 1991a, 1991b, and Lively 1999.

ability to see, then in acknowledging Pygmalion's own point of view we have accepted the vividness of another artistic creation. For Pygmalion is but a representation produced through the medium of Orpheus's song, and Orpheus in turn by Ovid's. Thus, the miracle of the statue's coming to life, remote as it is from the primary narrative, casts a transforming glow on all the intervening levels of representation. On the other hand, looking back at the saccharine description of the ivory statue's first experience of sight, "she saw her lover at the same moment she saw the sky" (10.294), we may decide that it really is too good to be true—again from Pygmalion's point of view. He has not seen what she has seen or seen that she sees, but has simply projected his own fantasies onto a subject who will never come to life because she can never speak in her own words. So too the tale fits Orpheus's own schema a little too perfectly—perhaps he simply made it up?—and, after all, this is nothing but a collection of unbelievable stories put together by Ovid. The ambiguities imposed by the narrative structure thus come to approximate, and to depend on, the dilemma of the realist image.

The Pygmalion episode, therefore, highlights the disjunction between two modes of viewing realist art, both of which Ovid makes available to his reader while also pointing out how that reader's response to images affects his response to the poem as well. Something more, however, is at stake in the Pygmalion narrative than an exploration of aesthetic response or establishing a program for Ovidian fiction. The story also shows how the question of viewing acquires a religious dimension that relates it very closely to the experience of rituals like sacrifice, as its narrative context suggests.

The Pygmalion story comes after two brief and, at first glance, fairly straightforward accounts of metamorphosis as an instrument of divine vengeance, both situated on Cyprus and involving the same divinity, Venus, who works the miracle for the sculptor. In the first instance, she turns the Cerastae into bullocks to punish them for sacrificing visitors at the altar of Jupiter (10.220–37); in the second, the Propoetides are punished for denying the divinity of Venus. They are first made prostitutes and then, as an extension of the same process, turned to stone as a result of their shamelessness (10.238–42). A reader beginning the Pygmalion story might well believe that, as in the narrative complex at the beginning of book 6, she was going to encounter yet another tale of punishment for questioning the priority of the gods set in the same locale.[46] Indeed, the traditional story of Pygmalion would have fit well in this context, for the

---

[46] Compare, for example, the tales of Arachne, Niobe, the Lycian peasants, and Marsyas, all set in Asia Minor.

only recoverable pre-Ovidian versions of the story describe Pygmalion as another violator of the divine, in this case by having sexual intercourse with a statue of Venus.[47]

Both the context of the episode and, quite possibly, prior knowledge of the story thus prepare the reader to pay particular attention to the interactions between men and gods in the narrative and so to be struck by the piety of Ovid's Pygmalion. This piety, of course, also (too?) ideally suits the rhetorical situation of the internal narrator Orpheus, whose entire song is addressed to a goddess, the muse, and carefully observes the hymnic proprieties by beginning with Jupiter. For Elsner, the religious issue in the story was bound up with the question of whether what the statue represents is a mortal woman or a goddess. By leaving this question aside, and by nailing down the mortal identity of the statue through the device of making the agalmatophilic viewer the very creator of the statue, who ought to know whether it is a goddess or a woman, Elsner suggests that Ovid "concentrates the story around the problem of realism which, while it is transgressive in making the marble or ivory flesh, is precisely *not* a problem of the human transgressing the divine."[48]

And yet much in Ovid's tale suggests that the two kinds of transgression are closely linked and that the response to statues indeed involves the boundaries between human and divine. For a start, the belief that the statue is alive and "wishes to be moved" is prohibited by *reverentia*, an emotion very much at home in defining the ideal relations between men and gods. To believe that the statue has come to life would indeed be an offense against the divine. It would be to locate the ability to make reality in the hands of a mortal as opposed to a divine craftsman. As such, the capacity to see a real maiden in the statue connects closely with the capacity to animate metamorphic images described in the first chapter, as well as the seeing of mortal countenances among the divine victims of the gods on Arachne's tapestry, who of course was punished specifically for failing to acknowledge the priority of the gods. At the same time, though, the text is equally adamant in saving the artist Pygmalion from the kind of transgression of which he was guilty in earlier versions of the myth. The bruise that Pygmalion fears will appear on "pressed" limbs offers a transmutation of the familiar story that the statue's lover had indeed left a mark on the object of his desire in the form of a semen stain preserved on the statue itself.[49] Despite its differences, the evocation of

---

[47] For detailed accounts of these other versions, both preserved in the contexts of Christian polemics against pagan image worship, see Elsner 1991b.157–59 and Rosati 1983.54–61.

[48] Elsner 1991b.158–59.

[49] The fear of the bruise fascinatingly transposes this earlier kind of staining because it requires an opposite sort of realism. The actual mark on the real statue left by the attempt at intercourse requires no assent to artistic illusion. Its origin may be perverse but it is not mi-

this earlier act of violation serves as a reminder that it is not only through accepting illusion that the boundaries between human and divine can be overstepped. For the Pygmalion who assaults the statue of Venus is perhaps guilty not only because of what the statue represents but because the statue itself is a sacred object. He is not necessarily to be imagined as someone who Ixion-like tried to rape a goddess; he is, rather, like the Cerastae, a defiler of religious rites. In terms of Ovid's statue, which has no sacred aspect, this other side of Pygmalion's transgression suggests a diametrically opposed way in which modes of viewing can violate the boundaries between gods and men, not because the viewer brings the images to life but because he does not, because the man-made artifact has taken over the role that ought to belong to the real—hence Pygmalion's castigation of *natura* (picked up again in the verb *nasci*, used in line 10.248 to differentiate his product from a "natural" one).

In this light what is particularly remarkable about Ovid's version of the story is its scrupulous avoidance of both kinds of impiety. The artist does not create a statue that comes to life; only Venus can do that. Nor has he accepted a substitute, so to speak, by actually consummating his passion for the artifact. Pygmalion's love for the statue as a narrative of courtship comes pretty far before the intervention of Venus. After the preliminaries of gifts and favors, he lays it on his bed and calls it the partner of his couch, but actual *coniugium* comes only after the goddess, and not the artist, has brought the statue to life. Desire then finds fulfillment only in a divinely wrought reality, and the narrative explicitly makes this point. Yet, as we have seen, in doing so it has risked its own authority among its readers. In fact, the role of Venus has proved among the most controversial aspects of the story and has prompted a variety of contrasting readings among recent scholars. For Barkan, for example, Venus's intervention is "merely a grace note" that, far from distracting from the miraculous capacity of human art to create living images, serves perhaps to exalt and dignify it: it is easily read through as a mere trope. Elsner by contrast, regards the intervention as crucial but not so much because it adds theological implications to the act of viewing as because it narrativizes the problems of the reception of artistic illusion, bringing the viewer's fantasy to life.[50] And these modern responses, while they perhaps do not formulate the issues involved in the same terms, no doubt mirror the hermeneutic challenge and surprise that this moment in particular would

---

raculous; in fact, the presence of the stain on the statue becomes a reminder that the statue is nothing other than a statue and, as such, cautions the viewer against mistaking it for a real woman/goddess. On the other hand, despite its easy translation into aesthetic terms, the mark Pygmalion fears leaving is one that could never be left on real ivory but requires seeing the statue as what it represents.

[50] Barkan 1986.76; Elsner 1991b.164–66.

have raised for ancient readers, at the point where the narrative leaves both the plane of events "that might have happened" and the authority of an established literary tradition, if indeed it was an Ovidian addition to a familiar story.

How then, to summarize, does the story comment on the act of viewing visual representations, and how does it link that experience to the reception of the text? It articulates for its reader a set of alternatives for responding to the ivory maiden, assent to illusion and an awareness of artifice, making both available to its reader without unequivocally either exulting in the powers of illusion (as, for example, Fränkel and Barkan) or providing a cold shower in the form of a reminder of the limits of art (Elsner). And it further charges the choice between these resulting views of art with religious and social implications by constructing a story in which the reader is made aware that the rewards of piety could so easily have been replaced by punishment for transgression. For human mimetic craft walks a tightrope here, with either of the views of art in play in the narrative liable to be read as an overstepping of limits. And the juxtaposition of the miracle within the story with the narrative's own embrace of the miraculous both makes the reader's view of visual arts dependent on a decision to adopt or reject the author's fiction and correspondingly makes the statue a paradigm for Ovid's own *ars*, which similarly invites either consciousness of mortal craft or participation in the represented fiction. What keeps art "pious" in the story is above all the good intentions of the audience, including the craftsmen themselves—for one result of making the artist predominantly a viewer in this story is to make other viewers artists, whose own response to the narrative becomes essential both for "bringing the statue to life" and for doing so without violating the limits of the human through hubris or idolatry. And this effect, which so closely resembles the involvement of the viewer in artistic reception described in chapter 2, receives further impetus here in the multiple authorship of the story, nested as it is within the song of Orpheus. Orpheus tells the story in a way that forcibly demonstrates the cooperation of divine power and human craft in suiting the narrative for his own audience. Ovid may be seen as doing so as well, especially when the text is read back through the lens of the exile poetry. But in both cases Ovid makes it easy for the reader to view the whole story through very different eyes, disbelieving the miracle of the transformation as mere fiction, penetrating the Orphic emphasis on the god's responsiveness to the desires of the artist,[51] and seeing through the Ovidian emphasis on the propriety

---

[51] One interesting way in which the narrator seems to foreclose assent to Orpheus's tale, or at least encourage the reader to think about discrepancies between levels of narration, is by placing the beginning of Orpheus's song just after the story of Cyparissus (10.106–42),

of creation. This chain of human "readers" must in each case work out the implications of Pygmalion's, Orpheus's, and Ovid's creations according to each reader's own preferences and preconceptions, and such an extended tradition of debate, bridging the difference between myth and present and image and text, becomes an important way in which art retains its religious dimension.

This religious dimension has many aspects. Philip Hardie, building on the text's suggestion that Venus herself is also directly present in the narrative in the form of a statue, links the debate over the reality of artistic images explored through the Pygmalion episode to their capacity to summon up the real presences of divinities. "The boundary between the suspension of disbelief operative in viewing works of art or reading texts and the worshipper's faith in the presence of his god is a fluid one."[52] In consequence, the reader by accepting the fiction of the statue's coming to life not only approximates the experience, and indeed the potential doubt, of the worshiper before the image, but opens the door to accepting the gods who animate Ovid's fictional world no longer as literary creations, the inherently unbelievable gods of myth, but as the present divinities of cult. At the opposite extreme from this we might imagine an interpretation that would treat religion very much as a figure for purely political issues. The gods, with their homes scattered along heaven's Palatine, as Ovid puts it, become stand-ins for the powers that be, in particular of course Augustus, the most powerful reader of the poem and one with a great deal at stake in protecting the borders between reality and representation from Ovidian incursions. But while there is no legislating on the degree of religiosity involved in Ovid's deployment of Venus here, by the very fact of raising these possibilities for the reader the poem facilitates a reflection on modes of divine interaction that itself qualifies the poem as a religious instrument.

And the figuration of these theological aspects of the text through questions about the power of images comes into greater relief through a second pattern of more explicitly religious imagery within which the

---

which has the same basic plot line as Pygmalion and echoes much of its language while also transparently calling to mind the experience of Orpheus with Eurydice. Cyparissus, himself a beloved of Apollo, has made a fetish of a sacred deer and adores it in ways that predict the various adornments and services Pygmalion offers the statue. When he accidentally kills the deer while hunting, he is consumed in grief. But rather than either allowing Cyparissus to die as he wishes, or bringing the lost beloved to life, the god in this story offers a "reality check" by reminding Cyparissus "to lament moderately and in proportion to the material" (*ut leviter pro materiaque doleret*, 10.133). This advice, especially given the artistic connotations of "*materia*," might well have been offered by Venus to Pygmalion, and if the literary connotations of *materia* are heard, would be a useful caution for Orpheus as well.

[52] Hardie 2002c.191, whose reading draws in turn on the fundamental article of Gordon 1979 on the religious properties of images in Greek and Roman culture.

Pygmalion story is embedded; this is none other than sacrifice. The experience of sacrifice, like Hardie's statue of Venus, provides another point of contact between a mythical tale and the immediate realities of religious practice. And sacrifice in turn initiates questions of identification and difference between the participant and the victim that replicate the problems of viewing raised by the artistic image.

The connection of Orpheus's entire song with etiologies of ritual practice has been observed by several scholars.[53] The death of Hyacinthus, the first major tale told by Orpheus, ends with the Spartan festival of the Hyacinthia, and the death of Adonis at his song's end includes Venus's proclamation of the Adonia as an annual commemoration of her grief. In the case of Pygmalion's tale, the explicit etiological motive involves only the name of the island (Paphos, from Pygmalion's son, 10.297) rather than any cult activity. However, the narrative is preceded by stories that do focus on ritual practice (sacrifice and, perhaps, temple prostitution), and its own narrative climax occurs at precisely the kind of festival whose origin closes the entire "hymn" of Orpheus, an annual festival of Venus.

If the subtle anachronism at work in associating the context for Pygmalion's story with a ritual that will only come into being to honor Pygmalion's great-grandson inspires a reader to think about the time relation between present and past implicit in etiology, she will find further encouragement in another pattern of imagery running throughout the episode. The ivory from which Pygmalion makes his statue has recently been taken as emblematic of the unbelievability of the miraculous narrative as a whole.[54] But what has not received equal attention in these discussions is that this ivory statue is quite literally surrounded by the antithetical material, horn.[55] In the story of the Cerastae, whose very name means "horned," the horns of sacrificial victims prompt the goddess's decision to turn the Cerastae themselves into bullocks. So at the very halfway point of Pygmalion's story the account of the festival of Venus similarly describes how "the heifers, with spreading horns covered in gold, fell at the altar, their snowy necks struck" (10.271–72). Horns also provide closure as the statue-maiden's parturition is dated at the time when "the moon's horns shall nine times have been brought to a full circle" (10.296). The last reference to time may at first seem to have nothing to do with ritual, except that the cyclicality of festivals receives particular attention in both the Hyacinthus and the Adonis stories (*annua*,

---

[53] First noted by Barchiesi 1999.117–19 and developed by Hardie 2002c.92–94.

[54] Esp. Elsner 1991b, also Liveley 1999.

[55] Though the linguistic presence of horn, sacrifice, and their various anagrams is observed and analyzed by Ahl 1985.244–45.

10.219; *annua,* 10.727, both emphatic, at the beginning of the line), and the birth of Paphos occupies the same structural position in Pygmalion's story that etiology does in the other two.

If ivory then signifies what is impossibly fictional and remote from everyday experience about the story (an association enhanced perhaps by the traditional use of ivory for representations of the divine), then horn brings it down to earth—or emphasizes that remoteness—by recalling the realities of both the human life cycle and the ritual practices that still today provide the means of contact between mortals and gods. This use of horn to signify what remains the same emerges especially from the Cerastae story, where it is the horns left behind from previous sacrifices that mark the new form of Venus's victims (note *relinqui,*10.236) and simultaneously define their textual presence in Ovid's poem (*Cerastae*).

But sacrificial ritual works to correlate present and past as more than just an allusion. I argued in the preceding chapter that Ovid's interest in the visual "transformations" between participant and victim in the sacrificial process provides an important area of overlap between the responses evoked by his own visualized descriptions of metamorphosis and the ritual experience of the contemporary reader. In the case of the Pygmalion story the density of sacrificial imagery connects this pattern of seeing likeness and difference with the viewer's response to artistic representations. The account of the Adonia already combines the kind of annual reenactment offered by ritual with the mimetic capacities of art, the language of which is strikingly present in the passage: the Adonia will provide a *mortis imago* as the celebrants enact *plangoris ... simulamina nostrae* (10.726–27). And though sacrifice per se was not a feature of the Adonia, the phrase *mortis imago* offers a link between the mimetic aspects of ritual and this practice, especially if we remember the account of the visual traces of sacrificial victims in the story of the Cerastae. Indeed, within the Pygmalion story itself comes a striking incentive to see the image as victim and the victim as image. While others have drawn attention to the similarities between the ivory statue and the ritual image of "Golden Venus" (10.277), she also shares a strong visual connection with the heifers, both in her costly adornment and, above all, in her snowy whiteness (*niveum* 10.247 ~ *nivea* 10.272).

To understand the significance of such a connection, let us look in more detail at the way in which the visual aspects of sacrifice are described in the Cerastae episode:

> *At si forte roges fecundam Amathunta metallis,*
> *an genuisse velit Propoetidas, abnuat aeque*
> *atque illos, gemino quondam quibus aspera cornu*
> *frons erat, unde etiam nomen traxere Cerastae.*

ante fores horum stabat Iovis Hospitis ara
†inlugubris sceleris† quam siquis sanguine tinctam
advena vidisset, mactatos crederet illic
lactantes vitulos Amathusiacasque bidentes:
hospes erat caesus! sacris offensa nefandis
ipsa suas urbes Ophiusiacaque arva parabat
deserere alma Venus. "sed quid loca grata, quid urbes
peccavere meae? quod" dixit "crimen in illis?
exilio poenam potius gens inpia pendat
vel nece vel siquid medium est mortisque fugaeque.
idque quid esse potest, nisi versae poena figurae?"
dum dubitat, quo mutet eos, ad cornua vultum
flexit et admonita est haec illis posse relinqui
grandiaque in torvos transformat membra iuvencos.

(10.220–37)

And if by chance you ask the city of Amathus, rich in metals, whether she would wish to have born the Propoetides, she would say no, as she would for those whose forehead was once made harsh with a twin horn, whence they take their name, Cerastae. Before their house stood the altar of Jupiter, protector of strangers; ... if some stranger should see this altar stained with blood, he would believe that milk-fed calves or young Amathusian sheep were sacrificed there. But it was a guest who had been slaughtered! Offended by these unspeakable rites, nourishing Venus prepared to desert her own cities and the Ophiusian fields. "But how have these pleasant places, how have my cities sinned?" she said. "What is their crime? Rather let the impious race pay the penalty with exile, or with death, or if there is anything between exile and death. And what can that be but the punishment of transformation?" And while she wondered what she should change them into, she bent her countenance toward the horns and was reminded that these horns could be left to those, and she changed their large limbs into muscled cattle.

The substance of this story unites issues from two earlier episodes that have been important in my argument. The motif of divine punishment for the murder of a stranger recalls Jupiter's punishment of Lycaon, the first animal metamorphosis in the poem as a whole.[56] As in that episode, from

[56] Orpheus interestingly replicates the first two metamorphosis narratives from the beginning of Ovid's own *carmen*, with the Hyacinthus story replacing Apollo and Daphne, but he does so in reverse order. This reversal, especially given the strongly marked connections between the Daphne story and the genre of elegy, confirms a pattern observed by Janan 1988.114 whereby Orpheus as the epic poet become love poet reverses Ovid's own progression from elegy to epic.

the god's perspective there is an important likeness between the victim and the new form in the transformation from large limbs to the rolls of muscle on the cattle.[57] But rather than being converted into an unmistakable predator, as Lycaon was, the Cerastae take on the image of the ideal victim of their actions, the cattle that are the proper sacrificial offerings. This substitution for the victim makes their punishment symbolically echo the experience of their own actual victims. For the "stranger" who would think that the blood on the altars was the blood of animal victims is surely about to find himself taking their place—he is another *hospes* ready for slaughter.[58] This moment when the viewer recognizes himself as the object of his gaze recalls the situation of Cadmus and the snake[59] and the whole dynamic of the victor seeing/becoming the victim that permeates the Theban narrative of book 3. In the discussion of that passage, I suggested that in a sacrificial context an overidentification with the victim inverted the socializing effect of sacrifice by making the viewer too readily perceive himself not as the agent of collective violence but as its object and hence an outsider. And here we find precisely such a point of view used in an explicitly sacrificial scene where the victim is indeed a stranger to the community. The goddess's transformation of the Cerastae then both replicates their own crime and undoes its damage. We now join in the condemnation of the killers, seeing them as "other" and as legitimate victims, while being assured that their new form indeed signifies who they are at last rather than appearing as an alien imposition. As a result, the possibility of proper sacrifice is restored.

A similar question involving the evaluation of an external form as being like what it represents also appears in the following story, that of the Propoetides, but here the narrative does not inspire such universal assent as it does in the case of the Cerastae. The Propoetides' original crime is denial of Venus' divinity. If the Cerastae destroy the distinction between participant and victim, their crime is the mirror opposite, for they assimilate the goddess and her human worshipers. The goddess punishes their disobedience by driving them to prostitution. The effect of this is perhaps dubious in light of the original offense; for, while the transformation demonstrates the power of the love goddess over mortals, it has the curious result of making them resemble promiscuous divinities still more closely.[60] The maidens' final transformation into statues is made to

[57] The recognizability of the victim plays an important role in the next narrative as well, where the petrifaction of the shameless Propoetides is noted as a "slight change" (*parvo discrimine*, 10.242).

[58] So Anderson 1972.494.

[59] Note that Ovid here uniquely deploys the epithet Ophiusian (transparently derived from the Greek ophis, "serpent") to describe Cyprus (10.229).

[60] So a desire to emulate the practices of the gods formed part of Byblis's specious self-exhortation toward sexual transgression (9.497–501).

appear as the natural extension of their shameless nature. Like Lycaon's transformation into a wolf, its aptness is conveyed through the impression that it happens spontaneously, without any intervention on the part of the god, as well as by the explicit narratorial (Orphic) comment that between statues and prostitutes there is but a slight difference. Hence too, perhaps, the rather strange claim that they prostituted their bodies (*corpora*) together with their appearance (*forma*), a phrase that suggestively deploys the programmatic terms of metamorphosis. In the first line of the poem, forms were said to be changed into new bodies. If that formulation allowed for a discrepancy between sign and substance, the insistence on the unity of *corpora* and *forma* here would seem to be a way of insisting that the Propoetides really are what they seem.

And yet, as Genevieve Liveley has recently underlined, the Propoetides were not by their nature shameless, though for the internal viewer Pygmalion this is indeed the root of their crime.[61] Again their exemplary, socially cohesive value comes from seeing the statues as the Propoetides; a quite different evaluation of the goddess's power comes from an awareness that the very behavior their transformation commemorates was imposed as a punishment by the goddess, and that their original crime can be construed as an exaltation of human capacities, which the mortal reader/viewer shares. Seeing a real presence within the stone maiden then involves a recognition of sameness that now has the potential to controvert rather than stabilize hierarchies.[62]

Questions of how to read metamorphoses, energized by the motifs of sacrifice, color the problems of viewing from the beginning of the Pygmalion story. For what we previously saw as Pygmalion's aestheticizing reading of images, reducing them to nothing other than representational artifacts, here corresponds to a reading of the Propoetides' metamorphosis that privileges final appearances, the shameless prostitutes of legend (cf. *feruntur*), over any internal living presence. Conversely, the reader's potential view of the statue as "real" offers a mirror image of the experience of the imaginary stranger viewing the sacrificial scene left by the crimes of the Cerastae. If such a person would have seen the altar of Jupiter, he would have believed that what he saw was not human; seeing the statue, "you" would believe that it was. There, a sense of security from danger was based on a mistaken assumption of difference; here, desire is kindled by a mistaken impression of sameness. As the stranger's loss of security goes together with a realization of the limits of human crime, a transgression that the Lycaon parallel suggests implies a defiance of the divinity, so here the ultimate frustration of that desire, to accept for the

[61] Liveley 1999.200–204.

[62] For an extended analysis of how another petrified scorner of the gods provokes similar questions, see the discussion of Niobe in the next chapter.

moment Elsner's reading of the ending, comes with a reminder of the limitations of human power.

My argument, then, is not for a rigidly schematic correspondence between the status of metamorphosed transgressor, sacrificial victim, and work of art. A case could be made that viewing the statue as a sacrificial heifer reveals the violent occlusion of an individual point of view required for an objectivizing perspective on the image as focus of desire.[63] A case could also be made the other way, that for the reader who has already seen the statue as human, the recognition of the heifers as like her provides an equivalent alienation from the sense of divine preeminence actualized by sacrifice. (Men can create life, too.) Different readers will be willing to entertain either or both points of view. But what I would insist on is that the Pygmalion episode reveals a degree of overlap between aesthetic and religious judgments that opens out the significance of Ovid's own act of poetic mimesis by at once pointing out and sharing in the capacity of representational art to approximate the effect of cult experience as a locus for defining boundaries between the human and divine.

II. Domestic Goddesses

The overlap between text and image we observed in the Europa episode points us toward another aspect of the nature of viewing in Augustan Rome that provides an important context for "reading" works of art within the poem. As we have seen, Ovid is by no means unique in asking his readers to visualize his narrative—that was standard rhetorical practice—but when we look beyond the literary context to consider the contemporary visual environment, this reaching out of the text toward the visual answers a tendency on the part of the visual arts to invite narrativization.[64] This can happen, for instance, when paintings depict scenes familiar from well-known literary narratives,[65] or, more distinc-

---

[63] This would be an extension of the general readings offered by Liveley and Sharrock (note 45 in this chapter), taking the statue as a figure replicating and exposing the male construction of women.

[64] For another example of the centrality of an effort to narrativize to the reception of mythological painting, see the suggestive discussion of Leach 1988.309–60.

[65] Let me be clear that this claim is not to grant the literary priority over the visual, as though images of Achilles were mere illustrations of the *Iliad*, but simply to observe that the images themselves were often of scenes that invited the reader to supply a before and after because of his knowledge of texts. Cf. Kuttner 2003.113: "What to feel and how to identify oneself in the iconic Roman artscape: paradigmatic literatures offered the scripts and the designed landscapes offered stages on which to impersonate these canonic stories." Kuttner goes on to make an observation that has largely inspired the subject of this section: "Story itself may generate lands and waters, as throughout Ovid's *Fasti* and *Metamorphoses*, which inhabited water gardens of the first century B.C." (Kuttner 2003.114).

tively, when the arrangement of pictures within the domestic environment gives a plot and order to a sequence of images that both guide and complicate their interpretation. As an example of the first kind of narrativization, one of the best, if most extreme, examples is to be found in the dining grotto of Augustus's villa at Sperlonga, as analyzed by Ann Kuttner.[66] This extraordinary complex offered a comprehensive sensory experience in which illusion and reality overlapped: a *triclinium* set in a natural grotto, reached by boat, and overlooking pools where, in place of the mosaic fish that formed a standard decorative motif for such spaces, swam real fish. The inside of the cave offered statue groups of the sack of Troy and scenes from Odysseus's adventures including the encounters with Scylla and Polyphemus, episodes that took place not only by the seashore but at a seashore very near the one viewed by the banqueters.[67] As Kuttner's reading suggests, here was an environment where the miraculous transformation of natural categories overlaps with the impression of entering a famous mythical narrative.

In addition to conjuring up a temporal narrative onto which static representations open an enticing window, the act of viewing itself can take on a narrative structure as the spectator tracks a path between the images that make up larger visual complexes, even when the scenes depicted do not invoke stages of a single story.[68] Bettina Bergmann's analysis of the House of the Tragic Poet at Pompeii provides the most telling explication of this element of Roman spectatorship.[69] The unusually rich and well-preserved painted decoration of this home contained more than twenty "panels" depicting mythological scenes, many relating to the *Iliad*. In the atrium on the left and right of the entranceway stood a now lost nude Venus (possibly with a male lover or possibly posing before Paris) and Jupiter and Juno embracing on Mount Ida. The other four panels in this room showed Achilles sending Briseis to Agamemnon; next to that, Helen fleeing with Paris; and, on the opposite wall, a picture of Neptune and Amphitrite beside a picture of the wrath of Achilles.[70] While four images, possibly five depending on how Venus was presented, do indeed form part of a Trojan cycle, the grouping of the pictures and visual echoes among the figures make possible more intricate patterns of comparison and contrast, which in turn bring to light thematic issues ranging

---

[66] Kuttner 2003.

[67] Ridgway 2001 provides a convenient survey of the material remains of the grotto and the current state of research. One might also note the recent argument of Andreae 1994 that Ovid's text itself provided the model for the iconography.

[68] See also Kuttner 2003.103–4 and Leach 2004.142–52.

[69] Bergmann 1994.

[70] Only the pictures from the right half of the room are extant, the Helen only partially; the others are reconstructed from nineteenth-century paintings of fragmentary remains. For a discussion of the reconstruction process, see Bergmann 1994.237.

from philosophical exhortations toward the restraint of desire (Juno, not Venus) to Roman foundation myths (Venus, not Juno), to women's rites of passage, here coded and contrasted by status: the divine Juno whose marriage with Jupiter is celebrated in the panel near the entranceway bears a close visual resemblance to the slave Briseis being forcibly separated from her captor Achilles. The central point about all these different combinations is that the story made up about the pictures depends on the visual choices the viewer makes and, more important, on his or her route among the various scenes.

What makes Bergmann's reading of viewing so suggestive for the transformation between poetic narrative and visual image that I am arguing Ovid's poem stimulates is that her model of reception is itself drawn from rhetorical techniques of memory and thus both depends upon and resembles patterns of literary ordering. This is the now much-studied mnemonic device by which, as a part of their rhetorical education, upper-class Greeks and Romans were taught to arrange elements in a narrative or argument by planting imaginary visual prompts in a specific architectural space, frequently a house (*Rhet. ad Herr.* 3.16–24). The sequence that the student adopts as he travels through this space with his mind's feet, so to speak, structures the order of presentation. As Bergmann argues, the way in which houses are conceptualized in this process and the visual experience of viewing real houses reciprocally affect one another: the efficacy of the memory technique depends after all on making imaginary spectatorship as real an experience as possible. The practice of using spatial order to establish connections between visual images dramatically complicates and enriches the disparate elements of a decorative program. The house becomes textual, and it also makes texts real by translating poetic images to the space where the drama of social interactions was played out. One of Bergmann's most telling visual echoes is the placement, in the peristyle, of a sacrifice of Iphigeneia directly opposite the *lararium* where the *paterfamilias* would preside over household sacrifices, creating an inevitable mythical parallel and, one hopes, contrast for the instantiation of status within the actual household.

In the concluding section of this chapter, I want to reverse Bergmann's perspective by going from visual ensembles back to literary ones, by demonstrating how one book of Ovid, the second, ending with the image of Europa previously analyzed, can be read as constructing its own house of memory. Lest from the start this seem a circular project of reapplying primarily literary patterns back from works of art to texts, let me point out that what I am attempting to show is not influence but precisely an overlap that encourages mental transference from one medium of reception to the other. I intend to demonstrate how Ovid uses visual details to generate connections and sequences among the very disparate episodes of this book much in the way that the decoration of the House of the Tragic Poet does. Obviously literary texts are capable of creating such thematic patterns without asking to be compared to visual artifacts—and Ovid's capacity for sophisticated cross-referencing between his stories requires no further demonstration—nor, as we have seen, does visual vividness imply the conjuring up of full-blown works of art. But if one model of responding to mythical ensembles like the *Metamorphoses* was in fact "memory houses" such as Bergmann describes, then it is valuable as an exercise in imagining ancient reception to try to read the text back through that paradigm. And indeed two of the characters who help frame the book, Callisto and Europa, were present as images in the House of the Tragic Poet itself. The payoff for making such a leap in this case will be to reveal a "domestication" of Ovid's text that not only brings a very remote set of stories "home" to a Roman audience by conjuring up their display in a familiar, everyday setting but also highlights their significance for issues that played out within the very spaces of the *domus*.

So incoherent has the complex of narratives that conclude book 2 seemed that one critic notoriously suggested that Ovid deliberately composed this passage to show how "unsatisfying" mythical stories become when the metamorphosis element is emphasized above everything else.[71] One aim of the following discussion is to turn this judgment on its head by showing how semiotically rich the passage becomes when we start precisely from the visual impressions the stories leave behind. The first half of this book is taken up by Phaethon's attempt to drive his father's chariot and the consequences of his death for his relatives: his sisters, who become poplar trees; his maternal relative Cygnus, who becomes a swan, and his father, who is so enraged at his son's death that he must be cajoled and bullied into resuming his regular function (2.400). As if to contrast with the longest continuous narrative of a single event in the poem, the rest of the book, via the hundred-line account of the rape of Callisto and Diana's transformation of her into a bear (2.401–530), becomes a mosaic of shorter stories whose narrative connections have baffled and fascinated readers.[72] As Juno flies back into the air, having successfully persuaded Ocean not to allow her rival Callisto, now transformed yet again into the constellation of the great bear, ever to find rest in the sea, the peacocks that draw her chariot prompt the transition to the

---

[71] Galinsky 1975.95 cited by Keith 1992.2.

[72] The narratological complexity of book 2 has received a book-length treatment by Keith, who provides a good review of earlier scholarship (1992.1–7). See also Tissol 1997.153–66, the comments of Wheeler 2000.37–40, 48–54, 70–85, and the many perceptive connections observed by Anderson 1996 and now Barchiesi 2005. Gildenhard and Zissos 2004 have recently suggested a thematic explanation of the organization of the book as a part of systematic devaluation of Athens in the poem.

tale of the raven, another bird whose appearance has changed (2.534). The raven was transformed from white to black for revealing the infidelity of Coronis to her lover, the sun god. On his way to complete this fateful mission, the raven is warned about the dangers of bearing bad news to the gods by another black bird, the crow (2.554). The crow had originally been a princess who was transformed into a (white) bird by Minerva to allow her to escape attempted rape by Neptune (2.569–88), but became black when she told her patroness that the daughters of Cecrops in Athens had unwrapped the basket in which she had placed the chthonic child Erichthonius (2.552–68).

The narrative now shifts to the consequences of the raven's revelation, as Apollo slays Coronis but snatches away his unborn son Aesculapius to be raised by the Centaur Chiron (2.596–632). Chiron's daughter Ocyroe, a prophetess, in the midst of telling the future of the child, is prevented from continuing by her own transformation into a horse (2.633–75). Chiron calls on the god of prophecy to undo the metamorphosis, but Apollo is not listening, being immersed in a pastoral erotic adventure in the western Peloponnese, in the course of which his cattle are stolen by Mercury. Mercury bribes the only witness, a shepherd named Battus, to conceal the theft, and when Battus tries to double his profits by revealing the culprit to the same god in disguise, he is turned into a statue (2.676–707). In flying away from exacting this punishment, Mercury sees and falls in love with Herse, one of the daughters of Cecrops. He enters her home at night to visit her but is stopped along the way by the same sister, Aglauros, who in the past had received a bribe from Minerva not to reveal the secret of Erichthonius. Aglauros now asks for a monetary reward from Mercury for helping his affair with her sister, and Minerva, disgusted by her mercenary spirit, sends Invidia (Envy) to infect her. As the girl becomes jealous of her sister, she refuses to allow Mercury into Herse's room and, in punishment, is also changed to a statue (2.708-832). At this point, Mercury is called away to assist his father in the deception of Europa, which ends the book.

The boundaries of the book already invite comparison between literary and visual arts in a way that enshrines the opposition between the mobile aspect of metamorphosis as process and its unchanging artifacts. For not only does this section of the poem conclude with the tableau of Europa; it begins with another formal ecphrasis, the description of the cosmos depicted on the doors of the sun's palace. This framing of the book with visual images thus highlights the tension between the stasis of images and the animation of narrative motion—as Phaethon enters the picture of order on the doors only to destroy it. But more than that, it equates the process of beginning the book with entering a *domus*, and so invites the kind of pictorial reading that I am proposing. The conceptualization of the text as domestic space is reinforced elsewhere by its contents. If the book begins with what is necessarily the most public and exposed part of the home, the doors, its penultimate episode takes place in its least accessible regions (*pars secreta domus*), the bedchambers of Cecrops's virgin daughters, whose arrangement is carefully delineated in the course of Mercury's visit (2.737ff.).

These contrasting views of the home already give shape to the inequalities involved in exchanges between gods and men: mortals approaching the home of a god of necessity do so by the front door, while gods materialize just outside mortals' bedchambers.[73] An appropriate mean between the supplicating mortal and the god driven by desire comes in another of the book's domestic visitations. When Minerva summons Invidia, a scene whose very nature confuses vengeance and desire as it blurs the power relations between the goddess of victory and the lowly personification of the emotions of the defeated, the episode's ambiguities are sketched by the description of Invidia's *domus* and the goddess's strange position in relation to it. The home itself is the mirror opposite of the Sun's palace, low as opposed to high and defined by the absence of light and fire (2.760–4). And by contrast to Mercury's easy penetration of the home of Cecrops, Minerva is forbidden to enter here. The motif of the *domus* then already helps point out that Minerva has come to a place where she has no tie of kinship (as Phaethon had to the sun), and in Roman social terms it was for the client to call upon the noble, not for the noble to come knocking on the client's humble dwelling.[74] So too the contrast with Mercury, who magisterially penetrates the recesses of the house for sexual gratification, highlights the uncertainty of Minerva's relation to Invidia. She is the superior but has come for a purpose that could be construed as giving an order or requesting a favor.[75] The balance between desire and repugnance, the arrogance of a master and the inferiority of a supplicant, emerges in the sideways glance with which Minerva both sees and does not see Invidia framed through the doorway of the home she will not enter.

If the settings of key episodes focalize events of the book from the perspective of one entering the *domus*, others, like the revelation of Callisto,

---

[73] On the visitor's position within and penetration of the Roman *domus* as markers of status and intimacy, see Wallace-Hadrill 1996.38–61.

[74] Though cf. Evander's praise of Hercules for not disdaining humble thresholds in *Aeneid* 8.362–65.

[75] Her situation is further elucidated by comparison with another divine visitation in the book, Juno's trip to the home of Ocean. There the "descent" implied in her visit becomes part of the rhetorical effect, as she wins sympathy for her plight by equating the catasterization of her rival Callisto with her own degradation and impotence. Note that there it is clearly Ocean who is granted the upper hand in the exchange, as the sea gods are said to approve her request with the Olympian verb *adnuerant* (2.531). Minerva by contrast is all business and takes care to frame her request as a terse command accompanied by the minimum necessary detail.

closely recall the kind of scenes one might well have seen depicted there. More important, though, Ovid achieves unity between geographically and thematically disparate scenes through a rhetoric of visual motifs very like those that gave coherence to the decorative programs of domestic interiors. To take Callisto again as an example, the instant where Jupiter sees her visually resembles Mercury's bird's-eye view of the Panathenaic procession that sparks his desire for Herse. Both take place in the kind of landscape beloved of Roman painting—the city view of Athens contrasting with the pastoral setting of Callisto. The visual connection is intensified by the description of Jupiter inspecting the walls of the sky (2.401) and the curved pattern of their journeys. (Again, the depiction of the winged viewer was a common visual motif in mythological painting.) Such a perspective opens out further thematic links both to another high flier, the tragically unwinged son of a god, Phaethon, whose disregard of his father's request contrasts with Mercury's unshakeable *fides* towards Jupiter (cf. 2.837), and to the bird's-eye views of real birds, like the crow and the raven, whose viewing becomes a voyeurism that leads to punishment rather than gratification.

So too, Callisto's meticulously described transformation connects her tale with other metamorphoses in the book: Coroneus's daughter is turned to a crow to avoid rape in another picturesque but contrasting landscape, the seaside, and Ocyroe, who has not suffered sexual violation, undergoes a sudden metamorphosis accompanied by loss of voice that is again meticulously cataloged. And the very animals created by metamorphosis conjure up another set of visual motifs: Ocyroe's metamorphosis into a horse, a form that differentiates her from her biform father, recalls the horses that lead to Phaethon's own demotion from his father as a result of assuming the prerogative of a god. More emphatically, birds, white like the swan and the crow before transformation or black like the raven, provide a similar motif. The Callisto episode thus ends with one of the most breathtakingly far-fetched narrative connections in the whole poem, one effected entirely through references to "painted" birds (*pictis*, 2.533). Juno's chariot is born by peacocks, as recently painted from the slaughter of Argus as the raven has been transformed to black. Perhaps, in looking down at Juno's chariot, a decorative detail outside the main narrative, we experience the equivalent of glancing from the self-contained "panel" of the Callisto story to the ornamental framework that surrounds it, only to discover a further set of visual connectives that unite both into an artistic whole. Indeed, in the House of the Tragic Poet the picture of Juno appeared above a painted peacock in the dado. The effect of the frame leaking into the narrative is further enhanced when birds appear not just as features in the story but in such "decorative" authorial additions as similes. Thus, Mercury, whose visual appearance itself contributes to and contrasts with the bird motif, is compared to a kite swooping down to snatch the organs burned for the gods at sacrifice (2.716–19).

Alternating with birds are cattle, which both recall the same ur-rape narrative of Io as the peacock and adopt the same color scheme, a gleaming white, as the crow, raven, and swan. Again we find the visual image provocatively echoed in a simile as well as in the main narrative. Thus, Apollo lamenting his murder of Coronis is likened to a heifer watching her calf (milky white) slain by the *victimarius* at a sacrifice (2.623–25)—another unifying link connecting Apollo's vengeance-cum-erotic-misadventure with Mercury's. The book's visual program also includes a pair of statues, Battus and Aglauros, of whom the latter, as off-white, contrasts with the birds and the cattle, while the former, being a shepherd, recalls a popular subject for actual statuary as well as complementing the pastoral element in the book's décor. Finally, we may note that—as in the House of the Tragic Poet portrayals of two contrasting goddesses engaged in sexual activity helped articulate the atrium's decorative program—book 2 offers two contrasting pairs of contrasting pairs: two quintessential virgin goddesses, the pastoral Artemis and the urban Minerva, take on the roles of avengers at the beginning and end of the book, while two celestial sons of Jupiter, who are anything but virginal, become its most prominent seducers.

As the preceding catalog shows, the reader prepared to "see" the scenes depicted in this book, as a Roman reader might well have been prepared to do by his previous experience of many of these stories depicted in visual media, finds prompts for comparison and contrast that place disparate tales in relation to one another and create the kind of open-ended thematic matrix that Bergmann's analysis has revealed in the House of the Tragic Poet. Another impetus toward the same way of reading, and another point of similarity to actual Roman mythological paintings, comes through the blurring of the boundaries of representation. Beyond the Third Style tendency to avoid "bounded" (*finitis*) images was another to present scenes in such a way as to incorporate the viewer into the image. Thus, Bergmann again, analyzing the representation of Actaeon viewing the bathing Diana in Pompeii's Casa del Frutteto, describes how the goddess's unwilling exposure to the viewer's eyes, together with the exaggerated size of the figure in relation to others, bring the painting's audience into the scene. This is but one example of how in the whole visual complex "the division between illusionistic prospects and … the actual lived space of the viewer dissolves."[76]

But if viewing as Europa means coming to see the bull as a real bull, for Ovid's audience of readers the additional step is required of mak-

[76] Bergmann 1999.88–89.

ing them see what the narrative suggests are real mythological figures as contemporary representations. Thus, in contrast to reading as Europa, we must also remember the perspective introduced in chapter 1, where we see the entire cosmos depicted in the first book, and its divine population, as sculptural figures.[77] Not only then will the reader be enticed into the illusionistic world of the poem, but she must be prepared to figure that world as part of her own "lived reality" through the capacity to see its scenes as art. A kind of retrospective viewing of book 2 as a painted image comes in the tapestry scene of book 6. For the resumption of the Europa tale at the start of Arachne's tapestry is but one of a number of visual links to this book, which, like the tapestries, focuses both on divine punishments for mortal overreaching and on the rapes inflicted by the gods. Minerva's tapestry after all connects with one of the most viewed prospects throughout the second book, the cityscape of Athens. And the viewer who comes forth to help Minerva find fault with Arachne's work is the same figure who came to look askance at the great accomplishment of Minerva in book 2, Envy. In that scene she sees the Acropolis "verdant with talents and riches and blessed peace" (*arcem / ingeniis opibusque et festa pace virentem*, 2.794–95): Minerva's tapestry literalizes those very attributes in "bordering the farthest edges of her tapestry with the peaceable [and presumably green] olive" (6.101).[78]

The overlap between Athens as image and Athens as city becomes yet more complex if we imagine that the "talents and riches" Invidia beholds on the Acropolis included the works of art that made it a famous tourist destination for first-century visitors and if we notice that Minerva's actions as seamstress bordering her tapestry recall the circular paths of Mercury the divine observer who circles around the city in book 2. Nor is it just in hindsight that the ambiguous representational status of the Athenian landscape stands revealed: the figures of Herse and her sisters are seen from above, twice, by different viewers in the book. First the crow sees them opening the basket in which Minerva has placed the chthonic child Erichthonius; then Mercury spies them as Basket Bearers

---

[77] Wheeler 1995.

[78] Correspondingly, we can see in the multiplicity of animal figures, and the very kind of visual patterning I have described here, an analogue to the compositional devices of Arachne's own crowded tapestry, which is remarkable precisely for its lack of a single unified narrative.

A final but very important demonstration of the link between the tapestry scene in book 6 and the narratives of book 2 results from Gildenhard and Zissos's (2004) demonstration of the importance of the crow's speech in Callimachus's *Hecale* as source and intertext for the Athenian references in the second book. This internal narrative of Athenian history also featured a scene that Ovid omits but Minerva the weaver magisterially restores—the contest in which she triumphs over Neptune as the presiding deity of Athens (*Hecale* fr. 70.10–11 Hollis).

in the Panathenaic procession.[79] Because the adult Erichthonius was often said to be the founder of the Panathenaia, this creates a notable anachronism.[80] But the question of whether to view the daughters of Cecrops as figures in a mythic past or as participants in the historical festival of the Panathenaia becomes even more pressing thanks to Anderson's suggestions that the women bearing burdens on their heads create a visual analogue to the Caryatids in the Porch of the Maidens, works not only accessible to any contemporary (or modern) tourist to Athens but also later reproduced in Roman domestic art as a way of denoting Athens.[81]

But what would be the implications of reading book 2 as a succession of interlocked visual images? One consequence involves the linearity of the reading process. One of the essential points Bergmann makes about the act of viewing in the homes she describes is the freedom it opens up for the viewer in tracking his own path among the representations on display. (Such freedom was not of course absolute but was itself dependent on the viewer's status and relation to the owner: not every visitor would have access to every room, and many would have had to take on board the interpretations of the host, as we find the guests at Trimalchio's dinner forced to swallow the freedman's mythology together with his food.) So in the case of the narrative complex in the second book, such an interpretative model allows the reader to make an almost infinite number of narrative connections between stories whose moral relationship to one another is conspicuously underdetermined by a narrative voice. And while of course texts too generate memories and refer back to themselves, the visual model of reception encourages a process of revision and completion that gives density to these internal references. Thus, if we think again of Europa as a picture, her own backward glance, which within the frame of the narrative is to the celebrations of young women surrounding her on the shore, may inspire the reader to look back along the wall of an imaginary gallery to a similar visual tableau, the moment when Callisto meets Diana accompanied by her nymphs or perhaps, again contrasting the urban and the natural, the daughters of Cecrops at the Panathenaia. And indeed such a visual link would be hardly surprising in a Roman domestic environment, where both Callisto and Europa were common

---

[79] If the Panathenaic procession conjures up for a reader the woven peplos that was presented to the statue of the goddess on that occasion, there is yet another embedding of the artistic images described later in the narrative in the literary "fabric" of the book.

[80] Commented on by Bömer 1969.407. For an analysis of temporal "deviations" in book 2 from a narratological perspective, see Gildenhard and Zissos 1999b.

[81] Anderson 1996.319. The most famous example of domestic Caryatids was at Hadrian's palace at Tivoli, but see Kuttner 1995.83 for the suggestion that they were already present in Brutus's villa and for a description of their role in the painted decoration of the Villa Farnesina.

subjects. In this case, the reader might notice that the Callisto story, as Ovid tells it, highlights precisely the scene that is elided in the story of Europa, the simultaneous moment of rape and recognition. This backward glance then would predict a much more distressing future for Europa than one would encounter simply by reading forward with a view toward the blessings of motherhood and the distinction of her offspring.

In addition to the interpretative freedom it allows—and the immediate presence it evokes for textual figures materializing as wall decoration—this mode of reading also highlights the thematic importance of viewing within the interlocked episodes, where vision itself connects both subjects and objects in ways that model the text's effect on its readers. Such an "infectious" power of viewing emerges most clearly in the figure of Invidia, whose name itself obviously links the emotion of envy with a complicated visual process.[82] Invidia feeds on visual images. The late gloss that connects the etymology of the term with gazing excessively on the well-being of others (Isid. 1.610) seems fully at work in Ovid's description of her "wasting away from beholding men's happy achievements" (2.780–81). But excessive seeing, which is also a literal viewing askance, as Envy looks with sideways glance at the departing Minerva (2.787), makes the envious herself a visual sign of such grotesqueness that she becomes unseeable, so that Minerva herself must turn away her eyes. (And Ovid's meticulous account of her has its own contagious properties, inviting the reader not to lament the success of superiors but to take visual pleasure in the miseries of the loathsome.) A consequence of the attention Ovid draws to the connection between Invidia and vision is to connect the emotion with a point of view both within the narrative and by implication for the reader/viewer. Not only does Invidia herself see Athens wrong, and here the idea of Athens as a visual or painted tableau seen by a succession of viewers becomes particularly helpful, but she makes those she infects see things differently. Thus, she works on Aglauros by setting a distorted portrait of her sister Herse before her eyes (2.803–5): the phrase *cuncta magna fecit* easily connects misreading as the result of powerful emotion with an optical distortion on the part of the "painter," Envy. The result is to have Aglauros herself turned to an artistic image, a statue that preserves the stain of her contagion. Perhaps by "magnifying" that stain, the reader is invited to enjoy a kind of superiority to Aglauros herself and is thus also viewing invidiously.

Envy's mode of seeing contrasts directly with other alternatives presented in the narrative, most obviously with that of the other viewer of the same Athenian panorama, Mercury. Indeed, Envy's attributes, the spiny staff and

[82] First discussed by Davis 1969.28–38 as summarized in Keith 1992.125–27. On the practical dynamics of *invidia*, see now Kaster 2005.84–103.

cloak of invisibility, make her appear to the viewer as a visual, or invisible, doppelgänger for the caduceus-bearing god. But if Envy sees everything with a profound sense of alienation, making over all happiness to others, Mercury sees with a proprietary greed (*avidus*) that easily translates desire to fulfillment. Thus, his view of Athens conjures up not satisfactions denied, but satisfactions ripe for the taking. And while hostile viewing distorts Envy and Aglauros by making them ugly, Mercury's complacent gaze translates into a self-satisfied improvement of his own appearance, the slight makeover that gives him greater confidence in his own attractiveness before presenting himself to Herse (2.731–36). And the very pattern of viewing the god adopts has its own significance, both within the text and in the space of the imaginary *domus*. Like Jupiter on the tour of inspection that leads to the fatal glimpse of Callisto, Mercury upon sighting Herse wheels around in a circle. The viewing of Mercury can itself be viewed as like both the divine proprietor's circuit of Jupiter and the obsessive fixation with a single image engendered by Envy, who is again literally a mirror of the god.

The shift between obsessive attention to a single image and the lordly survey of the whole reminds us again of the physical realities of viewing in the space of the *domus*, where itinerary plays a crucial role in determining meaning. But the gods' circular path and their bird's-eye view of the world have a further thematic significance. Bergmann elsewhere points out that Roman paintings commonly depict winged observers and that the bird's-eye view they would have enjoyed was itself a distinctive innovation of Roman painting. One possible way of accounting for the popularity of such a way of looking at landscape is that it reproduces so closely the ideal perspective of mastery and control from which the owner views his property, a point of view that shades easily into a designation of social and intellectual superiority. Thus, in his celebration of Pollius's villa at Sorrento, the poet Statius concludes by linking the lofty situation of the villa to the enlightened outlook of the owner: "We are a worthless crowd, ready to enslave ourselves to goods doomed to fail (lit. fall, *caducis*) and to hope always, but you from the lofty citadel of your mind look down on us wandering about and laugh at human misfortunes."[83] And so within Ovid's poem the god's secure elevation and circular motion powerfully contrast with the terrestrial perspectives of mortals. Nowhere is this clearer than in the contrast between Jupiter's circuit and Phaethon,

---

[83]   *nos, vilis turba, caducis*
deservire bonis semperque optare parati,
spargimur in casus: celsa tu mentis ab arce
despicis errantes humanaque gaudia rides.
      (Statius Silv. 2.2.129–32)

See the interpretation of Bergmann 1999.64–65.

who falls from just such a point of view, and for whom the possibilities of return and recurrence suggested by the sun's circular path (visually reechoed in Mercury's curved route) are tragically "foreshortened" by his one-way trip downward.

Finally to this catalog of points of view we may add both the interested gaze of the informer and, more directly connected to our artistic reconstruction of the narrative, the point of view of the victim of the god's sexual aggression, most tellingly adopted by Callisto. Here we begin by viewing her from the god's point of view as an attractive figure in a landscape,[84] a perspective encouraged both by the generic pastoral scene of which she is a part and by the language of Ovid's own description: her neck rests on a painted quiver (*pictam pharetram*, 2.421; a painting of a quiver perhaps?). But this external view of her becomes more complicated through subsequent scene changes, which Ovid introduces visually with the exhortation to behold (*ecce*, 2.441, as Diana appears; 2.496, for Arcas the hunter). In both of these cases, the figure who is introduced will in turn see Callisto, with devastating consequences, reproducing the pattern first introduced by the spectator Jupiter.[85] But the effect of inviting the reader to "behold" each new entrance is to disturb the connoisseur's view of her as image by placing the reader within the world of the painting. Thus, when we "behold" Diana, we are at once seeing a common image from Roman wall painting and seeing suddenly as a figure within that wall painting, and as one whose own sense of the truth of images has been traumatically shattered. Callisto, of course, rejects the easy recognition of Diana; Jupiter might again be concealed under her appearance. Again the viewing style of a character within the narrative communicates itself to the reader through the medium of an imagined act of visual reception.

The mental transformation of literary images to visual ones, then, not only gives a new immediacy to the way in which the text enmeshes the reader in a network of overlapping points of view; it also, as the preceding discussion suggests, clarifies the political consequences of such literary focalizations by projecting them into an imagined environment, the public rooms of a distinguished Roman *domus*, that offered a crucial stage for enacting hierarchical social relations.[86] Before going on to analyze how the thematic issues central to book 2 in particular graft themselves onto the environment of a Roman house, it is worth pointing out very briefly

---

[84] For a political reading of the erotic gaze directed to Roman panel paintings, see Fredrick 1995.

[85] And if any of these viewers had had the leisure or inclination to survey the whole Callisto cycle, their interpretation would perhaps have been different, as is explicitly stated of another potential viewer Juno (*adspiceres utinam … mitior esses*, 2.435).

[86] Wallace-Hadrill 1996, esp. 3–16.

how alive the *Metamorphoses* as a whole can be to the political function of Roman homes, and how often Ovid evokes the space of the contemporary house as the imaginary setting for some of his most fantastical episodes. In his first presentation of the Olympians in the poem, Ovid begins by depicting the gods as the denizens of very Roman homes (1.170–75): "This is the way the gods journey to the house of great Jupiter, a kingly dwelling. On the left and right, the atria of the noble gods, with doors open, receive the throngs; plebeian gods dwell in another neighborhood. But here the powerful and famous divinities have set their *penates*. This is the place that, if boldness were given to words, I would not hesitate to call heaven's Palatine." The passage is much discussed as an example of the kind of humorous anachronism that seems to keep Ovid's gods to a contemporary human scale. But what is equally important is the way that it not only builds on Roman ideas of the home as the extension of the public persona of its owner but also prepares the reader to correlate the spaces of the poem's mythical events with contemporary domestic settings, to see the gods at home. One may note that it is not only Invidia among the poem's allegorical figurations who is characterized through a vividly described domestic establishment; Sleep and Fama can boast of the "crowded house" so necessary to the prestige of a Roman noble.[87] Though the two "houses" are in many way mirror opposites—Fama's full of rumors, while Sleep's is without a sound—the atria of both conjure up the complex semantic and social environment of a Roman reception area. This emerges from the way in which space reveals preeminence: Fama is contrasted to the cheap crowd (*leve vulgus*, 12.53) who surround her, whereas Sleep, a Roman *pater*, reposes on a raised couch surrounded not by chattering masses but by the visual deceptions of dreams. The swirl of insubstantial representations are not at all out of place in a Roman atrium and not only as an analogue for the complex of insubstantial visual images that made up its decoration; this was indeed a real setting for rumor, for envy, and for deceptive dreams. Nor should we forget that Phaethon, the viewer whose entry into the Palace of the Sun plays an important role in establishing the domestic context for "seeing" in book 2, is no mere art lover. Rather his entry into this particular *domus* is motivated by the desire to appeal to its owner in order to raise his own status and make himself at home in the sumptuous palace.

Reading book 2 within the framework of a domestic setting then, beyond explicating its formal structure and modes of signification, offers a new way of relating its concerns to the social tensions of the world in which it was constructed, many of which would have played out under the eyes of the very same characters represented in Ovid's narrative. The

---

[87] Wallace-Hadrill 1996.91–117.

most recent and detailed analysis of the political significance of book 2 comes from Alison Keith's book-length study. Keith notes that a constraint on powers of expression connects the two plots most common among its varied episodes: tales of rape leading to metamorphosis, like Callisto's, highlight the loss of the power of self-expression, whereas stories of divine punishment for tale-bearing reveal even more clearly the constraint imposed from above on inappropriate uses of language.[88] She contextualizes this by invoking the imperial restrictions on freedom of expression imposed by Augustus in the last years of his principate.

But the domestic setting of these scenes allows us to realize that the restrictions on free speech form but one aspect of a much more pervasive conflict between high and low within the second book. And its relevance to contemporary social relations extends beyond the exchange between upper-class poets and princes. Book 2 presents a set of dramatis personae strongly contrasted in their status and capacities; nowhere perhaps are the consequences of being an Olympian god presented with greater starkness as the gamut of possible interactions between gods and mortals is explored, from sexual exploitation, to punishment, to efforts at establishing kinship and connection. The sexual appropriation of inferiors, to take one example, is a mark of power relations in the domestic as well as the mythological sphere, as sexual availability decreased in proportion to status. And the master's violation of slaves could doubtless introduce many further disruptions in the relationships within a Roman household. So Callisto's rape entails not only her victimization by Jupiter but also her punishment by Jupiter's wife and alienation from her own particular patron. As Anderson well observes, these are common elements in Roman comic plots, where, as in Plautus's *Casina* whose predatory protagonist is pleased to call himself Jupiter,[89] the figures involved in these domestic dramas sometimes have their own mythological pretensions.

But for every tale of violation and punishment, there is another—like that of the crow or the raven, or of Battus or Aglauros—in which an inferior attempts to exploit his or her proximity to the great for financial advantage or social promotion or to punish a rival. Like sexual politics, these complex interactions between patron and client, well known to us from satirical and moralizing literature, took place in the atria and *cubicula* of homes like that of the House of the Tragic Poet.[90]

[88] Keith 1992.135.

[89] Anderson 1996.282.

[90] Indeed, the image of the Olympian gods as *patroni* is also a crucial element of their first presentation in the poem, where Jupiter's concern for protecting the interests of the rustic demigods "not yet worthy of Olympus" has been seen by Habinek 2002.51 as evoking the traditional duties of a patron toward clients.

At the start of this chapter, I declared that its aims were to show how comparisons to existing artifacts could give greater immediacy and presence to the poet's text and how that text in turn could suggest to its readers new ways of construing their visual environment. So far in this reading of the second book I have concentrated on the first of these goals, showing how the model of viewing employed for the visual reception of mythological scenes both reveals new thematic connections in Ovid's arrangement of similar stories and constructs an environment that gives these themes an immediate relevance for their readers. Now, as the final element in this section, I discuss how Ovid's thematization of viewing in this book can echo and enhance the way in which actual painted images like those in the House of the Tragic Poet were read. There must have been great variety in the extent and manner by which different viewers related the scenes depicted in these elaborate interiors to the self-staging that took place in the rooms they adorned. Insistence on the pictures as a programmatic index of the status and story of the master, like the decoration of Trimalchio's house in Petronius, which introduces the freedman as hero directly into a mythological setting, stands at one pole, appropriating the world of myth for the exposition of here-and-now reality. At the other, we may imagine a mode of reception that stressed the difference between real and painted space, where, as we have seen, the very foreignness of the paintings in terms of both subject matter and artistry expanded the horizons of the viewer and reflected the taste and wealth of the master without necessarily requiring that he be literally put in the picture. It is interesting to imagine the case of a rape of Callisto depicted in the *cubicula* where a master takes sexual advantage of his slave. To what extent and for whom would the analogies in the situations be visible and what would the effects of this viewing be?

Ovid's text highlights above all the varieties of points of view available on such scenes and accentuates precisely how the viewing of images itself reflected differences in position—figuratively as well as literally—among its audience. At the same time, it potentially destabilizes the relationships each viewer enjoyed to the image. So in the case of Callisto, the sight of her as picturesque image ripe for possession, echoing both the way in which a proprietorial viewer might regard the painting itself as property and perhaps the way a "comic" master might enjoy projecting himself into the story by claiming Jovian powers over the nymphs of his household, comes under challenge as entering the picture means seeing as Callisto herself, in a gallery of mythological scenes that are anything but irrelevant or insignificant. Another way in which the book reveals patterns of viewing that might have an impact in the reception of actual images is the treatment of Invidia above all as a visual disorder. The similarities and differences between the point of view of the master and of the "worthless throng," to use Statius's phrase, must have been an important element in the way that domestic works of art were experienced. For guests and clients, the exercise of looking as a master on the scenes portrayed must have accentuated the realization, as for Aglauros and Invidia, that these scenes speak about and contribute to the contentment of another. In fact, we may see the punishments of Battus[91] and Aglauros as a particularly appropriate response to such viewing, and thus as forming an analogue to the way that Callisto transforms the perspective of the master. If we imagine seeing invidiously as a continual focus on the viewer's alienation from what she sees together with, in the real context of viewing works of art, a reduction of it to its material value, just as the invidious client sees not the bonds that connect him to his patron but the differences between them that reduce "friendship" to a simple economic transaction, then it is appropriate that those who act in response to it should themselves be transformed into material objects that can only be seen and not see.

[91] Battus is never explicitly accused of *invidia*, but it is important that both his status and his own visual activity are carefully delineated. He is not an independent shepherd—in fact, his work consists of watching (*servabat*) the pastures and excellent mares (*nobilium equarum*) of his master Neleus (2.689–90). He is not simply a sharpy out to take advantage of any situation that offers itself, but a social inferior for whom Mercury's request that he deny that he sees the rich herds the god himself is stealing connects closely with the nature of his own perpetual viewing. He spends his days watching someone else's possessions, as Aglauros watches the mental image of another's happiness.

CHAPTER 7

"Songs the Greater Image"

The kinds of interpretative decisions Bergmann and Elsner imagine being made by the viewer confronted with the painted images in the homes of the Roman elite emerge with even greater impact from the grand urban monuments of the emperor, those which were experienced by the viewer not as guest, client, slave, or master in the household but as citizen or subject of empire. In chapter 2, I argued that the political functions of complexes like the temple of Apollo on the Palatine resided not so much in the intricacies of the claims they communicated about the role of their ultimate producer, Augustus, but in the scope they gave for each viewer to work out his own position in the empire and relation to the center. But there sculptural programs were treated as similar to any other form of representation; no special attention was paid to the effect of their particular medium. Analysis of the Pygmalion story, though, has revealed the special efficacy of artistic images, sculpture in particular because of its coexistence in the same spatial realm as the viewer, as a means for constructing these relationships. The tension in ways of seeing raised by such an image between the artistic appraisal of the connoisseur and a recognition of what is depicted as real parallels the alternatives of distance and identification conjured up by sacrifice and so sparks a chain of contrasting implications for the viewer's relation to the artistic subject and its maker, and, in the right contexts, the gods.

This "imperial" aspect of representation is essential in Augustan culture and implies much more than the conqueror's ability to refigure the image of the conquered explored by modern colonialist studies. We have already seen how much of the experience of art inevitably connoted conquest simply because this was the ideal mechanism for making such works present at Rome in the first place. But an important corollary to this is the role that representations played in manifesting Roman power to viewers throughout the empire. For among the many other artistic experiments for portraying Rome's world domination, the Roman was trained to see the provinces of the empire as sculptural representations of women. Mourning allegorical figures, taking the visual form of a female captive either to be punished for rebellion or raised up through the generosity of the conqueror, featured on coins and items of houseware, as well as triumphal monuments, like the Forum of Augustus. Conversely, members of a community like Aphrodisias learned to imagine Roman power through a similar set of allegorical statues, including the representation of the female goddess Roma herself.[1]

This chapter analyzes how Ovid places his text in dialogue with the public display of images by the emperor. I first focus on the story of Niobe, a figure who played a significant role in the iconography of both major temples of the particularly Augustan god Apollo, as a freestanding group in the temple of Apollo in Circo and on one of the doors to the sanctuary of the temple of Apollo on the Palatine.[2] My analysis of Ovid's Niobe narrative attempts to fuse two lines of reading: one that deals only with art images as sources for Ovidian narrative without considering Ovid's own elaborate treatments of the problems of representation and another that uses artistic images primarily as ways to understand the poetics of Ovid's text without thinking of their effect as "real" real presences on the reception of Ovid's work. The second figure I discuss, Perseus, requires different treatment, for Perseus as a character, by contrast to Niobe, plays a relatively small role in Augustan iconography. Fragments of a terracotta plaque found near the temple of Apollo show the fight with Medusa, and the Gorgon's head appeared on the upper part of the shield of the cult statue of Mars Ultor.[3] Rather than drawing on a clear and prominent visual appropriation of Perseus, much of the effect of Ovid's politicization of the tale—in the broadest sense—comes from its unexpectedness. Perseus, the most fantastical and distant of the Greek heroes, and one with no genealogical or etiological connections to Rome or Italy, seems by his nature the one least likely to be seen as an Augustan prototype, and to view him from this vantage point forms another of the uncanny mirrorings of the familiar in the strange that punctuate that episode. Thus, the Perseus narrative offers a less specifically focused but ultimately even

[1] For details, see the groundbreaking discussion in Kuttner 1995.69–123.

[2] Evidence for the Niobids in the temple of Apollo in Circo comes from Pliny *HN* 36.28. On the decoration of the temple of Apollo in Circo, see esp. La Rocca 1985 and 1988. Viscogliosi's (1988.139) hypothesis on the arrangement of art works within the temple suggests that the Niobids would have been treated essentially as museum pieces, while Gros 1976.165 imagines them more closely integrated into the overall program. There is no hard-and-fast evidence that the statues were not in fact first displayed in the mid-republican predecessor of the Sosian temple (so also Schmitzer 1990.244), but whenever they were brought to Rome, Pliny's identification of them shows their connection with the restored structure. On the temple of Apollo on the Palatine, where the Niobids were not only present on the doors (Prop. 2.31.14) but adorning the handles of tripods dedicated by Augustus (for illustration, see Zanker 1988.87), see above all Zanker 1983 and now Galinsky 1996.213–24.

[3] Schmitzer 1990.239, who sees this as evidence of Perseus as a transparently Augustan figure.

more suggestive analysis of the power of images, as well as a final opportunity to study how Ovid's fiction measures itself against the real.

I. Reconciling Niobe

The Niobe narrative is ideal for exploring the relationship between texts and images not only because of her artistic "reality" in the city of Rome but also because the nature of her metamorphosis into a rock seems to create a link between narrative and monument. Although Ovid's stone Niobe is wafted to the slopes of Mount Sipylus, not the Palatine, the stone form taken on by the heroine provides an important visual "intertext" for her familiar image that invites comparison to actual monuments as well as opening up speculation on the priority of visual and literary representations. Reading Niobe, as it turns out, will require Ovid's audience to consider anew the nature of metamorphosis itself and how the alternatives it poses reemerge as challenges in responding to representational works of art: for the question of whether to see Niobe as what she has become takes on a special urgency, and one inevitably connected to the reader's actual experience of works of art, because what Niobe becomes through metamorphosis can seem indistinguishable from a statue. At the same time, the extratextual role of stone Niobes in defining and justifying Roman *imperium* makes it possible to relate these issues directly to the investigation of the political positioning of Ovid's text begun in chapter 2.

To set the stage for this investigation, it is important to notice the "imperializing" context within which Niobe appears in Ovid's narrative. The tales that begin Ovid's sixth book are striking for two contrasting kinds of sameness. First, the fates of Niobe, Arachne, Marsyas, and the Lycian farmers all strongly point to the same moral about the importance of humans' not infringing on the prerogatives of divinity. Denis Feeney in discussing the punishment of Arachne notes the ancient belief that because they were woven without *ars* but simply by the creative power of *natura*, spider webs were all the same.[4] And this repetitiveness seems to carry over into Ovid's narrative as well; for not only does the text, or at least one of its authorial voices, reproduce the same lesson, but it shows the stories themselves acting to impose conformity on their audiences. By making the transitions between these narratives hinge on the responses of internal speakers and audiences who are, or in Niobe's case should be, reminded by each story of further *exempla*, Ovid dramatizes what one might call the imperializing power of narratives to impose order by

[4] Feeney 1991.193–94, citing Sen., *Ep.* 121.23.

reminding listeners of their place. The metaphorical use of place to signify social position[5] emerges explicitly at the book's beginning: Arachne
challenges Minerva, although distinguished neither for rank (*loco*, 6.7)
nor for ancestry.

Already, though, it is hard to distinguish this vertical aspect of place
from a horizontal one; Arachne is, specifically, from the small town
of Hypaepae, whose "low" name (Greek for "under the mountain")
matches her status and prepares for the contrast with Niobe.[6] As Anderson notes, Ovid gives a virtuoso display of local knowledge with a flurry
of geographic references to sites in Lydia, the particular region of Asia
Minor where Hypaepae was located.[7] This concern with locality is the
second of the remarkable features in the narrative complex in book 6.
All of its major stories have a connection to one of the adjoining regions
of Western Asia Minor: Niobe's tragedy unfolds in Thebes, but she was
born in and returns to Phrygia. Lycia takes a turn in the tale of the peasants turned to frogs for refusing to allow Latona to drink, and Marsyas
returns us to Phrygia, where he, like Niobe, finally becomes a feature of
the landscape.

This geographic contiguity is sometimes treated simply as accidental
to the thematic identity that makes this one of the most clearly unified
segments of Ovid's narrative.[8] But its presence sets up two alternative
horizons for understanding the relationship between narratives, that of
Ovid's audience made aware of the universal significance of the issues
involved, and that of the audiences within the stories, who see these issues filtered through a network of local myth. The contrast in scale receives strong reinforcement in the difference between the imperial world
depicted on the tapestry of Minerva, with its clear center on the world
city of Athens and its "framing" *exempla* set at the margins of the composition, each of which also registers one of the cardinal points of the
compass, and the local specificity of Ovidian narrative. This tension between the universal and the local forms a second reflection of the impact
of empire within the text. As Simon Price has shown, the manipulation
of local myth within a larger Hellenizing frame gave individual cities a
crucial language for negotiating their own position in the larger empires
of both the Hellenistic and Roman periods.[9] Price draws attention to a
fascinating set of theater reliefs in the city of Hierapolis, from precisely
our region in southwest Asia Minor, that illustrate this phenomenon.[10]

---

[5] *OLD* s.v. *locus* §17.
[6] Rosati 2009.249.
[7] Anderson 1972.152.
[8] E.g., Anderson 1972.172 on the transition to the Niobe story.
[9] See Price 2005.
[10] Price 2005.118.

The reliefs portray the deeds of two important "local" gods, Apollo and Artemis, whose birth was located in Ephesus as well as at Delos, and include the presentations of local stories, the punishments of Niobe and of Marsyas. These images use depictions of myth both to relate local cults to those of nearby communities (here, Price suggests, the Apollo of Hierapolis appears as the iconic equal of the prestigious Artemis of Ephesos) and to constitute a kind of cosmic map of the ties that bind the local to the universal. For the next level of the frieze was focused on the figure of the emperor Caracalla, who had at his left a personification of the city of Hierapolis.

Because the sculptures date from two centuries after the *Metamorphoses* there is no question of their exerting any influence on Ovid's text (nor is influence in the other direction probable). However, the process that they illustrate, as Price argues, was an ancient one, and probably there was no period or place where the realignment of local myth with imperial iconography was more pressingly felt than in the Greek cities of Asia during the reign of Augustus. Thus, despite the anachronism, the reliefs provide a valuable perspective on the organization of Ovid's narrative precisely because they remind us that the local point of view his speakers represent was a historical phenomenon as well as a narrative device. And that seeing Apollo and Diana as the avatars of Roman power, the particular divinities of Rome's empire, must be balanced against points of view that would have to make the adjustment from seeing them as local figures.

Obviously the fraction of Ovid's audience who would have first thought of Apollo as, for example, the founder of Hierapolis was a pretty small one. But a much larger contingent of his first readers would have been aware of the existence of such a point of view, whether through travel or, more importantly, through the writings of Hellenistic authors and poets who loved to catalog precisely this kind of local myth. And here the imperializing transformation that Ovid's structure imposes on this material takes on a more recognizable literary aspect. Arachne's father Idmon, comes from Colophon, and Colophon was also the home of Ovid's best-known predecessor as a poet of *Metamorphoses*, Nicander. We know little of Nicander's writing, but it is argued by Forbes-Irving, and would plausibly reflect general Hellenistic tendencies, that his poem was much more concerned with relating metamorphoses to local cult practice throughout the Greek world.[11] We cannot say for sure whether there were specifically Nicandrian antecedents for the stories that Ovid collects at the beginning of book 6. He certainly told the story of the Lycian peasants (Antoninus 35), while adding the detail that, before returning

[11] Forbes-Irving 1990.24–32.

to punish the *coloni*, Leto was led by wolves to the river Xanthos, which is now sacred to Apollo. He also records a variant of the Arachne story, which interestingly replaced the Lydian setting with an Athenian one, and occurred not in his *Metamorphoses* but in his work on snakebites (*Theriaca* 11). This detail is perfectly compatible with his having told a different version in the other poem as well. But if it is not possible or necessary for my argument to establish Nicander as a consistent intertext throughout the narrative complex, it is easy to see him as a representative of a kind of locally based etiology that the epic dimensions and grand moral theme of Ovid's poem supplants. And in fact another distinguishing feature of many of all these stories is their fairly transparent engagement with the imagery of Hellenistic aesthetics, an engagement that allows Ovid's text to be read simultaneously as aligned to the perspectives of these Greek authors and as transcending them.[12] The rewriting of Greek etiology into Roman epic thus becomes part of the process that transforms local stories into reminders not to offend against the gods of imperial cult.

But what I have described as a conflict between imperial and local frames of reference here could also be conceptualized as a tension between the points of view of two localities. For in their sculptural form, two of the figures in Ovid's stories were also conspicuously present in the visual landscape of Ovid's Rome, the twin Niobes we have been discussing, and the statue of Marsyas, which stood next to the Comitium.[13] The divine triad of Latona, Apollo, and Diana, who play such an important role in all these stories, was of course on permanent display in the temple of Palatine Apollo, in the form of actual Greek cult statues transferred to Rome. In other words, by engaging a global vision of myth that places Rome at the center with the potentially disparate points of view imposed by geographic distance, Ovid's work once again replicated issues played out in the physical realities of the city.

Ovid's Niobe in particular raises themes that encourage the reader to connect it with the visual imagery of empire on display in contemporary Rome. In the context of temples erected to Apollo in the twenties BCE, the figure of Niobe was colored by her associations with the defeated Cleopatra and, as Ulrich Schmitzer has described, the particular features that helped characterize that Egyptian queen as other have also been put

[12] The opposition between classical (Minervan) and Hellenistic (Arachnean) aesthetics is widely recognized as a feature of the Arachne story (Leach 1974). For Niobe, see this chapter; for Marsyas, see chapter 2; and for the "muddy waters" created by the Lycian peasants, see Clauss 1989 and Myers 1994.83–90.

[13] On the political significance of this Marsyas, and especially on Marsyas as a numismatic emblem indicating the status of a "free city" within the empire, see Veyne 1961.

to work in Ovid's text.[14] Niobe's striking first appearance in the narrative, as she interrupts the festival of Latona to state her claim to divinity, highlights her foreignness and her associations with the institutions and garb of kingship and makes the perennial Roman connection between such institutions and the transgressive power of a woman. Thus, Niobe appears in Phrygian robes, flashing eyes described as *superbos* (6.169). Like Cleopatra, Ovid's Niobe stresses her divine descent, coupled perhaps with a suggestion of Ptolemaic incest: "Jupiter is my grandfather, and I exalt in having the same god as my father-in-law" (*Iuppiter alter avus; socero quoque glorior illo,* 6.176). Reference to Atlas brings a hint of the other African queen, Dido, and the *immensae opes* (6.181) on display in her home have reminded critics of the *barbarica ope,* of Cleopatra's fleet at Actium as depicted on the shield of Aeneas.[15] So her exaltation of the authority she wields harks back to the common link between *regnum* and the gender-reversing enslavement of subject peoples: she claims that "the Phrygians fear me"—as of course they would a tyrant—and the palace of Cadmus (*regia*) is *sub domina,* under the sway of a mistress (6.177–78).[16] But the most striking and significant link between the two figures, one not developed by Schmitzer, is that Cleopatra too seems to have connected claims to divinity with her role as a mother. The imagery of fertility appeared on the queen's coinage, including one where she is depicted suckling her son, and helped link her especially to the Egyptian mother goddess Isis.[17] Of course, the very names of Cleopatra's children by Mark Antony, Alexander Helios and Cleopatra Selene, call to mind the offspring of Latona.

But if one effect of this pattern is to activate all the terms of Cleopatra's barbarism as a means of giving the defeat of Niobe an ideological charge in the present, Ovid's Niobe seems equally to resist such an obvious characterization as foreign other. To start with geography, as a native of Sipylus in Asia Minor, Niobe is well qualified, in Greek Thebes, to play the domineering Eastern Queen. However, as the description of her gown as Phrygian reminds us, Sipylus is not so far from the homeland of Aeneas, often to be insulted as a Phrygian.[18] Indeed, her account of her own genealogy points to a further link with Rome's founder. She boasts of being the granddaughter of Atlas: *maximus Atlas est avus, aetherium qui*

---

[14] Schmitzer 1990.244–49.

[15] Schmitzer 1990.246, citing *Aen.* 8.685.

[16] The power of female dynasts becomes in Livy's account a defining feature of Rome's *regnum* in its last phase; Feldherr 1997. For Thebes in general as a mirror of Rome, see Hardie 1990.

[17] See Wyke 1992.102–3 for examples.

[18] E.g., at *Aen.* 12.99.

fert cervicibus axem (6.174–75). So too when the eastern stranger Aeneas claims kinship with the Arcadian king Evander, he does so through Electra, the mother of Dardanus, another daughter of Atlas: *Electram maximus Atlas edidit, aetherios umero qui sustinet orbis* (8.136–37). Not only are there links of kinship between the two figures, but the lines clearly resemble one another, with the words *maximus Atlas* and *aetherium(os)* occupying the same metrical positions. But recalling Aeneas's own genealogy reminds us of an even closer tie: Niobe is the daughter of Dione, the Homeric mother of Venus, making her Aeneas's cousin.[19]

When we move from Rome's Trojan progenitor to its contemporary *princeps*, another set of analogies with Niobe emerges. The most striking of these results from Ovid's amplification of Niobe's mythical crime, which is no longer simply comparison to the goddess Latona but the aim of supplanting her rival and claiming godhead for herself.[20] If this ambition of Niobe's exceeds mythical examples of hubris, it connects her to the problems of self-definition faced by Rome's *princeps* at this stage in his career. Indeed, the poem's final lines treat Augustus's divinization as the inevitable conclusion of his curriculum vitae, and in both cases the right to become a god rests at least partly on kinship. Niobe was daughter and daughter-in-law of Jupiter; Augustus, son of the god Julius. And as Niobe's claims to divinity are very much her own construction, Ovid points out the conundrum that Julius Caesar is deified precisely so that Augustus will be able to be the offspring of a god.[21] Niobe's glance at her opulent palace might recall how Augustus's own palace, conspicuously linked to the temple of Apollo, where of course Niobe herself was on display, establishes a special connection between the emperor and the gods. And even the reference to Niobe's beauty, the *digna dea facies* (6.182), suggests the iconographical sleight of hand by which the sickly Octavian propagated through statuary a face and posture that were indeed unchanging and worthy of a divinity.[22]

---

[19] Bömer 1976.60 notes the connection, though there are of course other genealogies of the mother of Aphrodite. In Niobe's case, as Schmitzer 1990.245 points out, Dione as her mother first appears in Ovid. Schmitzer uses the connection with Venus as another point of similarity with Cleopatra, who according to Plut. *Ant.* 26 met Antony dressed as Aphrodite and associated herself with Isis, recognized as an Egyptian Aphrodite. The most suggestive of the iconic links that Schmitzer establishes between Cleopatra and Venus was Caesar's placement of her in the temple of Venus Genetrix, encouraging perhaps the same conflation between her self-presentation and the genealogy of the imperial family that Ovid suggests here.

[20] Voit 1957.146–47; Forbes-Irving 1990.296: "Instead of the irresponsible chatterer of the epigrams we find here a god-defier on a grand scale." Yet Ovid's inflation of Niobe's crime goes perhaps even further than has been suggested. A Pentheus may challenge the divinity of Dionysus, but he does not demand, as Niobe does, to become a god himself.

[21] *Met.* 15.760–61, see Hardie 1997.190–92 and above, chapter 2.

[22] Zanker 1990.98–100.

The final, and most suggestive, point of contact between Niobe and Augustus, however involves the climax of her claim to divine status, her offspring. Before I treated the link between fertility and divinity as an essentially Cleopatran element in Ovid's Niobe, but it too is much more than that. For Augustus as well would prominently deploy the imagery of growth and fertility, as well as the propagation of offspring,[23] to depict the promise of his reign, but would also lose countless heirs and adoptive sons. Specifically his adopted sons Gaius and Lucius had both died in independent accidents in the decade before Ovid's poem. In his *Res Gestae*, Augustus's description of his own personal loss, *filios meos, quos iuvenes mihi eripuit Fortuna* (my sons, whom Fortune snatched away from me in their youth, *RG* 14), is given in language similar to what Niobe will use to predict the impossibility of hers: *maior sum, quam cui possit Fortuna nocere, multaque ut eripiat, multo mihi plura relinquet* (I am too great for Fortune to harm; though she should snatch away many things, she will leave me many more, 6.195).[24] Here, in distinction to what we might initially construe as the "anti-Augustan" effects of disclosing potential similarities between the *princeps* and a figure associated with a vilified rival, the resemblance stresses the ultimate humanity of both rulers, placing them on the same side in the battle to freeze the processes of change that open the door to Fortuna's depredations.

My point in drawing these connections is not to suggest that Ovid has fashioned his Niobe into a cryptic indictment of Augustan policy. Any reader of this speech who made the comparison between emperor and queen could easily find that it threw into relief precisely what Augustus does not do. He did not explicitly claim divinity, as a Hellenistic ruler might have done. On the contrary, his distinctive odor of sanctity came precisely from the scrupulous piety with which he acknowledges the gods, and these particular Latonan gods, as his superiors.[25] So too the reference to the royal palace reminds us that Augustus's *domus* explicitly did not claim distinction on the basis of wealth. And the elaborate costume and flowing hair of Niobe's own appearance in this scene would stand quite apart from the decorous clothing and restrained nodus hairstyle of an Augustan princess.[26] Finally, Augustus's language regarding the deaths of Gaius and Lucius shows an acceptance of the hazards of fortune that Niobe denies. But even if the symbolic language of Niobe's

---

[23] See most conveniently Zanker 1990.172–79.

[24] On the possibility of Ovidian allusions to the *Res Gestae*, see chapter 2, note 32.

[25] See Galinsky 1996.219 on the function of Niobe as *exemplum* in the temple of Apollo on the Palatine, who cites as the moral of the episode the dictum of Horace (C. 3.6.5) that "by holding yourself lesser than the gods, you rule, Roman."

[26] On the role of representations of women in the propaganda wars of the Second Triumvirate, see Kleiner 1992.

self-divinization is quickly diagnosed as precisely that which Augustus has rejected, her aim of using deification as a way of guaranteeing permanence in the face of change creates a more complex bond with the aging ruler. More important is the effect of having Niobe's claim presented in direct speech, indeed in a scene where the queen herself sets up a complex pageant relying on spectacle and rhetoric. Keeping Niobe in the role of negative exemplar to Augustus thus comes to depend on maintaining the priority of one representation over another—on keeping Niobe contextualized within the moralizing tendency of this part of the poem and the larger architectural context of Augustan Rome that records her as the deserving victim of divine punishment. The alternative is to perceive in Niobe's representational capacity a kinship between queen and *princeps* that levels the ideological playing field between them.

Niobe's role as an artist in her own right leads to the second part of my argument, which will point out how the different claims advanced about the status of Niobe rely on different modes of representation, and how, for the reader, interpreting her story means choosing between alternative models for construing Ovid's text. Because these representational alternatives are already delineated in the preceding encounter between Minerva and Arachne, I review quickly how their rival tapestries advance different political agendas by opening up different perspectives on the way artistic images convey reality. As Denis Feeney has pointed out, Minerva complements her diminution of humans to the role of cautionary *exempla* highlighting the permanence of the gods with a reliance on artistic realism to manifest the power of those gods in art.[27] *Sua quemque deorum inscribit facies; Iovis est regalis imago* (his own appearance marks each god, Jupiter's is the appearance of a king, 6.73–74). The divine images are doubly authentic—they are based on reality, in the sense that they really look like what they represent, and conjointly they convey the authority of the gods, whose power is operative in the real world. In answer to Minerva's moralizing use of metamorphosis and realism to reestablish the hegemony of gods over man, Arachne presents a catalog of the animal forms the gods have used to deceive the victims of their lust. Here, rather than being final, metamorphosis appears as a fleeting mechanism of deception, proof not only of the crimes of the gods but of the unreliability of appearances. Correspondingly, her art relies on a different aspect of realism, aimed not at guaranteeing images as true and reliable representations but at a verisimilitude that assimilates the viewer to the victim of divine deception: Jupiter here is not a king but a bull, and "you would think it was a real bull," *verum taurum ... putares* (6.104), just as Europa did.

[27] Feeney 1991.190–92.

Equally notable is that both artists' narratives are defective in contrasting ways. Minerva depicts a timeless hierarchy but totally omits the flow of human time, so that the victims of metamorphosis are never depicted as human beings but only as immortal signs of immortality. By contrast, Arachne uses the power of art to make an obviously transient moment seem to last forever—Jupiter, of course, will not appear as a bull forever, and the human countenances that art preserves unchanging will age and vanish.

Within the Niobe story a parallel to these two modes of representation emerges in the form of two rival utterances, and as in the Arachne episode both images seem to compete as programmatic guides to Ovid's own text, so here it becomes possible to ally the narrative voice with either of these speakers, but with radically different results.[28] The warning to worship Latona comes from the speech, directly reported, of Manto, the daughter of Teiresias, described as prophetic (*vaticinata*, 6.159), invoking the very term that Ovid will use to define his own poetic role in the poem's final line (*vatum*, 15.879). As a good *vatis*, Manto presents her speech as providing direct access to the language and will of a real-life divinity: "Latona orders this with my voice" (*ore meo Latona iubet*, 6.162). If we compare the voice of this *vatis* with that of the Ovidian narrator, we finds a pretty close match: we already know that the aim of the story will be to reinforce the moral of the Arachne narrative, and so again to emphasize the hierarchical patterns that subordinate men to gods, and that this hierarchy is presented as an extratextual reality (cf. 6.150–51). And Ovid's narrative too will offer direct depictions of the gods, cutting immediately from Niobe's boast to the scene of Latona begging her children for aid (6.204ff.).

---

[28] Further provocation to read the Niobe scene through the contrasting lenses offered by the tapestry images of the Arachne episdode comes from the thematic anticipations of her story in each of the four cautionary tales that frame Minerva's picture. Thus, Rhodope and Haemus in the first of these scenes undergo a kind of petrifaction (they are changed to mountains) as a result of calling themselves by the names of the Olympian gods (6.87–89). In the second episode, the Pygmy queen defeated by Iuno in an unspecified competition is gratuitously identified as a mother (6.90). The next figure, Antigone, another rival of Juno, shares with Niobe a royal heritage in Asia Minor (6.95–96). The final scene of Cinyras embracing the temple steps that were his daughters provides an exact mirror image of Niobe as a male parent, mourning children turned to stone, "seems to weep" (6.100).

Niobe's appearance, like that of her Vergilian analogue, Dido, seems to be as a figure stepping out of an artistic representation (with the temple of the Cinyras story perhaps tightening the connection). But here there is an added twist in the sudden shift from representation to reality because this tapestry figure herself appropriates an embroidered Phrygian cloth as an element of her own adornment, anticipating the reversals of perspective discussed later. For the importance of Dido's epiphany elsewhere in Ovid, see Hardie 2002c.183–86.

The second possible paradigm for the Ovidian narrator comes, of course, from Niobe's own speech, which in several features is not too far from recognizably Ovidian procedures. Interestingly, the lesson of Arachne is recounted by the poet as "to use lesser words," language that seems to link Niobe's offense precisely to her role as a verbal artist.[29] Ovid's descriptions of his own literary development as the evolution from small to large, in, for example, *Fasti* 2.3–4 and *Tristia* 2.63–5, where the *Metamorphoses* itself becomes his *maius opus*, invite comparison between Niobe's *verba* and the poetic text that contains them. Beyond the generalized opposition between the grand and the slight, a distinction that Ovid's poem conspicuously blurs, Alan Cameron has suggested that throughout Latin literature the "greatness" of a work relates directly to its panegyric function.[30] Such a connotation here further strengthens the connections both between Niobe's crime and her poetic performance and between that performance and the text that surrounds it. For Niobe's arrogance manifests itself in a perversion of a specific literary form, the hymn. Niobe deploys the traditional rhetoric of praise, as we have seen, to exalt herself while recasting the traditional hymnic narrative of the birth of Apollo to put blame on the goddess Latona.[31] Interestingly, this assertion of human superiority over the gods, which leads up to her poignant final neglect of the power of time to undo the signs of her triumph, itself depends on a truncation of the narrative that recalls the storytelling of Arachne. For just as the weaver never brings her tales to the end, so Niobe here omits the miraculous fixing of the island to the seabed that affirms Latona's divinity.[32] Her manipulation of the hymnic genre also provides an obvious point of comparison between Niobe and the hymnic narrator who has spent the better part of the last book recount-

---

[29] *verbisque minoribus uti* (6.151). For a similar poetological dimension to the succeeding narrative of the Lycian peasants, see Clauss 1989.

[30] Cameron 1995.466–71, though in the case of the *Tristia* passage designations of size and scale do seem to me operative in the use of *maius*.

[31] As described by Anderson 1972.177, see also Barchiesi 1999.124 and Fuhrer 1999.364, who catalogs precisely the hymnic elements in Niobe's self-praise.

[32] This also provides an important link to the Pierides, the human singers who challenge the muses to a contest of hymns in book 5, for they too end their song with the gods hiding (*latuit*, 5.331 ~ Latona?) concealed in the form of animals, rather than going on to narrate the defeat of Typhoeus. Other important thematic connections between Niobe and the Pierids are the latter's reliance on number over quality, at least as the Muses report (5.305) them, and the eastern, specifically Egyptian, emphasis of their praise of Typhoeus (for details, see Anderson 1996.531–32), which anticipates Niobe's eastern origins and perhaps her contemporary associations with Cleopatra. The "Egyptianizing" of the failed hymns in these books looks forward to the poem's final ostentatious reconfiguration of Alexandrian elements in the portrayal of Venus to serve Roman ends; see the important discussion of Barchiesi 1999.119.

ing a refashioned hymn to Demeter. Again, there are obvious differences between the two treatments, signaled not least by Niobe's omission of the prime Ovidian element of metamorphosis and Ovid's careful decision to place hymnic "big words" directly in the mouth of the muse of epic poetry.

But however much we may correct this impulse to hear Niobe's voice in Ovid's, just as we reject the notion of Niobe as Augustus, the exercise of making the equation discloses a resemblance between the two speakers that the reading of the story as an *exemplum* would like us to keep apart. The mortal and unimperial Ovid, even as he seems to anchor his narrative to reflections of those greater than himself, still appropriates the language and figures of external authorities and in doing so suggests that these authorizing images are perhaps no more than artistic constructs on the part of mortals. What we gain from the equation between Niobe and the poet, and again by extension Augustus, is a new perspective on those images that makes it possible to understand them less as representations of an external reality than as projections of human ambitions struggling to be accepted as real. Viewed like this, the very gods whose inclusion in Ovid's narrative differentiates it from Niobe's story and whose depictions in Apollo's temple perform a similar authorizing function have no authentic power outside of the representation. To make matters more confusing, they look a lot like Niobe herself. Niobe's own Arachnid view of images, where it is the human face that endures and takes precedence over the divine, becomes an essential corollary of Minerva's depiction of the gods. Making gods look like men inevitably makes men look more like gods. And so the first directly described image of Latona is of an angry woman seeking to obtain vengeance over a rival through her children (6.204–13). The view from the top down, where art accurately depicts real gods in human form as a warning to mortals, and from the bottom up where human beings immortalize their own countenances, creating gods in their own image, and where the face of the human artist is always visible, come to settle into one. And this is no mere metaphor, for Ovid's narrative here shows an extreme interest in verticality, as it moves back and forth between mountain and plain.[33]

The approximation of Niobe to the divine thus paradoxically becomes most visible just at the moment when the narrative would seem to have exposed her inferiority to Latona, when she is on the verge of being converted literally to a statue. And again this semantic doubling goes together with an emphasis within the text on problems of viewing and perspective. A brief glance at the death of the penultimate two daughters, whose

---

[33] Cf. *summoque in vertice Cynthi*, 6.204 ~ *planus erat*, 6.218.

removal finally reduces her, as she emphatically points out,[34] below the Latonan tally of two, helps make this clear:

> *latet haec, illam trepidare videres;*
> *sexque datis leto diversaque vulnera passis*
> *ultima restabat.*
>
> (6.296–98)

One hides, you might have seen the other tremble; with six given over to death and having suffered various wounds, the last was remaining.

The hiding daughter assumes precisely the characteristic pose of the exiled Latona and indeed seems to offer an etymological gloss for her name.[35] But Latona in a very different guise is lurking in the next line as well; the "death" to whom the daughters have been handed over is none other than Leto, the Greek name for the same goddess. This shift in perspective, by which the victim indeed comes to resemble the divine, while the divinity is reduced simply to the destructive force that alone keeps mortals from obtaining their due, occurs together with another little narratological reminder of Arachne's tapestry. You would see that daughter tremble, as on the tapestry you would believe that Jupiter's bull was a real bull. The introduction of the internal spectator once more accompanies a shift in perspective by potentially placing the reader in the story. As there seeing the bull as real meant adopting the point of view of the victim Europa, so here, I suggest, the "you" that you become is Niobe. The sympathetic perspective thus also coincides with the moment when the text itself seems most capable of producing the illusion of reality, the result of which is not only to be able to see Niobe's daughter with maximum vividness but to see as Niobe.

This fleeting reminder of the problems of illusionism is particularly suggestive here because it so closely prepares for the moment when Niobe herself becomes a work of art—the eternal stone figure that ends the narrative and, by extension, the actual sculptural figure on display in Rome. Before turning finally to consider how Ovid's narrative affects the reading of this real monument, and vice versa, it is important to recall just how problematic Niobe's metamorphosis had always been as a conclusion to her story. Why exactly does Niobe turn to stone? Do the gods transform her as the culmination of her punishment? Does the

---

[34] Cf. the stress on *unam* in lines 6.299–300.

[35] Fulgentius *Virg. Cont.* 104,13: *Latinus ... a latitando ... unde et Latona dicta est Luna quod nunc superna celet nunc inferiora nunc uniformis latitet.*

transformation happen spontaneously, or is it even granted to her by the gods as a token of compassion?[36] Ovid's own ambiguous description can accommodate many different possibilities. She grew stiff from evils, *deriguit malis* (6.303). The evils she committed, or the evils she suffered? One reading makes the stone commemorate Niobe's own transgression, fixing her into a perpetual reminder of the power of the gods to exact vengeance. The other, though, highlights the commemoration of her grief and her humanity. And if what is remembered is Niobe rather than her exemplary punishment, metamorphosis gives her the immortality she seeks at the beginning of her story.

The sign of Niobe becomes invested with these two different significations, coexisting in one image, and these differences enshrine not only the difference in points of view articulated in the tapestries that prepare for the scene but also different views of the "difference" that the figure of Niobe was meant to record in Augustan culture. In this connection too, it is important to remember that the tale of Niobe's historical analogue Cleopatra becomes especially difficult to deal with precisely at its ending, where the barbarian queen's brave suicide makes her at once sympathetic and heroic, and thus puts her beyond the reach of commemoration by Augustus, even as the fact of her death saved her from being displayed in a triumph.[37]

Although the development of the tale of Niobe prepares the reader to take this double view of the resulting image, Ovid's account of that image itself makes it a figure for perpetuating the ambiguities of the metamorphosis. The most striking thing about the stone Niobe is her contradictory nature as artistic artifact. She is at once totally inanimate and miraculously defies inanimacy. In comparison to ancient conceptions of the properties and ideals of statues, the stone is both too dead and too much alive. Ovid is at pains to present the final form of Niobe as the antithesis of her first appearance as a moving figure interrupting the rites of Latona with her boasting.[38] Her hair does not move, her face loses its color, and—the paradigmatic silence of statues—her tongue cleaves to her palate (6.303–9). A final element in the same pattern of inversion comes perhaps at the end of the catalog, where even the organs inside her have become stone: for this image controverts two Greek ways of figuring female fertility, as a soft wax tablet and as a fertile field. In this way, the stoniness of her internal organs points up the statue's lack of the very

[36] See Voit 1957.149 and Frécaut 1980.135–37, who also provides a résumé of other views.

[37] Wyke 1992.127, citing Pelling 1988.318–19.

[38] See also Forbes-Irving 1990.147.

creative capacity most essential to the immortal identity Niobe tries to establish for herself.[39]

Such inversions can indeed contribute to a reading of Niobe's petrifaction as the inevitable punishment for her hubris. But at the same time, they disconnect the stone precisely from the figure whom, if this is actually a statue, it ought to represent. A central paradox of statuary so frequently exploited in, for example, the ecphrastic writers in the *Greek Anthology*, is precisely that a statue's capacity to represent seems to give it properties it does not possess. So here Ovid's insistence that the statue does not move or speak and that "there is nothing alive in the image" (*nihil est in imagine vivum*, 6.305) reflects the hard facts of the statue as artifact,[40] but it also negates the very qualities that make it miraculous as art. However Ovid has a different kind of miracle in store. The immobile stone undertakes a remarkable journey as a blast of wind carries it from Thebes back to Mount Sipylus. So too Niobe, who had become so absent in the stone's figuration, persists not as an image but as a living presence. The stone, which remains grammatically feminine (cf. the participles in 6.310–12), continues to weep. Ovid thus emphasizes the complex semantic possibilities available to the viewer of the real statue of Niobe by disarticulating two contrasting ways of seeing. On the one hand, there is no illusionism at all: the viewer sees simply the dead rock that has replaced the living Niobe. On the other, there is an illusionism so complete that the role of art itself vanishes. Niobe weeps not because the rock seems to weep but as a continuing presence miraculously pouring forth real tears.

Niobe becomes an interesting figure for pointing out this possible gulf between reality and representation not just because of her iconographic importance as a statue in Augustan Rome but because throughout antiquity writers raise the question of what exactly you saw when you looked at Niobe. This uncertainty can take the simplest form in the mere question of whether a woman was figured in the actual rock on Sipylus. Thus, for example Pausanias, whose thoughts turn to the actual stone Niobe as a result of seeing a statue of her very like the one on display in Rome, a tripod embossed with Apollo and Artemis killing the Niobids, recalls how different points of view really did affect one's perception of the stone: "I myself saw this Niobe, having climbed the mountain at Sipylus. Close up she is a rocky crag, offering no appearance of any woman at all, much less a weeping one. But if you go farther off you seem to see a woman weeping with lowered head" (Paus. 1.21.3). The theoretical

[39] For writing and plowing as metaphors for female fertility, see Dubois 1988.65–85 and Steiner 1994.111–12. See also, on the contrast between the stone Niobe and the queen at the beginning of her story, Forbes-Irving 1990.147.

[40] On silence and immobility as the defining characteristics of statues in Greek thought, see Steiner 2001.136–151; on the contrasting illusion of animation, see Steiner 2001.44–50.

problem involved in matching Niobe with the stone appears in skeptical writers attempting to rationalize the metamorphosis story itself; thus, the comic poet Philemon has a character say: "I never believed Niobe was stone, nor now will I be persuaded that the stone was a human being: but rather, no longer able to speak on account of her evils, she is said to be a stone on account of her silence."[41] But more interesting still are the actual responses to stone images of Niobe recorded in the *Greek Anthology* that relate precisely to our problem of recognizing the living figure of Niobe in a stone image. The play between Niobe and the statue, between presence and absence, can be inflected in numerous ways. Thus, for example, an anonymous poet has a Praxitelean Niobe address the hearer as follows:

Ἐκ ζωῆς με θεοὶ τεῦξαν λίθον, ἐκ δὲ λίθοιο
ζωὴν Πραξιτέλης ἔμπαλιν εἰργάσατο.
(*AP* 16.129)

From a living woman, the gods made me stone; from stone, Praxiteles has made me a living woman again.

The idea that the artist in some sense challenges the gods as Niobe had done precisely in bringing the stone to life further suggests how the sympathetic recognition of Niobe in the statue can undo the image's exemplary significance. Notice too how the verbal artist, the anonymous epigrammatist, adds the finishing touch to her resurrection by restoring Niobe's power to speak. A poet much later than Ovid, Julianus of Egypt, takes precisely the opposite tack and relates the lifelessness of an actual image to the divine transformation that preceded the artist's work.

Δυστήνου Νιόβης ὁράᾳς παναληθέα μορφὴν
ὡς ἔτι μυρομένης πότμον ἑῶν τεκέων.
εἰ δ' ἄρα καὶ ψυχὴν οὐκ ἔλλαχε, μὴ τόδε τέχνῃ
μέμφεο· θηλυτέρην εἴκασε λαϊνέην.
(*AP* 16.130)

You see the true shape of the wretched Niobe, as if still mourning the fate of her children, but if she has not received a soul, don't blame this on the artist, for he portrayed a stone woman.

In this case the deadness of the statue, recording merely the shape of Niobe, is itself the perfect commemoration. But the simple equation be-

---

[41] ἐγὼ λίθον μὲν τὴν Νιόβην, μὰ τοὺς θεούς,
οὐδέποτ' ἐπείσθην, οὐδὲ νῦν πεισθήσομαι
ὡς τοῦτ' ἐγένετ' ἄνθρωπος· ὑπὸ δὲ τῶν κακῶν
οὐδὲν λαλῆσαι δυναμένη πρὸς οὐδένα,
προσηγορεύθη διὰ τὸ μὴ φωνεῖν λίθος.
(fr. 101)

tween bringing Niobe to life and undoing the gods' work, which I extended to adopting a perspective alien to the exemplary reading of the image, is complicated in yet another poem, by the Hellenistic Theodoridas, that most resembles Ovid's representation in its intricacy.

Στᾶθι πέλας, δάκρυσον ἰδών, ξένε, μυρία πένθη
    τᾶς ἀθυρογλώσσου Τανταλίδος Νιόβας,
ἃς ἐπὶ γᾶς ἔστρωσε δυωδεκάπαιδα λοχείαν
    ἄρτι, τὰ μὲν Φοίβου τόξα, τὰ δ' Ἀρτέμιδος.
ἁ δὲ λίθῳ καὶ σαρκὶ μεμιγμένον εἶδος ἔχουσα
    πετροῦται· στενάχει δ' ὑψιπαγὴς Σίπυλος.
θνατοῖς ἐν γλώσσᾳ δολία νόσος, ἃς ἀχάλινος
    ἀφροσύνα τίκτει πολλάκι δυστυχίαν.
                                    (AP 16.132)

Stand near, stranger, and weep beholding the thousand sorrows of the daughter of Tantalos, who had no door on her tongue, whose force of twelve offspring the arrows of Apollo and Artemis laid low. She, now having an appearance made up of stone mixed with flesh, has been changed to a rock. And lofty Sipylus groans. The tongue is a devious plague to mortals, whose unbridled madness has often given birth to unhappiness.

Theodoridas too highlights a division between flesh and stone that keeps Niobe from quite coalescing into a single image. But here, far from the sympathetic aspects of the statue alienating the viewer from the image's moral force, the more one sympathizes with Niobe—and notice how "you" are instructed to weep like the rock is weeping—the more vividly one experiences the sorrow that comes from disobeying the gods.[42]

This examination of other literary explorations of Niobe makes it clear that the connection between Ovid's poem and the visual imagery of Niobe is more than simple imitation;[43] rather we can see the poet engaging both with the contemporary didactic deployment of images of Niobe and with the tradition of meditating on the ecphrastic ambiguities of a statue of a stone maiden to accentuate thematic issues important within his own narrative. These issues include the question of whether the punished Niobe can also be seen as a figure for pity, whose ambitions to rival the divinity have their root in the essential condition of mortality and resemble those of the very prince whose monuments use her punishment

---

[42] For the treatment of the problem of the stone Niobe in Athenian drama, see Steiner 2001.147–48.

[43] That Ovid composed 6.298–99 to recapture precisely the pose of the Niobe now in the Uffizi (and sometimes argued to be a copy of the one on display in the temple of Apollo in Circo) was suggested by Bömer 1976.51 and Gros 1976.165, n. 85.

to legitimize his own reign, and of the very poet who tells her story. And as the exploration of the image highlights the ambiguities of the narrative, so Ovid's narrative charges the actual statues of Niobe with a new significance.

This reciprocal transformation of image and text points to two larger ways in which the fluctuation between picture and story becomes significant for understanding the function and nature of Ovid's narrative. The first involves the central phenomenon of Ovid's poem, metamorphosis. Both story and image reflect metamorphosis in different ways that controvert the seemingly obvious dichotomy between static image and evolving narrative.[44] In the case of stories, the fact that they move through time and so point out how characters undergo changes of condition makes them the ideal medium for representing metamorphosis. Indeed, in Aristotle's *Poetics*, the change of condition represented is an essential criterion for analyzing plot (*Poet.* 13). Niobe, of course, thinks that her life will have no narrative—that she will always be what she is, and correspondingly she herself does not tell stories all the way to the end. But once we know the stories, then the images have their own distinctive way of reproducing metamorphosis that verbal narrative lacks. That is precisely because images affect the viewer synchronically, juxtaposing new and old in the same instant. Once we have learned to see Niobe in the Niobe statue, or rather to accommodate different perspectives that subject the image to different readings, then it acquires the ability to present opposite states not one after the other but in shocking simultaneity. Niobe emerges as both victim and violator at once. As Ovid invests the image with such complex significance by telling the story behind it, at the same time his narrative acquires the ability to depict this contrast with the immediacy and the intensity of a visual image. One example of how he gives his text this iconic property comes from another of the episode's most studied lines, appearing halfway through Niobe's punishment after her seven sons have been killed: *Heu quantum haec Niobe Niobe distabat ab illa* (alas how much this Niobe differs from the former Niobe, 6.273). A wonderful pun since the second Niobe has "declined" from the nominative to the ablative, but also a key question for the entire narrative, capable of many answers from "not different at all since she still offends the goddess" to "halfway on the road to total desolation."[45] But the im-

---

[44] On the problems of representing metamorphosis in verbal and visual art, see Sharrock 1996.

[45] Tissol 1997.57–58 describes this "sinking downward" as a kind of linguistic proto-metamorphosis anticipating the effect of the final transformation before it has become visible to an outside observer. My own interpretation focuses more on the ambiguous likeness and difference between Niobe at the middle of her story and both her "before" and "after" states. In another important recent discussion of the line, Hardie 2002c.251 concentrates

portant fact for my purposes is that the line invests the word Niobe with the capacity to signify both states. Niobe, however we construe it grammatically or interpret the story it tells, has not changed at all; the same term signifies Niobe at both the beginning and ending as the statue itself records its likeness and difference to the arrogant dynast.

Finally, let us return from statues and narratives in the abstract to our starting point, the interaction between one particular narrative, Ovid's *Metamorphoses* and one particular set of statues, the images of Niobe infixed in contemporary temples of Apollo. Here too we will find not a simple question of models and reinterpretations, of an anti-imperial Niobe narrative planted like defacing graffiti on the monument of Caesar. Rather, just as within the text image and narrative mutually redefine one another, so within the real world into which Ovid's actual poem was introduced, the poet has made sure that the relative priority of these two representations of Niobe remains unclear in a manner that in itself plays on the episode's ostensible theme of the violations of the social order. Read according to Ovid's narrative sequence, the visual image comes last: this is a woman turned to stone. But in the real world the statues had been on display in Rome for at least thirty years when the poem was composed. The balance between our awareness of these two realities, the one created by Ovid's illusions and the one over which Augustus presides, make us look at what Ovid is doing in different ways. If we assume that the story is really an aetion for an image and motivated by the ending

---

on the distance the repetition introduces between the signifier Niobe, which undergoes no change at all, and its referent, Niobe herself, who will be radically transformed.

The possibility Hardie suggests here that the written "Niobe"—and, I would add, the sculptural Niobe—does not so much summon up the original Niobe as replace her emerges in another way from Ovid's portrayal of the metamorphosis. Ovid's account of Niobe's petrifaction has been central to the relation between metaphor and metamorphosis, and to arguments that seek to blur the boundary between the two by making of the metamorphic process a realization or literalization of a literary trope (Hardie 2002c.226–36, Pianezzola 1979, esp. 82–83, on Niobe). But at the same time, I suggest, the elision of the boundary here can act to remind the reader precisely of its importance. Pianezzola 1979.82 argues that when Ovid says in 6.303 that Niobe *deriguit malis*, "grew stiff with evils," this is not so much a narrative of her transformation but a preparatory use of a common metaphor for the effect of powerful emotion. If read in this way, the expression establishes an important continuity between the transformed image (and Ovid's text) and the actual experiences of Niobe as a human character. However, if we read *deriguit* as commencing the process of metamorphosis, and the reader will wait in vain for a clearer statement of her transformation as an event in the narrative, then it leaves open the possibility of imagining her transformation as something imposed from without that breaks the links between Niobe as subject and as image. Ovid's use of Niobe in this programmatic way for exploring the nature of representation of metamorphosis may result from the antiquity in literary historical terms of her exemplary function. As the story that Achilles tells to Priam in *Il.* 24.602–17, Niobe may be said to stand at the very beginning of literary representations of metamorphosis, or at least of their moralizing function.

point—it is there to reinforce a moral—then the poet himself emerges as a prophet comparable to Manto, whose words reveal the higher truth established by superiors. At the same time though, the poet seems to be describing the authentic Niobe, present in the audience's reality of Augustan Rome only as a representation, a statue. His Niobe is what Augustus is commemorating. The statues have now been animated by being reinserted into a narrative that highlights the instability of their significance. In this way Ovid's story seems to ensure that neither the *princeps*'s images nor his text can stand alone: both are linked forever in a continuous process of petrification and coming to life, as the artist perpetually places his art at the service of Augustus's empire and, Niobe-like, asserts his own.

II. Perseus: The Shadow

Ovid's Perseus narrative frequently disappoints its readers. The famous shower of gold by which the hero was conceived receives but half a line. The killing of the Gorgon is already over by the time our narrative begins, and the account Perseus himself later gives of it—twelve lines of indirect discourse—offers but a scant résumé. Such unexpected emphases can perhaps be explained as a reflex, almost a parody, of the conventions of Hellenistic narrative, a Hecale-like interest in novelty, intricacy, and setting the most frequently treated subjects in unexpected frames. But Ovid's priorities here also have two important thematic consequences that make the Perseus episode an ideal conclusion to this section's analysis of the representation of artistic images within the poem and to my larger arguments about how the poem stages the reception of its own fictions. First, by the time we meet Perseus he has already gained possession of the Gorgon's head. Thus, his distinctive power comes from his ability to effect metamorphoses, specifically to turn a series of opponents into stone statues. Second, Perseus's improbable history, like Ovid's fictions, frequently inspires disbelief and incredulity. And this disbelief actually becomes the force that drives the narrative, for it is precisely his audience's skepticism that calls forth his fatal image making, a power so miraculous that it cannot but be disbelieved in turn.[46]

My argument begins from the foregoing analysis of how the coexistence of Ovid's poem and the stone Niobes of the Roman cityscape destabilizes the meaning of both and specifically frustrates any final assertions about the statues' significance, their relationship to reality, and the moral they teach. A similar evasion of interpretative closure inevitably becomes

---

[46] On the theme of fictionality in the episode, see now the reading of Klein 2009, which appeared literally as this book was going to press.

a central point of the Perseus story, where each act of silencing dissenting voices inspires further skepticism. At first, Perseus's images would seem to be exempt precisely from any doubts about their relationship to reality. As Philip Hardie observes, their commemorative function appears absolute because they leave no gaps either between the identity of the victim and the image that recalls his defeat or between the act of victory and its commemoration.[47] Killing Phineus becomes identical with turning him into a statue of himself. But it is precisely the paradox at work in an unbelievable power to create authentic representations that allows it to raise such complex issues about the "power of images" in Augustan Rome, where monuments and celebrations served as the essential means of representing events and of imposing a view of history, by revealing how it depends on drawing a line between fiction and reality.

I begin by describing in more detail how Perseus is presented as a particularly Augustan figure in the poem. And the first similarity to stress between the emperor and the hero is that neither one is himself an artist. Unlike Pygmalion, Perseus has no ambitions as a craftsman per se—the last thing he would want is for his own images to come back to life. As his winged form takes him to the upper limit of human potential, so his divine parentage places him at the opposite end of the social scale from a mere craftsman like Daedalus, whom again he physically resembles. His sculptures are the by-product of his assertion of that status, a motive that dominates almost his every action and utterance in the poem. The images he leaves in his wake, then, memorialize not just the embedded presence of the victim but also the power of the victor.

In an earlier treatment of the civic and political role of visual display at Rome, I suggested that for a Roman imperator displaying the visual memorials of any victory was a kind of synecdochic extension of the victory itself; in the case of a triumph, such display becomes the literal completion of the journey that returns the victor to the very spot where he took the auspices in assuming his command.[48] As the commander will often have achieved victory by inspiring his troops with visual images, real or imagined, the visual commemorations of it replicate and extend his power and make him very much the author of the resulting monuments. The triumph too reminds us how plundered works of art—whatever their subject matter—acquire a specific value in Rome precisely as evidence of victory, *spolia*. One Augustan construction of the response to such booty, Cato's condemnation of the statues Marcellus brought as plunder from Syracuse in Livy's *History*, configures their reception as a

---

[47] See Hardie 2002c.179.
[48] Feldherr 1998.19–24.

struggle between the Roman narrative of conquest they commemorate and their own aesthetic desirability. Their craftsmanship makes them desirable and so instigates a cycle of avarice that will in the long run be as destructive to Rome as Rome was to any of its foreign rivals; thus, Cato describes the statues (*signa*) themselves as hostile (*infesta*).[49] This double link between art and victory, an association between the depiction and the event and the translation of other representational works of art into markers of Roman conquest, gives special point to the "functionality" of Perseus's *spolia* and to the connection between action and artistry noted by Hardie. Perseus might well be Cato's ideal artist, for not only is the very existence of his *signa* inseparable from victory but there is no craftsmanship at all to delight and seduce the eye.

What is more, like Augustus, another son of a god whose divine descent was always suspect, Perseus uses his extraordinary power only for the most pious ends: his last acts in the narrative settle old scores by paying off Proetus, the rival of his grandfather, and Polydectes, the king of the island where he and his mother had taken refuge, who had disbelieved in his divine descent. The very terms by which Augustus justified his participation in civil war as filial piety reemerge in the depiction of Perseus, who in the act of defeating Proetus is called "the redeemer and avenger of his dishonored parent," (*inmeriti vindex ultorque parentis*, 5.237).[50] And if these events were already a generation old by the time Ovid wrote, their commemoration was a highly topical issue, for the Forum of Augustus, with its central temple of Mars the Avenger was dedicated as recently as 2 BCE. So, as we have seen, Ovid describes his Perseus recalling, not performing, his most famous accomplishment. His narrative focuses around the visual effects of a *spolium*, for it is by this term, recalling precisely the kinds of objects that would be put on display by a victorious Roman general and which the temple of Mars Ultor was built to receive, that the statue-making head of the Gorgon is first described (*viperei referens spolium memorabile monstri*, 4.615). As a *spolium*, the Gorgon's head might equally recall another of Augustus's signal foreign victories, his defeat of Cleopatra, a similarly dangerous African female with unruly hair.[51]

[49] Livy 34.4.3.

[50] Other Augustan epithets of Perseus are noted by Schmitzer 1990.238–39: *genus deum* (4.609–10), *fortissimus* (4.769, 5.221), *victor* (5.237).

The interesting reading of the Perseus episode put forward by Neschke 1982 shows Ovid systematically remaking a Greek hero who relied above all on divine power to transcend human limits into an *exemplum* of the very Roman qualities of *virtus* and *iustitia*.

[51] Connections between Augustus's victory in the civil wars and Perseus's exploits were also made explicit on terracotta panels from the temple of Apollo on the Palatine. See Kellum 1985, cited by Schmitzer 1990.239.

These Augustan parallels gain prominence from the peculiar way that Ovid shapes the Perseus story and, in turn, give special significance to its emphasis on the use of visual images. In no other surviving version of the Perseus story does the motif of family revenge play such a large part as in Ovid's.[52] The expectation for vengeance is set in motion at the first mention of Acrisius in the narrative as someone who would learn by bitter experience the danger of doubting the divine paternity of both Perseus and Dionysus. Acrisius's role as a Pentheus-like doubter already creates the expectation that he will be punished (4.609–11), and given Perseus's important insistence on his paternity in the first narrated episode of his career, the encounter with Atlas (4.640), we may well expect that the grandson himself will be an agent of vengeance.[53] If Acrisius, contrary to these expectations, never appears again in the narrative, the twinned motifs of revenge and Perseus's need to prove that he is who he claims to be,[54] both set in motion by this introduction, will govern a number of its episodes. Atlas cannot explicitly deny Perseus's divinity, for his hostility is motivated by an oracle predicting that a son of Jupiter will steal the golden apples,[55] but he does call Perseus a liar for claiming to have killed the Gorgon. The fight with Phineus arises from a dispute over another reward (*praemium*, 5. 25), and here the challenger, who has unwittingly interrupted Perseus's story of the Gorgons, does explicitly deny the miraculous shower of gold by which Perseus was engendered (5.11). When the narrative comes full circle by returning Perseus to the scenes of his birth and first years, he faces down both a family enemy and a doubter: the specific crimes of Acrisius reemerge in his final two opponents Proetus and Polydectes, the king of Seriphus. Acrisius drove the god Dionysus from the walls of Argos despite his kinship; Proetus has similarly driven out his own brother Acrisius (5.5.238–39). Elsewhere, Polydectes' enmity toward Perseus was rooted in his own courtship of Danae; here though the primary offense becomes his disbelief in the story of the Gorgon (5.244–45), the same crime as Atlas. The description of Acrisius made us look forward to the avenging power of truth; *prasentia veri*, the "real presence" of what he doubted would "soon" make Acrisius

---

[52] Given both the many forms the Perseus story could take and the absence of any extended narrative other than those of the mythographers, this argument from silence by no means rules out earlier parallels.

[53] As of course he is, though unwittingly, in other surviving versions of the story, where Perseus accidentally kills his grandfather. See, e.g., Apoll. 2.4.4.

[54] The theme of disbelief in this episode is also treated by Wheeler 1999.183–84.

[55] Here, too, note the specifically Roman military terms in which this conquest is imagined, picking up on the account of Medusa's head: *spoliabitur* (4.644), *hunc praedae titulum* (4.645).

regret his crimes (4.612). And it is precisely proofs of truth, *pignora veri*, that Perseus offers Polydectes in the form of the transformative power of the Gorgon's head, at the conclusion of his story (5.247).[56]

But is it a conclusion? The last three of Perseus's exploits end suddenly, especially the account of the fight in Cepheus's palace, to which not a word is added after the description of the stone Phineus. Yet the impression that these perfect monuments engender finality because they leave nothing left to be said is itself undercut by the apparently infinite repeatability of the act. There is always another wrongdoer out there to turn to stone, and the narrative abandons Perseus not because he has overcome all his trials and settled down to live happily ever after, but because our internal audience, Minerva, has wandered off (5.250–52). Not only does this lack of an ending belie the irrefutable proofs of virtue that Perseus claims to provide; a distance also opens up between monument and meaning. Again, the image of Phineus makes this especially clear. Far from the fearsome, unjust, and incestuous barbarian rival the narrative depicts, the statue shows a humbled suppliant: "But nonetheless, the timid face and supplicating gaze, the lowered hands and obedient expression endured" (5.234–35). So too, as Anderson acutely points out, the possession of so powerful an advantage as the Gorgon's head casts doubt on the very heroism Perseus so desperately wants to prove.[57] Perseus's monuments, like those of Augustus, are always available to be read as fictions, and the disbelief they engender paradoxically provides the impetus to turn new dissenters into stone.

The doubly ironic use of the Gorgon's head, a miraculous *spolia*-producing *spolium*, as an incontrovertible and final proof of truth reveals how deeply Augustus's problems of representation are intertwined with Ovid's own. (The language in which Perseus's magical exploit is denied

---

[56] It is a very neat narrative trick on Ovid's part to set up the story with the expectation of punishment for a figure who never appears again, and to have his place taken (in the case of Proetus quite literally) by the punishment, as though long expected, of two figures who have never appeared in the narrative before. And by making this substitution Ovid is also (transparently?) sanitizing the life story of this Augustus figure whose actual murder of his grandfather is dropped from the narrative. Instead of assuming the crime of killing his grandfather, Perseus now gets to be his avenger (while simultaneously paying off the very crimes which the grandfather committed). As we shall see later in this section, the chain of substitutions, by which new victims take the place of old, is an important motif throughout the episode.

[57] For both points, see Anderson 1996.519, who uses the phrase "happily ever after." Barkan 1986.55 by contrast sees the final image of Phineus as a perfect embodiment of the latent cowardice of the character. However, the importance of the end of the *Aeneid* as an intertext further focuses attention on the moral and religious consequences of killing suppliants.

recalls the terms in which Ovid would disparage his own fictions. The story is a "lie," *mentiris*, 4.650, and "made-up," *fictam*, 5.246.) In making this point, I am not positing a generation of "Philippi-deniers" doubting the veracity of the emperor's claims to have avenged his father. Rather, the "problem of representation" is the same as that described in chapter 2: imperial representations themselves offer a context for voices other than the emperor's to emerge. Whether these voices dissent from or appropriate the authority of their creator, they challenge the *princeps*'s ability to manifest his power through images, to demand assent and promote civic unity as effectively as he did through the actual victories those images commemorate. And of the historicity of this phenomenon, we have a supreme example in the works of Ovid himself—not just the intervention of "fictions" in reconfiguring reality, which is the burden of my argument here—but in the *Ars Amatoria* where triumphs and monuments are refashioned both to signify and to accomplish the victory of love.

But the interaction of commemorative images and fiction is, of course, more complicated than a simple struggle for credibility and authority. It also clarifies how the real monuments of the emperor are pushed in the direction of fictionality. The power of the Gorgon's head is directly proportional to its unbelievability. So the more the emperor's images exalt and magnify his achievements, the harder they are to believe and, correspondingly, the more they require a form of representation that goes beyond producing a verisimilar image of what actually happened. Augustus may never have claimed to slay any Gorgons, but Perseus's dilemma applies to him in two related ways: first, part of the power of imperial display came from its capacity to bring directly before its audience's gaze peoples and creatures from the farthest edges of the earth, again the more exotic—the closer to the miraculous they become—the greater their prestige. And, second, spatial distance in this context offers a metaphor for the borders of the verisimilar. While Augustan art famously avoids the kind of baroque mythological excesses of the late republic, it nevertheless uses the language of myth, Apollo's presence at Actium, for example, to gloss imperial accomplishments as something beyond what can be described in merely historical terms. And here a couple of details about Perseus's adventures take on a particular significance: for him too the unreal is physically far away. Those episodes like his programmatic first encounter with Atlas, when he turns a mythical giant into a real mountain, that bring him farthest from apprehensible reality take place on the literal edges of the earth, and Ovid structures his narrative as the trip from there to here: we first meet Perseus making his way back from the slaying of the Gorgon, and the participle used there (*referens*, 4.615) links the physical carrying back of the trophy with "narrating" it.

The problem of how to domesticate the marvelous also features in one of the strangest of Perseus's deeds, and indeed one of the strangest metamorphoses in the entire poem, the creation of coral. After dispatching the sea monster, Perseus stoops to wash his hands, and "lest the hard sand harm the snaky head," he makes a soft bed for it by heaping up seaweed. But, of course, the seaweed absorbs the potency of the Gorgon and hardens into coral. The sea nymphs repeat this miracle (*factum mirabile*, 4.747) and cast the seeds of the transformed seaweed back into the water. So far a fairly generic etiological metamorphosis: some mythological event in the past offers an explanation for a feature of the natural world. But the distinctive point about coral is that the feature its miraculous origins explain is precisely the capacity for metamorphosis. Coral really does turn hard when it moves from the ocean into the air. These few lines then describe an iteration of metamorphosis itself that takes it from a single miraculous event performed in the past by a son of Jupiter, via the mediation of sea nymphs, to an empirical "hard fact" of natural science. It describes how the miraculous enters everyday experience: the plant turns to stone as it is lifted from one realm to the other, from sea to air.[58]

To demonstrate how Ovid's larger treatment of Perseus shows the instability of these translations from the marvelous to the real, we can examine the battle with the sea monster itself, turning first to show how, in Ovid's telling, this mythical victory at the edge of the earth takes on the recognizable form of a contemporary event, a naval spectacle. But if Ovid's text here gestures toward becoming real, it simultaneously exposes how much the glorification of Augustus relies on reconverting the visible to the miraculous. Among the most remarkable moments in this extraordinary combat is the ending, when the shores ring with applause and the sound goes up to the homes of the gods (4.735–36). For though we had been aware of the presence of Andromeda and her parents, we suddenly realize that an entire crowd has been watching this event from the shore. Within the narrative, this conversion to spectacle further enhances Perseus's glory, for unlike the killing of the Gorgon, which is apprehended only through a verbal report and is often disbelieved, this event is broadcast to an audience that measures the vertical dimensions of the cosmos at the very moment it occurs. But the presence of spectators within the narrative has the potential to change dramatically the terms

---

[58] The role of the sea nymphs here may make us think of the mutual miracle that begins Catullus 64, as the nymphs wonder at the ship, themselves emerging from sea to air. For a different reading of the passage, stressing how even the natural phenomenon of coral defies belief, see Klein 2009.197–98.

within which a contemporary audience reads the scene by assimilating it precisely to the kind of spectacle they might have seen at a *naumachia* or in an elaborate *venatio*. In this latter case, the coincidence between image and event experienced within the narrative begins to pull apart, for such spectacles were not, or not only, memorable in themselves; they also connoted or represented something else. Thus, the great *naumachia* put on by Augustus in which a Greek fleet faced off against the Persians, as it represents this distant historical reality, pretty transparently figures the battle of Actium as well, at which Augustus himself led the West to triumph over the East.[59]

The symbolic representations of victory in the games, though, could not match the kind of fantasy that was possible in other forms of depiction, above all literary description. Thus, the most famous poetic account of the battle of Actium, which struggles in turn to be made a real presence through its vivid ecphrastic context, diametrically reverses the properties of Ovid's description here (*Aen.* 8.671–713). There a historical event is converted to a mythic one: the geopolitical connotations of the battle, the triumph of West over East, and civilization over disorder, are realized through allegory. The bestial East emerges in a series of impossible hybrid divinities whose opponent, depicted in the form of a man, was the Olympian Apollo. In Ovid's text an event that can be nothing but make believe comes to occupy the apprehensible form of a spectacle and, by doing so, perhaps offers itself as a gloss on the real battle won by the emperor. If this connection is made, and there are other incentives to read the scene this way, not least its initial resemblance to the *Aeneid*'s boat race that with its bestialized combatants and moment of epiphany itself prefigures the Actian scene, then we might imagine that precisely as Perseus becomes more believable, he does so at the expense of the emperor, whose claims for his accomplishments are revealed in fully fantastical form. Or, for a believing audience, the miraculous victory of Perseus over the unreal, so to speak, realizes precisely the triumph of Augustus—making us see history in this miraculous guise.

This implicit comparison to spectacle concludes an episode that has already given special attention to the relation between being and seeming and the correlation between literary impressions, real perceptions, and public display. For the entire first half of the contest is visualized through

[59] One clue to connect this scene in the *Metamorphoses* with this event in particular comes from the way Ovid in the *Ars* describes that very spectacle: *Quid, modo cum belli navalis imagine Caesar / Persidas induxit Cecropiasque rates? (AA* 1.171–72). The two sides represent respectively the "sons of Perseus" and the descendants of a king who was half serpent, and the whole is "an image of naval warfare." The occasion for this *naumachia* was again the dedication of the temple of Mars Ultor, in 2 BCE, On the ideological significance of *naumachiae* in general, see Coleman 1993.

an elaborate and dense network of similes that define the protagonists and the space within which they fight:

> *Ecce, velut navis praefixo concita rostro*
> *sulcat aquas iuvenum sudantibus acta lacertis,*
> *sic fera dimotis inpulsu pectoris undis;*
> *tantum aberat scopulis, quantum Balearica torto*
> *funda potest plumbo medii transmittere caeli,*
> *cum subito iuvenis pedibus tellure repulsa*
> *arduus in nubes abiit. ut in aequore summo*
> *umbra viri visa est, visa fera saevit in umbra,*
> *utque Iovis praepes, vacuo cum vidit in arvo*
> *praebentem Phoebo liventia terga draconem,*
> *occupat aversum, neu saeva retorqueat ora,*
> *squamigeris avidos figit cervicibus ungues,*
> *sic celeri missus praeceps per inane volatu*
> *terga ferae pressit dextroque frementis in armo*
> *Inachides ferrum curvo tenus abdidit hamo.*
> *vulnere laesa gravi modo se sublimis in auras*
> *attollit, modo subdit aquis, modo more ferocis*
> *versat apri, quem turba canum circumsona terret.*
>
> (4.706–23)

Look, as a speeding ship with a sharp beak plows the waters driven by the sweating arms of young men, so does the beast, the waves parted by the force of its breast. When it was as far from the rocks as a Balaeric sling can traverse the heavens with its torqued lead bolt, suddenly the youth pushing off from the earth with his feet, leapt straight up into the clouds. When [as] the reflection/shadow of the [a] man appeared on the surface of the sea, the beast raged against the reflection. And as the bird of Jupiter, when it sees in a lonely field a serpent offering its blue back to the sun, seizes it from behind, lest it twist back its savage mouth, and plants his quick talons in his scaly neck, so Perseus driven headlong through the void in his swift flight attacked the beast's back and as it raged sunk his sword for the length of its hooked blade in its right shoulder. Damaged by this serious wound, the beast now raised itself into the air and now sunk back into the water and now turned about like a fierce boar whom the bellowing pack of hounds terrifies.

Appropriately for the coming evocation of a *naumachia*, the approaching monster is like a battleship; he is as far off as the range of a Balearic sling, and Perseus, in flying up on his winged sandals, is like the eagle of Jupiter pouncing on a serpent sunning itself. Finally the wounded creature thrashes like a fierce boar surrounded by dogs. While similes always play on the tension between likeness and difference of tenor and vehicle, the relationships between description and event in this passage simultaneously veer toward an anachronism that seems to haul the battle into the present day (especially the designation of the sling bolt as Balearic), and a closeness of reference that makes it unclear where simile ceases to be mere description. In a coralline metamorphosis, image becomes reality, and reality merges back into image. The first word of the description, *ecce*, already introduces this tension. For by compelling his audience to behold, the narrator at once pulls them back into the mythical world of Perseus and makes that world accessible to them in the form of spectacle. But what one is compelled to behold is not immediately that remarkable. It looks like a ship, not a monster. And if the final gesture toward spectacle summons up the viewing context of a *naumachia*, glossing a battle that aspired to being described as myth, then it is appropriate that the text's representation of the monster should contain an added twist. Because the image of the ship in the simile looks in turn like a monster, it possesses a *rostrum* attached to the front,[60] it leaves an incongruous "furrow" in the sea, and it is propelled by sweaty human arms. An extreme reading of this shifting image, then, would not so much offer a way of apprehending the strange through the familiar but expose the beast as a sham deception—just a ship with a fake snout stuck on (*praefixo*).[61]

If the first simile has the effect of defamiliarizing the real by opening the distance between tenor and vehicle, the second major simile, the eagle and the serpent, creates an impression of sameness that seems to make Ovid's representational figure an ideal medium for describing a distant reality. And the descriptive validity of this particular image is important because of the role it too played in contemporary depictions of empire. For Horace had used virtually the same simile in one of his most explicitly panegyric odes to describe Augustus's stepson Drusus's defeat of an Alpine tribe (C. 4.4.1–12). Drusus's resemblance to the eagle, though, is as nothing to Perseus's, who not only belongs to Jupiter directly through the fact of paternity but also actually has wings. The scales of the serpent aptly recall the scales on the monster's own back, and even the curved talons of the eagle mirror the hooked sword of Perseus.[62] Here again we seem to anticipate the metamorphosis of coral as the natural simply takes

---

[60] While it is metaphorically applied to the prow of a ship, *rostrum* originally designates the snout of an animal; see *OLD s.v.* § 1. For other monstrous ships in epic, see Hardie 1987.

[61] On the assimilation of ship and beast here, see now Barchiesi 2007.340.

[62] Indeed, though there is no semantic or etymological connection, the word for talon, *unguis*, itself looks like the adjective for curved, *uncus*, that had previously modified Perseus sword (and appeared in the same metrical position, 4.666).

over from the miraculous. In terms of its effects on the reading of impe-rial representations, perhaps this hyper-naturalization mimics a tendency in contemporary readings of Horace to see the serpent and the eagle less as amplification than as bestialization.

The potential confusion of image and reality raised by these curious similes figures in the action of the episode as well. After Perseus has sprung into the air, his reflection appears on the surface of the water, and the deceived monster makes a lunge at this reflection (*ut in aequore summo umbra viri visa est, visa fera saevit in umbra*).[63] But is the re-flection in fact merely a simile? Although the flow of the sentence ulti-mately reveals that *ut* much more probably marks a temporal clause, the tantalizing false impression of a simile never quite recedes, pulling the beast itself—which is, after all, imaginary—into the illusionistic world, trapping it "within the seen image" by making it "like the reflection of a man seen on the surface of the water." And one strong temptation to do so—despite the fact that it is also easily explicable as a common Ovidian epanalepsis[64]—comes from the verbal "mirroring" of the very words for reflection, *umbra ... visa*, chiastically arranged in line 713.[65] The twin realms of sea and sky seem to offer transforming reflections of one an-other, with no clear sense of where the original lies. Aptly, it is on the sea's surface, the point where coral too miraculously takes on its everyday hardness, that we become unable to separate reflection from reality. And indeed elements of the sea threaten to drag Perseus down, as the frothing monster sprays him with water and gore. At this point though, the play of images abruptly ceases, and we seem to move on to the solid ground of pure narrative. Appropriately this escape onto the literal rock, which at once coincides with the abandonment of his own miraculous ability to fly and makes possible his defeat of the miraculous beast, happens when

---

[63] A detail of Ovid's account noted by Vernant 1991.136, n. 46, in his discussion of the importance of reflection in the Medusa myth. I continue to prefer the ablative forms of *visa* and *umbra* over the accusative variants, though the latter have now been adopted in Tarrant's OCT. There is no doubt that the accusative is more appropriate if *saevit in* means simply attack, and the corruption into the ablative would be all too easy to explain. On the other hand, the simplification of the grammar comes at the expense of the kind of verbal game that we have seen Ovid play in describing Procne as "totally absorbed in the image of pain," *poenaeque in imagine tota est*. If the accusative is to be retained, the effect I describe here still operates through the ambiguity of the *ut* as temporal or comparative.

[64] Cf., e.g., 1.590–91.

[65] Though appropriately this is a purely visual effect—specifically a reflection, not an echo—because the quantity of the *a*'s is different in the two phrases and the ending of the first *visa* is prodelided with *est*.

For an excellent analysis of the effect of these lines, though one that concedes a little more control to Perseus than I would, see Barkan 1986.54. He reads Perseus's conscious manipulation of shadow and light to trick the monster as another example of how the hero wins his victory because of his mastery of metamorphosis.

Perseus himself has come to "doubt" his own wings (*credere*, 4.731). Yet, equally appropriately, this rock is not quite all there; it only partly and temporarily emerges from the surrounding sea.[66]

Having gotten our hero back to dry land, let me summarize the argument to this point. The connection I suggest between Perseus's production of images and Augustus's leads to a focus on two aspects of imperial self-representation. First, Perseus's own ability to produce images at the moment he obtains victory offers an ideal that makes clear by contrast the "space," both temporal and interpretative, that inevitably opens up between event and representation. Another problem with the credibility of images illuminated by the episode comes from a desire to magnify human and historical accomplishments by pushing them toward the miraculous and divine. Here twin dangers arise: the fantastic can come to seem banal—a sea monster emerging as a ship with a fake snout; or the real can seem incredible. Having concentrated first on the production of images and then, through a scene full of contrasting spectatorial perspectives, on their reception, I intend to continue that trajectory by analyzing how Ovid links the ambiguity of images to problems of recognition and identification similar to those that emerge in his own fiction. While the reading to this point has fit in with my emphasis on how the poet places his text in dialogue with other forms of imperial discourse, from here on I will be examining how the analogies between text and image give his poem access to the socializing powers of art.

The first step in this movement from spectacle back to fiction is a further examination of the figure of Medusa. She is at once the unbelievable creature, only present through reported narration, who provokes disbelief and the source of the power that provides proof in the form of images that seem to allow no room for incredulity. Yet the intervention of Medusa and the role of sculptural figures in the episode give a new and deeper significance to the issue of disbelief than emerged from the discussion in the first chapter, one that relates it to political realities at least as directly as the confrontation with Augustus's credibility does. For not assenting to fictions involves much more than an unwillingness to credit the authority on which they depend; it relies above all on a sense of difference between the viewing subject and the object seen. And here, although Ovid seemingly places the figure of Medusa in the narratological background of his account, he makes the broader mythical connotations of this figure in Greek culture central to his Perseus story.

---

[66] Thanks to the transformative power of similes, Perseus's combat with the sea monster bears an extremely close relationship to a later episode in the poem where a son of Jupiter competes for a bride with a watery creature also given to shape changing, the combat between Achelous and Hercules at the beginning of book 9.

J. P. Vernant's sweeping analyses of the significance of the Gorgon unite the two crucial themes that emerge from Ovid's account of the hero's disparate adventures: the production and uncertain status of images and their transformative, disruptive ability to absorb viewers into a chain of partial reflections with the power to alienate them from themselves. The face of the Gorgon itself, according to Vernant, provides an unaccountable mixture of different categories, at once human, divine, and bestial; beautiful and repulsive; face and genital.[67] For all its strangeness, gazing at this image becomes a process of recognition and of possession simultaneously, as the viewer not only sees himself as Medusa but sees as Medusa, thanks to the Gorgon's distinctive frontal orientation, its capacity to become the face in the mirror. Vernant thus glosses the experience of looking on the Gorgon by comparison with the mirror in the shrine of the goddess Despoina at Lycosura in Arcadia; when you looked in the mirror, you saw the images of the gods with great clarity, but your own image became blurred. The gaze of the Gorgon fascinates because by recognizing it as a reflection, you see yourself become an image; ultimately for Vernant it is a view of one's own mortality. And each person who has gazed at the face of the Gorgon becomes a new wondrous image, able to freeze and transform new viewers in turn, sentencing them to death as well, as it will turn out in Ovid's treatment of Medusa's commutative powers. For the purposes of my own argument here, the figure of Medusa suggests a further link between the potentially deforming processes of spectacle described in chapter 4 and the role of visual representations within Ovid's poem. One larger structural function of the Perseus episode within the work is to establish just such a connection, for his adventures link Ovid's Theban cycle, with its emphasis on the social and personal effects of reflection and recognition, to the focus on representation, verbal and visual, that extends from the song of the Muses in book 5 through the tapestry contest and the image of Niobe in book 6.

We might also note a further appearance of Medusa at the juncture between the Perseus story and the following panel of episodes delimiting the powers of art that establishes a special connection between the Gorgon and specifically literary representation of the sort Ovid practices. For Ovid makes the Medusa the grandmother of poetry. As Minerva arrives on Mount Helicon, the home of the Muses, the reason she gives for her visit is a desire to see the new fountain, the Hippocrene, so often figured as the source of poetic inspiration, "which the hard hoof of the Medusan flier has broken open" (*dura Medusaei quem praepetis ungula rupit*, 5.257). The next line is equally important: "I wanted to see the

[67] See esp. Vernant 1991.137.

marvelous deed" (*volui mirabile factum / cernere*, 5.258–59). Again Medusa, as "hardener" presides over the transition from the verbal to the visual (*fama ~ cernere*) and from the marvelous (*mirabile*) to the actual (*factum*).[68]

Having dealt with the motif of reflection in the Perseus episode largely in terms of the problem of representational accuracy, of whether images actually reflect what they represent, now I will show how, within the story, reflection acts to break down the distance between viewer and viewed. The most obvious example of this transformative power comes in what at first seems a jarring, ironic fashion, drawing attention, like so many similar touches in the poem, away from the mythical content to the authorial voice behind it.[69] As Perseus first catches sight of Andromeda, he "would have thought" that she was a marble statue (if she had not moved), and as a result of this misapprehension "he stands in wonder [*stupet*] and, captured by the image of her beauty, almost forgets to beat his wings" (4.676–77). Andromeda is not only herself a "statue" but threatens to freeze Perseus in his turn, with fatal consequences for the flying hero. A key word in this account of reciprocal petrification is "almost." This is not the actual story of Perseus's winged encounter with a statue-making female but, thanks to Ovid's language, seems close to it. He has substituted the erotic register of love poetry for the epic exploit anticipated, and Perseus wills the same transformation in his first address to her: "O worthy not of these [real] chains, but of the [figurative] chains by which desirous lovers are joined together" (another incidence, following the Atlas story, of Perseus's converting literal to figurative, and vice versa—and a pretty tactless comment under the circumstances).[70]

The next place where the theme emerges comes in the account of the battle in Cepheus's palace, though before the actual statue making begins. Here the figurative language of love used in the Andromeda passage begins to assume dimensions that are at once more real and more tragic and so prepare for the final reappearance of the treatment of visual reflection in the account of actual images. The first of Perseus's victims is the Indian boy Athis, whose death, like that of Vergil's Euryalus, is seen by his lover Lycabas (*vidit*, 5.60). Lycabas in turn challenges Perseus, shoots an arrow at him that sticks in the folds of his garment, and is cut down by the hero's hooked sword, "already made conspicuous [*spectatam*, 5.69] by the slaughter of Medusa." "Now dying he looked around for Athis with eyes already swimming in darkness." The fatal sight of the beloved, which makes the viewer Lycabas as dead as what he gazes upon, is enmeshed

---

[68] For a masterful discussion of these lines, see Hinds 1987a.3–24.

[69] Acutely analyzed in these terms by Anderson 1996.484.

[70] On the humor of the scene, see Solodow 1988.103–4.

in a number of the episode's thematic preoccupations. Again, the figure of the Medusa herself is seen but, appropriately, indirectly. We expect perhaps that Perseus will use the fatal head already at this stage in the combat, but again this expectation is deferred. Instead, he uses the sword that "was seen" in that episode, making his victim in that sense like the Gorgon herself. The emergence of the Gorgon's head, as we saw, was linked to the establishment of "hard evidence" so to speak, of Perseus's miraculous feat. We are not quite at that final stage of the "miracle," but already the interest in truth and fiction emerges; for Lycabas the viewer here is "no concealer of true love" (*veri non dissimulator amoris*, 5.61), with the word *veri* thrown into emphasis by hyperbaton and by its position at the caesura of the line. And the most important Gorgonic element in the passage, the figure whose gaze is as fatal for Lycabas as Perseus's hooked sword, is presented in ways that suggest that it has already become a work of art. For Athis's beauty receives no less than eight lines of description. It begins as though it were an ecphrasis, with the verb *erat*, and the account of his birth beneath the waves of the glassy stream of his nymph mother relates him to the world of images and reflections (as well, again, to fictions, for that is where she is believed—*creditur*, 5.49—to have born him). As the word *cultus* (5.49) doubly suggests, the adornment that magnifies his beauty involves the application of art to his final form—doubly, for statues too could receive the kind of anointing and decoration described in the context of religious cult.[71]

Finally comes the most direct example of the contagion of viewing in the episode, which now involves not someone "like" a statue but the real thing. Alone of the companions of Perseus, one Aconteus catches sight of the Gorgon's head and is turned to stone (5.200–202). His enemy, Astyages, believes that he is still alive and hacks at the stone with his sword, before he himself in his amazement turns to a statue that still seems to be alive. What is most striking about the description of Astyages here is that, while presumably he turned to stone because he saw the Gorgon's head, the efficacy of that magic token is never mentioned. Rather Astyages seems to absorb the stony nature (*naturam*, 5.205) directly from the image that he sees. And as Hardie has pointed out, the deception he experiences replicates a basic aspect of the deception practiced by all realist images—he thinks the statue is alive.[72] To reintroduce the terms of

[71] The *monilia* (5.52) anticipate those with which Pygmalion will dress his statue.

[72] Hardie 2002c.180 in fact argues that Astyages' misperception, characteristic of the naive viewer, forms the opposite of "the knowing credulity" experienced by the "normal" viewer of images, who is "amazed that what he knows to be marble seems to be flesh." I suggest that as in the Pygmalion story, Ovid's narrative does not allow the reader to rest comfortably in this position of knowing superiority but makes it possible even for experienced viewers to wonder at the metamorphosis wrought by the text in bringing representations

my own argument, his mistake is to see a likeness to himself in something whose representation makes it fundamentally different, and the likeness that he imagines comes to be realized but with destructive consequences for himself rather than his opponent. So too Phineus, at the moment before he also becomes stone, will recognize his own (*agnoscitque suos*, 5.212) among shapes that are actually different (*diversa*, 5.211). The dangers of reflection Vernant describes as operative in the Medusa's head are at work here as well even without her direct intervention.

Before I discuss the significance of the clearly tracked shift from erotic to martial associations of viewing, it is important to stress that, as in the Pygmalion episode, encounters with images here take place against a sacrificial backdrop that reproduces the reflexivity between viewer and viewed we have seen emphasized in the problems of recognition created by stone figures. In between the killing of the monster and the beginning of the tragic wedding banquet, Perseus erects three altars to the gods who aided him. He sacrifices a cow to Minerva, a calf to Mercury, and a bull to Jupiter (4.755–56). A representational likeness between god and victim was absolutely orthodox in Roman religion—so much so, perhaps, that it ought to go without saying here. The exchange, through resemblance, between top and bottom, sets the stage for an interest in sacrificial substitution throughout the battle narrative. Almost the first action in the fight sees Phineus ducking behind an altar to take refuge from Perseus's spear. Paetalus, struck in the neck with a club, dies "like a sacrificed bull" (5.122). Most horrible of all, Emathion, "a worshiper of fairness and fearful of the gods" (5.100), who, being too old to fight, rails against the weapons of the impious brawlers, is cut down as he too grabs an altar. His head falls into the flame itself with the tongue still cursing its killer (5.105–6).

The combat in book 5 offers a concentrated pastiche of all that is most gruesome in epic violence, and in that regard a fairly high incidence of sacrificial pollution is to be expected; it complements the motif of the corrupted feast as a classic topos of impious warfare. However, if we are willing to lend a little more weight to the sacrificial aspects of the combat, regarding them from the perspective of the sociological dynamics of sacrifice rather than primarily as a set of literary conventions, such imagery both accentuates the distinctive nature of this combat and links it to the interest in representation that we have been following. Not only is the battle between Phineus and Perseus a classic Girardian example of mimetic rivalry, the struggle between two figures for a single good, which in this case goes together with occupying the same role in society, as hus-

---

to life at the same time as Astyages replicates the innocent who sees only the represented, not the representation.

band of Andromeda and presumably Cepheus's heir; it also itself constitutes the imitative repetition of another conflict whose resolution should have been decisive.[73] For Perseus has already won Andromeda from one bloodthirsty, boundary-crossing suitor, and, as Cepheus points out, his defeat of that monster simultaneously checkmated Phineus's claims through his own failure to redeem her (5.16–25). The recursion of violence in the episode, especially when translated from the reasonably clear-cut victory of the celestial superhuman over the aqueous subhuman,[74] to a domestic combat that breaks apart essential human rituals signals what Girard[75] terms a sacrificial crisis, a moment when, because of the absence of differentiation, a society plummets into a chaos of meaningless and unstoppable killing. Sacrificial practice works to stop this cycle through a universally recognized act of substitution, where the animal victim stands in for one of the combatants, making it possible for the entire society to unite in the symbolic killing of a figure agreed to be the unique cause of violence in a guise that, because no longer human, invites no further retribution. In Girard's reading then, both the beginning and end of internal violence in a society depend on complex acts of recognition, on getting the right balance between seeing sameness and difference between perpetrator and victim. Too much sameness makes the victim a potential surrogate for the viewer and draws him or her toward a revenge that provokes further revenge and, in so doing, goes on erasing the boundaries between legitimacy and illegitimacy.

Scenes where the viewer gazing at a statue becomes what he sees, like Astyages' reaction to Aconteus, or Phineus's recognition of his companions at the moment of his own petrification (5.212), thus link the magical aspects of the Medusa's gaze to a very real and powerful force for social unification or dissolution. This reflective capacity of violence, where death uncannily doubles back on its own perpetrator or draws in new combatants through substitution or identification with a victim, recurs throughout the episode. When Phineus first dodges behind the altar, a substitute dies in his place, Rhoeteus, inadvertently struck down by Perseus's blow (5.38–40). Motifs of resemblance and substitution also color

[73] On "mimetic desire," see Girard 1977.143–68, esp. 145. For the sacrifice as a mimesis of an earlier act of violence that aims to a cycle of infinitely repeatable revenge, see Girard 1977, esp. 12–13, 26.

[74] I say "reasonably," because Ovid's narrative does not obscure a certain monstrous aspect to Perseus, whose tempting of the threshold of the sky (4.700) reflects the sea beast's lust for a human bride. And that beast, too, is an agent of Ammon (4.671), a figure who both is and is not the same as Perseus's Olympian father. All this shortly after Cadmus has just fulfilled the prophecy of book 3 by becoming a serpent (4.563–603).

[75] On sacrificial crisis, see Girard 1977. 39–67. For the productive application of this model to the situations of Roman epic, especially the *Aeneid*, see Bandera 1981.

the death of Lycabas, who makes what from the *Iliad* on was a classic error in picking up the weapon of the dead Athis and so shares his fate. That Aconteus should be the "one" (*unus*, 5.200) among Perseus's men to view the Medusa recalls the *Aeneid*'s emphasis on the one victim, like Palinurus, who gives his life for the many. And, in one of the strangest encounters anywhere in ancient epic, another substitute who would not have been drawn into the battle, Idas, is hit by Phineus's javelin instead of Perseus's (5.89–96). What begins as an echo of the death of Rhoeteus takes on a further reflexive twist as Idas, with an appropriately Gorgonic stare, threatens to settle the score by hurling the same weapon back at Phineus. This attempt to establish difference through substitution, where Phineus by feeling the force of Idas's blow in comparison to his own would "learn what an enemy [he] had made" (5.93–94), collapses in futility as Idas himself experiences the fate that he had predicted for his opponent, dying of his own wound in the very act of casting Phineus's weapon back at its owner. A specific link between such mimetic violence and the reflexive power of images comes in the account of Echemmon's demise (5.169–73). Echemmon, like Perseus and Phineus, misses his intended victim and strikes something else instead, not a human combatant but a column, a gesture that in turn looks forward to Astyages's attack on the stone Aconteus. A shard of the sword bounces back and wounds him in the throat, anticipating perhaps the stupefaction that Astyages himself will experience when he hears the echo from his marble victim. But the shard does not kill Echemmon; so Perseus has to finish him off, with the hooked sword of Mercury, making him a Gorgon in death.

These corrosive effects of a process of recognition that, by failing to establish difference, collapses crucial distinctions between self and other—a phenomenon we have now found at the mythical level in the figure of Medusa, who during this battle herself changes from enemy to ally,[76] and acted out in the account of the destructive consequences of violence in the episode—have implications not just for the viewers within the story but for the reader's of Ovid's text. For Ovid manipulates literary allusions in the passage, especially to Vergil's epic, to challenge the reader's own sense of distance from what he is reading. Many scholars have recognized how closely different aspects of the Perseus story echo points in the *Aeneid*. These echoes cluster around two phases of the narrative: obviously, the battle in Cepheus's palace replays the essential contest of the poem's second half after a foreign suitor arrives to claim a king's daughter.[77] The

---

[76] *auxilium ... ab hoste petam* (5.178–79).

[77] For a full treatment of the epic echoes in this section, see Keith 2002.240–45, with further bibliography. On the ending of the Perseus tale and the *Aeneid*, see Hardie 2002c.179; and on the use of the second half of Vergil's poem, Anderson 1996, esp. 498–519, who acutely notes references to and contrasts with the situation in *Aeneid* 7–12.

long deferral of the battle between Perseus and Phineus, and the latter's final act of supplication, sharpen the parallelism as well as further pointing to the patterns of sacrifice and substitution, whose importance in the conclusion of Vergil's poem has been much explored. The second group of references summons up the first books of the *Aeneid*, describing Aeneas's interactions with Dido in Carthage: as Hardie has suggested, Perseus's first perception of Andromeda as a statue coming to life recalls the way the Trojan hero sees Dido initially as an extension of the sculptures on the temple of Juno.[78] The African setting and a narrative pattern that puts the best-known exploit of the hero in his own mouth in the form of a personal reminiscence delivered at a banquet also encourage reading Perseus's story against the first four books of the *Aeneid*.

This crude map suffices to suggest how Ovid's deployment of Vergilian allusions in the episode replicate the cognitive challenges we have been tracing. First there is the simple process of comparing and contrasting the two texts. For Anderson has observed a number of crucial ways in which none of the figures at Cepheus's palace lives up to his Vergilian prototype. And figuring out the pattern of Ovid's allusions raises its own set of challenges. One could for example focus on the broadly progressive trend in the narrative, with Perseus too living through a complete mini-*Aeneid* from book 1 to book 12. And yet many elements of his story challenge such a reading. Most strikingly, Perseus never moves on from Africa as Aeneas has to in order for book 12 to be reached.[79] Rather his battle for preeminence takes place in this, from one perspective, much more compromising setting, as though we were reading an *Aeneid* where the love of Dido wins out, a difference that also has implications for understanding the Actian preechoes in the battle with the sea monster. And if we remember that Perseus finally does leave Africa to return home, this too significantly contrasts with the movement of the *Aeneid*, where, of course, the hero cannot and must not make such a return.[80]

But the act of plotting Ovid's Perseus against Vergil's Aeneas also allows the reader to revisit the strategies the earlier poet used to delineate the development of a distinctively Roman national identity. For as Ovid's reader cannot tell whether to place the hero in Africa or Latium, so too Vergil's text tempts the reader to see the arrival at Latinus's court as a replaying of the poem's first books. Ovid thus borrows and further complicates the process of differentiating between the special destiny of Rome and the various foreign roads-not-taken that the *Aeneid* sets in

[78] Hardie 2002c.183–86.

[79] The first Persean tableau, showing a winged figure's encounter with Atlas, makes the reader particularly aware of this difference, for it was against such a backdrop that Mercury descends to spur Aeneas's desertion of Dido (*Aen.* 4.246–51).

[80] See the essential discussion of circularity in the *Aeneid* by Quint 1993.50–96.

motion. Again there is a figure for this confusion of forward motion and circularity in the story of his adventures that the hero tells at an African banquet—one of the most Vergilian moments in the episode and one that has at its focus the face of Medusa herself. Perseus's tale of his encounter with the Gorgon is framed by potential anachronisms, nothing flamboyant like Ovid's calling the Milky Way the Palatine of the gods, but suggestions to the Ovidian audience that the conditions created by the narrative itself have been projected back to its beginnings, so that the world of Perseus's experience and the world after Perseus fold back in to one another. Thus, Perseus begins his account, as Ovid does, with a reference to Atlas (4.772). But he describes Atlas as a geographic feature rather than an anthropomorphic figure as he should have been before Perseus made a mountain of him. So too Perseus ends (again predictive of the larger tale as Ovid frames it) with Minerva, already sporting Medusa's head on her aegis, although the hero clearly still has possession of it (4.799–804).[81] These temporal distortions gain their disorienting effect by blurring the contrast between a mythical space of flying heroes defeating monstrous opponents and the familiar world where Atlas names a mountain chain and the goddess Minerva was depicted with a Gorgon's head. When Perseus tells of his first glimpse of the island of the Gorgons, he describes seeing "statues of men and beasts here and there among the fields and roads" (4.779–80). Beyond the curious similarity to a contemporary Roman garden landscape, which might well contain such *simulacra*,[82] the setting, with a transposition indoors, and minus the wild animals, anticipates where we will leave Perseus at the end of the very conflict into which the narrative directly leads, a room filled with the stone likenesses of two hundred men.

And while neither Ovid's reader nor the internal audience of feasting Ethiopians can have any foreknowledge that Perseus's adventures have brought him full circle to the point where they began, the next section of his prehistory, in which he answers the question of why Medusa alone of her sisters had snakes intertwined among her hair, might have recalled to them a familiar moment from their own recent past (4.790–804). Medusa too emerges as a subject, rather than simply an agent, of metamorphosis. She was originally not unseeable but beautiful, and her hair was the part most worthy of being seen. So desirable was she that the god Neptune raped her in the temple of Minerva, and in punishment for this violation, for which she was hardly responsible, the goddess turned her hair to serpents. This etiology, and Ovid makes Perseus use all the narra-

---

[81] Both anachronisms are noted by Kenney 1986.402 and by Anderson 1997.402–6, and discussed by Bömer 1976.222 and 227.

[82] A comparison developed by Kuttner 2002.

tological and generic markers deployed to juxtapose present and distant past in that genre, allows its audiences to see, so to speak, the quintessential face of the monstrous other as the same as that of their own princess Andromeda, another maiden subject to violation by a creature of the sea who, while being punished for something for which she bears no particular culpability, is especially concerned to redeem her own reputation through narrative.[83]

The Gorgon's head, here perhaps most terrifying because it is not monstrous, sits at the core of a series of internal representations and, like the similarly situated syrinx discussed in the first chapter, contains the power to collapse the distinction between the fictive and the real, bridging the distance between the experience of the internal Ethiopian audience and Ovid's Roman audience, both of whom are looking into a narrative mirror where the familiar seems strange and a tale about an "other" suddenly approximates the realities of the present. As we have seen, this effect of narrative also becomes disquietingly familiar if it is read as itself miming representational strategies and social practices central to the maintenance of the contemporary Roman state—self-expression through the language of sculpture and the affirmation of unity and legitimacy through sacrificial ritual, both of which, as representations, open the door to a similar recognition of the self in the face of the conquered that can fragment as well as unify. It is no accident perhaps that, just after the appearance of this Gorgon's head in Perseus's account, the festival celebrating union (*coniugalia*, 5.3) turns to internal violence, and the distinctively human ritual of the wedding reverts to the bestial (*festa* 5.3 ~ *fera* 5.4).[84]

It is time now to step back from the narrative to ask about the consequences of Ovid's exposure of what happens when stories come true for understanding the political role of his own fiction and, more specifically, his poem's evocation of sculpture. First, it is remarkable how the dynamic of recognizing figures represented in statuary traced in Ovid's narrative of the battle in Cepheus's palace runs precisely counter to the

---

[83] Andromeda overcomes her modesty and tells Perseus her identity "lest she seem unwilling to confess faults that were her own" (4.685–86). It is also no accident, I think, that the first detail that transforms Andromeda in Perseus's eyes from a statue back to a maiden is the breeze moving her hair (4.673).

We may also note that Ovid's version of Medusa's early history, with its temple setting and emphasis on the responsibility of Neptune for the action (*vitiasse*, which can connote a ritual lapse is here uniquely used as a metaphor for rape in the poem), adds a sacrificial aspect to both figures, who suffer as substitutes for others. In the case of Andromeda, who is distanced from the crime of her mother, the punishment seems unjust and rallies viewers to her defense.

[84] The simile comparing the disruption of the banquet to a stormy sea subtly signals this link between representation and present by recalling the figure of Neptune as the violator of Medusa within Perseus's story.

claim Perseus, the internal commemorator, makes for it. Within the context of the battle, petrifaction is above all a way of enforcing a distinction between friend and enemy. "If any friend is present, let him look away," is Perseus's injunction as he lifts the Gorgon's head (5.179–80). Only foes, this implies, should turn to *simulacra*, and vice versa. As Perseus's own success and fame require these inherently ambiguous artifacts to be read in particular ways by particular audiences—as recognizable likenesses of themselves perhaps by other potential opponents, who will thus be warned of their own fate if they challenge Perseus, as commemorations of Perseus's triumph over violators of justice by everyone else—so too he relies on a particular reading of what it means to realize fictions. For the hero Perseus on the one hand owes his prestige to bringing the fabulous into the present, while on the other denying that it is a *fabula*, a lie, or a story. The kind of disorientation that results not from framing the marvelous in a solid bulwark of normality but rather from allowing the unbelievable to reshape the present, or to make the fabulous recognizable as an aspect of that normal reality, plays no part in his scheme. Thus, the Medusa he defeats is not an innocent woman but a terrifying monster, and, in a different sense, the sea creature that he defeats is not a ship with a snout attached. An anti-Persean reading of his life story can be generated either by an excess of distance—those deeds are not true but are indeed fictions—or by an excess of identification with the fictional.[85]

We can see one aspect of how monumentalization and the control of what is believed work together by looking more closely at the fate of one of Perseus's stone foes, and this will be a bridge back to the original starting point of this discussion, the reading the poem offers of artistic monuments in the public sphere. The third of Phineus's allies to fall victim to the Gorgon's head is the Egyptian Nileus, "who falsely claimed that he was the son of the sevenfold Nile and had even embossed seven rivers on his shield, partly of silver and partly of gold. 'Behold,' he said, 'the origins of our race! You will bear great consolation for your death to the silent shades to have fallen at the hands of such a great man'—the last part of his words were suppressed in mid-utterance, and you would

---

[85] A historical example of such an identification with the marvelous comes in the curious crowd response to Pompey's staging of the killing of elephants in his games of 55 BCE. Not, obviously, a mythical creature on a par with Gorgons, elephants were nevertheless important as a symbol of the conquest of far-off Asia brought before the eyes of an audience of Romans. When these elephants were killed in the arena, their groans are said to have sounded so human that the crowd was frightened and appalled by their death and so turned against Pompey (Plin. *HN* 8.21). In addition to the agency of sympathy at work here, perhaps in taking on a human voice, so to speak, Pompey's creatures had become too fabulous for their master's own good.

think that his open mouth wished to speak, but it offered a path for no words" (5.188–94). Of all Perseus's foes, Nileus is the most like him in his attempt to fight fire with fire, to defeat one image with another image. But this is only the beginning of the resemblance between the two figures because the very image at the center of Nileus's shield not only looks like the Medusa's head with its winding rivers but in fact also stakes a claim of identity with Perseus. When Nileus speaks of "our" race, this is no mere poetic plural, for Perseus too, the Danaeius hero, as he is called in the first line of the fifth book, is also very much a Danaid hero, a literal son of Egypt, descendant of the only Danaid who did not kill her Egyptian bridegroom on her own wedding night. And Perseus now plays out the mirror image of that scene as a suitor who is foreign because he is a Greek in an African land. The author's almost italicized insistence that Nileus's story is a fiction (with *ementitus*, 5.188, emphasized by enjambment), while superficially rebutting the Egyptian's own claims to superiority over Perseus, simultaneously suggests a more dangerous potential for assimilating hero and victim. It is important to note that Nileus too, like any challenger was interested in creating a difference between Perseus and himself, and that difference has to do with the quality of silence (*tacitas*, 5.191, thrown into relief by both metrical position and extreme hyperbaton). Perseus responds not with words but by turning Nileus to stone, a form of monumentalization more absolute than Nileus's not only because it emphatically shuts his mouth but also because it leaves no scope for fiction, for the representation to be anything less than what it seems to be. Beyond that, in silencing Nileus, he has won the battle for difference. It is not Perseus but his rival who suffers the fate of becoming like the image that he attempts to impose on another in a reflexive action that mimics the deflation of Idas's earlier boast. In another sense, the triumph of reality over fiction involves stopping the chain of "sacrificial" recognitions that blur the boundaries between victor and victim and so rob victory of its semantic certainty.

The defeat of Nileus also instantiates more directly than any other moment in this elaborate story the relationship between verbal and visual artifacts as we encountered it in the previous discussion of the Niobe episode. While not silenced by death, Perseus's absence of utterance contrasts dramatically with Nileus's boast; not only are deeds stronger than words, but the perfect image needs no other narrative explication. It is what it seems to be and, importantly, is nothing more than what it seems to be, not a representation conjuring up the absence/presence of Nileus but a fact in itself, a perpetual deed of Perseus. And yet when statues are viewed, their self-sufficiency vanishes. When "you" look at Nileus, you do recognize a person there, and in assenting to the idea that this is a representation, you come to believe—as one might believe a fiction—that Nileus will speak (*adapertaque velle ora loqui credas*, 5.193–94).

In actuality, then, as the episode as a whole shows, there is no such thing as a statue without text or a reality that does not conjure up some measure of fiction in the act of being viewed. Nor do texts live quite apart from monuments. In fact, the Nileus episode not only makes present internally generated images—the shield of Nileus, which is on different levels a product of both Nileus's and Ovid's artistry, and the stone figure of Nileus himself—but gains meaning from a complex network of external referents that are at once verbal and sculptural. The mixed metals of the shield, which Ovid goes out of his way to mention (5.189), perhaps recall the blazon of the most famous Roman epic shield, Aeneas's in *Aeneid* 8. At its center was another water image crafted in both silver and gold,[86] the defeat of Cleopatra at Actium, which obviously also answers the claim to Egyptian supremacy made here.[87] But the narrative reference to the Danaids simultaneously alludes to one more of that poem's most important sculptural artifacts, the belt of Pallas, the presence of which as a *monimentum* in the possession of Turnus prompts Aeneas to take revenge (*Aen.* 12.945). The importance of the belt for the Perseus scene as a whole has been briefly discussed by Hardie, who finds in Perseus's threat to Phineus that he too will be a *monumentum*, a reminder of this final moment in the *Aeneid*. Building on a claim of Michael Putnam, who notes not only that the belt of Pallas inspires action in the poem but that it and the poem depict the same thing, the deaths of young men, and in the case of Turnus a would-be bridegroom, Hardie suggests that the effect of verbal and visual image coalescing, already predicted in the *Aeneid*, is taken to a new level of reality in Ovid by the direct creation of an image, the statue of Phineus, through a narrated event.[88]

But this is only part of Ovid's rivalry with the *Aeneid* in the realization of ecphrases. First, he has integrated his echo into an episode that comments precisely on the connection between representation and violence. The role of the belt of Pallas in the *Aeneid* mirrors the importance of what we might call representational reciprocity in Ovid's battle, the danger of becoming one's own image and, in that way, coming to resemble the defeated. As Idas and Nileus see their boasts cast back on themselves, so Turnus is destined both to share the fate of his own victim, Pallas, and

---

[86] *Aurea* (*Aen.* 8.673); *argento* (*Aen.* 8.674).

[87] The river Nile itself is also featured on Aeneas's shield at 8.711–12, though anthropomorphized. Interestingly, as the image of Nileus seems to demand that one supply an imaginary utterance, so the Nile on the *Aeneid* shield is shown "crying out," *vocantem* (*Aen.* 8.712).

[88] Hardie 2002c.179, citing Putnam 1998.205.

to become like the image that he bears. And, as in Ovid, it is the representational capacity of the image, here made inseparable from its monumental value—for what it shows, a dead young man, now looks like what it reminds Aeneas of, the death of a different young man, Pallas—that opens the door to future violence.

Beyond this thematic integration into the much darker mirror of the *Aeneid* produced here, Ovid also competes with Vergil in the authenticity with which his text depicts that crucial image. The actual scene on the belt of Pallas is described as follows: a band of youths slaughtered on the very night of a wedding and bloody chambers, *una sub nocte iugali / caesa manus iuuenum foede thalamique cruenti, Aen.* 10.497–98. While the *Aeneid* does in some measure reproduce aspects of the scene, that is nothing to the closeness with which Perseus's own battle does, as is indeed appropriate given Perseus's own special connection to the events described. And if Ovid has realized in narrative the scene on Pallas's belt, at the same time, to extend Hardie's original point, he has also done without the intermediary services of Clonus, son of Eurytus, in turning the scene to art, for he has created a scene that produces its own representation.

If Ovid rivals Vergil's text in terms of both the realism and the reality of the image he offers, bringing the embossed scene to narrative life and at the same time creating artistic representations inseparable from the original, that is but one of the ways in which he approaches Vergil's poem as much as an artifact as a text. For from Perseus's first glimpse of Andromeda as statue, to the belt of Pallas, to the Shield of Aeneas, Ovid's text evokes Vergil's poem through the visual images that that poem in turn has created. In other words, Vergil's poem is entered by means of its own poetic power to generate images that count as real. And yet, in the case of the Danaid tableau, it is not just a question of whether to see Vergil's poem as image, for the Danaids, as we have seen, also existed as an actual sculptural image in Rome in the temple of Palatine Apollo; even as Ovid competes with Vergil in the vividness with which he turns poetry to stone, he is also renarrativizing the sculptures of Augustus, giving them their own capacity to speak.

What the triangulation of Ovid's scene with both the textual artifact of Vergil's *Aeneid* and the real monuments of Augustan Rome suggests is a double process in which Ovid's poetry aims simultaneously at "monumentalization" and at the conversion of monuments back to the more fluid context of narrative. Ovid thus measures his authority against both kinds of *auctores* by turning Vergilian fable into hard fact and giving human expression to Augustan marble. And this way of reading the episode helps clarify how Ovid's figuration of his own personal authority, studied in the second chapter, coexists with the distinctive political efficacy of Ovid's text in allowing its viewers to entertain multiple perspectives on scenes that are—and are not—also images affirming the construction of Roman *imperium*.

One final device Ovid uses to articulate these different points of view, as well as to remind the reader of his own personal role in crafting the scene, has to do with the contrast between erotic and martial sensibilities throughout the episode. We have already observed how the process of petrification evoked alternatively the experience of the lover and the warrior. The tension and overlap in imagery and diction between poetic descriptions of these aspects of experience was of course a phenomenon central to practically all contemporary poetry, elegiac or epic. When Perseus looking at the chained Andromeda mentally opposes her too real bonds with the metaphorical bonds of love, his train of thought is thus one that any experienced reader would be conditioned to share. But Ovid's deployment of this effect here deserves attention because of the way that he integrates it with the larger question of the relationship between texts and monuments. As elegiac and epic codes offer their own distinctive transformations of reality into poetry, revealing the same image "chains" or "wounds" from radically different perspectives, so Ovid has linked the doubleness of his central figure of the alterity emerging from artistic creation, Medusa's head, to this generic metamorphosis as well. For, as Perseus's story reminds us, the Gorgon could inspire love as well as terror. And even in her present form, her head is not all scales and fangs. Rather, Ovid specifies that every other hair has turned into a snake (*alternos inmixtos crinibus angues*, 4.792).[89] Perhaps one may even detect a generic pun in the "alternating" coiffure of the Gorgon recalling the alternating lines of elegiac couplets. The last suggestion becomes more plausible in light of the preceding verse, where *unus ... ex numero procerum* can mean not only "one of the throng of heroes [interrupted asking ...]" but also "[asking] according to (moving away from?) the meter of heroes," that is, dactylic hexameter.

Beyond possessing this double aspect herself, Medusa bestows it on her creations as well. Philip Hardie has observed that Perseus's final taunt to Phineus couples references to two very different functions of statues: to commemorate victory and to provide erotic replacements conjuring up absent loved ones: "No, I will produce monuments to last through all eternity and you will always be gazed upon in the home of *my* father-in-law so that *my* wife may console herself with the image of her beloved"

---

[89] See the comments of Anderson 1996.495: "Bömer protests that the picture does not fit the traditional frightfulness of the Gorgon, but that is Ovid's point. The poet has slipped out of the epic mode, and he is now combining the elegiac and the aetiological."

(5.227–29).[90] Perseus's irony in the last line, though, points to the pattern that we have already observed throughout the narrative as a whole: the capacity of "statues" to petrify lovers merges into their destructive capacity in war. But the lover's response to the vision of the beloved contrasts with the experience of a Phineus or an Astyages in ways that reinforce the tensions we have seen in the responses the poem generates to images. The effects of petrifaction bear different consequences when read against the different generic codes of epic and elegy. So, for example, when Perseus almost forgets to beat his wings at the sight of Andromeda, the gesture recalls the dangerous "stilling" of the epic hero who is distracted and turned away from his aims, as Aeneas was by Dido. By contrast, the desirability of Athis, described in an ecphrasis that seems to forestall the coming destruction of the battle, is suddenly "shattered" as the hero Perseus smashes in his face with a wooden beam. This generic transition is also signaled by the placement of Perseus's erotic viewing at the beginning of the story and the erection of *monumenta* at its end, for while the glimpse of a statue can often provide the beginning of a love story, the proper role for statues in a historical narrative is to impose finality on a successful campaign or to instantiate the glory already won at home by a victorious politician.

Once again, this contrast in whether to take statues as the starting points for elegiac desire or as the ultimate ends of epic accomplishment is not just an issue in the reading of texts but also in viewing the monuments of the Roman city. We have already seen how Propertius elegized the sculptural decoration of the temple of Palatine Apollo. That poem was framed as a fictive conversation. "You ask me why I am late," it begins (2.31.1). If we imagine the fictive addressee here as the poet's lover, then he has substituted the viewing of Augustan monuments for a lover's meeting. And yet, as he tells it, the temple itself offered both a rival and a substitute for the beloved in the form of a whole "crowd of women," who were none other than the Danaids.[91] And this bevy of femininity appears all the more striking because it emerges from a setting of markedly imperial significance, a portico set with columns of "Punic" marble, a reminder, when described this way, of Rome's defining victory as well as an evocation of the first book of *Aeneid*. For here, as in the moment when the sculpted Penthesilea on Carthage's temple of Juno seems to come to life as Dido, the effect of Propertius's account is to suggest not statuary decoration but a throng of real women enjoying the colonnade.

[90] Hardie 2002c.178–79.

[91] ... *Poenis digesta columnis, / inter quas Danai femina turba senis* (Prop. 2.31.3–4). *Poenis* also paronomastically recalls the punishment of the maidens for their disobedience, which, it has been suggested, was central to the political iconography of the complex (see chapter 2).

But the remapping of the new Roman city as a setting for erotic adventures was most sweepingly accomplished by Ovid himself in the first book of the *Ars Amatoria*, (1.67ff.), where the new monuments of the emperor were imagined as places to find a lover (again the beginning of the erotic adventure). Such an elegiac view of actual *monumenta* provides an interesting possibility for relocating the fabulous meeting of Perseus and Andromeda to a contemporary Roman space.[92] The sight of a barbarian maiden, whether as a real woman in the context of a triumph or as a sculptural representation—as, for example, the allegorical figures on the shield of the Prima Porta Augustus—was central to the Romans' visual experience of their imperial success. Among the most recent manifestations of this pattern, as Kellum has argued,[93] was the display of caryatids in the attic level of the Forum of Augustus, where they alternated with other elements easily glossed as symbols of conquest, shields bearing the heads of Jupiter Ammon.[94] There is nothing especially erotic about caryatids, and their heavy dress was an important part of their iconography.[95] But their upright posture, their association with captivity, and the presence of Jupiter Ammon in the narrative background to Ovid's scene make possible the visual juxtaposition that I have been describing. And the questions that Perseus asks Andromeda would be precisely those a Roman viewer might ask in making sense of these allegorical images: "What is the name of your country, and your own, and why are you wearing chains?" (4.680–81).

This distinctive erotic pattern of reading images may compete with a memorializing, imperial signification, or it may be that for other readers it realizes an element of eroticization already latent in the choice to represent conquest by reducing defeated people to female slaves. Conversely, what seems a striking juxtaposition in interpretative context may also point, as in the Pygmalion episode,[96] to the extent to which the representation of love in much Latin discourse involves a certain amount of objectification, if not actual conquest. But the degree of competition between these perspectives involved in the reading of images should not obscure the important connections that unite the lover's and the hero's

[92] Of course, as we have seen, the episode was also already presented in the painted decoration of many a wealthy Roman house.

[93] Kellum 1996.171 and 1997.167–68.

[94] It is unclear how many of the shields bore this figure as opposed to other male heads. The imitation of this design in the forum at Merida in Spain showed Ammones alternating with the heads of Medusa (Kuttner 1995.251, n. 71).

[95] According to Vitruvius 1.1.5, the Greeks made the women of the medizing city of Caryae retain their matrons' robes as a further reminder of the state from which they had fallen.

[96] See Sharrock 1991a.

capacity to create images. A key point about the chained Andromeda's metamorphosis into a statue is that it is hypothetical. So too Athis may be presented as though he were a work of art, but Perseus's club quickly destroys that illusion together with Athis's appearance.[97] In both cases, the lover makes the interpretative mistake of treating real people as statues, only to have movement—and, particularly, the possibility of death, threatened in the case of Andromeda and tragically accomplished in the case of Athis—correct the lover's error. Thus, Perseus, whose statues are real statues, can seem a greater artist than the lover-poet, who only comes close to such a miracle. But mortality again imposes a limit on the permanence of those images as well and not just because, as ancient poets perpetually remind their audiences, time destroys even bronze and marble. As the lovers see reality transformed into statues, so warriors in the poem like Astyages, and Phineus make the mistake of seeing statues as people. Even miraculous statues must be viewed by human eyes, and this always involves a possibility of experiencing the absence caused in this case emphatically by death in personal and human terms, of the viewer experiencing this death as his own. And if few viewers of Augustan monuments were actually turned to stone by the sight, if the Ovidian reflection of this experience seems to distort the real phenomenon it reflects, that just proves again that fact is not always more powerful than fiction.

[97] I am assuming for the sake of this argument that the luxurious description of Athis's beauty in 5.49–54 is focalized through the gaze of his lover.

Conclusion

Keith Hopkins describes the operation of Roman ritual as follows:

> Rituals cumulatively, throughout each year and each lifetime, provided Romans with a system of action and knowledge by which they negotiated standardized and repetitive ways of dealing with powerful imponderables, such as sexual appetite, hierarchy, and sickness. Sacrifices, for example, joined humans with their gods, gladiatorial games confirmed Roman superiority over defeated enemies and highlighted the risks of cowardice in battle, the Lupercalia helped delineate the multiple differences between men and women and their mutually problematic sexuality, the Saturnalia dealt with slaves by subverting rank and temporarily giving slaves the power to command .... This whole array of Roman rituals ... was like an orchestra with each ritual standing for a single instrument. None of them can be understood alone, by itself. Each ritual depended on the others. To be sure there was no conductor, no ritual dictator. Each citizen could play or hear different tunes on each instrument.[1]

More than any specifically literary formulation, this vision of civic and religious ritual has inspired my understanding of Ovid's poem. That work too makes up an enormous whole whose parts echo and define each other in ways that no single analysis can catalog for they depend on the different journeys individual readers make through it, noting linguistic and thematic links and contrasts, responding differently to each transformation as they identify differently with the figures in the narrative. Like Hopkins's ritual participants, where these readers end up depends to a great extent on where they start from, on the degree of knowledge they bring, on their status, ethnicity, and gender. For some readers the journey may ultimately take them back to where they started, confirming assumptions about who they are in their relations to others; for different readers their experience of the poem may reshape understandings of what it means to be a slave, a woman, a Roman, a human.

The analyses I offer here are a mixture of the prescriptive and the exemplary. I have tried above all to draw attention to several devices Ovid uses to deepen the poem's hermeneutic complexity and to show with

---

[1] Hopkins 1991.485.

some examples how attention to these devices can increase the breadth of the work's meaning. This breadth involves both the range of issues that we allow the poem to be about and the variety of positions in relation to them that it makes meaningful.

My central methodological claim starts from the work's most emphatically unifying feature, metamorphosis itself. Each metamorphosis raises a question of recognition: is the new form the same as what it replaces? Our answer to this question will not only help determine whether we read a story as fundamentally tragic or comic but also shape our conception of the place of the narrative itself within the world of experience. For the move from form to form takes us from an exclusively narrative presence—Daphne, Procne, Marsyas—to one that makes up a part of the here and now—a laurel tree, a swallow, a spring. Ovid's specific strategies for narrating transformation both sharpen and deepen this connection between reading metamorphoses and reading *Metamorphoses*. By highlighting alternative narrative focalizations in such programmatic stories as Daphne, Io, and Lycaon, Ovid establishes a link between the perspective we adopt on transformation and our ability to see events through the eyes of different figures within the narrative. This makes clear how reading transformation and reading the story within which it is embedded depend on one another. More fundamentally, it also opens new bridges between the reader as subject and the text by showing how the questions of likeness and difference raised by metamorphosis extend from whether Daphne is the laurel tree to how I the reader am and am not Daphne. Because metamorphosis itself had an important role in establishing a taxonomy of narratives that would have made the stories Ovid tells by definition unbelievable, his emphasis on transformation also possesses a programmatic, self-reflexive quality stressing the link between interpreting a transformation and interpreting narrative. This intrinsic connection between subject matter and form also draws attention to how Ovid's poem challenges the rules by which a Roman reader was trained to make sense of a story, even as the metamorphic products it describes are simultaneously real and unbelievable.

Ovid's way of constructing the response to his own narrative through metamorphosis provides the link between reading and experiences like the rituals Hopkins describes. It is thus the bedrock for my expansion of the text's political capacities. For I argue first that the connections Ovid's techniques establish between poem and reality invite reexamination of how real a text can become, of how dynamically it can shape the readers' response to and participation in the world around them. But there is yet a closer connection between Ovid's narratology and such political and cognitive modes as religious ritual, gladiatorial spectacle, and other forms of visual display: the recognition of identity and difference that Ovid makes central to reading also lie at the core of the political functions of those experiences. How sacrifice affects our understanding of the relationship between men and gods or between the individual spectator and communal authority depends, I believe and have tried to demonstrate, on the degree of likeness and similarity we recognize between ourselves and the victim. How gladiatorial spectacle configures civic identity depends on how the audience identifies with the figures on the sand. How the viewer construes the meaning of a work of art depends on how he sees it, as, for example, an object signifying primarily its own appropriation, or as a representation of alternative subjects. Thus, in making a similar process of identification crucial to the act of reading, Ovid gives the poem a political dimension in two ways, both by stressing a key functional similarity between reading and these other forms of response and by putting his text in dialogue with them, so that Ovid's poem can shape how its audience responds to the material spectacles and rituals around them. His story of Niobe allows one to read Augustus's image of her with new eyes. Pythagoras's view of sacrifice helps focus the ways of viewing generated by metamorphosis onto the actual experience of sacrifice. Of course, this exchange works both ways: Ovid's staging of his relationship with an emperor who always is and is not textualized reveals at once the transformative power of art, the artistry of power, and how the realities to which his poem refers determine the meaning of his text even as his text lets us see them as new.

But the ritual analogy with which I began also highlights fundamental differences between texts and acts that will have made the claims in the preceding paragraph hard for some of my own readers to accept. Reading is not doing, and if we ever lose track of the distance between them we become less, not more, responsive readers of Ovid's poem. The gap between a poem, of which at least nine-tenths is explicitly about Greek myth, and the contemporary practices of Augustan Rome raises two related questions: how can you establish that the poem refers to the present, and then what precisely is the payoff of this recognition—how and within what limits does "reading" translate into "participation"?

I start with the question of reference. As we have seen, the ending point of a metamorphosis narrative juxtaposes the unbelievable past and the undeniable present, and the structure of the poem as a whole does so at least as urgently. The impulse to read the work as a collection of individual stories drawn from Greek myth struggles with the form Ovid emphatically embraces at its start, that of epic, which organizes those stories within a larger narrative trajectory whose end is indeed the present. Making the connection, then, between distant and near, foreign and Roman, fictional and real, becomes the challenge that the poem imposes by virtue of Ovid's choice to write not another episodic *Heroides* but an epic, the genre whose claim to speak authoritatively, to matter in the present, was after all one of the features that define it against Ovid's previously elegiac compositions. That is not to say that the episodic approach to the poem does not also receive encouragement from the text (the number of translations that use subheadings to designate different stories makes it clear that the poem cannot not be read in this way as well); but even if the work's formal ambiguities do not mandate a reading directed toward the Augustan present, they do justify the reader in asking what such a connection might look like.

The poem's beginning prompts the same questions as its ending point. Book 1 contains three extensive narratives belonging to the most common and familiar kind of metamorphosis tale, the transformation of an individual into an object, plant, or animal: Lycaon, Daphne, and Io, all set in the mythical, Greek, past. Yet Ovid begins the first and ends the second with explicit references to Augustus, while commenting on the phenomenon of reading in the third. In doing so, he highlights the potential of these stories to refer to the political life of the present and further justifies us in adopting a similar perspective on other mythical stories, asking how such connections might be made even if they are not made explicitly, as in the case of Perseus.

But to look only at how the text refers to the here and now is but half the picture, for it was an essential characteristic of contemporary political iconography and ritual dramatically to expand its own frame of reference and specifically to redeploy Greek myth as a means of describing the present. To take a striking and now familiar example, the temple of Apollo on the Palatine makes a range of mythical references as extensive and rich as any book of Ovid's poem available for understanding a recent historical event, the battle of Actium, and the political order that results from it. Religious rituals show a similar malleability: Mary Beard has demonstrated the transformation of the festival of the Parilia from a shepherds' festival to purify the flock to a commemoration of Rome's foundation.[2] Her analysis is based on Ovid's *Fasti*, where the poet describes his own participation in the ritual (4.725–26) and then turns from what was done to why it was done. This exploration of what the Parilia means takes him from the pastoral realities of the ritual and prayer to the story of Romulus and Remus, but along the way he also considers explanations drawn from science (the conjunction of fire and water that creates life) and explicitly rejects as unbelievable an allusion to two of the myths that he refers to prominently at the beginning of the *Metamorphoses*, the flood and the fire that destroyed Phaethon. Ovid here poses Greek myth as something that some bring up in explaining the festival, even if he rejects it. But

[2] Beard 1987.

there is far more to the explanation and its rejection than that. For in the reference to disbelief we recognize the characteristic terms in which Ovid cites his own transformation tales as unbelievable. The raconteurs the author does not believe become those who tell his own stories, and this hint may make us recognize that the entire passage explaining the Parilia constitutes a *Metamorphoses* in miniature, beginning with creation, incorporating myths like Deucalion, before moving on chronologically via Aeneas to Rome's foundation and a prayer for its future stability under Augustus. There can be no better illustration of how Ovid imagines his narratives do intervene, via ritual, in the interpretation of the present, even as he highlights the barriers that they must jump over to do so.

Any such references or glosses, however, do not simply impose a particular point of view on contemporary experience, whether affirmative or subversive. Because of the inherently prismatic effect of reading metamorphosis, the text rather exposes and explores alternative responses, transferring them to the experiential realm that each story both does and does not signify. Such "transference," though, is the stage of my argument that must remain ultimately unprovable. Obviously we have no access to the psychology of any specific ancient reading. But more important, the twin "reality" effects I have described, moving into the text through absorption into its fictions and seeing that narrative as a part of the phenomena of real experience, are each presented only as one alternative for responding to the poem—and indeed themselves pull in opposite directions. Like Argus, some in Ovid's audience may vigilantly keep the fantastic within its bounds—and the same episode that illustrates this approach to fiction simultaneously cautions us against too simply categorizing it as misreading. But just so, many participants in a sacrificial ritual will never have lost sight of the victim's bovine form. And as Hopkins's model of ritual suggests, even this reaction constitutes a specific kind of participation, productive of a distinctive positioning in relation to the set of oppositions (e.g., human-divine, male-female, Roman-foreign, leader-follower) that animate and politicize ritual experience. This is why I call my readings exemplary: they are meant as possible readings, possible, though, because they develop a logic of reading and take up questions that the text invites.

But the interpretative process that transformation sets in motion is political also in the questions it raises about the nature of authorship and—via a semantic overlap that the Latin word *auctor* makes apparent—of authority. As I discussed in chapter 2, Karl Galinsky presents authority—cognate with the very name *Augustus* chose for himself—as a defining issue for all forms of cultural expression under the first emperor. But authority constitutes more than the subject of the art, literature, and ritual he describes. In Galinsky's view, the media through which authority is discussed themselves project and manifest authority, as polysemy gives way to authorial guidance in articulating their meaning. Similarly, Keith Hopkins, in the passage with which I began, significantly speaks of a "symphony," not "polyphony." He goes on in the sentence just after I ended my quotation to make a stronger claim about the unitary meaning that emerges from ritual performance: "Even so, out of the diversity and apparent cacophony, collective rhythms emerge. Diversity of experience and understanding does not preclude a recognizable score which was identifiably Roman."

My own reading of the poem parts company with both these "authorities" in its reluctance to define a similar authorial score. Indeed, several of the passages analyzed here have featured divine figures attempting to impose a political meaning on stories in which they themselves appear as characters—Jupiter on Lycaon, Apollo on Daphne, Minerva on Arachne. But in each case we have also seen how interpreting the resulting metamorphosis, again taken as a programmatic gesture for reading the poem, while not necessarily refuting these claims, nevertheless presents them as themselves subject to response and as part of a broader spectrum of readings. At the same time, Ovid notoriously makes his own authorial position in relation to these internal narrators uncertain, itself a subject of interpretation.

Each of these three divine figures has been plausibly identified as "Augustan," Jupiter and Apollo via specific analogies in the text. If these internal authorities at the poem's beginning seem to figure Augustus, the real center point for Roman *auctoritas*, so the work ends by staging an attempt to bring the outside in, textualizing Augustus himself. As a result of this dialogue between authorship and authority, the figures of emperor and poet each enter into a hermeneutic dance, as the struggle of one to control the other depends in turn on the limits of our assent to the text. That Ovid questions his own authorial capacity in this process—as opposed to projecting a unitary alternative voice—renders his destabilization of the concept of authority in both its textual and political aspects yet more radical. My interpretation in turn reflects an image of Augustan culture centered less on the *princeps* per se than on the issue of response to the *princeps*, on how the presence of such totalizing claims to authority changed the terms in which all members of that society could project their own position, which was now increasingly subject to judgment as "like" or "different," "for" or "against" Augustus.

It is a truism in Ovidian studies that criticism of the *Metamorphoses* is continually transforming itself in response to the intellectual climate in which the poem is read. The self-conscious artist of the new critics long cohabited with the anti-Augustan dissident of more historicizing readers. Deconstruction brought an emphasis on inconsistencies and tensions that make the poem resistant to closed readings while new historicism inspired investigation of how this poetic openness figured in the text's exchanges with its cultural context. Readings of many literary works have doubtless followed a similar path. But I think the *Metamorphoses'* continually addresses the present—and not just our present—with special urgency. And this has to do with more than its obvious hermeneutic complexity or its own emphasis on change. Its multiple internal narratives highlight the poet's narrative cleverness, but they equally stress the pressures of reception: how do stories told about distant cultures and times from contrasting moral perspectives, told by gods to mortals and by mortals to gods, told about women by men and about men by women, communicate across such differences? So Ovid's poem explicitly relates stories from a foreign culture in a medium that resists straightforward application to a historical present while nevertheless building these stories into a trajectory that connects the long ago and far away with the here and now. And these tensions are, as we have seen, conveyed through a set of narratological devices that, despite their changing significance over time, are still universalizable in that they generate questions about representation only in their telling.

My own response to the poem has itself been shaped by the shifting critical interests of the decades during which it was written. For this was, in general, a period in which many of the barriers within literary studies were challenged as critics in different ways explored the limits of textuality. "Neo-Aristotelians" such as Wayne Booth and Martha Nussbaum restated the claims that literature can teach ethics.[3] And the contemporary "ethical turn" in deconstruction has led a school that more than any other challenged the notion that a text can ever "mean" to reexamine literature's ability to refer to the world outside.[4] The role of literature in articulating the conditions of colonialism has inspired reexamination of how reading can be political, specifically how literature allows both writer and reader to adopt different social roles, escaping from and reaffirming their positions through the transformations texts allow.[5] I have drawn on none of these ideas explicitly in building my own arguments about Ovid, but I think it is important to record them in ending this book, and not just as a further caveat about the potential limitations of my own perspective nor, I hope, in a meretricious gesture toward "rel-

---

[3] Booth 1988; Nussbaum 1990.

[4] The phrase is Baker's (1995). Key primary texts are Miller 1987 and Derrida 1992.

[5] The bibliography is too enormous to summarize, but the position of Kristeva 1988 seems particularly productive for developing the strategies of reading Ovid's fictions put forward here. See also the summary in Rye 2000.

evance." All authors reveal expectations about how their works will be received, but the historical and cultural changes of the period when he wrote led Ovid to investigate the political role of literature and the ways in which reality and representation configure one another with particular energy and brilliance. The results of his investigation have much more to tell us about literature than my book could suggest.

Ahl, F. (1985). *Metaformations*. Ithaca.

Alpers, P. (1996). *What Is Pastoral?* Berkeley.

Anderson, W. S. (1963). "Multiple Change in the *Metamorphoses*." *TAPA* 94: 1–27.

———. (1972). *Ovid's* Metamorphoses: *Books 6–10*. Norman, Okla.

———. (1989a). "Artists' Limits in Ovid: Orpheus, Pygmalion, and Daedalus." *Syllecta Classica* 1: 1–11.

———. (1989b). "Lycaon: Ovid's Deceptive Paradigm in *Metamorphoses* 1." *ICS* 14: 91–101.

———. (1996). *Ovid's* Metamorphoses, *Books 1–5*. Norman, Okla.

Andreae, B. (1994). *Praetorium Speluncae: Tiberius und Ovid in Sperlonga*. Stuttgart.

Auguet, R. (1972). *Cruelty and Civilization: The Roman Games*. London.

Baker, P. (1995). *Deconstruction and the Ethical Turn*. Gainesville, Fla.

Bal, M. (1985). *Narratology: Introduction to the Theory of Narrative*. Toronto.

Bandera, C. (1981). "Sacrificial Levels in Virgil's *Aeneid*." *Arethusa* 14: 217–39.

Barchiesi, A. (1989). "Voci e istanze narrativi nelle *Metamorfosi* di Ovidio." *MD* 23: 55–97.

———. (1991). "Discordant Muses." *PCPS* 37: 1–21.

———. (1997a). "Endgames: Ovid's *Metamorphoses* 15 and *Fasti* 6." In D. H. Roberts, F. M. Dunn, and D. Fowler, eds., *Classical Closure*, 181–208. Princeton.

———. (1997b). *The Poet and the Prince: Ovid and Augustan Discourse*. Berkeley.

———. (1999). "Venus' Masterplot: Ovid and the Homeric Hymns." In P. Hardie, A. Barchiesi, and S. Hinds, eds., *Ovidian Transformations: Essays on Ovid's* Metamorphoses *and Its Reception*, 112–26. Cambridge.

———. (2005). *Ovidio:* Metamorfosi, *Volume I (Libri I–II)*. Milan.

———. (2007). *Ovidio:* Metamorfosi, *Volume II (Libri III–IV)*. Milan.

Barkan, L. (1986). *The Gods Made Flesh*. New Haven.

Bartsch, S. (1994). *Actors in the Audience*. Cambridge.

Barton, C. A. (1993). *The Sorrows of the Ancient Romans: The Gladiator and the Monster*. Princeton.

Beard, M. (1987). "A Complex of Times: No More Sheep on Romulus' Birthday." *PCPS* 33: 1–15.

———. (1996). "Le mythe (grec) à Rome: Hercule aux Bains." In S. Geourgoudi and J. P. Vernant, eds., *Mythes grecs au figuré: De l'antiquité au baroque*, 81–104. Paris.

Beard M., and J. Henderson. (1998). "The Emperor's New Body: Ascension from Rome." In M. Wyke, ed., *Parchments of Gender: Deciphering the Body in Antiquity*, 191–219. Oxford.

Beard, M., J. North, and S. Price. (1998). *Religions of Rome*. Cambridge.

Beard, M., J. North, and S. Price. (1998). *Religions of Rome.* Cambridge

Bergmann, B. (1991). "Painted Perspectives of a Villa Visit: Landscape as Status and Metaphor." In E. Gazda, ed., *Roman Art in the Private Sphere: New Perspectives on the Architecture and Décor of the Domus, Villa, and Insula,* 49–69. Ann Arbor.

———. (1994). "The Roman House as Memory Theatre." *Art Bulletin* 76: 225–56.

———. (1995). "Greek Masterpieces and Roman Recreative Fictions." *HSCP* 97: 79–120.

———. (1999). "Rhythmus of Recognition: Mythological Encounters in Roman Landscape Painting." In F. de Angelis and S. Muth, eds., *Im Spiegel des Mythos: Bilderwelt und Lebenswelt,* 81–107. Wiesbaden.

Bernbeck, E. J. (1967). *Beobachtungen zur Darstellungsart in Ovids* Metamorphosen. Zetemata 43. Munich.

Bernsdorff, H. (2000). *Kunstwerke und Verwandlungen. Vier Studien zu ihrer Darstellung im Werk Ovids.* Frankfurt.

Bettini, M. (1991). "Sosia e il suo Sosia: Pensare il 'Doppio' a Roma." In R. Oniga, ed., *Plauto, Anfitrione,* 9–51. Venice.

Bieber, M. (1961). *The History of the Greek and Roman Theater.* Princeton.

Bilinski, B. (1958). *Accio ed i Gracchi. Contributo alla storia della plebe e della tragedia romana.* Rome.

Bloch, M. (1986). *From Blessing to Violence: History and Ideology in the Circumcision Ritual of the Merina of Madagascar.* Cambridge.

Bloomer, M. W. (1997). *Latinity and Literary Society at Rome.* Philadelphia.

Bömer, F., ed. (1969–86). *P. Ovidius Naso:* Metamorphosen. 6 vols. Heidelberg.

Booth, W. (1988). *The Company We Keep: An Ethics of Fiction.* Berkeley.

Boyd, B. W. (2006). "Two Rivers and the Reader in Ovid, *Metamorphoses* 8." *TAPA* 136: 171–206.

Bradley, K. R. (1994). *Slavery and Society at Rome.* Cambridge.

Bretzigheimer, G. (1993). "Jupiter Tonans in Ovids 'Metamorphosen.'" *Gymnasium* 100: 19–74.

———. (1994). "Diana in Ovids 'Metamorphosen.'" *Gymnasium* 101: 506–46.

Brown, R. (1987). "The Palace of the Sun in Ovid's *Metamorphoses.*" In M. Whitby, P. Hardie, and M. Whitby, eds., *Homo Viator: Classical Essays for John Bramble,* 211–20. Bristol.

Buchheit, V. (1966). "Mythos und Geschichte in Ovids *Metamorphosen* I." *Hermes* 94: 80–108.

Burkert, W. (1983). *Homo Necans.* Trans. P. Bing. Berkeley.

Burnyeat. M. (1997). "Postscript on Silent Reading." *CQ* 47: 74–76.

Bynum, C. W. (2001). *Metamorphosis and Identity.* New York.

Cahoon, L. (1996). "Calliope's Song: Shifting Narrators in Ovid, *Metamorphoses* 5." *Helios* 23: 43–66.

Cameron, A. (1995). *Callimachus and His Critics.* Princeton.

Champlin, E. (2005). "Phaedrus the Fabulous." *JRS* 95: 97–123.

Clausen, W. (1994). *A Commentary on Virgil,* Eclogues. Oxford.

Clauss, J. J. (1989). "The Episode of the Lycian Farmers in Ovid's *Metamorphoses.*" *HSCP* 92: 297–314.

Cole, T. (2004). "Ovid, Varro, and Castor of Rhodes: The Chronological Architecture of Ovid's *Metamorphoses*." *HSCP* 102: 355–422.

Coleman, K. M. (1990). "Fatal Charades: Roman Executions Staged as Mythological Enactments." *JRS* 80: 44–73.

———. (1993). "Launching into History: Aquatic Displays in the Early Empire." *JRS* 83: 48–74.

Coleman, R. (1971). "Structure and Intention in the *Metamorphoses*." *CQ* 21: 461–77.

Courtney, E. (1993). *The Fragmentary Latin Poets*. Oxford.

Curley, D. (1997). "Ovid *Met*. 6.640: A Dialogue between Mother and Son." *CQ* 47: 320–22.

———. (2003). "Ovid's *Tereus*: Theater and Metatheater." In A. Sommerstein, ed., *Shards from Kolonos: Studies in Sophoclean Fragments,* 163–97. Bari.

Curran, L. (1972). "Metamorphosis and Anti-Augustanism." *Arethusa* 5: 71–91.

———. (1978). "Rape and Rape Victims in Ovid's *Metamorphoses*." *Arethusa* 11: 213–41.

Currie, H. M. (1981). "Ovid and the Roman Stage." *ANRW* 2.31.4: 2701–42.

Dällenbach, L. (1977). *Le récit spéculaire: Essai sur la mise en abyme*. Paris.

Davis, N.G.G. (1969). "Studies in the Narrative Economy of Ovid's *Metamorphoses*." Ph.D. diss., Berkeley.

Degl'Innocenti Pierini, R. (2002). "Il barbaro Tereo di Accio: Attualizzazione e funzionalità ideologica di un mito greco." In S. Faller and G. Manuwald, eds., *Accius und seine Zeit,* 127–39. Identitäten und Alteritäten 13. Würzburg.

Derrida, J. (1992). *Acts of Literature*. Ed. D. Attridge. New York.

Devereux, G. (1976). *Dreams in Greek Tragedy: An Ethno-Psycho-Analytical Study*. Berkeley.

Dörrie, H. (1959). "Wandlung und Dauer: Ovids *Metamorphosen* und Poseidonios' Lehre von der Substanz." *AU* 4.2: 95–116.

Dubois, P. (1988). *Sowing the Body: Psychoanalysis and Ancient Representations of Women*. Chicago.

Due, O. (1974). *Changing Forms*. Copenhagen.

Dupont, F. (1985). *L'acteur-roi*. Paris.

Eck, W. (1984). "Senatorial Self-Representation: Developments in the Augustan Period." In F. Millar and E. Segal, eds., *Caesar Augustus: Seven Aspects*, 129–67. Oxford.

Edwards, C. (1993). *The Politics of Immorality in Ancient Rome*. Cambridge.

Elsner, J. (1991a). "Cult and Sculpture: Sacrifice in the *Ara Pacis Augustae*." *JRS* 81: 50–61.

———. (1991b). "Visual Mimesis and the Myth of the Real: Ovid's Pygmalion as Viewer." *Ramus* 20: 154–68.

———. (1995). *Art and the Roman Viewer: The Transformation of Art from the Pagan World to Christianity*. Cambridge.

Erasmo, M. (2004). *Roman Tragedy: Theatre to Theatricality*. Austin.

Faber, R. (1998). "Daedalus, Icarus, and the Fall of Perdix: Continuity and Allusion in *Metamorphoses* 8.183–259." *Hermes* 126: 80–89.

Fabre-Serris, J. (1995). *Mythe et poésie dans les* Métamorphoses *d'Ovide*. Paris.

Fairweather, J. (1987). "Ovid's Autobiographical Poem, *Tristia* 4.10." *CQ* 37: 181–96.

Fantham, E. (1990). "*Nymphas ... e navibus esse*: Decorum and Poetic Fiction in *Aeneid* 9.77–122 and 10.215–59." *CP* 85: 102–19.

———. (1993). "*Sunt Quibus in Plures Ius est Transire Figuras*: Ovid's Self-Transformers in the *Metamorphoses*." *CW* 87: 21–36.

———. (2004). *Ovid's* Metamorphoses. Oxford.

Farrell, J. (1992). "Dialogue of the Genres in Ovid's 'Lovesong of Polyphemus' (*Metamorphoses* 13.719–897)." *AJP* 113: 235–68.

———. (1999). "The Ovidian Corpus." In P. Hardie, A. Barchiesi, and S. Hinds, eds., *Ovidian Transformations: Essays on Ovid's* Metamorphoses *and Its Reception*, 127–41. Cambridge.

———. (2004). "Ovid's Virgilian Career." *MD* 52: 41–56.

Feeney, D. (1991). *The Gods in Epic*. Oxford.

———. (1992). "*Si licet et fas est*: Ovid's *Fasti* and the Problem of Free Speech under the Principate." In A. Powell, ed., *Roman Poetry and Propaganda in the Age of Augustus*, 1–25. Bristol.

———. (1993). "Towards an Account of the Ancient World's Concepts of Fictive Belief." In C. Gill and T. P. Wiseman, eds., *Lies and Fiction in the Ancient World*, 230–44. Exeter.

———. (1998). *Literature and Religion at Rome*. Cambridge.

———. (1999). "*Mea tempora*: Patterning of Time in the *Metamorphoses*." In P. Hardie, A. Barchiesi, and S. Hinds, eds., *Ovidian Transformations: Essays on Ovid's* Metamorphoses *and Its Reception*, 13–30. Cambridge.

———. (2004). "Interpreting Sacrificial Ritual in Roman Poetry: Disciplines and Their Models." In A. Barchiesi, J. Rüpke, and S. Stephens, eds., *Rituals in Ink: A Conference on Religion and Literary Production in Ancient Rome Held at Stanford University in February 2002*, 9–22. Stuttgart.

Feldherr, A. (1997). "Livy's Revolution: Civic Identity and the Creation of the *Res Publica*." In T. Habinek and A. Schiesaro, eds., *The Roman Cultural Revolution*, 136–57. Cambridge.

———. (1998). *Spectacle and Society in Livy's History*. Berkeley.

Fitzgerald, W. (2000). *Slavery and the Roman Literary Imagination*. Cambridge.

———. (2007). *Martial: The World of the Epigram*. Chicago.

Forbes-Irving, P.M.C. (1990). *Metamorphosis in Greek Myths*. Oxford.

Fowler, D. P. (2000). *Roman Constructions: Readings in Postmodern Latin*. Oxford.

Fränkel, H. (1945). *Ovid, a Poet between Two Worlds*. Berkeley.

Frécaut, J. M. (1980). "La métamorphose de Niobé chez Ovide (*Met.*, VI, 301–312)." *Latomus* 39: 129–43.

Fredrick, D. (1995). "Beyond the Atrium to Ariadne: Erotic Painting and Visual Pleasure in the Roman House." *CA* 14: 266–87.

Frontisi-Ducroux, F. (1996). "Andromède et la naissance du corail." In S. Geourgoudi and J. P. Vernant, eds., *Mythes grecs au figuré: De l'antiquité au baroque*, 135–65. Paris.

Fuhrer, T. (1999). "Der Götterhymnus als Prahlrede—Zum Spiel mit einer Literarischen Form in Ovids 'Metamorphosen.'" *Hermes* 127: 356–67.

Galand-Hallyn, P. (1994). *Le reflet des fleurs: Description et métalanguage poétique d'Homère à la Renaissance*. Geneva.

Galinsky, K. (1975). *Ovid's Metamorphoses: An Introduction to the Basic Aspects*. Berkeley.

———. (1996). *Augustan Culture*. Princeton.

———. (1998). "The Speech of Pythagoras in Ovid's *Metamorphoses* 15.75–478." *PLLS* 10: 313–36.

———. (1999). "Ovid's *Metamorphoses* and Augustan Cultural Thematics." In P. Hardie, A. Barchiesi, and S. Hinds, eds., *Ovidian Transformations: Essays on Ovid's* Metamorphoses *and Its Reception*, 103–11. Cambridge.

Gavrilov, A. K. (1997). "Techniques of Reading in Classical Antiquity." *CQ* 47: 56–73.

Gildenhard, I., and A. Zissos. (1999a). "Somatic Economies: Tragic Bodies and Poetic Design in Ovid's *Metamorphoses*." In P. Hardie, A. Barchiesi, and S. Hinds, eds., *Ovidian Transformations: Essays on Ovid's* Metamorphoses *and Its Reception*, 162–81. Cambridge.

———. (1999b). "Problems of Time in Ovid *Metamorphoses* 2." In P. Hardie, A. Barchiesi, and S. Hinds, eds., *Ovidian Transformations: Essays on Ovid's* Metamorphoses *and Its Reception*, 31–47. Cambridge.

———. (2000a). "Inspirational Fictions: Autobiography and Generic Reflexivity in Ovid's Proems." *G&R* 47: 67–79.

———. (2000b). "Ovid's Narcissus (*Met.* 3.339–510): Echoes of Oedipus." *AJP* 121: 129–47.

———. (2004). "Ovid's Hecale: Deconstructing Athens in Ovid's *Metamorphoses*." *JRS* 94: 47–72.

———. (2007). "Barbarian Variations: Tereus, Procne, and Philomela in Ovid." *Dictynna* 4.

Girard, R. (1977). *Violence and the Sacred*. Trans. P. Gregory. Baltimore.

Gordon, R. L. (1979). "The Real and the Imaginary: Production and Religion in the Graeco-Roman World." *Art History* 2: 5–34.

Graf, F. (1988). "Ovide, les *Métamorphoses*, et la véracité du mythe." In C. Calame, ed., *Métamorphoses du mythe en Grèce antique*, 57–70. Geneva.

———. (2002). "Myth in Ovid." In P. Hardie, ed., *The Cambridge Companion to Ovid*, 108–21. Cambridge.

Griffin, J. (1977). "The Epic Cycle and the Uniqueness of Homer." *JHS* 97: 39–53.

Gros, P. (1976). *Aurea Templa. Recherches sur l'architecture religieuse de Rome à l'époque d'Auguste*. Rome.

———. (1981). "Les *Métamorphoses* d'Ovide et le décor interieur des temples romains. Un essai de définition du dernier art "baroque" hellenistique." In *L'Art décoratif à Rome à la fin de la République et au début du Principat*, 353–66. Collection de l'École française de Rome 55. Rome.

Gruen, E. (1992). *Culture and National Identity in Republican Rome*. Ithaca.

Gurval, R. A. (1995). *Actium and Augustus*. Ann Arbor.

Habinek, T. N. (2002). "Ovid and Empire." In P. Hardie, ed., *The Cambridge Companion to Ovid*, 46–61. Cambridge.

———. (2005). *The World of Roman Song*. Baltimore.

Hano, M. (1986). "A l'origine du culte impérial: Les autels des Lares Augusti. Recherches sur les thèmes iconographiques et leur signification." *ANRW* II.16.3: 2333–81.

Hardie, P. (1986). *Virgil's Aeneid: Cosmos and Imperium*. Oxford.

———. (1987). "Ships and Ship-Names in the *Aeneid*." In M. Whitby, P. Hardie, and M. Whitby, eds., *Homo Viator: Classical Essays for John Bramble*, 163–71. Bristol.

———. (1990). "Ovid's Theban History: The First Anti-*Aeneid*?" *CQ* 40: 224–35.

———. (1992). "Augustan Poets and the Mutability of Rome." In A. Powell, ed., *Roman Poetry and Propaganda in the Age of Augustus*, 59–82. Bristol.

———. (1993). *The Epic Successors of Virgil*. Cambridge.

———. (1994). *Virgil Aeneid Book IX*. Cambridge.

———. (1995). "The Speech of Pythagoras in Ovid *Metamorphoses* 15: Empedoclean *Epos*." *CQ* 45: 204–14.

———. (1997). "Questions of Authority: The Invention of Tradition in *Metamorphoses* 15." In T. Habinek and A. Schiesaro, eds., *The Roman Cultural Revolution*, 182–98. Cambridge.

———. (1999). "Metamorphosis, Metaphor, and Allegory in Latin Epic." In M. Beissinger, J. Tylus, and S. Wofford, eds., *Epic Traditions in the Contemporary World: The Poetics of Community*, 89–107. Berkeley.

———. (2002a)"Another Look at Virgil's Ganymede." In T. P. Wiseman, ed., *Classics in Progress*, 333–61. Oxford.

———. (2002b). "Ovid and Early Imperial Literature." In P. Hardie, ed., *The Cambridge Companion to Ovid*, 34–45. Cambridge.

———. (2002c). *Ovid's Poetics of Illusion*. Cambridge.

Harries, B. (1990). "The Spinner and the Poet: Arachne in Ovid's *Metamorphoses*." *PCPS* 36: 63–82.

Hershkowitz, D. (1999). "The Creation of the Self in Ovid and Proust." In P. Hardie, A. Barchiesi, and S. Hinds, eds., *Ovidian Transformations: Essays on Ovid's Metamorphoses and Its Reception*, 182–96. Cambridge.

Herter, H. (1958). "Ovids Verhältnis zur bildenden Kunst." In N. Herescu, ed., *Ovidiana*, 49–74. Paris.

Heslin, P. (2007). "Augustus, Domitian, and the So-Called *Horologium Augusti*." *JRS* 97: 1–20.

Hinds, S. E. (1985). "Booking the Return Trip: Ovid and *Tristia* 1." *PCPS* 31: 13–32.

———. (1987a). *The Metamorphoses of Persephone*. Cambridge.

———. (1987b). "Generalising about Ovid." *Ramus* 16: 4–31.

———. (2001a). "Cinna, Statius and 'Immanent Literary History' in the Cultural Economy." In E. A. Schmidt, ed., *L'histoire littéraire immanente dans la poésie latine. Entretiens Hardt* 47: 221–65.

———. (2001b). "Landscape with Figures: Aesthetics of Place in the *Metamorphoses* and Its Tradition." In P. Hardie, ed., *Cambridge Companion to Ovid*, 122–49. Cambridge.

———. (2005). "Dislocations of Ovidian Time." In J. P. Schwindt, ed., *La représentation du temps dans la poésie augustéenne / Zur Poetik der Zeit in augusteischer Dichtung*, 203–30. Heidelberg.

Hoefmans, M. (1994). "Myth into Reality: The Metamorphosis of Daedalus and Icarus (Ovid, *Metamorphoses*, VIII, 183–235)." *AntClass* 63: 137–60.

Hofmann, H. (1971). "Ausgesprochene und unausgesprochene motivische Verwebung im sechsten Metamorposenbuch Ovids." *AC* 14: 91–107.

———. (1985). "Ovid's *Metamorphoses*: *Carmen Perpetuum, Carmen Deductum.*" *PLLS* 5: 223–41.

Hollis, A. S. (1970). *Ovid:* Metamorphoses *Book VIII*. Oxford.

Hopkins, K. (1991). "From Violence to Blessing: Symbols and Rituals in Ancient Rome." In A. Molho, K. Raaflaub, and J. Emlen, eds., *City States in Classical Antiquity and Medieval Italy*, 479–98. Ann Arbor.

Hopkinson, N. (2000). *Ovid:* Metamorphoses *Book XIII*. Cambridge.

Horsfall, N. (1981). "Some Problems of Titulature in Roman Literary History." *BICS* 28: 103–14.

Isager, J. (1991). *Pliny on Art and Society*. Odense.

Ishøy, H. (2006). "Bimsstein und Stirn, Horn und Nabel. Zu den Beschreibungen der Ausstattung der Papyrusrolle in römischer Poesie." *Hermes* 134: 69–88.

Janan, M. (1988). "The Book of Good Love? Design versus Desire in *Metamorphoses* 10." *Ramus* 17: 110–37.

———. (2004). "The Snake Sheds Its Skin: Pentheus (Re)Imagines Thebes." *CP* 99: 130–46.

Johnson, W. R. (1976). *Darkness Visible: A Study of Vergil's* Aeneid. Berkeley.

Joplin, P. K. (1984). "The Voice of the Shuttle Is Ours." *Stanford Literature Review* 1: 25–53.

Kaster, R. A. (2005). *Emotion, Restraint, and Community in Ancient Rome*. New York and Oxford.

Keith, A. (1992). *The Play of Fictions: Studies in Ovid's* Metamorphoses *Book 2*. Ann Arbor.

———. (2002). "Sources and Genres in Ovid's *Metamorphoses* 1–5." In B. W. Boyd, ed., *Brill's Companion to Ovid*, 235–69. Leiden.

Kellum, B. (1985). "Sculptural Programs and Propaganda in Augustan Rome." In R. Winkes, ed., *The Age of Augustus: An Interdisciplinary Conference Held at Brown University April 30–May 2, 1982*, 169–76. Louvain.

———. (1996). "The Phallus as Signifier: The Forum of Augustus and Rituals of Masculinity." In N. B. Kampen, ed., *Sexuality in Ancient Art*, 170–83. Cambridge.

———. (1997). "Concealing/Revealing: Gender and the Play of Meaning in the Monuments of Augustan Rome." In T. Habinek and A. Schiesaro, eds., *The Roman Cultural Revolution*, 158–81. Cambridge.

———. (1999). "The Spectacle of the Street." In B. Bergmann and C. Kondoleon, eds., *The Art of Ancient Spectacle*, 283–300. New Haven.

———. (forthcoming). "Whips, Cockfights, and Foundlings: Playing Enslavement at the House of the Vettii."

Kennedy, D. (1992). "'Augustan' and 'Anti-Augustan': Reflections on Terms of Reference." In A. Powell, ed., *Roman Poetry and Propaganda in the Age of Augustus*, 26–58. Bristol.

Kenney, E. J. (1973). "The Style of the *Metamorphoses*." In J. W. Binns, ed., *Ovid*, 116–53. London.

Kenney, E. J. (1976). "Ovidius Prooemians." *PCPS* 22: 46–53.

———. (1986). Notes to *Ovid: Metamorphoses*. Trans. A. D. Melville. Oxford.

Klein, F. (2009). "*Prodigiosa mendacia vatum*: Responses to the Marvellous in Ovid's Narrative of Perseus (*Metamorphoses* 4–5)." In P. Hardie, ed., *Paradox and the Marvellous in Augustan Literature and Culture*, 189–212. Oxford.

Kleiner, D.E.E. (1977). *Roman Group Portraiture: Funerary Reliefs of the Late Republic and Early Empire*. New York.

———. (1992). "Politics and Gender in the Pictorial Propaganda of Antony and Octavian." *EMC* 36: 357–67.

Knox, P. (1986). *Ovid's* Metamorphoses *and the Traditions of Augustan Poetry*. Cambridge.

Konstan, D. (1991). "The Death of Argus, or What Stories Do: Audience Response in Ancient Fiction and Theory." *Helios* 18: 15–30.

———. (1998). "The Invention of Fiction." In B. Chance, R. Hock, and J. Perkins, eds., *Ancient Fiction and Early Christian Narrative*, 3–17. Atlanta.

Kristeva, J. (1988). *Étrangers à nous-mêmes*. Paris. Translated by L. S. Roudiez as *Strangers to Ourselves*. New York, 1991.

Kuttner, A. (1995). *Dynasty and Empire in the Age of Augustus: The Case of the Boscoreale Cups*. Berkeley.

———. (1999). "Culture and History at Pompey's Museum." *TAPA* 129: 343–73.

———. (2002). "Turning to Stone: Emotional Sculpture and Designed Landscape in Ovid's *Metamorphoses*." Paper presented at "Aetas Ovidiana: Ovidian Themes in Contemporary Latin Studies," Trinity College, Dublin, March 22–24.

———. (2003). "Delight and Danger in the Roman Water Garden." In M. Conan, ed., *Landscape Design and the Experience of Motion*, 103–56. Washington, D.C.

Lada-Richards, I. (2007). *Silent Eloquence: Lucian and Pantomime Dancing*. London.

Lana, I. (1958–59). "L'Atreo di Accio e la leggenda di Atreo e Tieste nel teatro tragico romano." *AAT* 93: 293–385.

Larmour, D.H.J. (1990). "Tragic *Contaminatio* in Ovid's *Metamorphoses*: Procne and Medea; Philomela and Iphigeneia (6.424–674); Scylla and Phaedra (8.19–151)." *ICS* 15: 131–41.

La Rocca, E. (1985). *Amazzonomacchia. Le sculture frontonali del tempio di Apollo Sosiano*. Rome.

———. (1988). "Der Apollo-Sosianus-Tempel." In *Kaiser Augustus und die verlorene Republik*, 121–36. Mainz am Rhein.

Laslo, N. (1935). "Reflessi d'arte figurata nelle *Metamorfosi* di Ovidio." *Ephemeris Dacoromana* 6: 368–441.

Latacz, J. (1979). "Ovids 'Metmorphosen' als Spiel mit der Tradition." *Würz. Jbb.*, n.s., 5: 133–55.

Lateiner, D. (1984). "Mythic and Non-mythic Artists in Ovid's *Metamorphoses*." *Ramus* 13: 1–30.

Lausberg, M. (1982). "*Archetupon tes idias poieseos*: Zur Bildbeschreibung bei Ovid." *Boreas* 5: 112–23.

Leach, E. W. (1974). "Ekphrasis and the Theme of Artistic Failure in Ovid's *Metamorphoses*." *Ramus* 3: 102–42.

———. (1988). *The Rhetoric of Space: Literary and Artistic Representations of Landscape in Republican and Augustan Rome*. Princeton.

———. (2004). *The Social Life of Painting in Ancient Rome and on the Bay of Naples*. Cambridge.

Lee, G. (1953). *Ovid,* Metamorphoses *I*. Cambridge.

Liapis, V. (2006). "Achilles Tatius as a Reader of Sophocles." *CQ* 56: 220–38.

Little, D. (1972). "The Non-Augustanism of Ovid's *Metamorphoses*." *Mnemosyne* 25: 389–401.

Liveley, G. (1999). "Reading Resistance in Ovid's *Metamorphoses*." In P. Hardie, A. Barchiesi, and S. Hinds, eds., *Ovidian Transformations: Essays on Ovid's* Metamorphoses *and Its Reception*, 197–213. Cambridge.

Lyne, R.O.A.M. (1984). "Ovid's *Metamorphoses*, Callimachus and l'art pour l'art." *MD* 12: 9–34.

MacMullen, R. (1974). *Roman Social Relations*. New Haven.

Marchesi, I. (2005). "Traces of a Freed Language: Horace, Petronius, and the Rhetoric of Fable." *CA* 24: 307–30.

McKeown, J. C. (1979). "Ovid *Amores* 3.12." *PLLS* 2:163–77.

Meuli, K. (1946). "Griechische Opferbräuche." In *Phyllobolia: Festschrift Peter Von der Mühll*, 185–288. Basel.

Miles, G. B. (1995). *Livy: Reconstructing Early Rome*. Ithaca.

Miller, J. (1993). "Ovidian Allusion and the Vocabulary of Memory." *MD* 30: 153–64.

Miller, J. H. (1987). *The Ethics of Reading*. New York.

Morales, H. (1996). "The Torturer's Apprentice: Parrhasius and the Limits of Art." In J. Elsner, ed., *Art and Text in Roman Culture*, 182–209. Cambridge.

Morgan, L. (2003). "Child's Play: Ovid and His Critics." *JRS* 93: 66–91.

Murgia, C. E. (1986). "The Date of Ovid's *Ars Amatoria* 3." *AJP* 107: 74–94.

Myers, K. S. (1994). *Ovid's Causes*. Ann Arbor.

Neschke, A. (1982). "Vom Mythos zum Emblem. Die Perseuserzählung in Ovids *Metamorphosen*." *AU* 25.6: 76–87.

Newlands, C. E. (1995). *Playing with Time: Ovid and the Fasti*. Ithaca.

———. (1997). "The Metamorphosis of Ovid's Medea." In J. J. Clauss and S. I. Johnston, eds., *Medea: Essays on Medea in Myth, Literature, Philosophy, and Art*, 178–208. Princeton.

Newsom, R. (1988). *A Likely Story: Probability and Play in Fiction*. New Brunswick, N.J.

Nicolet, C. (1991). *Space, Geography, and Politics in the Early Roman Empire*. Ann Arbor.

Nicoll, W.S.M. (1980). "Cupid, Apollo, and Daphne (Ovid, *Met.* 1.452ff.)." *CQ* 30: 174–82.

Nussbaum, M. (1990). *Love's Knowledge: Essays on Philosophy and Literature*. Oxford.

Oliensis, E. (1997). "*Ut arte emendaturus fortunam*: Horace, Nasidienus, and the Art of Satire." In T. Habinek and A. Schiesaro, eds., *The Roman Cultural Revolution*, 90–104. Cambridge.

———. (1998). *Horace and the Rhetoric of Authority*. Cambridge.

Oliensis, E. (2004). "The Power of Image-Makers: Representation and Revenge in Ovid *Metamorphoses* 6 and *Tristia* 4." *CA* 23: 285–321.

Otis, B. (1970). *Ovid as an Epic Poet*. 2nd ed. Cambridge.

Pavlock, B. (1991). "The Tyrant and Boundary Violation in Ovid's Tereus Episode." *Helios* 18: 34–48.

———. (1998). "Daedalus in the Labyrinth of Ovid's *Metamorphoses*." *CW* 92: 141–57.

Pelling, C.B.R. (1988). *Plutarch: Life of Antony*. Cambridge.

Pianezzola, E. (1979). "La metamorfosi ovidiana come metafora narrativa." *Quaderni del circolo filologico-linguistico padavano* 10: 77–91.

Piccaluga, G. (1968). *Lycaon: Un tema mitico*. Rome.

Price, S. F. (2005). "Local Mythologies in the Greek East." In C. Howgego, V. Heuchert, and A. Burnett, eds., *Coinage and Identity in the Roman Provinces*, 115–24. Oxford.

Purcell, N. (1999). "Did Caesar Mime?" In B. Bergmann and C. Kondoleon, eds., *The Art of Ancient Spectacle*, 181–93. New Haven.

Putnam, M.C.J. (1995). *Virgil's Aeneid: Interpretation and Influence*. Chapel Hill.

———. (1998). *Virgil's Epic Designs: Ekphrasis in the Aeneid*. New Haven.

Quint, D. (1993). *Epic and Empire*. Princeton.

Rawson, P. B. (1987). *The Myth of Marsyas in the Roman Visual Arts: An Iconographic Study*. Oxford.

Ridgway, B. S. (2001). "The Sperlonga Sculptures: The Current State of Research." In B. S. Ridgway and N. T. de Grummond, eds., *From Pergamon to Sperlonga: Sculpture and Context*, 78–91. Berkeley.

Robinson, T. M. (1968). "Ovid and the *Timaeus*." *Atheneum* 56: 254–60.

Rosati, G. (1979). "L'esistenza letteraria. Ovidio e l'autoconscienza della poesia." *MD* 2: 101–36.

———. (1983). *Narciso e Pigmalione: Illusione e spettacolo nelle* Metamorfosi *di Ovidio*. Florence.

———. (2001). "Mito e potere nell'epica di Ovidio." *MD* 46: 39–61.

———. (2002). "Narrative Techniques and Narrative Structures in the *Metamorphoses*." In B. W. Boyd, ed., *Brill's Companion to Ovid*, 271–304. Leiden.

———. (2009). *Ovidio: Metamorfosi, Volume III (Libri V–VI)*. Milan.

Rye, G. (2000). "The Impossible Ethics of Reading: Identity, Difference, Violence, and Responsibility (Paule Constant's *White Spirit*)." *French Studies* 54: 327–37.

Santini, C. (1998). "Segni grafici e metamorfosi." In I. Gallo and P. Esposito, eds., *Ovidio da Roma all'Europa*, 37–54. Quaderni del dipartimento di scienze dell' antichità. Università di studi di Salerno 20. Naples.

Sauron, G. (1982). "Discours symbolique et formes décoratives à Rome à l'époque augustéenne." *MEFRA* 94: 699–713.

Scheid, J. (1984). "La spartizione a Roma." *Studi Storici* 4: 945–56.

Schmidt, E. A. (1991). *Ovids poetische Menschenwelt: Die* Metamorphosen *als Metapher und Symphonie*. Heidelberg.

Schmitzer, U. (1990). *Zeitgeschichte in Ovids Metamorphosen: Mythologische Dichtung unter politischem Anspruch*. Stuttgart.

Schönbeck, H.-P. (1999). "Erfüllung und Fluch des Künstlertums: Pygmalion und Daedalus bei Ovid." *Philologus* 143: 300–16.

Segal, C. P. (1969). *Landscape in Ovid's* Metamorphoses. Hermes Einzelschrift 23, Wiesbaden.

———. (1972). "Ovid's Orpheus and Augustan Ideology." *TAPA* 103: 473–94.

———. (1994). "Philomela's Web and the Pleasures of the Text: Reader and Violence in the *Metamorphoses* of Ovid." In I.J.F. de Jong and J. P. Sullivan, eds., *Modern Critical Theory and Classical Culture*, 257–80. Leiden.

———. (1998). "Ovid's Metamorphic Bodies: Art, Gender, and Violence in the *Metamorphoses*." *Arion* 5: 9–41.

———. (2001). "Intertextuality and Immortality: Ovid, Pythagoras, and Lucretius in *Metamorphoses* 15." *MD* 51: 63–101.

———. (2005). "Il corpo e l'io nelle *Metamorfosi* di Ovidio." In A. Barchiesi, ed., *Ovidio: Metamorfosi Volume I (Libri I–II)*, XV–CI. Milan.

Sharrock, A. R. (1991a). "Womanufacture." *JRS* 81: 36–49.

———. (1991b). "The Love of Creation." *Ramus* 20: 169–92.

———. (1994a). "Ovid and the Politics of Reading." *MD* 33: 97–122.

———. (1994b). *Seduction and Repetition in Ovid's* Ars Amatoria II. Oxford.

———. (1996). "Representing Metamorphosis." In J. Elsner, ed., *Art and Text in Roman Culture*, 103–30. Cambridge.

Solodow, J. (1988). *The World of Ovid's* Metamorphoses. Chapel Hill.

Spahlinger, L. (1996). *Ars latet arte sua: Untersuchungen zur Poetologie in den* Metamorphosen *Ovids*. Stuttgart.

Steiner, D. T. (1994). *The Tyrant's Writ: Myths and Images of Writing in Ancient Greece*. Princeton.

———. (2001). *Images in Mind: Statues in Archaic and Classical Greek Literature and Thought*. Princeton.

Stroh, W. (1968). "Ein missbrauchtes Distichon Ovids." In M. von Albrecht and E. Zinn, eds., *Ovid*, 567–80. Wege der Forschung 92. Darmstadt.

Sumi, G. S. (2002). "Impersonating the Dead: Mimes at Roman Funerals." *AJP* 123: 559–85.

Syme, R. (1960). *The Roman Revolution*. New ed. Oxford.

Tarrant, R. (1982). "Editing Ovid's *Metamorphoses*: Problems and Possibilities." *CP* 77: 342–60.

———. (2002a). "Chaos in Ovid's *Metamorphoses* and Its Neronian Influence." *Arethusa* 35: 349–60.

———. (2002b). "Ovid and Ancient Literary History." In P. Hardie, ed., *The Cambridge Companion to Ovid*, 13–33. Cambridge.

Theodorakopoulos, E. (1999). "Closure and Transformation in Ovid's *Metamorphoses*." In P. Hardie, A. Barchiesi, and S. Hinds, eds., *Ovidian Transformations: Essays on Ovid's* Metamorphoses *and Its Reception*, 142–61. Cambridge.

Thiem, J. (1995). "The Textualization of the Reader in Magical Realist Fiction." In L. P. Zamora and W. B. Faris, eds., *Magical Realism: Theory, History, Community*, 235–47. Durham, N.C.

Tissol, G. (1997). *The Face of Nature: Wit, Narrative, and Cosmic Origins in Ovid's* Metamorphoses. Princeton.

———. (2002). "The House of Fame: Roman History and Augustan Politics in *Metamorphoses* 11–15." In B. W. Boyd, ed., *Brill's Companion to Ovid*, 305–35. Leiden.

Todorov, T. (1975). *The Fantastic: A Structural Approach to a Literary Genre.* Trans. R. Howard. Ithaca.

Vernant, J. P. (1988). *Myth and Society in Ancient Greece.* Trans. J. Lloyd. Chicago.

———. (1991). *Mortals and Immortals.* Princeton.

Veyne, P. (1961). "Le Marsyas 'colonial' et l'indépendence des cites." *RPhil* 35: 87–98.

———. (1988). *Did the Greeks Believe Their Myths?* Trans. P. Wissing. Chicago.

Vian, B. (1963). *Les origines de Thèbes: Cadmos et les Spartes.* Paris.

Viarre, S. (1964). *L'image et la pensée dans les 'Métamorphoses' d'Ovide.* Paris.

Vincent, M. (1994). "Between Ovid and Barthes: Ekphrasis, Orality, Textuality in Ovid's 'Arachne.'" *Arethusa* 27: 361–86.

Viscogliosi, A. (1988). "Die Architektur-Dekoration der Cella des Apollo-Sosianus-Tempel." In M. Hofter, ed., *Kaiser Augustus und die verlorene Republik*, 136–48. Mainz.

Voigtländer, H.-D. (1975). "Die Idee der Ich-Spaltung und der Stil der 'Metamorphosen' Ovids." In J. Cobet, R. Leimbach, and A. B. Neschke-Henschke, eds., *Dialogos: Für Harald Patzer zum 65. Geburtstag*, 193–208. Wiesbaden.

Voit, L. (1957). "Die Niobe des Ovid." *Gymnasium* 64: 135–49.

von Albrecht, M. (1961). "Zum Metamorphosenprooem Ovids." *RhM* 104: 269–78.

Wallace-Hadrill, A. (1982). "*Civilis Princeps*: Between Citizen and King." *JRS* 72: 32–48.

———. (1996). *Houses and Society in Pompeii and Herculaneum.* Princeton.

Webb, R. (2005). "The Protean Performer: Mimesis and Identity in Late Antique Discussions of the Theater." In L. Del Giudice and N. Van Deusen, eds., *Performing Ecstasies: Music, Dance, and Ritual in the Mediterranean*, 3–11. Ottawa.

Welch, T. S. (2005). *The Elegiac Cityscape: Propertius and the Meaning of Roman Monuments.* Columbus.

Wheeler, S. M. (1995). "*Imago Mundi*: Another View of the Creation in Ovid's *Metamorphoses.*" *AJP* 116 (1995): 95–121.

———. (1999). *A Discourse of Wonders.* Philadelphia.

———. (2000). *Narrative Dynamics in Ovid's* Metamorphoses. Tübingen.

———. (2002). "Ovid's *Metamorphoses* and Universal History." In D. S. Levene and D. P. Nelis, eds., *Clio and the Poets: Augustan Poetry and the Traditions of Historiography*, 163–89. Leiden.

Wickkiser, B. L. (1999). "Famous Last Words: Putting Ovid's Sphragis Back into the *Metamorphoses.*" *MD* 42: 113–42.

Wilkinson, L. P. (1955). *Ovid Recalled.* Cambridge.

Williams, G. D. (1996). *The Curse of Exile: A Study of Ovid's Ibis.* Cambridge.

Wise, V. M. (1977). "Flight Myths in Ovid's *Metamorphoses*: An Interpretation of Phaethon and Daedalus." *Ramus* 6: 44–59.

Wyke, M. (1992). "Augustan Cleopatras: Female Power and Poetic Authority." In A. Powell, ed., *Roman Poetry and Propaganda in the Age of Augustus*, 98–140. Bristol.

Zanker, P. (1983). "Der Apollontempel auf dem Palatin. Ausstattung und politische Sinnbezüge nach der Schlacht von Actium." *Anal. Rom.*, suppl. 10: 21–40.

———. (1988). "Augustan Political Symbolism in the Private Sphere." In J. Huskinson, M. Beard, and J. Reynolds, eds., *Image and Mystery in the Roman World*, 1–13. Gloucester.

———. (1990). *The Power of Images in the Age of Augustus*. Trans. A. Shapiro. Ann Arbor.

Zeitlin, F. (1986). "Thebes: Theatre of Self and Society in Athenian Drama." In P. Euben, ed., *Greek Tragedy and Political Theory*, 101–41. Berkeley.

Zumwalt, N. (1977). "*Fama Subversa*: Theme and Structure in Ovid *Metamorphoses* 12." CSCA 10: 209–22.

Index of Passages Cited

General Index